GLIMPSES OF EMPIRE

A
CORONA
ANTHOLOGY

Anthony Kirk-Greene

I.B.Tauris *Publishers*
LONDON • NEW YORK

Published in 2001 by I.B.Tauris & Co Ltd
6 Salem Road, London W2 4BU
175 Fifth Avenue, New York NY 10010
www.ibtauris.com

In the United States and Canada distributed by St. Martin's Press
175 Fifth Avenue, New York NY 10010

ISBN 1 86064 3981

A full CIP record for this book is available from the British Library
A full CIP record for this book is available from the Library of Congress

Library of Congress catalog card: available

Typeset by The Midlands Book Typesetting Co, Loughborough, Leicestershire
Printed and bound in Great Britain by MPG Books Ltd, Bodmin

Contents

List of Illustrations

Foreword

BY
HIS EXCELLENCY THE RT HON SIR RICHARD LUCE DL

The British Empire is long gone. Former British colonies have been transformed into the Commonwealth of nations. The few remaining territories wishing to remain under British responsibility are now known as the United Kingdom Overseas Territories.

A significant stage of British history has therefore ended. On 25 May 1999 a moving ceremony took place in Westminster Abbey in the presence of Her Majesty The Queen and the Duke of Edinburgh. It was a Service of Commemoration and Thanksgiving to mark the end of Her Majesty's Overseas Civil Service, the Centenary of the Corona Club and the Golden Jubilee of Corona Worldwide.

At the same time a book *On Crown Service* was published giving the history of the old Colonial Service (later known as HM Overseas Civil Service). The author was Anthony Kirk-Greene, the leading historian of the Colonial Service, who also had the experience of serving as an administrator in Nigeria.

It is therefore entirely welcome and appropriate that Anthony Kirk-Greene should have compiled, edited and written an introduction to this book *A Corona Anthology*. *Corona*, published monthly from 1949 to 1962, kept Colonial Service officers well informed on policy debates and political events at home and up to date with the many challenges faced by the Service in some 40 or so colonies around the world.

This is a time when we can look at our colonial role historically and with impartiality. *Corona* gives a rare insight into many aspects of colonial life, thus enriching knowledge of our colonial past. This Anthology gives an excellent glimpse of the historical value of *Corona*.

Governor and Commander-in-Chief
GIBRALTAR

Introduction

Corona, the Journal of Her Majesty's Colonial Service (from 1954 Her Majesty's Overseas Civil Service), was published monthly from February 1948 to December 1962. It was reprinted *in toto* in 1977–8, at a price which emphasized its rediscovery by academic researchers on the Colonial Empire a decade beyond the closure of the Colonial Office in 1966 as well as causing many one-time readers to regret that they had not kept their original copies.

Probably just because so many of these readers were resident abroad somewhere in the Empire, experiencing the traumatic upheavals of colonial service life in frequent transfers, unpacking and repacking loads, departure and return from leave to a new house or a fresh station, split family life, etc., it seems that few of the thousands of subscribers had space or time to retain their monthly copy of *Corona*. Not many were ready to add habitually to their 'permanent' possessions in the peripatetic life of the colonial civil servant. Some passed it on to a friend or the Club library; others cut out the articles they wished to keep and threw the rest away. In some cases white ants or mildew wrought their destructive toll on paper possessions. To quote the lament of a former member of the Malayan Civil Service who may be speaking for many,

> I wish I had been able to keep my copies, but an active HMOCS career [he served in four territories in South East Asia and the Far East] was not the best way to build up a library, so they were jettisoned – something I have always regretted.

Like the thirteen volumes of the associated but unlinked contemporaneous *Corona Library*, also published by HMSO, each of which was designed to provide an up-to-date narrative picture of the colony, a set of *Corona* has today a positive scarcity value. A complete run of the original Journal is not easy to find in university or public libraries – all at a time when the last decade of the 20th century has been characterized by a positive re-awakening of interest in and books about the Colonial Empire and its Civil Service.

It was way back in 1972 that I suggested a *Corona* anthology to Jack Tawney, its former editor and before that a senior administrative officer in Tanganyika, with whom I was then working as the Oxford Colonial Records Project's research officer in oral history. It was my hope that, on his third retirement, such a venture would capture his interest, for he was also a fine writer in his own right and an enthusiast for Colonial Service history. Nothing came of this initiative, however, and with my teaching commitments in the University it was not until I started work on my history of the Colonial Service, *On Crown Service*, in 1997 for the official commemoration of the end of the Colonial Service and HMOCS in May 1999 that I felt the moment was appropriate to resume the project of a *Corona* anthology as a complementary publication.

In this I was encouraged by a letter from Roderick MacLean, who wrote to say that

> An idea occurred to me this morning while taking my shower. An attractive idea to mark the Corona Club centenary might be a facsimile reproduction of some or all of the former HMOCS magazine *Corona* (Letter to author, 24 April 1997).

"To us in the service", he added, "*Corona* was our *Blackwoods*".

With the knowledgeable and eager co-operation of my publisher, Dr. Lester Crook of I.B. Tauris, and with the imaginative technical co-operation of their Steven Tribe, this Anthology is now offered not only to fellow historians of and researchers into the Service but also to former colleagues in the Colonial Service and HMOCS as a reminder, half-nostalgic, half-historical, of the days when they too used to look forward to the monthly arrival (however late it came by surface mail) of the next issue of their buff-coloured *Corona*. It remains a matter of conjecture which page or kind of contribution the reader turned to first as he opened his or her *Corona*... unless, of course, it happened to carry a contribution by oneself.

The selection of any anthology, be it Palgrave's once-ubiquitous school-text *Golden Treasury* (1861), Robert Bridge's pocket volume of philosopher-poets *Spirit of Man* (1916), or Field-Marshal Wavell's inspirational *Other Men's Flowers* (1944), immediately encounters three determining questions. Of what is it an anthology? For whom is it intended? And whose anthology is it?

Ultimately, of course, every anthology reflects the predilections and preferences of the selector. As Wavell put it with characteristic modesty, "I ask no one to applaud my choice. I do not always applaud it myself, but a part of me from which I cannot dissociate myself, my memory, has made this selection" (Memorial edition, 1955, 15). Yet within that choice certain principles must obtain if the final product is to be something more than a ragbag. Is it to be a would-be Golden Treasury of all that is best in the defined corpus? Is it to be an unashamedly personal collection, say of all the poems that Wavell could repeat from memory, or of all the passages from prose and poetry which Lord David Cecil, Professor of English Literature in the University of Oxford, reckoned in his *Library Looking Glass* (1975) to be the most illuminating instances? Or is it perhaps to be John Hadfield's wider-ranging literary sub-collections, *A Book of Beauty*, *A Book of Delights*, and *A Book of Pleasure*? Or maybe a narrower, single-topic anthology, like the elegant articles in André Simon's *A Wine and Food Bedside Book* (1972)?

In the present case the Anthology, assembled by one who has spent fifteen years in the Colonial Administrative Service and then thirty-five researching and writing about it, has been designed simultaneously to achieve two purposes. One is to reflect the multiple aspects of life in the Colonial Service, a Crown civil service operating in nearly forty territories across the oceans from South Georgia through Malta and Cyprus to Mauritius and the Gilbert and Ellice Islands and in over twenty separate professional departments from the Audit to the Veterinary Service. The other objective is to recall and record, forty-five years beyond the end of the Colonial Service and its transformation into HMOCS (itself now closed), the insiders' views – and hence a primary source – on what such a life was all about. The Anthology thus assumes the dual task of recalling to those who were in the Service some of the major moments and memories of their experience, and of presenting an authentic insight for later generations for whom such a respected, sought-after and rewarding career is no longer an option yet who wish to understand what the Colonial Service did, how and why they did it, and what the socio-political milieu of the job was.

Putting behind me the easy temptation of choosing only my favourite pieces, I have been deliberately guided in my choice by the imperative of equity, seeking to ensure that as far as possible there is at least one excerpt on every territory in the then Colonial Empire and on as many branches as possible of the Colonial Service. Furthermore it has been purposely widened to take note of what to many readers was the essence of *Corona*, what might be called 'the Lighter Side', as well as to give examples of those personal features like "For Your Leave", "News of Your Friends" and other Agonies, all of which could mean so much to those working overseas and looking forward to home leave. Through the vast range and variety of its contributions, the Journal became an accurate mirror of Colonial Service life. A study of *Corona* offers an authentic contribution to and a profound insight into the history of the Colonial Service and the work of its men and women overseas.

So much for the rationale and content of the anthology. What of the original corpus? *Corona* was designed as part of the 1947 package deal of Colonial Office reform put together by the influential new Secretary of State Arthur Creech Jones and his visionary Assistant Under Secretary of State for Africa, Andrew Cohen. The declared aim was to enable the post-war, new-look Colonial Service to shake off its alleged parochialism and broaden its horizons (intellectual as well as practical) by having its own journal for the dissemination of knowledge and ideas and for the exchange of experience and opinions on colonial administration and development. Other items in that turning-point package deal included proposals for the post-war re-orientation of Colonial Service training; the critical dispatch on Local Government which replaced the pre-war credo of indirect rule and Native Administration; the inauguration of the annual Colonial Office Summer Schools on Africa Administration at Cambridge University under Ronald Robinson, reviving and elaborating on the pioneer Oxford University Summer Schools on Colonial Administration organized by Margery Perham in 1937 and 1938; and the establishment of an African Studies Branch in the Colonial Office. There were already, of course, partly comparable journals, like the professional *Overseas Education*, the wider-targeted *New Common-wealth* and *Crown Colonist*, and the authoritative *Times Colonial Supplement*. Furthermore the *Journal of African Administration* had been launched with the similar aim of keeping the Service in touch with new ideas, aimed primarily at the Colonial Service in Africa where three-quarters of the Service were posted. But *Corona* was to be the first attempt to offer the entire Colonial Service a worldwide journal of its own, to be written for and predominantly by its members.

Corona's maiden issue appeared in February 1948. Its birth had been announced by Creech Jones in his address to the annual Colonial Club dinner in the previous June, an occasion at which the Secretary of State customarily took his Service into his confidence. He had it in mind, he said, to appoint an editor to launch a Colonial Service journal, "to keep members of the Service informed about the recent pronouncements and developments in colonial policy and practice". Now he contrib-uted a foreword to the new Journal, in which he emphasized that in the complex and internationally scrutinized post-war world the Colonial Service could no longer "perform independently – each of us working in comparative isolation in our own office, our own village, our own district, or even our own Colony or Protectorate" (1, Feb., 4). To succeed, he went on,

> we must exchange our information and pool our ideas; we must profit from the experience of others in avoiding the pitfalls which lie in front of us, and appreciate how our own actions may create difficulties elsewhere to the detriment of the common task.

Hence the importance of *Corona* providing

> a ready means whereby such knowledge, gained from day to day by officers at work in the field, may be put into a common pool from which all their colleagues may draw with advantage.

What was more, *Corona* would help to keep the Colonial Office in touch with what the Colonial Service was doing and thinking: "We here, I may say, do not intend to keep out of the arena". Creech Jones concluded by appealing to members of the Colo-nial Service to make it their journal: "we want individual officers to have the greatest possible freedom and encouragement in making their contributions". Twelve years later, that rationale was reinforced in a notable editorial:

> *Corona* encourages that catholicity of outlook [which was so great a part of the Service's tradition] by covering as wide a range as possible of work and experience in the Colonies... Its backbone has always been the wish, for example, of the Forestry man in Tanganyika to know how his opposite number is getting on in British Honduras, or of the North Borneo Policeman to understand the problems facing the Force in Sierra Leone (XII, 404)

The name had, of course, already been appropriated by the Corona Club, the Colonial Service's social club, founded by Joseph Chamberlain in 1900 with the proposal that "An Annual Service Dinner shall be instituted, with a view of affording Officers on leave from the Crown Colonies the opportunity of a social meeting with each other, with the Officers of the Colonial Office [and later the Crown Agents], and with past Crown Colony Officers". *Corona* was also the choice of Sir Frederick Lugard for his Nigerian gubernatorial steam yacht built in 1902 (of which a model was still on display, in 1998, in the Crown Agents office in Grosvenor Gardens), reputedly so named to commemorate King Edward VII's coronation. For the Secretary of State himself, "the happy title of the Journal turns to a new purpose an old word standing for the unity and association of all those who serve the peoples of the Colonial Territories" (I, Feb.,3). But *Corona*'s founding editor, Kenneth Bradley, is on record in his autobiography *Once a District Officer* (1966) as admitting his dislike of the name, without ever being able to come up with a better one for his "house magazine". If in 1949 it was an older generation who connected it with cigars, a younger one linked it with the delivery of soft drinks of the 'Tizer the Appetizer' variety.

Corona was published every month for fourteen years, the final issue appearing in December 1962. In terms of the present Anthology, this means that it has been distilled from 167 monthly issues, averaging 480 pages a year or nearly 7,000 pages in all. The Anthology thus represents less than 5% of the total material to hand. An enforced alteration of the Journal's sub-title came in 1952, from "His Majesty's" to "Her Majesty's Colonial Service", and again in October 1954 to "The Journal of Her Majesty's Oversea Service" following the publication of the White Paper *Reorganization of the Colonial Service* (Col. No. 306); and to the ultimate "Her Majesty's Overseas Service" in 1956. The editor declined to adopt the correct name of "The Journal of Her Majesty's Overseas Civil Service" on the grounds that the previous "Colonial Service" was the accepted shorthand for the full title of "Colonial Civil Service" and hence "Civil" should not appear in *Corona*'s new title either (VI, 364). Otherwise, apart from changing the colour of its cover from light blue to light buff and suddenly improving its typeface in the May issue of its final year, *Corona*'s format over fourteen years underwent only minor alterations, cosmetic rather than substantive.

The early habit of opening with a rather ponderous article, e.g., a two-part treatise on the psychology of public administration by H.A.C. Dobbs, "Administrator and Specialist" (I, Nov., 17; Dec., 18) or a contributed piece on "Colonial Economic Development" (I, Feb., 17; March, 18), was quickly dropped. In 1955 the digest of colonial debates, "Parliament", was more attractively restyled "Beneath Big Ben". From time to time the journal opened with a message from the Secretary of State, especially in the New Year, or with an editorial regularly in November to carry the editor's Christmas wishes to readers. There might be half a dozen articles of 3-6 pages and three or four shorter ones, perhaps just a page apiece.

The articles were nearly always signed, with a useful biographical note on "Contributors to this Issue" in each number, but a few were specially contributed or reproduced from sister publications like *The Times, Economist, Listener, Colonial*

Development, Optima, the BBC and Chatham House, and now and again – for the lighter kind of article – from *Punch* and *Chamber's Journal* (*Blackwood*'s stories were too long to reprint, and in principle the editor was against publishing fiction). Most issues carried one article in lighter vein and a short poem. From time to time a letter featured under "Correspondence", and now and again letters appeared generated by articles published. Among the regular features were brief book reviews; "News of Your Friends" (marriages, births, deaths, promotions, transfers, gubernatorial appointments, and the extensive biannual Honours List); a calendar of sporting and cultural events in Britain headed "For Your Leave", including plays and films; and a page of Agonies, principally hotels and accommodation to let for officers and their families coming home on leave – at rates unbelievable to today's re-readers! The personalia were free but Agonies were charged at 5/- a line (VIII, 241). Besides four full-page photographs, always of good quality (often from the Colonial Office's Information Department), or four pages of frequently outstanding drawings linked to the centre-page article, each issue also carried several line drawings, both artistic and cartoon-like. Examples of these personalia, along with photographs and drawings, are to be found on the pages that follow. Space considerations preclude reproduction of any of the book reviews usefully published in each issue of *Corona.*

Every volume was accompanied by an index for the year, listing the title of articles published (but, short-sightedly in retrospect for the historian, without the authors being separately listed alphabetically) and of books reviewed, verse, illustrations, and what were called Regular Features – Parliament, News of Your Friends, Monthly Chronicle, For Your Leave, etc. At the end of each issue came several pages of commercial advertisements, on schools at home or banks and books overseas, pensions and life assurance companies specializing in Colonial Service clients, tropical outfitters, car hire, and holiday accommodation, e.g. the regular recommendation of the multiple activities at Thorpeness, "on the lovely healthy Suffolk Coast: Solves the Problem of Where to Stay on your Next Leave". Further examples are included on the following pages. From time to time 'relevant' advertisements were carried to help keep the Colonial Service in touch, e.g. announcements about the Hansard Society (III, 27), the Royal Institute of Public Administration, Royal Empire Society etc. The annual subscription in 1949 was 14/-, including postage, rising by 1/6d (7.5p) in 1952. After a lengthy apology from the editor over the increase of 6d per copy in 1957 (IX, 403), it was still no more than 28/- (£1.40) a year by 1962, postage included. *Corona* was published by Her Majesty's Stationery Office, whose distributionary role provided a light-hearted article by an HMSO staff member, "The Journal Goes Out" (VIII, 438)

Every issue carried two Service warnings. On the first page came the disclaimer that

> The Secretary of State does not necessarily endorse any opinions expressed in this journal nor does any of its contents necessarily represent the official policy of either the Secretary of State or the Government of any Colonial territory.

This was followed on the last page by the General Orders-like reminder that all manuscripts submitted by civil servants must be accompanied by an assurance that they had been approved in accordance with the regulations. Despite the bold reference in an editorial announcement to "usual rates" and "normal publication fees", at least one regular author remains convinced that no fee was ever paid to in-Service contributors.

The first editor was K. (later Sir Kenneth) G. Bradley. He had started what was to be a distinguished Colonial Service career as a District Officer in Northern Rhodesia in 1926. In 1939 he was appointed the territory's Information Officer, before being transferred to the Falkland Islands as Colonial Secretary in 1942 and then as Under Secretary in the Gold Coast in 1946. His flair for public relations was recognised in 1948, when the Colonial Office offered him the post of editor of the new *Corona*. After leaving the journal in 1953, he became Director of the Imperial Institute and oversaw its successful move to Kensington High Street, opened in 1962.Bradley was knighted in the following year. His literary output put him in the front rank of writers about the Colonial Service life with the widely acclaimed and reprinted *Diary of a District Officer* (1943), followed by *Once a District Officer* (1966). In the latter he has a whole chapter on his *Corona* assignment, which for the journal's historian is usefully supplemented by his article "Midwife to Corona" (IX, 406)

The second editor, who came into the chair in 1953 originally as a three month stopgap but in the end for ten years, was John (Jack) J. Tawney. If *Corona* was very much Bradley's conception, it grew up as very much Tawney's baby. After Oxford, Tawney joined the Colonial Administrative Service in 1930 and was posted to Tanganyika Territory, as it was then officially known. He became a deputy Provincial Commissioner in 1948, retiring in 1952. Following the closing down of *Corona* in 1962, Tawney was offered the new job of Director of the Oxford Colonial Records Project based at Queen Elizabeth House, Oxford. The project closed in 1973, by which time Tawney, with the assistance of Ivan Lloyd-Phillips (Gold Coast, Palestine and Malaya), had helped to build up what today, in Rhodes House Library, has become the largest and richest archive of Colonial Service personal papers in Britain.

This selection from the fourteen volumes of *Corona* published between 1948 and 1962 is limited to material on the Colonial Service. (see Contents page for sub-sections). A subsequent, complementary anthology dealing with the Colonial Office, Colonial policy and Colonial affairs in Parliament, the transfer of power and early retirement, is in hand. In each excerpt, the reference to the location of the article in the original volumes is indicated, e.g. III, 77; IX, 432. In the case of extracts from Vol.1, the month is also given, since annual pagination for the whole volume was introduced only with Vol.II.

Under the critical Section (b), "The Colonial Service at Work", it is striking how relatively few contributors to what was the Journal of the whole Colonial Service came from the score of professional Departments when set beside the wealth of material on and by members of the Colonial Administrative Service. In some instances, such as Audit, Judicial, Medicine, Forestry and Survey, it is hard to find more than a handful of articles over the whole fourteen year period. What has been reprinted in the Anthology should be looked on as representative of the material to hand and in no way exhaustive of its wide coverage. Together, the articles, and above all the comparative experiences of fellow officers in other territories, ensured that *Corona* could be of real value in arousing and sustaining the targeted Colonial Service's 'awareness' of what was going on beyond the confines of their own bailiwick.

Besides the principal themes identified here, certain other articles were published which, though of interest to Colonial Service members then, may forty years later be too tangential to qualify for reproduction in a space-limited Anthology. For instance, as part of its horizon-widening remit *Corona* reproduced articles on the colonial policy of other colonial powers, such as Portugal (I, Nov.11), francophone Africa (II,13), Indonesia (II, 89) and the Belgian Congo (II,130). The Congo reappeared on the eve of its independence in 1960 (XII,18). There were also articles on non-mainstream 'colonial' territories like the Sudan (I, March, 13; III,260), Papua New Guinea (III,418 and XIII,104, with a special editorial disclaimer), Haiti (III,340), Burma (IV,15), Ethiopia (V,310) and South Africa's Bantustans (XIV,376). Several treated of the experience of Colonial Service officers in the USA (IV,347; IX, 427), but curiously perhaps, in view of the palpable anticolonial views of the United States in the 1950s, nothing was included on America's own dependent territories such as the Philippines or the mandated territories of Samoa and the Marshall Islands.

Expectedly, there was on occasion an air of the colonial 'flavour of the month'. For instance in 1948, when the Malayan Emergency was well under way, two heavy-weight contributed articles on "Disorders in Malaya" were carried (I,Feb.,12: May, 12), followed by two more, this time by Harold Ingrams, on the major cold-war topic of "Communism and the African" (I,July, 3; August, 11). Considerable coverage was given to Britain's 'Colonial Month' and its associated 'Colonial Weeks' throughout 1948 and 1949. Again, in the mid-1950s there were pieces, often official, on Mau Mau and later on the Central African Federation. Some of the professional and descriptive articles on, for example, colonial economics, soil erosion, veterinary research, the role of the Public Works Department (PWD) in the Gambia or Dominica or on Telecommunications planning in Nigeria, can read too heavily to justify inclusion in a latter-day Anthology. Others were too topical or too ephemeral to stand the test of time. Against that, a return to the original corpus suggests that there is enough material in the fourteen volumes of *Corona* to be able to design a separate volume of "Collected Anecdotes", along the lines of Blackwood's celebrated *Tales From the Outposts* series, about the lighter side of life in the Colonial Service, or to put together a separate collection of "Colonial Service Poems" to supplement the retrieval project recently sponsored by the Overseas Service Pensioners' Association (see *Overseas Pensioner*, 77, 1998, 33–38). Brief comments on the material now selected for reprinting in this Anthology are to be found in the introduction to each sub-section.

Before turning to the text of the Anthology proper, attention should be paid to *Corona*'s editorial policy and procedures. Exemplified by the contributions that follow, this is the core of what *Corona* was — or was not – all about, in the eyes of the editor as well as in the minds of its members. *Corona* was, of course, a brand new Colonial Service venture, an official journal without being under Colonial Office control. It was made sternly clear at the front of every number that the contents were not to be taken as necessarily representing official policy. The editor went one stage further by stressing that although *Corona* was housed in the Colonial Office in Great Smith Street, it was not a Colonial Office organ (IX,404). For all that, colonial officers were required to accompany their manuscripts with an assurance that they had been officially approved for publication by their own governments. The requirement is significant in the context of what could/would (or not) be published. Not until February 1958, after ten years, was this warning modified to read "articles of a type requiring approval under regulations..." – much to the relief of contributors of the humorous anecdote and lighthearted reminiscence.

Both Bradley and Tawney were ready to show themselves responsive to readers' views. Bradley regretted that the maiden issue did not quite live up to all that had been "cheerfully prophesied" in the introductory brochure [not seen], regretting in particular the lack of any Correspondence opportunity, but he promised to develop that and other "missing features". He also agreed that there should be an Agony Column of personal notices and advertisements:

> In these difficult times [1948] members of the Service can help each other in many little ways and particularly by making available to each other some of the scarce necessities of life, ranging from flats to uniforms (I,Jan.,5).

However, the editor balked at the idea of becoming a sort of Universal Aunts. While proud to announce a "free information service", he cautioned that despite *Corona*'s close co-operation with the Women's Corona Society he could not guarantee results: "many people do write to us about schools, flats and houses; they have also asked us about training for ballet dancers and for help in historical research" (III,3). His successor, on his own initiative, reminded readers how "a number of retired Colonial Service officers have already taken up appointments in preparatory schools" and suggested that others might like to write to the Incorporated Association of Preparatory Schools (VII, 476). On another occasion he regretted that he could not engage in correspondence with all the golf clubs in the UK to find out which (if any) would be prepared to offer special terms to officers on leave, but from his own knowledge he gave the address of the secretaries of three willing clubs (XIII,40).

An important declaration of editorial policy appeared in April 1950, under the heading "Purely Domestic", in which it was acknowledged that what had started as a sideline to help those on leave was now a major business of the Corona office (II,157). This was followed not only by an increase in Agonies notices but by special editorial contributions on "Holidays Abroad" (II, 195) and "Petrol, Points and Prices" (II,235), together with a series of five articles in Vol.II by J.J. Tawney titled "On Leave Now", replacing "In England Now" and supplementing the regular "For Your Leave" calendars of coming events.

Notices of engagements, weddings, births and deaths could be inserted without charge. Deaths of serving officers were later editorially separated from those of retired ones. It was rare to publish an obituary, so that those recording the assassination of Duncan Stewart as Governor of Sarawak (II,79) and of Sir Henry Gurney as High Commissioner to the Federation of Malaya (III,478) provided an additional Service emphasis to the enormity of the twin tragedies. The non-Colonial Service profile of Professor Ida Ward of the School of Oriental and African Languages was, too, very much an exception (I,Dec.,37). The announcement of a memorial fund for Sir John Thorp, who as Governor of the Seychelles lost his life while attempting to save some children in difficulties when swimming (XIII,480), recalls the similar all-but tragedy of Sir Evelyn Baring's ocean rescue at Malindi while Governor of Kenya (XI,405). "From the News" was expended into the monthly "Chronicle", a move qualified by the editor with the remark that *Corona* was not a newspaper and so its news was, like its "Parliament" report, more of a record than news: "Both of them will always be laggards but between them they may help you to keep things in perspective" (II,3).

Initially the editor remained cautious about handling government reports and generally steered clear of reproducing official press releases, but over the years his selection from constitutional conferences and Parliamentary White Papers established what is today a useful record of colonial policy. The editorial comment that "it is not for us to review the Secretary of State's annual report to Parliament" (a public document published by HMSO) seemed to some readers to be a sign of leaning over backwards (II,288). Against this, the editor did not hesitate to come out quite directly in wondering whether the Secretary of State's 1956 elaboration of the establishment of HMOCS and the creation of a Special List (*Statement of Policy Regarding Organization*, Cmd. 9768) was going to be enough to halt the sinking Colonial Service morale:

> The need is twofold.. to reassure officers already in the Service and to secure the flow of the right type of entrant. Mr Lennox-Boyd hopes that young and women and men might now be encouraged to join the Service with easy minds. We feel, however, that they will want more than a White Paper to attract them.

> We know of young men, seemingly well qualified, and in some cases with a family tradition behind them, who are keen to join the Service but who, after examination of the printed proposals, are not yet sufficiently reassured to make it their career. One cannot blame them, any more than one can blame those serving officers who so rightly want some counterweight of security as the pendulum of progress swings towards uncertainty (VIII,283).

Once again, towards the end of its life, when the Service was beginning to feel insecure over its future, the editor had to defend himself over what some saw as *Corona*'s lack of political comment:

> During its thirteen years *Corona* has had few editorials. It is difficult, if not impossible, to comment on matters within the journal's scope without becoming political – indeed, the Overseas Service itself is now entwined with politics and its very existence is a political issue. But because the journal is tied to the Service and because it exists under the aegis of Whitehall and is sometimes, though wrongly, thought to be a Government mouthpiece, politics have been kept as far as possible from our pages...
>
> It has been suggested that conditions have now so changed that some political comment should appear in the journal... [Yet] however strongly we support individual freedom of expression elsewhere, so long as *Corona* remains the journal of the Overseas Service we feel it must avoid anything which might show partiality – and politics are the stuff of partiality (XIII,404).

The editor's postbag must have been a full – and a difficult – one. In 1954 the new editor disclosed a revealing insight into some of the comments received from readers (VI,59) "We want to be amused – a touch of *Punch* perhaps" was balanced by "I hope the serious aspect of the magazine will be maintained and that it will not give way to any demand for lighter fare", while "A lot of the matter, e.g. 'News of Your Friends' is a waste of newsprint"was countered by "We could do with more about people". Another reader felt that the ground of *Corona* was largely covered by other publications. Yet another gave vent to a *cri de coeur*: "Drop all these fanny [sic] articles and let's have something from the bushmen – if there are any left, which I am beginning to doubt". The editor was taken to task for refusing to give a lead to the Service over the issue aired in press and parliament in 1954, that when the time came for the Colonial Service to be closed it should be replaced by a genuine Commonwealth Service. The allegation of "a dumb *Corona*" was, the editor retorted, simply not true:

> We have given the matter a lot of thought but we don't think the time has yet come to write about it. At present the Commonwealth Service is an idea only, and not even the idea has attained official stature. *Corona* is not, emphatically, a mouthpiece of official policy, but it would be of little value to add to unofficial expressions of opinion which have appeared elsewhere and which may be expected to continue in the future (VI,163).

At a later period, after the Special Lists 'A' and 'B' had been introduced and the linked issue of lump sum compensation for premature retirement had been well chewed over within the Service, one reader reiterated the call that *Corona* ought not only to indulge in political comment but also carry information about comparative conditions of service: "Officers in one territory know very little of the conditions of the service, pay, housing, etc. of their colleagues in other territories... The Service's only magazine should fill the gap" (XIV,120).

The editor disagreed with the plea for "a voice to express and air grievances" and stood by his principle that, while he welcomed "critical articles...to provoke argument", *Corona* was definitely "NOT a show-window for chips on individual shoulders or for personal grouses" (VII,403). For him, as he expressed it when the dramatic news of the end of the Colonial Service was announced in 1954, "this is going to be a lengthy game, and the kick-off is not the time to comment on the run of the play. That is why *Corona* for the present remains silent, but watching with the deepest interest, on the touchline" (VI,164).

Another reader drily wrote "I find it not a little droll that after fifteen years' service in India and the Sudan where the benign Governments provided *Corona* free of charge, I now become a member of the Overseas Service and for the first time have to pay for its journal" (VII,142). However, he conceded that at £1 a year it was money well spent. The editor was persuaded to transfer the Parliamentary record away from the opening pages, for despite its admitted importance in *Corona* readers felt that, along with certain indigestible articles, they were "confronted with some pretty solid chunks of prose as soon as one opens the paper"(VII,8). Another criticism came in the Correspondence columns, where John Loxton from Kenya dismissed most of *Corona*'s articles as having "a limited appeal to the rank and file of the Service" – the very group targeted in the original venture. Noting that most of his non-subscribing friends only looked at "Promotions and Transfers" and then put it down, he recommended that "'our' journal would be more sought after if it contained more information on matters that affect large numbers of us personally, e.g. our conditions of service... The Service Journal is the proper place for circulating such news" (VIII,240). C.R. Niven, a senior administrative officer from Nigeria, thought that *Corona* should respond to Africanization, Malayanization, etc., by becoming a forum for the exchange of ideas between members of the new local public services and the Overseas Service (IX,120). None of this deterred the editor from citing his prize *Corona* quote from a headmaster who had recently taken out a subscription: "It will be something, too, to be able to hold up a copy of *Corona* in the classroom and say 'Here is a journal written for and by the men who administer this great family of nations'" (VIII,6).

From the beginning, the editor let it be known that his preference was for articles informing other members of the Service of what was going on. "Nearly everyone in the Service has something interesting to say which will be useful to his colleagues, and this rather than literary quality, is our criterion. So do not let modesty deter you". (I,Sept.,3). It did not, and in the event he frequently got both. He repeated the call two years later, asking for more articles from readers "about their jobs and about the problems which the Service has to face. The quality of *Corona* depends on its contributors" (III,443).Articles were either submitted or reproduced, with, according to internal evidence, some specially commissioned by the editor. In the early years many of the last group were deliberately slanted towards officers coming home on leave. With a continuously wary eye on *Corona*'s financial heal:h, the editor realized that to include contributions from those defined in the colonial vocabulary as 'unofficials' would likely result in more subscriptions. Articles, which were in theory restricted to 1,500 – later generously raised to 1,600 – words (though the principle was frequently breached and its disregard often connived at by allowing an article to appear in two or even three parts) came from journalists, academics, missionaries, MPs and Fabians, as well as – and predominantly – from within the Colonial Service. Apart from articles, the editor declared his interest in receiving drawings and photographs. "We are particularly anxious", an editorial ran in April 1950, "to get in touch with more photographers and artists in the Service. Many a light is, we are sure, hidden under a distant bushel, and we would very much like to give our artists an opportunity of having their work published in *Corona*" (II,123). Once again, he could not have been disappointed in the quality of much of what he received.

For a journal published in the 1950s, and from a Colonial Service that was essentially a male career, *Corona* is characterized by the encouragement and attention it gave to – to quote the now dated title of a six part series it ran as early as 1951 – "The Distaff Side" (III,passim) This was focused on Britain and leave, but it was not long before contributions from the field, whether by wives of officers or by women officers, could be reckoned on as a regular feature. For social historians of the Colonial Service this, as with Charles Allen's revelatory *Tales from the Dark Continent* (1979) and *Tales from the South China Seas* (1983), or A.J.Sherman's *Mandate Days* (1997) and Derek Hopwood's *Tales of Empire* (1989) for the Middle East or June Knox-Mawer's *Tales from Paradise* (1986) for the Pacific, adds an extremely important dimension to Colonial Service life and to the value of *Corona* as a source.

However satisfied the editor was with the quantity and the quality of contributions, by the mid-1950s he was beginning to be worried at the imbalance in the numbers and territorial origin of *Corona*'s subscribers. Hence his launching of "Exercise Corona", based on the premise that *all* members of the Service might be expected to take some interest in *their* journal, inviting subscribers and governments to campaign for more readers (VII,40). Three of the smaller colonies, Cyprus, Gibraltar and Dominica, promptly produced no less than 300 new subscribers, followed by first time subscribers from New Hebrides, North Borneo, Trinidad and British Guiana. Hong Kong managed to triple its subscriptions, so that by Christmas 1955 *Corona*'s new subscribers exceeded the total recorded in any previous year. It is unfortunate that HMSO no longer has a record of subscriptions or of the number of copies of *Corona* it printed; nor did the editor ever publish a list of the number of subscribers by territory.

In the next year the editor thought up another plug for his publicity drive by announcing a "Corona Competition" (VIII,80) A prize (of three guineas) was offered for the best true story under the title "My Strangest Half Hour". Entrants had to be past or present members of the Colonial /Overseas Service, and the stories had to relate to occurrences during their service overseas within the past twenty years. They had, too, to be certified true! The judge was S.H. Evans, Head of the Colonial Office Information Department. The winner was A.F. Giles' "The Caller" (IX,39), with the well-known author J. Darrell Bates's "Lunch for Three Hundred" *proxime accessit* (IX,157). There followed an offer to print stories of interesting public personalities appearing in unlikely places in the Colonies, limited this time to one thousand words. F.D. Hislop's account of how he once entertained 'the' Dr. Jung in an up-country station in Kenya in 1925 (XII,236) was matched by D.C.C. Trench on how he looked after Eleanor Roosevelt in the Solomon Islands in 1944 (XIII,159). A later ploy to stimulate subscriptions was to include a brief preview of what articles were going to be published in *Corona* in the following issue (e.g., XII,226) While most contributions were signed, the editor was ready to accept pen-names (Kojo, Corin, Kwelu were among them) and now and again plain initials by the shyer or more modest (e.g. W.J.S.S., quickly identifiable by the Northern Nigerian cognoscenti as the wife of a senior Resident, and 'M.W.K." in II,107 and 187 respectively).

As the Gold Coast and Malaya approached independence, the editor began redirecting his thoughts away from the Colonies to the Commonwealth. In May 1956 *Corona* ran an article on "The Commonwealth Takes Shape" (VIII,177), derived from three substantial background pamphlets prepared by the Reference Division of the Central Office of Information. A little later the editor commissioned no less than eight successive articles, "Commonwealth Diary"(XII,152, ff.) from the Editor of *New Commonwealth*, Don Taylor. In another reorientation mood, the regular feature "For Your Leave" was amplified in 1956 with three issues (appropriately each covering one term of the academic year) of "Letter from Oxford" (VIII,98ff.) by Michael Taafe, the pen-name of a former Tanganyikan Provincial Commissioner (and author), now teaching Swahili to the Overseas Service Courses at Oxford. Another lecturer on the Oxford courses, G.E. Masefield, had published an article in the very first issue of *Corona* on "Colonial Aims" (I,July,21), which was responsible for a substantial amount of reaction under Correspondence. The Oxford Colonial Service programme continued to make its mark with a letter from the Course Supervisor, H.P.W. Murray (XI,120), notifying members of the Colonial Service Club there that the well-loved Joy Bourdillon was about to retire after seven years as the Club's warden, and also conveying the news that the subscription for Harry Smith, the Club's barman for thirty years, who retired in 1957 – "more than one departing Cadet has returned to greet an unforgetting Smith as a Governor" – (IX,304) – had passed the £500 mark. The editor was, it seemed to feather-ruffled Cantabs, too loyal an Oxford man (and robustly proud of it) ever to include or seek out Colonial Service news from the Other Place apart from one lighter-hearted piece on the Cambridge Summer School and another on the Second Devonshire Course at Cambridge by two N. Nigerian administrators (VIII,75;150).

Rightly, given the eclecticism of his readership, the editor turned his face against anything like a special issue focused on a single theme. Nonetheless, now and again in the early days a monthly issue did include more than one article on the same topic, for example community development (I,March), trade unions in the colonies (II, August)

and soil erosion (five articles in five consecutive issues). On the other hand, towards
the end of *Corona*'s life the editor, possibly as part of a Colonial Office campaign to
raise the profile of the new HMOCS and stimulate recruitment, and in step with his
predecessor's propaganda pamphlet *A Career in the Oversea Civil Service* (1955),
commissioned a series of articles on the work of "The Administrative Officer Today"
(Vol.XI), covering N. Nigeria, N. Rhodesia, Fiji, Uganda, Barotseland, West Indies
(not many DO jobs for Britons there), and Tanganyika (no less than three altogether,
by editorial licence: after all, was that not his own original territory?). For these the
purpose was not to discuss district administration in general terms but rather "by
recording personal experiences from a variety of places, to build up a picture of the
many differing duties and responsibilities still [1959] required from a branch of the
Service which is particularly susceptible to change' (XI,85). Special attention and
welcome were promised to junior officers who sent factual rather than theoretical
accounts of their life and duties in provincial administration. Unfortunately, in terms
of HMOCS's steadiest demand for applicants, where the decline of the expatriate
administrative officer cadre was balanced by a sharp increase in the number of professional officers required, the Series was never extended to the new-look work of the
current Agricultural, Educational, Medical, etc. officer. In one of the final volumes a
short attempt was make to redress the balance, when a single issue contained contributions on the Zanzibar Prison Service, the Aden Magistracy, medical work in the Windward Islands and the Police in Sierra Leone (XII,June).

The announcement in August 1962 that *Corona* was going to close by the end of
the year (XIV,286) came as a shock to its hundreds of subscribers and potential
contributors. In the event, a close reading of editorial reflections reveals that *Corona*'s
demise was not as sudden as it seemed. As far back as 1959, the editor had warned
subscribers: "We must be realistic: independence for Colonies means contracting
circulation for *Corona*" (XI,5). In one of its few substantial editorials (a lack on which
the editor congratulated himself), the view was aired in November 1961 that, given
the transfer of responsibility for HMOCS recruitment from the Colonial Office to the
new Department of Technical Co-operation and the likelihood of "a new stream of
men and women coming out to work in countries in which the [career) Service has
held the field until now", it might well be that "in those circumstances *Corona* should
no longer be addressed principally to the Service" (XIII,404). With self-government
already achieved in so many former colonial territories over the past five years and
with a contract HMOCS replacing the permanent career Colonial Service since 1954,
there was a clear perception at both home (Whitehall) and abroad (in the territories)
that the new conditions of service brought new tasks and new recruits, whose basically short-term commitments in turn brought new interests. That often spread, too, to
a change in the kind of things they wanted to read about in 'their' magazine, including
more tomorrow and less yesterday or even today. With all that had so dramatically
taken place on the colonial scene and in the established Colonial Service in the 1950s,
the original *Corona* was no longer going to make sense or exercise the same appeal
for the new, non-career Service of the 1960s.

In a further defining editorial nine months later, by which time the die had been cast, the editor firmed up his belief that <u>Corona</u> was "dependent on the Colonial Service for its existence" and hence its future would clearly be in jeopardy "if the Service became a casualty of changing Colonial conditions" (XIV,287)."That" he concluded, "has now happened." Indeed, he conceded, "for some time it has been unrealistic to think in terms of a journal designed for the Service in 1949".It had been hoped that a merger might have been effected to allow *Corona* to adapt to "present-day purposes", but no willing partner was found. Rather than face a future character-ized by "a growing inability to preserve those intimate links with the Service which were a reason for our existence", the decision had been taken to "close our pages while our name still strongly represents those servants of the Crown who made up the Colonial and Overseas Services" (XIV,288). *Corona* would accordingly terminate at the end of 1962.

In today reading and re-reading all 7,000 pages, the question inevitably arises of how far *Corona* turned its readers on, above all in the critical first issues, and so spurred them into taking out an annual subscription. In the event, time and positive editorial-izing were to show that *Corona* not only really did establish itself as the journal of the Colonial Service but also attracted subscribers and contributors from outside the Service. Yet perhaps because of that catholicity of contributors, who were in no way confined to the Colonial Service or the Colonial Office, it would be misleading to look to *Corona* for trying to establish anything like a profile of Colonial Service opinion or the quintessential mindset of the Colonial Service. Indeed, one might well argue that to expect to find such a phenomenon as the hypothetical 'attitude' of the Colonial Service towards its work could in itself be no more than a speculative enterprise among such an individualistic and independent-minded body of men and women as the Colonial Service. It was rare enough to find a provincial or territorial unanimity over local policy, let alone anything as monolithic as a Service one. To get, as it were, under the skin of the Colonial Service, far more rewarding are the insights to be derived from the newsletters etc. of the various territorial Civil Servants' Associa-tions, generically and affectionately known within the Colonial Service as the 'Bolshie Societies'. In the event, these records too remain an unexplored source for local civil service history.

A house magazine is not the same thing as an activist journal or newsletter. As we have seen (pp. 19–21), the editor rejected any suggestion that *Corona* should become a forum for discussing conditions of service or terms of compensation. He was adamant that the one thing *Corona* would never be was a 'trade union' outlet: not "a voice to express and air grievances" and definitely "NOT a show-window for chips on individual shoulders". Nor should it be overlooked that every article written by civil servants required clearance by their government in accordance with local regula-tions. Few controversial articles appeared, and those that did – not always from Colo-nial Service officers – were generally more critical of practice than of policy and rarely generated much support in the scanty correspondence pages. It was description rather than debate, information and not instigation, which characterized the contents of *Corona*. In the end, as with every society's or association's journal, what *Corona* did was to express the views of those who cared to write for it. Beyond lay a far larger body of the silent, content to listen and to learn rather than to argue and to advocate. *Corona* was happy to cater for the majority of its readers and they seemed happy to go on paying for what they got.

Even on the major crises of colonial policy in the 1950s, such as the handling of the Malayan insurgency, the roots of Mau Mau and the role of grassroots Colonial Service officers in promoting the imposed Central African Federation, it was official statements and White Paper abridgements rather than thoughts from within the Colonial Service that characterised *Corona*'s presentation of such traumatic events. A similar reticence or reluctance can be observed over the lack of articles taking up the broader issues of the political impact of socio-economic development, like compulsory soil erosion measures, the appropriate goals of higher education initiatives, the conflict between Western and traditional medicine, and the whole cultural downside of 'development' *pur sang*.

Yet overall there can be no doubt that, for all *Corona*'s contemporary appeal to Colonial Service officers and their families, today it is its intrinsic and unique contribution to the history of the Colonial Service, at work and at leisure, *en poste* and on leave, which through its 'points of entry'has enhanced its original ongoing value to that of constituting a primary and hitherto under-exploited tool for research into the Colonial Service.

The December issue of Volume XIV, the final appearance of *Corona*, remains a particularly important one. Many of the contributors were, significantly, drawn from the Great and the Good. The doyen of the Colonial Office and long-time 'uncle' (to Sir Ralph Furse as 'father') of the Colonial Service Division, Sir Charles Jeffries, looked back with an essay on "The Colonial Service in Perspective" (456); the final Permanent Secretary of the Colonial Office, Sir Hilton Poynton, looked ahead in "Speculation in Church House" (456); the long-time Colonial Office visionary and first Permanent Secretary of the new Department of Technical Co-operation, Sir Andrew Cohen, discussed "Other Times, Other Needs" (467); and no less than three one-time Secretaries of State for the Colonies, the current Duncan Sandys and two of his best-known predecessors, Arthur Creech Jones and Viscount Boyd, all added importantly to the plethora of look-backs and farewell messages addressed to, in Duncan Sandys' words, "The Service – Past and Present" (447).

The editor, too, contributed his own "Goodbye" (XIV,496). He dwelt with justifiable satisfaction on how *Corona* had reached far beyond its Colonial Service readership, with regular subscriptions from American and Australian as well as Ghanaian and Tanzanian Universities. He also quoted obituary tributes from some of the readers, full of expressions like "sorry", "regret", "heart-broken" and "sadly miss'. In one case *Corona* was apparently looked on by a professor of Public Administration as "a practical expression for the teaching of administrative theory" (XIV,496).

The editor's final words, after thanking the Colonial Office for its cordial hospitality and *Corona*'s indefatigable secretary, Diane Morris, for having typed more than ten million words for the printers, were addressed to the backbone of the enterprise, the Journal's contributors. Following up his message to them when he took over from K.G. Bradley ten years earlier, when he had written:

> we have, of course, had disappointments – no editor is ever satisfied. Quality can always be improved; many a valuable contribution to the professional and political aspect of colonial administration from serving officers does not even get written, let alone sent to us, for reasons which we quite understood but are not valid (V,43),

Tawney once more addressed "those who made the journal – our contributors":

> Although we believe they enjoyed writing and drawing for *Corona*, a special word of thanks is due to them. How understanding were those whose pet pieces were returned with a letter of regret; how long-suffering when their published work showed a scandalous amount of editorial interference; how civilly did even those react to a blue pencil who, during their Service days, slashed red ink onto other people's compositions. And if sometimes a few of those who had promised contributions became deaf and dumb as deadlines approached, how gallantly did others respond when asked to fill a gap at short notice (XIV,497).

It is, too, to *Corona*'s long-time and dedicated editor that we may properly turn for the final word in this Introduction. His prophetic hope in 1962 makes as noble and as pertinent a conclusion to this <u>Corona</u> Anthology as it did for *Corona*'s epitaph nearly forty years ago;

> When the Service has disappeared it will still be possible to read the records of its doctors, administrators and policemen; road makers, foresters and vets; firemen and nurses;geologists, tax gatherers and men who ran railways;auditors and meteorologists; labour officers, agriculturists, social workers, sanitary inspectors specialists, school mistresses and many others.
>
> Even if the history of the Service is never written, much of what it did will be found in these unemotional pages by people who left home to work for other people. Their stories are evidence that neither expediency nor personal distress blinded their original obligations.
>
> If *Corona* helps to make that clear, its fourteen years of life will have served their purpose (XIV,268).

AHM Kirk-Greene
St. Antony's College, Oxford

31 May 1999

Acknowledgements

In acknowledging the kind permission of the Controller of Her Majesty's Stationery Office in whom Crown copyright vests to reproduce the material contained in this anthology from *Corona*, I should like to make three points. First, permission to reproduce the material was granted a quarter of a century ago to the publishers Kraus Publications of Lichtenstein for their reprint of the entire *Corona* magazine. Both editions have been consulted for this Anthology. Secondly, though neither in that case nor the present has it been possible to identify any third party contributors who, despite the regularly printed notice that *Corona* and not the contributors retained the copyright, might not have vested their copyright in the Crown, in the absence of the *Corona* files we should like to take this opportunity of also thanking all original contributors for articles or illustrations reproduced in this Anthology. Finally, in acknowledging HMSO's confirmation that there are no objections on the grounds of Crown copyright to reproducing this material, I should in particular like to express my appreciation to Anne Battley, Copyright Officer HMSO (Cabinet Office), for her personal interest and the dedicated way in which she has handled the issue of the Crown copyright of *Corona* material.

(a) The Colonial Service at Large

While particular aspects of the Colonial Service at work and at leisure, sampling nearly every territory and every department, form the focus of this Anthology, from time to time *Corona* featured contributions which covered the Service in a more general way. These included such items as the Queen's message to her Colonial Service on her accession to the throne; Sir Ralph Furse's keynote address to one of the Cambridge Summer Conferences and Sir Charles Jeffries' lookback at the Colonial Service in 1962; reflections from serving officers on the purpose and philosophy of colonial government; the changing pattern of recruitment in the 1950s; and reports of the annual gathering of the Colonial Service's social club, the Corona Club, and the Women's Corona Society. An article "Why Study the Colonial Service" was written – unexpectedly perhaps — by an American scholar, Robert Heussler, who successfully did just that for the Administrative Service in Nigeria, Tanganyika and Malaya, as well as on its recruitment and training at Oxford.

CORONA

The Journal of His Majesty's Colonial Service

VOLUME I	November, 1949	NO. 10

CONTENTS

First Things First

THE last speech of all at the Cambridge Summer Conference was made by Sir Ralph Furse, and many of those who heard it thought that it was the most important contribution of all and were sorry that it had not been made on the first evening instead of on the last. Nobody, moreover, had a better right to give this message to the Colonial Service than Sir Ralph, and we hoped that he would interpret our long applause not merely as our agreement with what he said but as our tribute of respect and affection for himself.

We ourselves are convinced that Sir Ralph is right. Material progress is only valuable as a means to a higher end. What, precisely, *is* our purpose? The blind cannot lead the blind. We must try to clear our vision and we need each other's help. When you have read what Sir Ralph Furse said to us, perhaps some of you will feel like making your own contributions through the pages of *Corona.*

Sir Ralph began by pulling the Chairman's leg. Like the Almighty, Mr. Cohen moved "in a mysterious way." Had he not chosen, to wind up the Conference, the one man there who knew least about the subjects of discussion and was too deaf to hear more than a tenth of what had been said?

"But," he added, "this is not the first time that I have detected some resemblance between Mr. Cohen and the Almighty! I well remember the last day of the first of these Conferences three years ago. Mr. Cohen was billed to make an important speech after Hall. Some of us spent the afternoon visiting the Rural College at Impington. We were driving home about 6 p.m. along the road over there, the other side of that ditch that Cambridge men call a river. I happened to look out of the window of the bus and caught sight of Mr. Cohen stamping up and down the Backs like a bull elephant with toothache. I could see him almost literally clutching at the skirts of some idea which he wanted to crystallise for his speech and which was equally obviously eluding him at the moment. I could not help thinking of the picture of the Almighty walking in the Garden in the cool of the evening wondering where that damned elusive apple had got to."

Sir Ralph went on to say that he did not believe Mr. Cohen had yet found the apple, nor had anyone else—British at any rate—who had been engaged on the problem of Colonial Administration. But in his view it was vital to find the apple, and to find it soon. "For the apple I am thinking of is the fruit of the tree of knowledge of what is good or evil for Africa."

He could not help feeling that in our attack on the problems of Colonial Administration we had "set our sights too low." "Have we not busied ourselves overmuch with material needs—communications and production, hospitals and infant welfare, mass education and the like? And when we have strayed further afield have we not rather limited ourselves to objectives such as the establishment of the Pax Britannica and the rule of British justice? All these things are important—do not misunderstand me there—but they are not enough.

"All of you know the African much better than I do, but I cannot bring myself to believe that he is so different from ourselves, that he will be content if we provide him with an extra pint of milk a week, and an expert Trade Union' leader per 100,000 of the population to organise his strikes for him in a nice, tidy way. For he has a soul, just as we have, and anyone with a soul needs the higher and more intangible values—religion and beauty, art and music, the dance and drums; and that something which, I believe, stirs in the blood of a Masai *moran* when he fingers his spear, just as it stirs in the blood of a Highlander when the pipes are playing."

A civilisation must be evolved for Africa in the modern world, but we could not "hand it to them ready made on a plate." The only people who could work out such a civilisation were the Africans themselves. All we could do, but it was a very big thing, was to create a "climate" in which Africans could evolve "a good civilisation and not a bad one, a civilisation in which individual Africans can lead a good life and be happy."

Turning to the African officers present, Sir Ralph said: — "You are the future leaders of your people. But I believe that for the present the most valuable rôle you can play, and the one in which you should be principally used, is what the Army would call reconnaissance and liaison. You should be particularly well qualified to tell us what Africans really want. But if you are to undertake this rôle, then a very heavy responsibility will be laid upon you. For nothing is more dangerous in battle than faulty information. You must not only tell us what the educated Africans want—we know a good deal about that already—or what the primitives want—we know something about that too. You must also tell us what the intermediate mass of what I might call the partially-educated Africans want. This mass is continually growing, and, in the words of an African, will be the petrol that will drive the African car."

"And now," Sir Ralph went on, "may I say a word to the British officers? I have interfered pretty considerably in the lives of a good number of you.

And therefore I have felt very responsible towards you, especially in the rather grim times through which you have been passing and are still passing. For I feel that in asking you to put the crown on British achievement in Colonial Administration, we may have asked many of you to put upon your own heads something which must often feel rather like a crown of thorns. And so I have been thinking a lot in recent years, trying to see an aspect of what you are doing which, while not presenting a false view, might bring some comfort. I offer the following suggestion for what it may be worth.

" I believe that what we are really trying to do in the Colonial Service and in the Colonial Office is to write the last and most difficult chapter in the record of a great experiment on which the British people, whether they always knew it or not, have been engaged since the time of Humphrey Gilbert—and that, if my history is correct, must be nearly the last 400 years. That experiment is nothing less than the greatest experiment in the association of free peoples which is recorded in history."

In the speaker's view there had been five British Empires. One had been lost in France in the Middle Ages. Another had been lost in North America " through insensitive statesmanship." A third was created in the white Dominions —Canada, Australia, New Zealand, South Africa. " We have not lost that—yet anyway—because we learnt our lesson from number two, but it has changed into something which can no longer be called an ' Empire,' and is no longer so called." We had made a fourth empire in India and were now watching Hindostan and Pakistan, who had slipped their cables and were sailing out over unfamiliar seas.

" We were left with the fifth British Empire—the Colonial Empire which you administer. And it will be the last, for there is nowhere else to go. This is the last chance the British will ever have of doing something for which, with all their mistakes and all their blunders, and even their crimes, they have shown a peculiar genius."

Imperial thinkers of the older school had more than once expressed the hope that as the British Commonwealth evolved, it might provide the whole world with a model on which to arrange its affairs in peace. But they—Sir Ralph felt—were thinking mainly in terms of the white Dominions. That was no longer enough. Since the fall of Singapore, to take a convenient date, what with the improvement of communications and the great movements that are sweeping across the world, " no working model will do which does not bridge the frontiers of colour." " That," he added, " is where we come in. Other colonial powers—especially France—can show a rich experience and a great record of achievement in the administration of what are called dependent peoples. We too have had some experience in that line. But we have also had the experience, which no other race possesses, of having brought to nationhood overseas communities of European origin and then of having retained them—so far at any rate—in free and willing co-operation within the family of the Commonwealth. With that unique record and unique experience behind us we dare not falter in this the last and most difficult lap of the race. We may fail, but we dare not falter.

" And if, by any chance, we do succeed: if we can successfully fulfil our own trust, and if in so doing we provide the world with an effective working model, then the name of the British Colonial Service will be remembered in honour for a thousand years after this fifth and last British Empire has faded away and changed into something the pattern and lineaments of which we cannot yet discern.

" But first we must find that apple. And to remind myself of that, when Mr. Canham—as I hope he will remember to do—sends me my printed copy of the proceedings of this Conference, I am going to take a red pencil and at the bottom of the last page I shall put a large question mark, and then write these words: — ' What shall it profit the African if *we* save his soil and *he* loses his soul? '."

One Tour

by J. G. HUDDLE

IN his recent and notable autobiography, *Arrow in the Blue*,* Arthur Koestler reflects on the way in which the course of his life has veered, sharply and unpredictably, between two contradictory poles. "I have," he writes, "a vivid image of the arrow, whose timeless flight through space was, in one way or another, always present in my mind, splitting lengthwise into two. The two halves have a repellent effect on each other, their orbits become deflected; they continue their flight in opposite directions, one symbolising Action, the other Contemplation." I quote this observation because I think that the unique and outstanding merit of the Colonial Service as a career is the opportunity which it offers to strike a satisfactory means between the rival claims of "action" and "contemplation," to use Koestler's terms. The many problems with which the Colonial Service is faced in the various territories are complex, arresting and of obvious international significance; yet constant and widespread contact with the people themselves, at every level of society, is of undiminished importance and the scope for initiative and local action on the ground remains ample. It is the resulting marriage between differing elements so rarely compatible in other careers that seems to me to be the final justification of the Service as a career, a justification that remains unaffected by the glosses placed upon this career by modern developments and which I propose in a moment to discuss.

As I am now completing only my fourth year of service, having spent approximately half that time in East Africa and half in Malaya, it is clear that I could have nothing to offer from my apprentice's experience which would be of assistance to qualified and experienced officers in the Service. My reason for writing is less specific than that. I am one of the post-war generation of Colonial Servants who have never known the atmosphere of security, of assuredness, that must have been the background to the careers of the majority of British Colonial Servants in the earlier years of this century. Even before we arrived in our Colony or Dependency my generation learnt, from the conversation and attitude of Colonial students at the Universities, that the very basis of our careers and policies as Colonial Civil Servants was now being challenged; the colonial scene in which we were to be cast was dynamic rather than traditional.

I am sufficiently new in the Colonial Service to recall much of the attitudes which I and my contemporaries brought into it at the beginning, yet I have now obtained, perhaps, just sufficient first-hand knowledge to discern the nature and outlines of the Colonial Service as a career. For this reason I have chosen this moment, at the end of my first tour, to try and think out where I stand; and it may be of some interest to others to know the reaction of a beginner to the present situation in the Service and his estimate of the prospect which it offers. I well realise my actions may be as superficial as my experience; but they may at least be symptomatic.

I have mentioned the absence of security and assuredness, now characteristic of the Colonial Service as a career. This, of course, is a symptom of a world trend towards revolutionary developments in social and political life, but it is a trend to which colonial territories are peculiarly exposed. I feel that this fact of instability is the most important aspect of the Colonial Servant's career at the present time (I would emphasise that I am not concerned simply with any insecurity in his tenure of office, but with the dynamic nature of the whole colonial landscape, political,

* *Arrow in the Blue*, Arthur Koestler. Published by Hamish Hamilton & Collins, 1952.

social and economic, in which he finds himself); and I consider that the generation of Colonial Service Cadets, of which I am one, was on the whole unprepared for this state of affairs. Perhaps this was because of what we ourselves insisted on imagining, despite all the signs to the contrary. Perhaps it was because, from what we were told during our training, we built up a picture of careers far too much of a piece with the "traditional" colonial picture derived from the "golden age" of the District Commissioner, of the years from the turn of the century up to the Second World War (brief though this period is in relation to the whole long history of British expansion overseas). Whatever the reason, I feel that we had built up in our minds a picture which failed by a considerable margin to do justice to the intriguing but exacting realities with which we were bound in the end, almost wherever we went, to be faced.

To describe, for instance, this revolutionary period in colonial affairs in which we were to participate, as the finest phase in a culminating process of tutelage, of "training our future masters," seems to me to have stopped considerably short of accuracy. It does not appear, for one thing, to take sufficient account of the insatiable iconoclastic pressure of the nationalists, who will not wait to be trained. Of course, we can produce, on the basis of our premises, compelling arguments to resist the more irresponsible of the nationalists' claims; but such arguments can hardly contend with the degree to which outside political considerations, in the United Kingdom and in international affairs, now dictate or at any rate influence the direction of colonial policies, quite independently of the intrinsic merits of the case. These facts, and the hostility and suspicion which, from certain quarters and widely varying degrees, press against the Colonial Servant must, it seems to me, be fully realised; they must not be something that comes upon him unawares and which consequently he greets either with resignation (literal or otherwise!) or appeasement. We must continue to work on the end of our branch, neither deterred nor deflected by the activities of persons—doubtless "all honourable men"—who are busy sawing off the branch at the trunk-face.

To be realistic, which I am trying to be, is not to embrace pessimism, still less to show any lack of respect for the colonial heritage to which we are the heirs. Some people now talk glibly and critically of the "crumbling Empire." What seems so remarkable to me, however, is the durability and adaptability of our imperial heritage in this dynamic age. This resilience is not ultimately dependent on mere power (in which we need not be ashamed to admit ourselves nowadays to be "second-rate") and it is perhaps for this reason attracting the increasing interest and respect of an outside world which, until recently, has been prone to dismiss British colonial policies as mere imperialism.

Malaya is an outstanding example of the peculiar strength of the British Empire at the present time. Faced with an armed insurrection, the United Kingdom and Malayan Governments have provided the necessary military strength to combat it. But others could have done that. The British alone, I suggest, could have brought this military strength to bear in the manner required, combining it all the while with enlightened civil administration and a susceptibility for local nationalist feelings. Uniquely and adaptably comprehensive in another way, the Malayan Government's policies have extended the rights and position of the Chinese community in Malaya; yet the linchpin of our position, in these critical years of the "emergency," has been the loyalty of the Malay community, and this could not have been retained but for the respect won from the Malays by the administration of the Malayan Civil Service in the first half of the century. It is part of the British colonial genius to provide for each facet of policy men devoted to their own particular speciality yet capable of keeping a balance—soldiers who are sensitive to the needs of the civil administration, Resettlement Officers concerned with the welfare of their Chinese villagers who can appreciate the need for the occasional application of unpleasant security measures, and so on. And from the distilled wisdom of centuries of imperial experience, Britain can supply to all these facets a guiding touch that can hold all together to achieve, in Malaya, what is perhaps unique amongst the many current struggles against militant Communism through South-East Asia and the Far East, namely advance and success not merely on the military but also on the social and political fronts.

Indeed, it seems likely that these two latter aspects now constitute the most likely lines of fruitful advance in Malaya. In the part of Malaya where I served for a short time it seemed that the armed struggle with the terrorists was stabilising itself, at a lower level far more favourable to the force of law and order than that which prevailed until very recently. Owing to growing security force pressure, particularly in the realm of food control, the terrorist gangs concentrate now merely upon carrying on their own existence and building up supplies, only mounting "incidents" when provoked or when everything happens to be in their favour. In the context of their past these gangs are still most formidable and they can still demonstrate their strength in savage, well-planned forays. It remains essential to hold the favourable military position which has been built up with such difficulty and at such cost. The main line for future advance, however (implicit in the Malayan Government's policy throughout the emergency but now assuming greater relative importance), lies, it seems to me, in the isolation of the Communist terrorists from the people of Malaya by progressive social, political and economic policies, so that the terrorists come to occupy in the minds of the Malayan population the same position of odium and resentment that gangsters do in normal civilised states. We must remove altogether from these terrorists the "Robin Hood" mantle which makes them to some extent a contrary pole for popular loyalties, disturbing the onward march of the Malayan peoples towards a united nationhood. In this light it can be most clearly seen, as General Sir Gerald Templer has so firmly emphasised, that there can be no division between "emergency" and "non-emergency" in the affairs of Malayan government.

Looking back on a tour spent partly in Uganda and partly in Malaya, it seems to me that one factor making for a profound difference between the attitudes of the two administrations is the missionary tradition and influence in Uganda and the virtual absence of it in Malaya. This is connected with an impression which I formed very soon after my arrival in Malaya from East Africa. In comparing the two territories I was mainly struck by the fact that the relations between the Europeans and the non-Europeans in Malaya seemed to be far easier and fuller than in Uganda (and, I imagined, other African Dependencies as well); this, I might mention, was in 1951 before the Mau Mau outbreak in Kenya and at the peak of the Malayan emergency. The European in Malaya sits, it seems, more easily and less demandingly among the Malays and other races domiciled there than does his counterpart in East Africa. After all, it is bound to make for greater tension if the colonising race not only lays claim to superior techniques but also asserts its right and duty to transform and uplift the very soul of the dependent peoples. I realise, however, that this is only one explanation of the greater racial tension in Africa; the more primitive stage of society at which the colonising countries found the African peoples, as compared with the Malays and Malayan Chinese, is obviously also of importance.

In Malaya, the task of the British administrator can from one point of view be regarded as that of an umpire, holding the balance in the race between different communities and striving to compensate for their various strengths and weaknesses *vis-à-vis* one another; here, inevitably, the taunt is invited, "Divide and rule!" In Africa, on the other hand, it might be said that we are concerned more to control the forces which we have evoked and to teach the Africans that they have to wait, that they must prove their fitness before we can allow them to taste the very things for which we have given them appetites; as a result, in Africa we are sometimes called repressors. Whether in Malaya or Africa, however, I found considerable similarity in the suspicion with which articulate, educated non-European opinion regarded British activities and actions. This suspicion, it seems to me, is as inescapable a part of the colonial background as cold weather in an English winter; the British Colonial Servant, however sure he is of the strength of his case, must accept this fact with as much patience as he can muster. The fashionable and widespread *malaise* of anti-Government feeling in the colonial territories is not a nationally conceived attitude, which could be met squarely with logical arguments; rather it is the powerful emotional and cultural reaction of a newly born political consciousness to events and situations as it finds them. In the climate of world opinion, to-day and in the foreseeable future, there are few grounds for hoping that anything we do or say can ever wholly dislodge this hostility from its place in colonial consciousness. And before we, as Colonial Servants, fall into despair at the unreasonableness of colonial opinion, we should perhaps be careful not to overlook the fact that we are too close to these controversial affairs to be ourselves always free from some personal, emotional involvement in them which might influence and. distort our own judgements.

It seems to me that one way through the tense and complicated situation which I have tried to outline is to be found on a personal basis. At the level of personal contact, where it is established that one has the interests of the African (or of the Malayan) really at heart, the opportunities for achievement are great. It might be said that, whereas on the plane of Constitutions and Legislative Councils we are dealing in impermanencies and abstractions, in the effect that our example and friendship has on individuals we are dealing in the indisputable basic currency of the future—human lives, which will influence and create the social and political institutions of the dependent territories and determine the use to which they are put. Such ultimate issues of transcendent importance as whether, for example, a territory, when it achieves independence, will choose to stay within the British Commonwealth may very well be determined in the realm of individual human relationships in the present; whereas the devising of a new constitutional device, however brilliant, to solve some pressing political difficulty may have little or no effect, in the future, on such grave matters.

This approach, of working where possible in terms of individuals, will separate us off from the approach, characteristic to-day of some highly influential British newspapers and periodicals, which superimposes upon the colonial scene a structure of political life and attitudes having little relation to the facts. By a process of faulty analogy, and derived from a well-supported and deeply rooted school of British historical writing, this approach looks in every situation for the "progressive" elements. It tries to discern in the "politics" of an African Dependency the same holy progression, in the face of unenlightened and reactionary government opposition, from medieval heretics, through Levellers, Whigs and Chartists to Fabianism and Social Democracy which it holds (perhaps superficially and inaccurately) to be the real theme of British history. Such an approach has many dangers. It identifies the worthwhile with the so-called "progressive." Upon those who, often on dubious grounds, qualify for this label, is conferred a dangerous immunity from frank appraisal and criticism, while those who cannot be brought under the "progressive" label (and they are clearly of substantial importance in the more backward societies) are discounted. In its extreme ascendancy, such a theory would hand over each territory without delay to a bad charade on European Parliamentary democracy, and all the traditional virtues, the quiet but promising beginners, the competent apprentices and true nascent leaders, would be thrown to the winds. Nor would it take long for the charade to give place to a play far more sinister and disastrous, with little relation to the liberalism that it was meant to represent.

I have already mentioned the analogy (and I am sure it is not an original one) of the Colonial Servant working on, "regardless" one might say, at the end of his branch whilst, at the other end, events on a quite different plane are sawing off his branch at its base. Dangerous, if well-intentioned, misconceptions of the nature of political life in the dependent territories comprise one of the factors with which the Colonial Servant has to reckon in this way. As far as possible, however, it seems to me that we should refuse to allow ourselves to be so much harried, whether it be by the academic but radical conclusions of international commissions or by angry resolutions passed in the heady atmosphere of political meetings at the English seaside, as to be distracted from our main concern, which is to encourage and deal with the good, wherever it is found, and to reform, or if necessary to overcome, what is harmful and bad.

It is in the tremendous importance and scope for individual influence that there seems to me to lie the great attraction of the Colonial Service as a career. Nowhere else, perhaps, are such huge demands placed upon an individual, partly because, even nowadays, a European is still such a rarity in Asia and Africa (at any rate outside the few big towns) and partly because of what the colonial peoples have learned to expect from the example of past British Colonial officials. The opportunities which the Colonial Servant has for exerting his personal influence are in fact limited only by his inclinations. Our policies, our ten-year plans, even our local development schemes, may be bitterly opposed, but it is more rare for our friendship to be refused.

One of the main ingredients, it seems to me, of Western Christian philosophy (as opposed to the disastrous, totalitarian perversions from it mainly of the last hundred years) is emphasis on the primary importance of the individual, on the sacredness of his dignity and rights and on the vital importance of his holding firm, whatever the external difficulties, to what he conceives to be right. Politics, affairs generally from the community point of view, are recognised to be unpredictable and definitely secondary (causally and in importance). If this is so, it bears out my case: although the traditional colonial framework and attitudes may be undergoing rapid transformations, the function of individual service remains as broad and as vital as ever. The Colonial Servant can only "speak right on," true to what he holds to be right, even though all his world comes crashing down about his ears; which one does not imagine it will.

Horsburgh Light, Singapore

What's in a Name?

by G. F. SAYERS

"THE Colonial Service," said my tutor at Oxford, "now, that's where you get a C.M.G. after twenty years and a K.C.M.G. after thirty years, isn't it ? And what," he added, "do you call yourself when you're in it ?" Appointed to what was then—before the first world war—the East Africa Protectorate, I found myself termed an Assistant District Commissioner ; a full-blooded, high-sounding title suggesting that you held a commission from somebody, which, in fact, you did not and implying, correctly, a certain vagueness about the scope of your duties. Had an attempt been made to define them, it would have been easier to set out what they did not include rather than what they did, for they comprised, among other things, the dispensation of justice, the collection of revenue, the construction of roads and bridges, the planning and building of houses and offices, the prescription of medicines—indeed, about every service that one can render to mankind. The only drawback to the title was that, being composed of ten syllables, it was invariably contracted to A.D.C. which led people at home to confuse one with the Governor's Aide-de-Camp. Sometimes, too, the initials went wrong, as when the daughter of a Kenya settler announced me as "the A.B.C."

But it was a sight better than the title borne by one's colleagues in a nearby Protectorate, i.e. Collector. This was a blatant admission that one was expected to be a tax gatherer and nothing else. Here, indeed, one could detect the sinister influence of the Treasury, struggling to reduce the annual grant-in-aid from Whitehall, judging the ability of the administrator by the size of his revenue receipts.

Had fortune directed one's steps to the other coast of Africa, one might have found oneself among the "Residents," a title intended to emphasise the self-effacement of an Administration working behind the scenes in the powerful Emirates of Nigeria. In theory, at least, the Resident's function was to advise rather than command. They were cogs in the wheels of indirect rule rather than the driving belt of the machinery. They had one snobbish advantage over us, these Residents. They could head their notepaper "The Residency," which sounded grand to folks at home. It conjured up visions of Eastern palaces with the Union Jack flying over the battlement—a fanciful picture since, as a rule, the flag drooped listlessly in the breathless, shimmering haze before a modest bungalow of waitle and daub and thatch. But there was the same cachet about "The Residency" as there was about "The Manor" at home—so much so that one Provincial Commissioner in East Africa, where Residencies were unknown, adopted the heading on his notepaper—to the annoyance of the Secretariat !

Commissioners, Collectors, Residents—these were not the only titles by which the Administration was known. There were, as well, scattered over the Empire, District Officers, Native Commissioners, and even just plain Administrative Officers whose degrees of seniority were denoted by numbers and who were listed, like railway travellers, as Class I, II or III. Whatever they were called, they were all doing the same job and doing it supremely well. At least, members of what later became the Colonial Administrative Service could not complain that their Governments had fallen victims to the modern craze for uniformity and standardization. In one respect we of the Colonial Service were modest compared with our opposite numbers in the Sudan. Having climbed to the top of the Administrative ladder and taken charge of a Province, we were content to be called "Provincial" or "Senior Commissioners," as the case might be, whereas our Sudanese colleagues styled themselves "Governors." This was all right by us, but very confusing to maiden aunts to whom all Governors were "Excellencies" with stars on their breasts and ribbons on their shirt-fronts.   Nevertheless, it was embarrassing, having modestly answered "Never," to the question "When are you going to be a Governor ?" to be told, "Oh, but the Vicar's son is one already" ; and Aunt Belinda went on to murmur, "but of course he's a clever young man."

This diversity of titles was not confined to the Administration.   In the departmental line, too, there were different names for people doing the same job.   In the Public Works Department you might be an Executive Engineer, a Works Superintendent or a Supervisor of Works.   In the Police you had a choice between being an Inspector-General or a Commissioner.   The general rule seemed to be the smaller the Colony the more resounding the title.   The head of the Police, for example, in one of Africa's more insignificant territories was not content to be the Commissioner ; but must needs tack a "Chief" on to it.

Colonial railways, almost alone of departments, preserved some uniformity, mainly because their staff structure was modelled on the home railway system from which their personnel were recruited.   Traffic Managers managed traffic, whether on the Great Western or the Kenya-Uganda Railway : Chief Mechanical Engineers had much the same function, whether in Atbara or Crewe.   And it goes without saying that the boss had to be the "General Manager" irrespective of the length of line he controlled.   This could have surprising results.   There used to be a railway in Zanzibar which meandered through the streets of the capital to the suburb of Bububu, half-a-dozen miles away.   Nevertheless, it boasted a General Manager who, thanks to the courtesy of our British Railways, invariably enjoyed free travel anywhere in the United Kingdom when he came on leave—a courtesy he promised to reciprocate should, say, Sir Felix Pole or Sir James Milne find occasion to visit Zanzibar !

In those days the "Directorship" complex had yet to manifest itself.   This was the child of the first world war when anyone who was anybody was a Director of this or a Deputy Director of that.   But Colonial Governments soon caught the infection and modest men like Game Wardens blossomed out into Directors of Game Preservation.

There were occasional exceptions to this rash of "Directorships."   Those charged with the inspiring task of caring for our Colonial forests, have always been content to stick to the title of "Conservator."   They, at least, sensed that nature could be preserved, but would jib at being "directed."   And there was another department which eschewed grandiloquent titles, namely the Government Press responsible for publishing our Gazettes, Hansards and Laws.   In Britain the Stationery Office is under a Controller who, by Letters Patent, is "the Queen's Printer."   His opposite number in the colonies is content to be known as "The Government Printer"—and what more sensible and dignified title than that ?

So, after studying some of the old Colonial Staff Lists, you may ask, "What's in a name ?"   Those of us who gave our best to the job, whatever we might be called, would reply, "A rose by any other name would smell as sweet."

Colonial Aims

by G. B. MASEFIELD

THERE is nowadays much discussion of " colonial aims," which have even become a subject of formal teaching at the universities. Such discussion has, however, tended to confine itself to the aims of the Administrative Service. On these lines several masterly and idealistic expositions of our colonial aims have been made by British representatives both at home and abroad. But the same degree of attention has by no means been paid to the aims of the scientific or technical services in the colonies.

This is the more to be deplored because there is in fact a considerable divergence between these two sets of aims, between the administrator's and the scientist's dream of what a colony might be or ought to be. This divergence is no doubt partly the reflection of an inevitable difference in viewpoint between men educated in the humanities and those educated in science. There is no reason to suppose that the two sets of aims are irreconcilable; but their differences should be realised and deserve reflection, since they are responsible amongst other things for a certain amount of human tension and friction within the Colonial Service.

To the Briton who is offered an administrative post in the colonies, the first question to be settled with his conscience is whether his country has any right to engage in colonial administration at all. Has she (he may ask himself), by reason of her political experience, economic strength, or military power, something to offer backward peoples which will genuinely assist their development, and which cannot be better provided by any other power? It may be assumed that he will have answered this question in the affirmative before joining a colonial administration. As a serving officer in the colony, his immediate objectives will be to provide efficient government, maintain financial solvency, keep peace and order, offer impartial justice and so on. As a more distant goal, he will strive to educate the people for whom he is responsible towards self-government, so that it may be conferred upon them at the earliest practicable moment. And at the back of his mind may be the splendid ideal of calling into being new democracies to redress the balance of a world over-shadowed by dictatorship. Engrossed by these noble visions, he has some tendency to regard merely as a nuisance the technical officer who bothers him for money and for the expenditure of the scanty store of time, energy, and resources which are at Government's command, on projects which do not directly contribute to the realisation of his particular dream.

Different in many respects is the dream of the technical officer. For him equally there is a question of conscience before he accepts his post whether modern physics and chemistry, biology and the applied sciences have something to offer to under-developed peoples; whether we are right in superimposing these scientific disciplines on the existing culture of colonial races. To the trained scientist, this question can have only an affirmative answer; though it may be noted in passing that the feeling of primitive peoples themselves is by no means always in sympathy with this answer. Like the Administrative Officer, the scientist has his immediate objectives in the colony, which may take such forms as a reduction in infantile mortality or the eradication of trypanosomiasis from an area. But behind these he also has his more visionary ideal. An Agricultural Officer who is spreading the use of scientific methods among primitive peasants does not feel that his sole aim is to increase their incomes or material well-being; more important in the long run is their introduction, through the easy medium of the homely biological facts around them, to some conception of western thought and modern science. The scientific worker cannot be regarded as a mere materialist when he has at heart the inculcation of such grand principles of science as the necessity for accurate observation, and the experimental outlook. These modes of thought will do, he thinks, at least as much as any other to free primitive man from the grip of superstitious fear and to expand his mental horizons so that he can eventually take his place in a world of wider culture.

This technical officer has been trained in sciences which know no frontiers, has been taught to accept with equal avidity research findings which come from Russia, Germany, France, Italy, or America more often than from home; and he looks for final approval of his work, not to the British or colonial public, but to that small international body of colleagues who know enough of his particular scientific problems to understand the significance of their solution. To him professionally, it matters nothing whether he works under the British, French, or Liberian flag as long as the government will provide him with funds and assure that minimum of law and order without which scientific work cannot proceed. As a professional, he is not interested in democracy or dictatorship; nationalism and the advance towards self-government do not touch him closely, for he knows that British technical advisers will be the last to leave and will be required even after British Administrative Officers have been dispensed with. He therefore in his turn is sometimes tempted to regard the Administrative Officer as a mere nuisance, fussing about things which are not vital, stingy with the money, and encumbering his pet projects with unnecessary rules and regulations.

I have here emphasised on purpose the possible divergence of these two viewpoints. In fact, they can of course be largely reconciled. The technical officer, whom we have been considering as a disembodied professional, is also a Briton with a natural belief in the British way of life; and the Administrative Officer has, with the ever-widening basis of modern education, much more know-ledge of science than he did in the past. Steps can be, and are, taken to increase this sympathy on both sides—by giving Administrative Officers more training in science, by including among them a proportion of men with science degrees, and by giving technical officers more opportunity to study colonial history and politics. There is every hope that in the future the divergence between the two points of view can be reduced to no more than a friendly rivalry; but in the meantime, the chance of friction is not abolished by ignoring its possible sources, nor by giving a one-sided presentation of our colonial aims, which ignores the ideals and aspirations of whole sections of the Colonial Service.

(We are glad to publish Mr. Masefield's article because it ventilates a difficult and important question. There is, however, undoubtedly more to be said, and we hope that our readers will contribute to the discussion—*Editor*.)

Reality or Idealism ?

by P. G. COUTTS

FROM time to time, amid the welter of routine and paper that inevitably surrounds most of us these days, come brave efforts designed to bring to our consciousness our greater aims as a colonizing people.

Our superiors, having a broader and more comprehensive view than we have, pluck us by the sleeve, pull us from our labours at our individual trees, and ask us for a while to ponder the majesty and meaning of the Imperial Wood. Provincial officers, trying to break the deadening chain of over-administration, beg us to see our District problems as a whole, and by informal discussion to hammer out new approaches and new techniques to win the waywardness of the people with whom we deal, or to grasp firmly signs of their improvement.

Our Governors, wrestling with everlasting demands for facts, enormous sums of money and pages of reports, pause and, having paused, see purpose in it all and remind us, by circular in kindly terms, or in after-dinner speech, that in the long run we are dealing with men and not machines. And finally, the Peripatetics from Home—God bless them—come out, ostensibly to learn how we fare, but in fact teaching us that from Whitehall more than anywhere it can be seen that personal contact and a human approach are paramount.

What is so often the essence of this advice ? What is the golden thread which runs through all these attempts to rekindle our imagination, the thread on which our traditional reputation and our hopes for the future depend ? It might be defined as Imperial Benevolence—leadership mellowed by humanity—giving place, as the people advance, to the helping hand. In such a thread, which has run throughout our imperial history since we learned our American lesson, we may discern three strands.

The first strand, and the easiest to break, is that of Impeccable Race Relations.

Have you ever noticed how those trained in authority never seem to have any difficulty in remaining friendly without losing their dignity ? Our unalterable duty towards other races is surely to treat them as they would be treated, with respect and consideration. Kipling, a man for various reasons now neglected, had something to say on the subject of Kings and Common Touches. How true it is today that none of us can dare to lose that Common Touch. Too few of us really get to know our fellow peoples : and often, if we have two peoples to deal with, we hold to one and despise the other, to our loss and theirs. We have an unenviable reputation of being poor mixers and execrable linguists : until we can overcome our prejudices, we are unlikely to overcome our main problems.

A second strand in our thread is Courtesy. Downright good manners have been one of the bulwarks of our colonial ship ; two wars have done their best to stove the bulwark in, but I hope it still holds. "Manners makyth man." Many people in the colonies who could not understand this famous motto, but whose appreciation of human conduct is very shrewd, would say that it is profoundly true and of the highest importance. Yet how easy it is to forget our manners, and in the heat and confusion of the day to bundle someone unceremoniously out of the office. The amount of progress lost through churlishness is incalculable : yet the amount made through courteous reception, letters promptly answered, or thoroughly annoying matters dealt with as if they were enjoyable, must be equally great. The unofficials who leaven our society could tell us a few things about the difference good manners make to them. By our laziness (for that is all it amounts to) we do allow our customers to feel that our shop is the last place they want to visit because the people behind the counter have not the good manners to make their visit a pleasant one.

The third strand, which binds the other two together, might be described as Kindliness. The other two strands have a passive flavour : we can be sympathetic and bland, but many are born thus and find it comes naturally to them. To all of us, the third means positive effort, a conscious attempt to stir ourselves and our minds from their habitual lethargy, a striving to do the decent thing, when it would be easier and simpler, perhaps, to do nothing. All of us must have a thousand and one opportunities every day of doing Wordsworth's "nameless, unremembered acts," yet how often we fail, and what opportunities are lost! For there is in us all a strain of common decency which can rise to the moment yet again and again fails us when our consciousness is lazy and we decline to act. Yet, whatever our jobs, whether it be telling a gang of men to do more work, or searching for different kinds of truth in Laboratory or Court, our duty must lead us to innumerable chances to do good. "Basic Christianity," the vague term used for us these days to describe something we can't describe, has yet a significance —we all know what it means. Never was it more vital than now that we should put it into practice.

As I pondered these thoughts first, wandering idly over that colonial microcosm of wasted effort, famous triumphs and bad tempers, the Station Golf Course, it occurred to me that I was setting up "an all time high" for hypocrisy. I, who every day loosed my tongue at offenders and every hour mentally kicked the office boy down the office steps—I, epitome of all that these thoughts did not stand for, thinking of committing them to paper! Yet perhaps that is precisely why I did set them down, because I realise how constantly we need to be reminded of their truth. Too often our Chief Clerk, conscience, brings them to the fore : lazily we scrawl our initial on them and then toss them idly into the Out Tray of our memories.

Not so long ago the godfather of our Service hit the nail on the head when he asked us "What shall it profit the African if *we* save his soil and *he* loses his soul ?" In a colonial world becoming increasingly material, bewildering in its variety and scope, and occasionally disillusioning in its unexpectedness, these words bring inspiration and hope.

Parochialism

by J. F. R. HILL, C.M.G.

I T is easy to be wise after the event. I can imagine readers saying: "More musings from another old horse that has gone out to grass." Nevertheless, when one has recently left the Overseas Service it is undoubtedly easier to see in a more balanced perspective the administrative efforts of the past. The horizon lifts and Colonial problems appear in a wider context, no longer confined within the boundaries of a single territory.

There is one fault, it seems to me, of which many of us have unwittingly been guilty. My chief experience has been in Tanganyika where I spent some 28 years, and therefore it is of that territory that I write now; but it will be for readers to decide if this article has a wider application, and if the fault can also be laid at their door.

The fault is parochialism. It is not a new fault; it has existed for years and it still remains. Some recognition of it now may help our efforts in the years ahead.

So far as Tanganyika is concerned, the territory has been fortunate inasmuch as not only has it had a first class Civil Service, but the early years of British rule were spent in close and careful administration, which provided an excellent and stable foundation for progress, based on an intimate knowledge of the territory's people. But it was difficult not to have a limited outlook, and not to be somewhat complacent during the period between the two world wars. The Africans were peaceful and poor; there was no political feeling, and interest in this sphere was limited to tribal quarrels or complexities, to boundary disputes or to hereditary bickerings among the leaders. Tribes knew very little about one another, for there was only a modicum of movement and travelling between the different parts of the country; indeed, Tanganyika was no more integrated than the Balkan States are today. So that the Administration had little to worry about, and the three cardinal rules for the District Commissioner—thou shalt collect thy tax, thou shalt not have a famine, and thou shalt not embarrass thy Government—were not so difficult to comply with, even. if famine was sometimes a serious bogey.

The result was that not only the Provincial Administration, but also technical and departmental officers, sometimes with time to burn and always with too little money to spend, could not avoid a certain measure of complacency. I do not think that the central Government realised the situation, for what existed at district level existed too at provincial and territorial levels. I am not suggesting that there was a lotus-like existence; on the contrary, there was intense enthusiasm in nearly all ranks—but energies were directed largely to local and petty problems, and not enough thought was given to the wider aspect of affairs, and to the future. The District Commissioner seldom thought beyond the confines of his own district, Provincial Officers seldom compared their problems with those of neighbouring provinces, and even the central Government had sparse contact with the policies and ideas of neighbouring territories. Close relations were, of course, made difficult by lack of communications, which meant that contacts involved comparatively long absences from one's station.

Thus during the period when there was *time* for thinking, and when the pressure of work was not so intense as it is now, energies were directed inwards rather than outwards; in other words, parochialism was paramount. I feel that too much attention may still be given by most officers, whether the most senior or not, to routine and petty affairs at the expense of the wider aspect of current trends outside the officer's immediate orbit.

It is easy to make this charge, and I know that the immediate riposte will be: "What nonsense! We now have District Commissioners' conferences, technical officers conferences, innumerable conferences at Headquarters, East African High Commission services, and so on. We simply haven't got time to do more. If there is to be even more interchange of views and thoughts, and more visits to each other, or if you expect us to spend more time reading about the affairs of others, then we shall not only suffer from mental indigestion, but we shall perforce neglect our practical duties."

That is very true. But where the mistake has been made in the past and is still being made, I feel, is that we expect officers to do far too much; we count on them to attend to the veriest minutiae of administration, and at the same time to sit back and think. The result is often that they have to attend meetings or conferences with half digested thoughts and unprepared views . . . have there not been occasions even in the highest executive body in the territory, when decisions of the greatest importance have had to be taken hurriedly, because its members have had insufficient time to study and deliberate on the memoranda that are heaped on them at the last moment ? Throughout the Service there is far too much rush . . . and rush is the begetter of parochialism.

One solution to the problem would be to achieve a much greater degree of delegation, and decentralization. I suppose that this last word has been more used and abused than any other in the bureaucratic vocabulary, and yet with little effect. Decentralization is needed not only at the highest level but at all levels. But everyone seems to be fearful of the consequences, however much lip service is paid to the theory. I remember one head of a major department complaining that he was unable to allow a greater measure of authority and decision to his officers in the field because they were comparatively *young* and inexperienced. I argued that unless they had the responsibility, they would only grow *old* and inexperienced. Risks of mistakes from youth or inexperience have got to be taken from time to time, but is this not far better than to have the leaders always cluttered up with routine detail and entangled with red tape ?

In Tanganyika the first step in the right direction was the inauguration of the Membership system, the purpose of which was to have a senior officer responsible to the Governor and to advise him on the policy of the subjects in his portfolio. This system has now been extended with the promotion of Members to the rank of Minister and the appointment of Assistant Ministers, with the idea that the former shall busy themselves with policy and matters of importance only. But the policy of decentralization needs to be carried much further and to be extended to a greater degree in local and district affairs. It is curious that the first British officers in charge of Districts were called District Political Officers, and that only after a number of years was the title changed to District Officer and, later, District Commissioner. It would not be inappropriate if the wheel were to turn in full cycle and the title 'District Political Officer' to come into being again. For District Commissioners are inevitably becoming more nearly akin to Political Advisers, and as time goes on must shed much of their executive functions.

That the reins of centralization are still drawn too tight may be, in my personal view, largely due to the fact that too little attention has been paid in the past to the training of junior or subordinate local staff. Until recently there has been no major attempt to promote organized training for the young men (and why not some women, too ?) who would be willing and suitable for posts in Government service.

And since there has been no regular channel, the Government has relied on the haphazard collection of such staff as is recruited from time to time. And once these men are in Government employ, what opportunity is there for onward training? We talk a lot about "training within industry": when I was in Tanganyika I do not think I ever heard of "training within the Government."

I am no apostle of 'Africanisation at all costs', but it does seem to me that decentralization and delegation depends largely on an accelerated use of local staff and that we must face the fact that past efforts to fit local men for sub-professional or non-professional posts have not only been inadequate but have been a direct cause of placing too many different straws on the willing camels' back. And that is where I came in . . . overweighted by straws (or paper), how can the Overseas Service officer see his job in its widest context and avoid parochialism?

Does it matter, you may ask? Of course it does. I am appalled by the ignorance of so many officers (and this includes myself), of the policies and practices even of Tanganyika's neighbours . . . Kenya, Uganda, Nyasaland, Northern Rhodesia, the Belgian Congo and Portuguese East Africa. How often, with all our local pre-occupations, have we looked at West Africa or the Far East in relation to ourselves?

Today the need is to look at Colonial affairs in the context of the Commonwealth and not only from the viewpoint of a particular Colony. I doubt if anyone, from Cadet to Governor, would quarrel with that statement . . . but I wonder how many of the Cadets who at this time of year are starting their overseas service, will have a chance to do so?

The Buck

by R.O.H.

Across the sloping orange land
　　We bump upon our way,
To where the moss-green cedars climb
　　To cliffs of silver-grey.

The tan buck with the polished horns
　　Knew not he was to die,
Sees not, now his throat is cut,
　　The sunset in his eye;

Nor sees blue mountains move across
　　Beyond the northern plain,
Nor the far-gleaming pools of grass,
　　Sunlit after rain.

Swifter than the yellow leopard,
　　Catapult to start,
He travelled not so swiftly
　　As a bullet through the heart.

(b) The Colonial Service at Work

Corona was never a recruitment publication: its appeal lay four square to those who were already in the Colonial Service, not to those who might be thinking of it as a career choice. Yet for one of the most intimate insights into what the job really involved and what life in the Colonial Service was all about, the pages of *Corona* provide, today as tellingly as fifty years ago, a unique source. Written at the time and not, in the way of published memoirs, many years after the event, and contributed voluntarily by grassroots members from within all branches of the Colonial Service, here is the authentic voice of the Colonial Service as it was spoken and heard at the time. The excerpts, which rightly form both the core and the largest selection of the Anthology, are divided into three parts.

PART i: THE ADMINISTRATIVE OFFICER

Part (i) deals with the Administrative officer. To mark its tenth birthday, *Corona*'s editor commissioned a number of contributions on "The Administrative Officer Today". An extensive selection from this major series is included here, along with further articles from other issues of the journal.

PART ii: THE PROFESSIONAL AND DEPARTMENTAL OFFICER

Part (ii) deals with contributions by and about Departmental officers. Too many (there were twenty branches in the Colonial Service) to allow for an extensive coverage of the Colonial Service's work, they have here been classified into five professional groups: Health and Medicine; Natural Resources; Education and Social Services; Engineering and Public Works; and Law Enforcement Services. Personal accounts by women officers in Nursing and Education have been included under the separate Section, "From the Woman's Viewpoint".

PART III: ON SPECIAL DUTY

Many members of the Colonial Service would at one time or another have found themselves assigned 'on special duty'. The catalogue of such temporary postings was as vast and varied as the range of responsibilities involved while on so-called 'normal duty', so that together they demonstrated that the one word that could never be applied to a job in the Colonial Service was 'routine'

'Special duties' covered such postings as secondment to the Colonial Office (the conventional practice of 'beachcombing') or to vice-consular duty; a posting to Government House as Private Secretary or A.D.C. to His Excellency, or even, during the pressures of a Royal Visit, as additional P.S.; responsibility for supervising a national census or a general election, or for setting up a Trade Union organization or a museum; as aide to a UN Visiting Mission; to establish an information service or a public relations department, design an adult education programme or a fertilizer or 'Grow More Food' campaign; to organize and direct special training courses; to act as chairman of a commission of enquiry or as secretary of a Colonial Office mission; and so on and so on, virtually without end in the final decolonizing decade of bureaucratic change and policy innovation. Some welcomed such an opportunity and saw it as part of that variety of responsibility which had long been one of the attractions of a career in the Colonial Service; others grumbled but still enjoyed it; a few remained disgruntled at the break in their routine work. The contributions selected make it plain that being assigned 'on special duty' hugely widened the range of material on work in the Colonial Service experienced by and offered to readers of *Corona*. Finally, as D.C.C. Trench's article shows, the heroic exploits of the Coast Watchers and their local colleagues in the British Solomon Islands during the Japanese invasion of 1942 form a unique story of the Colonial Service in wartime.

Pagan Battle

TO all those members of the Service who are bowed under the burden of their files and to all those who are preoccupied with Politics and Progress we commend the following. It is a slightly shortened version of a District Officer's report written from Gwoza in Nigeria on the 15th March, 1950 and published by the Public Relations Department in Lagos in May.

For some time the most troublesome people in the Gwoza District have been the people of the Ngoshe and Bokko villages. Fights, affrays, murder and theft have been common and there are many villages who have serious scores to pay off against Ngoshe.

On Saturday, 4th March, during a beer party at Ngoshe, an Ngoshe man wantonly killed a man from Zeledva. The news reached me on Sunday morning and at the same time I heard that the people of Zeledva were marching towards Ngoshe to attack them. I took the District Head, my messenger and one Policeman and drove to Ngoshe. We arrived as the two armies were approaching each other. All the men were in full war equipment—helmets, body-clothes, shields, poisoned spears and bows and arrows. I would estimate the number as from two to three hundred from Ngoshe and rather more from Zeledva. We got in between the two armies, but we were unable to prevent battle being joined on the right flank. This went on for some time until one Zeledva man was killed and several wounded on both sides. The Zeledva men disengaged and removed their dead and wounded and then withdrew altogether into the hills. After making sure that no further trouble was likely that day we returned to Gwoza.

During the evening news came through that Zeledva were marshalling all their kinsmen and allies for a large scale attack on Ngoshe. The District Head had collapsed with high fever, and I left for Ngoshe during the night with my messenger and an escort of one Sergeant and twelve Nigerian Policemen. Arriving at Ngoshe early on Monday I was met by Lawan Boujje. After discussing the matter with him, I called for the Dulamas and elders of Ngoshe. They admitted that the initial fault was theirs and they had no wish to fight Zeledva. At the same time, all the men of Ngoshe were dressed in full war regalia and fully armed and were ready to attempt to repel any attack. The Bulamas finally agreed that they would produce five cows as *diya* to be paid to Zeledva, and would disperse their warriors. The payment of *diya* is the normal settlement of any blood feud and fighting never takes place after *diya* has been paid.

The five cattle were collected and the Ngoshe warriors dispersed. I went with the Ngoshe Bulamas, who were unarmed, to the foothills from where the Zeledva warriors would approach. The cattle were tethered in a prominent position from where they could be seen by any approaching party. At this stage I told the Sergeant of Police that under no circumstances would fire be opened unless we were personally attacked.

In due course very large numbers of men were seen approaching. An intermediary was sent forward to call for the Bulamas and elders. These came and I went forward with Lawan Boujje and my messenger to meet them. I pointed out that this was no way to settle quarrels, which should be brought before the Pagan Court. I then said that the people of Ngoshe had admitted their fault and had brought five cattle as *diya*, which I pointed out to them, and had also dispersed their warriors. The Zeledva Bulamas said that, in these circumstances, there could be no fight between them, but before taking away the cattle they must consult their people, who would certainly agree. They returned to their men, who had now collected among the rocks in the foothills. I estimated that there were more than a thousand of them. At this time I told the police to withdraw some little distance.

Shortly afterwards the Bulamas returned and I went forward to meet them again. They stated that they had consulted their people, who had agreed to the acceptance of *diya,* and that they would collect their cattle and go back home. My messenger went off to collect the cattle, and at that moment the war-cry was raised on the right of the Zeledva line and men started to charge forward at us with spears and shields at the ready. I retired to the police escort and the Bulamas rushed back in a vain attempt to stop the attack. It was not possible, however, and all along the line men started to charge forward at us with their flanks converging towards us. I considered that the situation was now dangerous.

When the attackers were about seventy yards away I told the Sergeant to fire one round in the air above their heads. He did so and the line wavered and then came on. The Sergeant immediately fired two more rounds and two men fell, at an approximate distance of forty to forty-five yards. Had the Sergeant not fired I would have been forced to tell him to do so. No Ngoshe men were in sight and we were the only possible objective.

Immediately the two men fell the remainder turned and fled. Of the two men hit one was killed and the other superficially wounded. It was, of course, not possible to take an accurate low aim at men running with shields in front of them. The constables behaved in an exemplary manner. The Zeledva men removed the body and all the attackers dispersed.

I remained at Ngoshe for a further thirty-six hours to ensure that there was no other outbreak. On the morning of the 7th Zeledva sent me a message to say how deeply they regretted their treachery and to appeal for clemency in any punishment they might be given. The investigation proceeds.

Kenya

A DISTRICT TEAM AT WORK*

by FERGUS WILSON, M.B.E.

I

IT is clear that an essential ingredient of progress in the colonial territories is co-operation : co-operation between all those who are in any way responsible for development—Administrative and technical officers of Government, representatives of Missions, business men, and representatives of the people themselves. Another form of co-operation of equal importance is that between Government officers and the mass of the people. The most important fact to be realised by all is that ultimately we are dealing with persons rather than problems. Without genuine and cordial personal relationships much that we strive for and plan will be brought to nought. Hence the importance ot the field officer and of such institutions as the District Team, for these form the vital link between Government and the people. Nowadays there is much talk of the necessity for agrarian revolution, community development, and various other aspects of raising the general productivity of under-developed areas. It is well to remember that it is upon the District field officer—be he District Commissioner, Agricultural or Veterinary Officer, doctor or missionary—that the hinge of development ultimately turns.

The emergence of District and Provincial Teams represents the logical development of an association which has existed for many years between Administrative Officers and the various technical officers of Government departments and unofficial representatives in many Districts and Provinces. Whereas in the past the District Commissioner would consult his colleagues and advisers as and when he thought desirable, nowadays it has, in many places, been found necessary to set up a properly constituted body or team. This team meets at regular intervals to discuss problems and plans, its deliberations and decisions are recorded, and its considered opinions and advice can be of great value to senior officers and to Government itself. Those who have worked in East or West Africa will be familiar with changes in plans which accompany the all-too-frequent changes in District and Provincial staffs : one officer is keen on road construction, another on the erection of Welfare Centres, a third on opening of more schools, and so on. District and Provincial Teams can play an invaluable part in developing a balanced and progressive local policy within the broad framework of Government policy, and also in ensuring reasonable continuity for local policy and plans.

The description which follows is of the work of the North Nyanza District Team which took shape and developed into its present form under the chairmanship of Mr. C. H. Williams, O.B.E., now Provincial Commissioner, Nyanza Province, Kenya. Elsewhere, the actual form and possibly the functions of District Teams will differ widely as will their composition, depending a great deal upon the degree to which Africans are assuming responsibility in the conduct of their own affairs. It would be a great mistake in this, as in many other matters, to be dogmatic as to the precise form teamwork should take but there can be little doubt that the principles underlying the idea offer real possibilities in many areas. The essential ingredients for the successful functioning of a District or Provincial Team are simple : a wise and capable chairman ; a group of individuals who are prepared to co-operate wholeheartedly ; some measure of financial independence ; and the general support of the Local Native Councils and the people. It is important that the team should constantly be aware of the need for developing and main-

*Based partly on a lecture given to the Institute of Rural Life at Home and Overseas.

taining a sense of confidence in its capacity by the practical results which it produces and by the constructive advice and carefully considered opinions which it expresses.

The team idea in practice.

It is important that the team should be as representative of the major interests of the area—District or Province—as possible. The Chairman is the Senior Administrative Officer. It is not too much to say that success or failure rests in a very large measure with the Chairman. The Senior Officers of the various technical departments are members and local Missions, business interests, and the people themselves are represented. This may mean a somewhat large gathering with the result that deliberations tend to occupy lengthy periods. In such cases it has sometimes been found to be of great practical value to select an executive core of not more than four or five persons to meet more frequently, to deal with day to day business and to prepare material for the regular meetings of the full team. Such an organisation certainly increases efficiency.

What are the main functions of such a team ? The first duty is clearly to co-ordinate the aims and work of the various departments and agencies in the District. The work of many departments is very largely inter-dependent : health depends much upon improved diets which involve both Agricultural and Veterinary Officers ; education must obviously bear some close relation to the rural life and pursuits the "educated" must ultimately follow ; the layout and upkeep of roads bears closely upon problems of economic development, as well as matters of soil conservation. The job of the Team is to bring together all viewpoints, complementary as well as conflicting, and to evolve an over-all balanced plan of development. As most of the members are practical men responsible for getting things done they will ensure that plans are shorn of all theoretical and high-sounding trappings and are reduced to clear, simple, and practical measures. Thus armed, the Team is able to present a "united front" to the people. Continuity, so essential to progressive development, is also largely assured, for, although individual members of teams may be replaced, the Team and its over-all plan goes on. Flexibility is also essential to the successful prosecution of our work and again this is introduced by the fact that all members of the team are in day to day contact with the practical problems and changing situation in the field. A good District Team may well be compared with a Brigade Operational Headquarters in a forward area in wartime : in constant touch with the changing situation ; co-ordinating the work of all units under the command ; sending back reliable and vital information to higher formations.

There is little real incentive to expend thought and time in the preparation of District Development Plans if the Team is aware that hundreds of miles away some financial committee's blue pencil hangs like a Sword of Damocles over draft estimates of expenditure. District and Provincial teams only really begin to function when there is some degree of genuine devolution of financial authority. When they feel that they are being entrusted with certain expenditure the careful consideration of plans and the pursuit of a practical development policy becomes a reality. In this regard the local Agricultural Betterment Funds, raised through the Marketing Boards by the proceeds of crop cesses, and belonging to the District from which the crops were sold, has given a tremendous impetus to the work of District Teams in Kenya. It is difficult to overestimate the importance of this aspect of District or Provincial teamwork : the granting of a measure of financial authority implies confidence and confidence nearly always draws out the best both in committees and in individuals.

It may well be asked whether District Team loyalties and ideas may not clash with those of individual members to their various departments. In practice this has not been found to be the case. Senior technical officers of Government are welcome guests at team meetings, whilst it is often the practice for copies of team minutes to be sent to Provincial or more senior officers. Thus the work of the team is made to fit into the vertical scale of departmental organisation as well as the horizontal scale of inter-departmental co-operation. Many theoretical snags disappear when people of good sense and goodwill are determined to work together towards a common goal.

Methods of working.

Many "Schemes" and plans have failed, with consequent adverse effects upon the confidence of the people, owing to lack of sound information. The recording and collection of information relating to all aspects of the District is an important function of the team. In this connection the Uganda District Agricultural Books commenced some twenty-two years ago at the instance of Mr. (now Sir Geoffrey) Clay present a unique and invaluable record of progress and conditions upon which it would be difficult to improve. The carrying out of simple surveys and the collection of all relevant information forms the basis upon which District planning can alone be carried out with any hope of real success.

Now comes the planning of a year's work ahead. For various reasons it is wise to plan well in advance : seeds, tools, and materials have to be ordered ; propaganda must precede campaigns ; nurseries must be constructed for the supply of seedlings or planting material ; above all, Chiefs, elders, and technical assistants must have a clear idea of what lies ahead. The preparation of the annual draft estimates of revenue and expenditure usually brings the matter to a head and in connection with these a simple plan of campaign is sketched out. Appendix I is an example of the type of programme produced in North Nyanza District.

When the draft programme is prepared, a three-day conference is arranged to which all Chiefs, Senior Agricultural Instructors, Senior Veterinary Assistants, certain Medical Dispensers and others are invited. During those three days the programme is thoroughly explained and discussed. Where necessary it is amended and in its revised form it represents a working plan upon which all are clear and are in general agreement. The idea that Chiefs should form their own Location Teams is also fostered, for co-operation at all levels is of great importance. This annual conference is also the occasion for some local demonstrations together with the lighter social side which is all important.

Individual campaigns are dealt with in a similar manner although the meetings in this case are shorter and take place at Location headquarters. Effectiveness is achieved by concentrating upon single objectives at any one time in any given area. Once the team has agreed upon a plan of campaign it forms the subject of a simple operation order signed by the District Commissioner and District Agricultural Officer. This serves the purpose of confirming verbal instructions in clear and simple terms ; it is also a further demonstration of unity of aim and purpose. The District Commissioner issues copies to his Chiefs and Headmen whilst the Agricultural Officer does the same for his staff. A typical operation order is attached (Appendix II). It is produced in the local language.

Campaigns are useful to achieve limited objectives but unless there is something deeper underlying the whole work, they achieve little of permanent value. Underlying the whole of this work, therefore, is the long term objective of "better farming." It is true that we do not know the answers to many of the agricultural problems of different regions of Africa. Much remains to be discovered only by patient research and experiment. But there are also many simple improvements which can be tackled and indeed must be tackled without delay : contour layouts, strip cropping practices, the making and use of manure, improvement of pastures, conservation of water supplies, the integration of livestock and animal husbandry, and the trial of grasses for leys under African farming conditions. With these and other considerations in mind, the team presses on continually

in its efforts to gain the confidence of responsible public opinion and the co-operation of leading and progressive farmers in trying out and demonstrating improved
methods.   Thus each Location is encouraged to adopt some specific line of
improvement and is later visited by parties from other areas.

There are many plots of land under government or Local Council control
where improvements and practical demonstrations can be unostentatiously
developed.   A market provides the opportunity for combining sanitary measures
of collecting refuse, slaughter-waste and dung to make into compost.   Trees and
grass can be planted and a nearby school plot can demonstrate what astounding
crops result from really heavily composted bananas.   A sharp bend in the road
or at cross-roads where P.W.D. funds are spent in slashing weeds, bush, and tall
grass, can be cleaned and levelled with graded slopes on steep banks and planted
to valuable erosion preventing grasses which cover the ground, never need slashing
and will, in due course form an invaluable reservoir of planting material.   In
these, and a hundred other ways, gradual steady progress in improved use of
land and resources can be taught.   Since schools, prisons, co-operative societies,
Missions and other interests are represented on the District Team, advance on
a broad front is possible, and that overworked word "propaganda" is supplanted
by practical visual demonstration.

Educational tours, financed from Agricultural Betterment Funds, have proved
of great value.   Selected parties of elders, farmers and others are taken to see
work and progress in other districts.   Alternatively, they may be taken to see the
results of over-cultivation or over-stocking and erosion.   Visits such as these
have paid dividends in the shape of support for our work far exceeding the time
and trouble expended in their organisation.   A local newspaper, produced by a
member of the team, which has struck a happy balance between "propaganda"
and local news, has achieved real popularity and is exerting a definite influence
upon public opinion.   It is sold at a subsidised price and, therefore, valued far
more highly than a free publication.   Work with films and local broadcasts
complete the picture.

Rondel of Pity

by RAYMOND TONG

Be not afraid of pity.
Regret not the tears you shed
for the disinherited,
the outcasts of this city.

Say not that the trinity
of Faith, Hope and Love are dead.
Be not afraid of pity.

For he who fears to pity,
who turns with an eyeless head
from the dying in his bed,
dies already in his stead.
Be not afraid of pity.

With acknowledgements to *English*.

On Tour in Sarawak

by I. A. N. URQUHART

DISTRICT Officers in Sarawak scarcely ever do their tours by car because there are so few roads—only 160 odd miles of all-weather roads in a country the size of England, and most of them are in or near the towns. Indeed, the Government of Sarawak has often been criticised by people not responsible for spending the country's revenue, for not building more roads. However, there are difficulties.

The country is very roughly cigar-shaped, and one-half of it (divided along its length) has a long sea coast backed largely by swamp forest, while the other half consists of steep jungle-covered hills and mountains. The countryside is traversed across its width by many large, tidal and often navigable rivers with cultivated areas along their banks. Any roads intended to join up the main towns by the shortest route would have to cross these rivers and creeks where they are still wide and deep, and traverse the intervening swamp forest, where there is no road building material. The alternative would be to build the roads inland, where they would have to cross the chains of steep-sided mountains that lie between the rivers, and, though they might open up new country, there would be no towns along their route. In either case, maintenance of the roads would be difficult and costly. The main goods to be transported in Sarawak are imperishables such as rubber, pepper, sago, timber, rice, dried fish, tinned food, cloth etc., which can be carried much more cheaply by slow river transport than by road.

Such conditions, which make for few roads, provide delightful travelling conditions for the District Officer on tour. He leaves his station for several days at a time and, outside the bazaar areas where there may be a government resthouse, he will stay in the houses of the local people, be they Chinese, Dayak, Malay or others, and thereby really get to know them. He has none of the rush and bustle of the District Officer in more civilized countries with better communications and it is impossible for him to say "I can just afford the time to take the car and spend half an hour in your village, but I must be back for tea." In Sarawak it is very difficult indeed for anyone to catch up the absent District Officer with unwanted news from headquarters, for he will have set off in a fast boat, with the tide in his favour, for the "ulu."

"Ulu" to the European who never leaves the capital means "impenetrable jungle coupled with discomfort and/or romance among the head hunters." To the local people it means "up river," and to the District Officer it also has the added meaning of a temporary freedom from the hampering restrictions of a doubtless necessary bureaucracy and a feeling that he is really doing the job for which he joined the Colonial (now Oversea) Service.

Down river, the District Officer probably sets off in a government launch or a big long-boat made out of a huge tree and driven by an outboard engine. The down river areas are mostly well cultivated and fairly prosperous; the river is wide, muddy and dull, and the banks are low and swampy. A few of the Sarawak rivers have very fast flowing tides and bores several times a month, but to make up for this they have no bars; most of the rivers, however, have bars at their mouths but no bores.

Visiting villages in these down river areas may sometimes be pleasurable, is normally dangerous, and rarely romantic. The danger comes first. After skilful, barefoot Sarawakians have tied up the craft some few feet from the banks, the District Officer, with an attempt at great dignity, steps out of the boat on to the end of the mud covered log that has long ago been laid down to serve the locals as gangway-cum-wharf. He spends a little time, to the accompaniment of encouraging sounds from his staff and hosts, trying to get his balance on this log. If he is a wise and experienced District Officer, he will be barefoot and wearing his oldest clothes; if he isn't he will by now have slipped off the log into the shallow water and mud while all those around are shrieking at him "Look out! Be careful!" Eventually, hot, flustered and sweating profusely, he struggles up the log and arrives on terra firma, and can look back to see Sarawakians walking briskly and confidently up and down the slippery log as they fetch his kit ashore.

The District Officer's pleasure at meeting his down river people will be tempered by the thought that the difficulties of walking up the log were much less than those of the descent to be made when he returns to his boat. Indeed, he probably exhorts the village elders to build a good wharf and gangway to ease the burden of their daily lives. The villagers nod politely but cannot see any advantage in this when a log has long been so suitable, especially if it has "happened to float" down to them from one of the rafts of the nearest timber firm and has cost them nothing.

The joys of travelling through swamp forest are so well known, since excellent films have portrayed it from Africa to India via Devil's Island and Malaya, that I needn't describe them here. But travelling up river is a great contrast. Here the water is clear and shallow and the river, flowing swiftly between mountains, is interspersed with rapids and large deep pools. The big outboard or launch is replaced by a smaller one with a lower powered engine and this is eventually exchanged for a couple of "perahus". The District Officer, cross-legged and balanced precariously in the narrow craft, sits as still as possible while the sun or rain beats down on his pallid chair-borne features and the crew alternately paddle or pole him up the smoother parts of the river or haul and pull the boat up the rapids.

In his early days the District Officer used to offer to help in the paddling or poling, and with the hauling at the more difficult places, but now that he is better known in the district the Sarawakians politely order him to sit still and not be a nuisance—they can do deceptively easy things which Europeans should rarely attempt. In rough water they can stand up to pole a boat without rocking it or shipping water, but the European finds it difficult enough to sit still even in smooth water. The Sarawakian, leaping lightly from a boat into fast moving water on to an invisible bottom of slippery stones and hidden depths, rhythmically hauls the boat into smoother water before leaping no less lightly back into the craft. Even if the European is barefoot and wearing the minimum of dress, he is clumsy at all these manœuvres, incapable of estimating depths when he jumps out of the boat, which he does with little grace, much pain to his feet and considerable obstruction to his crew. After he has got back awkwardly into the boat and sunk heavily into his seat, he finds about a bucket of water has come in with him and has splashed over most of his bedding and spare clothes.

It is not surprising, then, that there are those who think the Colonial Office ought only to recruit P.T. experts and Commando trained officers for service in the "ulu" areas of Sarawak, and that the First Devonshire course should include a compulsory period in the parks and rivers of Cambridge, London and Oxford under a Sarawakian from the "ulu."

This is not an article on what the District Officer does and eats and sees when he stays in Chinese rubber gardens, Malay fishing villages or Dayak long-houses, so I will confine myself to travelling. Up river it really is delightful to step out of the cramped boat on to a shingle or sandy bank, stretch one's cramped limbs and then dive into a deep, clear pool of mountain water. The crew, who ought to be exhausted after their efforts, show little signs of tiredness and while some miraculously get a fire going, others bathe or sit talking animatedly. And after the bathe, how delightful to relax in the shade of a tree, to eat and drink to the sights and sounds of the river gurgling on its way. At times like this one can well understand the romance of travelling in the "ulu."

However, all good things must come to an end, and eventually one must leave the boat where the river has become too shallow for even a native "perahu," and carry on on foot. A notched tree trunk set at a steep angle is the usual ladder by which one leaves the river side for the top of the bank. The notches are very small and ideal for prehensile bare feet, but not designed for European footwear. Should the European discard his shoes, he will not automatically be able to imitate the smooth ascent of the experienced Sarawakian—indeed he may find the sharp edges under the bridge of his foot so excruciatingly painful that he will lean forward to transfer his weight to his hands. Even so, it is easier to go up these native ladders than down them, unless a swift uncontrolled descent on the base of one's spine with a splash at the bottom can be considered easy.

For a short distance on reaching the top of the bank everything is fine. The District Officer, striding unencumbered along a well-worn footpath, can just keep up with his heavily laden porters. "Ulu" Sarawakians, however, eschew the flat and uninteresting and soon the assault course begins. As a loosening-up exercise one is led up a steep and slippery hillside with the embryo path giving way to notched sticks at the more precipitous parts. Sooner or later the top is reached, when inevitably there follows a descent down the other side. This is usually done wildly and snatching at twigs and blades of grass as one's speed gathers momentum. For a while, at the bottom, there is a variation as the party moves in single file up a river bed. The guide churns up the mud so that those behind can't see where they are putting their feet, and bits of gravel in the shoes worm their way into a position of torment under the foot or between the toes.

Soon the stream narrows and becomes rocky and slippery and a fall is painful. The District Officer struggles to keep up in these unhappy conditions, often on all fours like an ungainly ape, until the stream bed becomes too uncomfortable for even a Sarawakian and the guide follows a track through the jungle. The stream rushes and bubbles over sharp pointed rocks some thirty or more feet below, when the party comes to a bridge that would be frowned upon by the P.W.D. It is composed of a narrow ironwood plank, worn smooth by time so that there is not the slightest corrugation from which the foot can get a grip or the eye take comfort. The plank is tilted to one side and slopes down to the far bank. It is wet from rain and bounces up and down in the middle. There is no handrail and no evidence to show that it will support the weight of a man. The new District Officer feeling he must keep up the good name of his kind refuses help and advances, pale and tense, to the middle of the plank. Here the bridge becomes too much for him; slowly and tremblingly he completes the passage on all fours. The more experienced District Officer puts his hands on the shoulders of a man in front while another coming behind holds his hips. After being thus shepherded across, he sits down to recover his equipoise and to answer frank questions such as "If you're like this here, how on earth do you manage when walking in the countryside of London?"

So the journey by land goes on until a distant cock-crow is heard—only ten minutes to one's destination, one thinks, and then for a cool bathe in a limpid pool, clean clothes and rest on a blanket on the floor of the longhouse with a drink at hand. In fact, exuberance is premature, for the District Officer has not yet reached half way, and the cock-crow that heralded freedom from aches, fear and pain came from a hut where an old crone shooed her hens from the paddy drying in the sun.

Now the guide leaves the shelter of the damp jungle for an uncultivated hillside under long grass, which keeps out any breeze but gives no protection from the sun. At intervals the guide finds it easier to leave the prickly grass and walk along the burnt out remains of felled jungle trees lying on the hillside. The District Officer walks confidently along the trunks of these prostrate giants, but sooner or later he steps on to a weak part which all the porters avoided—and down he goes. This so affects his confidence that when he comes to the end of a tree, he prefers to jump to the ground and climb up on to the next one instead of jumping lightly from one to the other as the heavily laden porters do.

Everything ends, however, and eventually the District Officer's only desire in the world is realised; he has reached his destination and can relax—collapse might be a better word.

The return journey is much the same except that shooting the rapids is quicker, more fun and less exhausting than going up them, and in due course one is home again. The comforts of roominess, chairs, beds and other pleasures make one vow to stay there for a while and do no more touring for the nonce.

However, the next Secretariat Circular and the sight of the work that has accumulated in one's absence soon alters that. After a few days the District Officer is happily planning his next trip into the "ulu" areas of Sarawak.

Echo

by RUTH BULMAN

Now the shy buds have pierced their sheaths of green,
And blossoms float in the white light of Spring;
But to the raddled eye that has known Africa,
These colours are too gentle, and too clean.

Hibiscus! Royal flower of the Hibiscus. Morning
    Glory bursting with brief life,
Blue, blue Jacarandas: Cassias all the way to the bazaar
Where there is dirt and brilliance, where colours shriek
On the dark, silk skins of the women!
I hear their voices now, rich and abandoned,
Hot, lazy earth smells creep on an English orchard.
    The pruned boughs hold for a space
Little, scented temple-flowers, falling in broken bells upon the grass.
The twisted pear swells lofty as a mango tree
    Where the fruit-bats gorge at night.
Far off, the hills clap snow to their stern brows,
And rise, untamed, the Mountains of the Moon!

Bird-song makes tremble where the lilacs trail,
Sweet timbre shivers the white light of Spring,
But to assaulted ears that heard the dawn in Africa,
These voices are too tender and too frail.

"Ulendo"

by MICHAEL LEONARD, M.B.E.

IN some West African and in the High Commission territories, I believe they call it "trek", in all of East Africa "safari", in Ghana, Nigeria and no doubt Malaya "tour", in the Pacific and the West Indian Islands, where the same performance is largely by boat it may well be "cruise", but in Nyasaland it is *ulendo*. The word is appropriate—*lendo* with its connotation of the oddity, meaning strange and in this context carrying overtures of Noel Coward and mad dogs and Englishmen, and the U making it into a journey, as well as in local society making it a very "U" occupation and pastime.

No doubt the same applies elsewhere but for a harassed Field Officer the soft answer that turneth away the wrath of superiors is "I was/am/will be on *ulendo*." It can be used to explain an incomplete or late report, absence when a V.I.P. or an auditor is due, why the flag is torn, and the official rest house dirty. Granted most superior officers have used the same gambit in their time, but the excuse is invaluable to gain a breathing space, if not as a final answer, and can, with experience, be played to cover manifold sins of both submission and commission.

The beauty of the excuse is that it may well be true and that from every Colonial Secretariat, I have no doubt, there issue from time to time, circular letters exhorting and ordering officers in the field, in earlier more direct days "to get to know the natives", and in our more bureaucratic and "democratic" days "to administer more closely and evaluate local opinion at the grass root level." One is urged to concentrate on the most enjoyable and rewarding part of one's job.

Nyasaland generally, and especially the Northern Province, is probably one of the pleasantest places in the Colonies for *ulendo*. The scenery is delightful and there is considerable range within comparitively short distances. From the rolling Vipya grasslands it is only some 30 miles through tumbled forested foothills to the lake shore plain, and in some places the mountains fall almost sheer into the lake. The lake shore itself contains infinite variety, wooded rocky bays, long sandy beaches, reedy river mouths and curious shaped peninsulas and islands. The country is sparsely populated and the itinerant official is, apart from missionaries, the only European seen over large areas of country. As his visit gives an opportunity to complain about the impersonal "they" who impose taxes and natural resources regulations, to lobby a personal grievance and even to sell some produce, it can be a welcome change to the boredom of bush life, and in any case gives material for interminable conversation and speculation, food for gossip and even be the occasion for a more than usually lively beer drink after his departure.

Planning an *ulendo* under such conditions can have the entertainment of a walking tour in more civilized countries, except that favourite pubs cannot be included nor are there often maps of much value. Such maps as there are were, until very recently, those produced by people who had walked over the country and were more of the "there be dragons here" variety than the immaculate glosses of the Ordinance Survey. Distances are more apt to be expressed in "carrier-time" than miles and certain routes adjectively annotated.

In theory every village in a district should be visited at least once a year. Chiefs' headquarters, sub-treasuries and courts must obviously be visited regularly, and there are seasonal reasons for going to other areas—early preparation of fields for food crops, early planting in grain areas, tax drives, anti-bush fire propaganda in the dry weather and checking of tax census in the wet weather early in the year before anyone starts paying in earnest. Then there are the special *ulendos;* explaining to one's parishoners the latest constitutional proposals and methods of elections, looking for a new road line, checking forest reserve boundaries, dealing with an inter-village boundary dispute, breaking in a cadet and even conducting a "visiting fireman", scientific, anthropological, sociological or political and merely "swanning" to see people, bugs, birds, schools, minerals, or just so that one can go away and write a book.

The choice of route is comparatively limited by the fact that to cover the whole district some overall plan must be followed. This district is broadly quartered and as each of two or more officers do about ten days a month by foot or boat it is possible to cover the whole 3,000 square miles in a year. Because of the size there is room for manoeuvre and preference within a block, and until the whole has become familiar reference is made to *ulendo* books which are kept at District Headquarters. These are informal and often individual gazetteers of each section and can provide entertaining and informative reading. They tend to reflect both the time of year in which they were amended or compiled and the writers' personal preferences.

"Village Headman scruffy and useless, camp site unshaded, a six hour flog to get here, food and water poor and full of mosquitoes."

"Very steep climb which took carriers two hours, but a superb view and camp site. Locals amiable but dumb and as it was full moon drummed all night."

"Good bathing but boat anchorage dangerous, the smell of drying fish and cassava permeates everything and Khungu fly flew in at sundown".

"Tomasi was plastered again and the carriers had nowhere to sleep."

Seasonal needs and comfort must also be considered; nothing is more wearisome than trudging through deep, dry lake shore sand in the October and November heat, nor sliding up and down muddy and steep forest paths in a rainy March across the grain of the country, and an unwise choice of route may well mean that sufficient carriers cannot be found, or those who set out will desert. Luckily the country is so diverse in character that it is possible generally to go when the going is good and to do highland *ulendo* during the hot dry weather and the lake shore and low foothills in the rains and cold season.

Once the route has been fixed, the unsuspecting victims of one's choice have to be told and a messenger is sent out to let the Chiefs and village headmen know what is in store for them. This has the disadvantage of giving dubious clerks time to balance their books and impenitent tax defaulters warning of the approach of their nemesis, but it does ensure that food is prepared for carriers, camp sites cleared and the scattered population told that their chance to let off steam to the Boma has come round, without the trouble of a long walk. Messages are also sent to other village headmen to ask them to send in carriers to supplement the permanent carrier team at the Boma. This team is the dozen or so station hands, usually a motley collection of ex-tax defaulters, local layabouts, potential messengers and stranded wayfarers who, when not carrying, cut the grass and do a hundred and one other jobs under the desultory supervision of Boma Messengers. They are issued with a uniform and have a certain status; the best are not very reputable, but they are invaluable on *ulendo*, especially as carriers are hard to get. They can carry the heavy outer fly of a tent or a cumbersome bundle of tent poles over miles of broken country at a jog trot and still have the energy at the end to argue about food issues, seduce the local lovelies, and walk a few extra miles for a beer drink. They are often quarrelsome, always cheerful and cannot be put off by rain, flood, hail or mud.

The rest of the entourage is made up of men sent in by village headmen—one soon learns to ask for more than you hope to receive, and those who appear can and do vary in age, stamina, dress and willingness to a marked degree. Some are semi-professionals who turn up time after time and often end up in the team of station hands, replacing those whose transgressions have brought about their dismissal. In some districts it is the custom for women to volunteer as casual carriers, which poses a variety of problems, though the men like their cooking.

Having fixed the route, warned everyone, acquired carriers, detailed messengers and clerks, organised one's cook and/or one's wife, packed everything up, comes the start. No matter how experienced everyone is and how carefully everything has been planned the start is always chaotic. The bundles, boxes, bedding rolls, bits of tent, the bath with the cooking pots inside and a bedraggled chicken perched on the piece of corrugated iron used for a stove, the chairs and the official *ulendo* box are all finally assembled in one place and the carriers let loose on them.

As one seldom walks out directly from the Boma, the chaos starts again as the carriers fight for room in the lorry which takes them to the jumping off place and all try to get into the lifeboat at the same time. The wise man leaves this initial shakedown to the messengers and driver and boat crew, and in any case it is always precisely at this point that an important but unannounced visitor arrives or an urgent signal demands a return to the office. An hour or so after the time fixed for departure you finally get away, and at long last you are perched in the stern of an overcrowded boat, wedged in the front of an overloaded lorry or merely striding up the first hill to catch up the carriers. It is a moment of moments, the point of no return when the rememberance of the unfinished tax account, the impending visit of the next goggle of M.Ps., the next batch of court cases and the check of the sub-accountant's cash can be sloughed off—there is nothing you can do about it; you are on *ulendo*.

At camp on the first day there is always a muddle but after the tent is up, the local dignitaries greeted, food produced and distributed and lunch finished, there is time to relax and wonder how the village meeting can be persuaded that contour bunding on steep slopes is not merely a devilish intention to raise revenue by fining backsliders but will really improve crops and stop erosion; how to put over the latest constitutional proposals in a language which contains few abstracts and is not adapted to express the subtle difference between two-tier, one-tier and qualitative franchise, and whether the oft repeated assurance that the Government is doing its best to produce schools, hospitals and roads, and that the manufacture of more bank notes is not the answer to the problem will stand any greater chance of acceptance than it was the last time you produced this particular bromide to the man who wanted to know why he should pay tax anyway.

After the first day the normal routine is established and for the next weeks or so the pattern is roughly the same—early breakfast, the dismantling of the tent, the carriers starting off, payments for food and flowery farewells, the dew on the grass and the transient morning freshness in the air. The walk in the growing heat, camp at midday, checking tax census and records, long involved conversations with Chiefs, clerks, messengers and villagers, the payment of remittances, the afternoon meeting and a stroll or shoot till sunset. Bath and evening meal, further long discussions with the Chief or headman, *ulendo* diary to write, books to read, a dance to watch and so to bed.

Each day is slightly different, there are detours from the main route to inspect schools, look at fields of crops, ravaged hillsides and possible road lines; a visit to some hot springs or a waterfall or to see the line of a fiercely contested boundary In the evening the local Malipenga band may prance, posture and drum, a Viseksi choir come and sing with their accompaniment of seed rattles, or one may be persuaded to go out flare fishing in an unstable dugout canoe.

On foot *ulendo* through the less accessible areas there is time to stand and stare, time to talk, to be talked at and to, time to listen to curious legends and unravel involved inheritance systems which lie behind a bogus claim to a patch of fertile soil. A long dry walk in the November sun to find the village water supply —a water hole in a dry river bed—makes the need of a well a reality. A detour to see a forest-edge plot ravaged by pig and monkey, or a lakeside rice field flattened by hippo, brings home the need for a hunter or the organisation of a local hunting party. An appreciation of the cheerfulness and fecklessness of what has been called "an ignorant man and his wife with a hoe" begins to grow and a great respect for the resource, good manners and kindliness of the ordinary villager. The noble savage living in idyllic bliss is a figment of a city-dweller's imagination nor do the daily marches resemble the parade through exotic be-orchided jungle glades to be seen in certain African films nor the sweaty animal-menaced, tsetse-fly haunted sagas to be seen in others. There are always snags in even the pleasantest day's march; heat, rain, floods, cold and the inevitable last long hill before reaching camp can always provide irritants, as can the over-long meeting, the incredible incomprehension, real or assumed, of the audience and the swarm of night insects that forces a retirement to bed under a mosquito net.

The people can be delightful or dim, surly or splendid, seditious or just plain stupid, but in retrospect and in some no doubt patronising and infuriating way, they become "our people". One knows them, curses them, praises them, defends them illogically to strangers, prosecutes some and is accused of persecuting others, but if one's masters and fates are kind, and one can stay long enough in a district, one can do something concrete for them. *Ulendo* can give one the perspective to know what are the needs and what can be done. The two seldom equate and it is perhaps arguable as to who reaps the greater benefit from this exercise—the administered or the administrator.

The day when household furniture was taken on *ulendo* and one lived in grass houses and dressed for dinner have gone. The coming of the jeep and the aeroplane, V.H.F. and bulldozer, the pollster and the politician, the Information Department handouts and the Nationalist broadsheets are sounding the death-knell of *ulendo*. Carriers will not carry, villages boycot meetings and there is no time for quiet amid the shouting of slogans, the demands for rights and the denial of responsibilities, but nevertheless

> . . . Whatever comes
> One hour was sunlit, and the Most High Gods
> Can boast of no better thing
> Than to have watched that hour as it passed . . .

Up-Country A.D.O.

by H. P. A. WALKER

THE curtain rises on a white house in a fishing village on the East Coast of Malaya. This village is the administrative headquarters of a 2,000 square mile sub-district, which includes several hundred miles of more or less navigable river and an island 33 miles in circumference 60 miles out to sea. The life-lines are the ancient ones of rivers and sea, with a series of coastal tracks severed by wide unbridged rivers as the contribution of the modern age. The people, as of old, live at the river-mouths and along the river banks. Near the coast they are Malay fishermen and Chinese shopkeepers. Up-river, aborigines and Malays practise shifting and settled cultivation and trade in jungle produce such as cane and jelutong—from which latter chewing-gum is made.

There are no other Europeans within 50 miles and among the scattered population of 8,000 the number that can speak English does not run to double figures— a clerk, a police inspector, four hospital assistants who run dispensaries, and the virtually self-taught son of a leading Chinese shopkeeper, the first villager to have been appointed a Justice of the Peace.

As the sun rises and shines through his low bedroom window the Assistant District Officer emerges rather reluctantly from under his mosquito net and potters around, typing out a confidential letter, doing some shopping by post and cleaning a carbine borrowed from the Home Guard for protection against bandits, crocodiles and tigers on river and jungle journeys. A shower and breakfast of cornflakes and coffee is followed by a half-mile stroll down an avenue of coconut palms to the small office where a smiling "Good morning, Sir," from the clerk and a solemn "Selamat pagi, Tuan," from the office-boy greet him at the door.

The mail has got through today, but before there is time to open it the tubby Home Guard Adjutant, Syed Ali, bustles in to report that a shopkeeper, Ah Boon, failed to turn up for guard duty last night. Although there has not been any bandit trouble locally for some years, discipline must be preserved, and a few platitudes together with a fine of $5 (which goes to the Home Guard Welfare Fund) will probably meet the case.

Following on at once is Ramasamy, an Indian who wishes to renew his licence to run a coffee-shop. There is no objection, and providing he passes the necessary medical inspection (which will involve him in a 40 mile trip each way and take at least two days) the licence can be renewed.

It is still not possible to open the mail, for hot on Ramasamy's heels is Abdullah, an aggrieved fisherman, complaining that last night the source of his livelihood, his big fishing-net, was eaten by one of Ramlah's buffaloes. This is sure to be a troublesome case, as Ramlah will inevitably deny that it was her buffalo which did the damage, a fact that Abdullah will find hard to prove, as there are very few villagers who can recognise one buffalo from another—frequently even the owners have no idea which ones are theirs.

A temporary respite and letters can be opened. The first is from the Medical Officer, requesting that a suspected aborigine leper 50 miles up-river be taken to hospital for examination. This will call for delicacy, as aborigines can fade into the jungle with their blowpipes very easily if they get wind of anything so unpleasant as compulsory evacuation to hospital—not but what there is growing confidence in the Government's medicine since Batin (headman) Pa Tipah of Krau consented to his daughter being taken 100 miles away for treatment (and she returned walking for the first time in years).

The other letters include routine correspondence on applications for land, issue of licences to tap rubber, collect turtle eggs or bird's nests, and numerous applications for identity cards for 12-year-old children; also for replacement of ones lost when boats capsized, or houses were burnt down.

There's Lim passing the window. Not difficult to guess what his errand is ... yes, it turns out as suspected. Soh Koon, the other pork-seller, has again broken the agreement whereby they were to slaughter in alternate weeks. Last time Lim was the culprit and Soh Koon the complainant.

Back to the letters. The next one (barely literate) is a complaint against the headman of Tanjong Kerdau village who (according to the letter) oppresses the villagers in general, and specifically has just stood by and watched others do the work of building a community hall for which the Government has provided the materials on an undertaking from the locals to do the construction. The letter is signed for a change—but it is twenty to one that the signatory will prove to be non-existent, or if there is actually a person of that name he will deny point-blank that he wrote the letter, saying either that he cannot write or that the writing is totally different from his.

Here is an Audit Query. Revenue was not paid in to the Treasury on the last working day of the month and an explanation is required. Paying in revenue involves a two-day journey here. The A.D.O. can hardly afford so much time every month, nor does he see how he can spare his one clerk. Better discuss this with the District Officer.

Now a letter from the D.O. agreeing to the dismissal from office of Batin Tomin. This was a strange day, 140 miles up-river, sitting on a tree trunk with two tribes of aborigines ready to fly at each other's throats on either side of him awaiting a decision—Batin Tomin with his melancholy, spiteful face and old withered body, pointing an accusing finger in the best Rider Haggard manner at his sturdy rival, Batin Chatang, who he alleged was attempting to kill him by a combination of magic and poison.

Time for lunch and flight from an unusually tiresome bunch of sand-flies. As the A.D.O. reaches for hat and stick (an Irish thorn, believed by locals from its resemblance to a rare Malayan wood to have magical powers—an old island medicine-man offered him $100 for it, though it was bought for five shillings in Ireland, and that was a wicked price!) his clerk comes in with a plea for more file-covers, there not being even any paper left to make temporary ones. Requests by letter for these from the D.O. have produced no results. Memo: raid the District Office on the next visit to headquarters.

Too hot to eat much for lunch—a spoonful of rice, a few vegetables and a bit of fish. Coffee, a cheroot and the day before yesterday's *Straits Times* that came with the morning mail.

Now off to Bendang, about four miles along the coast, to discuss the formation of a proposed co-operative society to plant rice, and also to try to settle a dispute between a meek teacher and a fierce villager over an alleged assault by the latter. Anyway, this is less serious than the last spot of trouble in Bendang, when a girl was attacked by her mother-in-law with a hatchet!

A Land Rover whose seats floated away when the vehicle was inadvertently driven into a river by the previous A.D.O. carries his successor along the sandy track to the river bank where it is abandoned for a small sampan that is rowed or sailed across according to the direction of the wind.

A short walk up the sandy beach and through the few shops to the Malay Penghulu's office, where the necessary business is transacted. The dispute does not prove capable of solution and is later taken to court, where the villager is fined and has to pay damages to the teacher. As he has no money at the time, the teacher lends it to him to save him from being sent to jail!

An agitated rice-planter from another village bursts in to complain that for the last few nights elephants have been laying waste his crops. Elephants are one of the worst problems, as, unlike the other major pests, wild pig, monkeys and rats, there is very little that can be done about them, though a constant watch and the use of firebrands and crackers sometimes scares them off. Fortunately an elephant rifle has recently arrived from England for the Game Ranger, and the A.D.O. is able to promise fairly speedy assistance.

Visits to the small Chinese school with its 24 pupils and the rather bigger Malay one with 200 pupils elicit that the former wishes to close a well to make a basket-ball pitch, while the thatch roof of the latter is badly in need of repairs.

Before leaving, the A.D.O. has a cup of coffee with the Penghulu and a few locals in a Chinese coffee-shop and the conversation turns to stories of the Japanese occupation. By the time the A.D.O. arrives home it is too late for a game of badminton, and instead he prints some recent photographs in a bathroom converted into a dark room by the light of a kerosene lamp. Some are semi-official ones taken far up-river, where photographers do not exist, for the purpose of identity cards; others are for his own album—sinking a sampan after removing all the contents to pass it under a fallen tree in the river, attractive aborigine ladies whose sartorial accoutrements extend only as far up as the waist, a view through palm trees and casuarinas of the transparent waters of a bay on one of the islands, and a homely one of a stray cat his 'boy' has adopted.

Then a shower, change of clothes, and off to teach English to Malay children at the night school. This is run by his clerk, but on occasion the A.D.O. takes a hand. Tonight he bears with him an old gramophone. His own voice is tuneless, but accompanied by music, the words of 'The Teddy Bears' Picnic' will probably stick as well as most of what is learnt from *The Simple English Reader*, so that the diversion will not be without pedagogic value.

And so back to supper of curried fish and corned beef and cheese and biscuits, and then a few letters home to be written before bedtime. One further interruption yet, however: an informer to give details of some bandits he has seen at Jerkoh, said by their aborigine guide to be on their way to Pulau Sering. The lateness of the hour, the informer's conspiratorial tones and the furtiveness of his manner make the A.D.O. wonder if he will dream that he is Clifford 60 years ago, and similar intelligence is being delivered to him about disgruntled chiefs who are ready to come out in revolt. . . .

The District Officer in Kikuyu Areas

(Reprinted, with permission, from "The Times British Colonies Review".)

THE pattern of a district officer's life in a Kikuyu tribal area is rapidly changing. No longer are these areas the backwoods, where life goes on unperturbed by outside thought and the hurly-burly of the present-day world. The advent of education and the ease of communications have brought entirely new horizons to people who thirty years ago lived in a most primitive state. These new horizons beckon the young and perhaps frighten the older generation; it is not surprising that a gulf appears between the two, and the young tend to throw off the discipline of the old. Nor can the elders any longer hold the young under the discipline required in days of inter-tribal warfare. What appears to the young men as a life of ease and excitement turns out to be a hard life, and suspicion of government plans soon sets in. The older men find this new way of life brought to them also, but they in their turn tend to be suspicious of those who bring it. Such a situation is fertile ground for new political doctrines, the seeds of which may be implanted from afar.

This is the setting in which the district officer of to-day finds himself, and in some ways it presents him with his greatest problem: a vast and barely literate population, with a young minority, more highly educated, swept up in the surge of progress. It is the duty of the district officer to cater for both these widely different classes of Kikuyu society at the same time, patiently seeking to remove the imagined grounds of suspicion.

Daily at the district office many an elder, clad only in a red blanket, seeks help on some intricate land dispute, which has already been argued for days before the African court elders. Waiting with them will be smartly dressed young men inquiring about the extension of a bursary, the chances of an apprenticeship in Nairobi, or about joining the Army.

The junior officer is freer than his District Commissioner to travel in his district, or in that part of it allotted to his special charge. Most of his time is devoted to meeting and talking with the people in their villages. He tells them at his *barazas* what government policy means in "bricks and mortar" to them: what they with the Government have to do to bring about improvement of the countryside and of their lives. He hears their problems, and, after sifting the oriental wheat from the chaff, he will generally be able to deal with them on the spot.

The district officer makes a point of meeting the chief and the locational advisory council together, for here is the executive head, and also the leading elements of the area, with whom he can discuss the current parish problems. In the advisory council there is a mixture of young and old. There will be schoolmasters, traders, farmers, elders of the mission schools, a stonemason or carpenter or two—perhaps some thirty in all. To-day many attend wearing the badge of the Home Guard, their rifles slung over their shoulders. They have many subjects for discussion with the district officer, and he with them. The agenda may include the election from among their number of a councillor for the African district council, the construction of a new road, an application to the district council for a dispensary, or the raising of a local rate to build a new school classroom at a mission school in their area. This is what matters, and the district officer knows it. He tries to inculcate a sense of self-help and to allay any inherent suspicion of Government's intentions; no district officer will leave this gathering until he has heard the last word on each subject.

After his meeting with the locational council, the district officer, accompanied by the chief and an African agricultural instructor, will walk to see the latest soil conservation work being done by communal labour, turned out on the orders of the clan or headman; then on to see the latest developments made by a young farmer and to a school smallholding. He returns late to his house in the reserve, where his companions may be a European police inspector, an agricultural officer, and a Kikuyu livestock officer. There is still much to be done. His efforts to get the old men to dispose of their surplus stock have met with so little success although he and the livestock officer have tried every means possible to persuade them of their folly. He discusses this with the livestock officer. There is little doubt that more teaching, example and persuasion are needed before the conservative peasant will see the advantages which the district officer strives so hard to put across, but it is equally certain that his enthusiasm, coupled with the quickened intelligence of the minority of young farmers, will sooner rather than later bear fruit.

In these critical days there is one vital task for each district officer in the Kikuyu tribal areas: he is in charge of the Kikuyu Home Guards. He has formed and trained them, watching for the right man to command, and watching too for infiltration of undesirable elements. He has often led them in operations with the armed forces against their fellow tribesmen in the Mau Mau gangs. He has taught them to send out patrols and to construct their strong points where they can rally for defence, and from which they can sally forth to harry and destroy the gangs.

Several times a week the district officer will visit each Home Guard unit in his area. He will discuss their tactics in the fight against Mau Mau. He will check the membership lists of each unit with its commander and his special henchmen. He will also check their weapons and ammunition. He may find that a closer liaison is required between a Home Guard unit and the nearest police post, and this he will discuss with his police officer. In these days these two officers are very much in each other's pockets, and, as the police officer is often new to the job, the district officer can advise him on tribal custom and idiosyncrasies, the sources of potential trouble, and, in particular, he can pass on much intelligence, particularly political intelligence, to him.

The district officer may deplore the fact that he has to devote so much of his time to the operational campaign against Mau Mau. He firmly believes that he has a much fuller armoury for success than the weapons he issues to the Home Guard. He sees many of the development schemes on which he was previously engaged slowed down or even stopped altogether in consequence of the activities of Mau Mau gangs. The truly progressive Kikuyu are usually the members of his Home Guard, and it is for the resumption of these schemes and their future progress that these men are fighting. It is on these Home Guard members, too, that, after the emergency ends, much will depend when a full-scale reconstruction can be undertaken. This fact alone makes the district officer insistent on quality rather than quantity in his Home Guard. It is also through such men that the hearts of the numerous waverers will be won over to loyalty. Through the Home Guard, too, the district officer has the opportunity to inculcate a sense of pride in a tribe that, because of Mau Mau, has so sadly lost it.

Meanwhile, the District Commissioner translates the policy of the Government to suit the conditions of his district, keeping in closest touch with his technical officers to ensure that the development of the district goes smoothly ahead, or as smoothly as the emergency permits.

Especially important are the meetings with the chiefs, to whom will be added other leading Kikuyu, so that the District Commissioner, short circuiting official reports, may keep himself fully informed. The chiefs will differ greatly one from another; some will be men of the old school, who have escaped the ultra-conservatism of their fellows, while others will be "coming" men. These men are no politicians, and yet they are the real leaders of the people. They are well aware that present-day trends are difficult for young and old alike. They are, however, eager to lead their

The accompanying illustrations are of Masailand.—Ed.

people forward and they are increasingly aware of the need to carry them with them, but they sincerely ask that they may have strong executive power in order to fulfil their rôle, and that it may be given to them with full and continuing support; tribal discipline must be fully enforced among the young. Probably through no channel is the Government better advised about the real opinions, reactions, hopes and fears of the people than through the chiefs.

To the chiefs, however, can now be added the slowly growing number of African district officers. These men, who take their places side by side with their European counterparts, are playing an important rôle. They must be men of exceptional personality and possess powers of leadership.

The District Commissioner can also, in his position as president of the African district council, assess opinion in his district. An elected majority may well sometimes not be in sympathy with the views expressed to the District Commissioner by the chiefs elsewhere. The scope of these councils is wide, covering as it does many aspects of education, public works, agriculture, health services, community development and so forth, with a budget of £60,000 or more.

The emergency, needless to say, has increased the functions of the District Commissioner, and to ensure complete co-ordination he takes the chair several times a week at meetings with the district police superintendent and the senior military officer engaged in operations in his area. He endeavours to make sure that any operational plans made will not have undue adverse political effect on the district as a whole. The restoration of peace will increase the task of economic and political development. But in some ways the emergency itself has helped; it has thrown up outstanding local leaders, and it has revealed weak links in organisation and personalities. The elimination of a few political malcontents, too, mostly with the barest of education and seeking only their own advantage, has sometimes made possible development and progress which only they, by their heckling of an illiterate population, had hitherto prevented.

Of all the functions of the District Commissioner probably the most important is that of chairman of the meetings of his district officers and technical officers, European and African, commonly known as the district team. Here most of the planning and co-ordinating is carried on, and it is on the harmony of this team that much of the progress of the district depends. Throughout the emergency the team has sought to keep its many projects alive, often only with the greatest difficulty and after the team's case has been strongly represented by the District Commissioner to the emergency committee of police and military officers. Sometimes a scheme has had to be shelved for operational reasons, but always there is the fullest recognition that the plans of the team must go on, Mau Mau or no Mau Mau.

As Africans of calibre come forward to share to the full in the administration of a district the interest in the work increases, and there is no district officer who does not long to be rid of the emergency, and of Mau Mau, so that all the plans for development and the handing over of an ever-increasing share in their administration to the Kikuyu themselves can go on; but all this must be set upon a foundation of order, well and truly maintained.

D. C. Ocean

by G. WYN JONES

[In his article *The Prince in the Pacific* (*Corona*, March, 1960, p. 94) Sir Alexander Grantham said . . . "Ocean Island is really a phosphate factory in a South Seas setting . . ." Here the District Commissioner gives an account of a day's work on the island.—Ed.]

OCEAN ISLAND is the westernmost island in the Gilbert and Ellice Islands Colony, and it is the only island in the administration which is not a low-lying atoll or reef island. A steep hump of rock which rises precipitously from the depths of the Pacific to a height of about 250 feet, Ocean Island has been a major source of phosphate for sixty years. Its rich deposits contain the highest grade of phosphate ever discovered, and inevitably the island's life is dominated by the mining operations of the British Phosphate Commission.

The position and responsibilities of the District Commissioner are consequently unique. He and the Superintendent of Police are the only senior Government officers stationed on the island (the Medical Officer is employed by the Phosphate Commission). There are over 200 junior Government staff and their families: the rest of the 2,500 population, Europeans, Chinese and Gilbertese and Ellice are employees of the British Phosphate Commissioners.

Despite this apparent homogeneity, and despite the lack of an indigenous population and of native administration as it is known elsewhere in the Colony, the day's work can present the District Commissioner with an interesting variety of tasks. It is not an exacting station—the office work is light by today's standards—but a few times a month come the 'shipping days' and it is then that one can appreciate the Olympian peace of a Secretariat. We are predominantly Australian here and many fine ships ply between Ocean Island and Melbourne or other Australian ports.

At dawn the telephone shrills and the breezy voice of an Assistant Harbour-master shouts that the *Triaster* is just approaching the buoy and will be tying up in twenty minutes. A face-hacking shave, a quick shower and into the Landrover. It is only a mile or so to the boat harbour and the drive clears away the last of the cobwebs. In the Government village the Postal Messenger who is going to collect the mail leaps on board. He grins a welcome.

The sea is not too bad this morning, and the Medical Officer and the D.C. make it from the launch to the ship without loss of dignity—for once. On board, the Purser promptly placates them with steaming coffee and the customs and immigration formalities are then seen to. Before leaving the passenger decks the D.C. violates the morning-after recuperation of any passengers bound for Tarawa, the Government headquarters 200 miles away, and tells them when to be ready to disembark. They look incredulous when shown the Colony ship they are to travel in—she is lunging and rolling vigorously in a light sea off shore. A quick chat with the Master to collect any safe-hand mail there may be and then another launch out to the small ship from Tarawa. It's *Nareau* this time, an old stager by now and a ship of eighty-five feet with a reputation for cutting 'good sailors' down to size. A leisurely exchange of views and gossip, a gloomy glance at a mail bag bulging with mail from the Secretariat and the Chief Postmaster, a leap from sponson to launch, and then ashore for breakfast. Everyone else is just rubbing the sleep out of their eyes. One misses the B.B.C. news by three minutes and can get only the Luton Girls' Choir and the weather forecast for Lower Hutt. Ah, well, it's a shipping day and only to be expected.

At a few minutes to eight, down to the office to have a look at the official mail, and to see how the postal staff of two are withstanding the strain of two incoming and two outgoing mails and of last minute customers who want to send Money Orders to Hong Kong and British Postal Orders to Iraq. The telephone starts its never-ending summons. Mrs. Toolate asks if the mail is closed and what is the airmail rate to Japan *via* New Zealand? The Hardware Store states there is no crystal-green Spred, will Bergermaster Berkshire Green do? The Commission's Manager wants to know if a penny to a pound raffle which the Golf Club wishes to run would be legal, and may he bring along a VIP guest from *Triaster* later on?

Then it's time to meet the passengers who are coming ashore at nine. A sheep dog exercise of growls and cutting out movements to segregate the Tarawa passengers and despatch them in a launch to *Nareau*. They go, very reluctantly and anxious about their heavy luggage—see the stevedores about this, and then a swift there-and-back trip to *Nareau* to tie up the last loose ends. There is then time to have a look at the manifests and to send a telegram to Tarawa to say that *Nareau* is on her way and whom and what she is carrying.

In the office the morning telegrams have just arrived. The Chief Postmaster is petulant about an error in a Money Order list. The Secretariat have a query on royalty payments on phosphate exports and want to book some passages for Australia and New Zealand. There is an obviously garbled message authorising salary payments to a Wireless Operator on the scale of a Managing Director, and for some obscure reason the Superintendent of Works wants to know how many telephones on a manual exchange we have on Ocean Island. The telephone takes the hint and starts ringing again. Someone wants to make arrangements for a driving test. The Medical Officer says he has a mental patient who may need certifying. The Commission's Labour Inspector recites a list of queries—a Workmen's Compensation Agreement has to be signed, a contract to be terminated, a case of sorcery is causing him worry and he gives the background of the man who is undergoing mental treatment. The Postmaster comes in to ask when the hundred odd parcels which have arrived, mainly for the Chinese spare-time hawkers, may be assessed for customs duty—a tedious job.

A constable appears with the charge-sheets for the Court to be held later in the week. A couple of interesting looking assault and adultery cases, the sorcery one referred to by the Labour Inspector and the usual plethora of traffic and other minor offences. The constable also stays to give a short and biased account of how the Police cricket team lost to the Scouts in the competition the previous Saturday, and then salutes and leaves. A Gilbertese messenger from the Commission's Accountant by-passes the main office and thrusts an envelope forward. It turns out to be a batch of Certificates of Essentiality for goods which are to be ordered in the *Triaster* mail that day. The top certificate is to cover twelve gross "Chamber pots, enamel, twelve inch". One supposes they are essential: the 'purpose for which required' is described as 'incentive goods'. One signs.

The harbourmaster calls to ask when it would be convenient for the Master of the charter vessel, which is lying off waiting for *Triaster* to sail, to register a Note of Protest. The D.C. agrees to do it on board. Ocean Island is not loved by ships' Masters. The currents are tricky and to load phosphate the ships are pulled in under a cantilever loading arm to within one hundred and fifty feet or so of the reef. The sea bed falls away steeply and three hundred yards from shore "B" berth boasts the deepest moorings in the world—243 fathoms. Everywhere the reef is too close to relax and there is always the mute warning of *Kelvinbank*, broken in two on the coral two hundred yards away.

And then home to lunch. There is a Tarawa family going on leave by *Triaster* and they give the latest gossip and news while they eat, at the same time rhapsodising over the salad and fresh frozen foods which Ocean Islanders can enjoy. All too soon it is time to go back to the office. *Triaster's* papers are cleared and the passports stamped, and then the only shipping duty left is the Note of Protest. By this time *Triaster* is lying off and the tramp is under the cantilever shrouded in a cloud of phosphate dust as the greyish-brown wealth is poured into her holds. The crew can find nowhere free of the choking grit and look very sorry for themselves. However, the Master proves to be a pleasant fellow and is discovered in olive green bathing trunks hosing down the deck near the bridge. With a long white beard the effect is striking. A pleasant ten minutes are spent on board, chatting about the propensities of ships to pursue mooring barges and of the latter for getting in the way of ships, and about the expense of educating children. A signature, a stamp and seal and then back to shore.

On the drive back to the office there are a series of calls in the main administration block of the Phosphate Commission: on an island where almost all the public services are provided by an independent body, there is a continual need to maintain close liaison with the management and various departmental heads, and one is very dependent on their goodwill. The views of the Civil Engineer on the repairs to the Government Rest House are not reassuring, but the gloom is lightened somewhat by the ability of the Mechanical Electrical Engineer to take the Landrover into the Commission garage the following week for undersealing. But this tour of the offices unfortunately exposes the flank to a reference to Lions who have their tails tweaked by All-Blacks, followed by a barbed word of congratulation at being able to beat India at cricket—"you must have sent a rugby team out by mistake to play us Aussies"—life is difficult in a predominantly Antipodean community when their sporting tails are up. But back to the files.

Some files are restless by their very nature, and today's selection consists mainly of the perennials which spend their working life being carried from bays to dips to desks to bays until they collapse limply, very much the worse for wear, into well-earned retirement in archives. Accountancy (audit query), Medical (epimediological return due), Vital Statistics (a birth or a death to register), Ceremonial and Visits (wonder who's coming now), Education (secondary schools entrance examination due soon), Labour (always something here), a Personal File (probably only an increment certificate), Shipping (two or three of these without fail), and then they're finished.

A sudden entrance in the outer office—"Anything else for me?"—and an exit quick enough to anticipate any incipient reply. Into the car, past the Court House, Post Office, Wireless station and War Memorial, through the village, pick up three-year-old daughter who has been watching volleyball (the Government team lost and the men will have to catch all the flying fish for the feast next Saturday), past the playing field, between the mango trees and away up the hill. Call at the Rest House to see if the transients are settled in, past the Police House, the Commission School (for European and Chinese children—there are about thirty skilled Chinese artisans from Hong Kong on the island) and, at last, home and a cup of tea and the enticing prospect of an hour or so on one of the beaches (or, if we feel energetic, golf on a nine-hole course, or floodlit tennis later). A drive round the east coast and then a nice long drink with the newly-arrived magazines and newspapers. That is the one traditional pleasure of Colonial administrators that has not changed. It is also an interesting variant on the well-worn concept of an empire where sun ne'er sets that for every hour of the twenty-four there must still be at least one weary Overseas Civil Servant welcoming the setting of the sun with a nice long drink.

And now it's the turn of D.C. Ocean. That was his day!

Evocation

by MARJORIE M. RANSOM

In swelt'ring, sun-baked towns;
From humid jungle's avid mouth
Or shimm'ring, arid desert wastes;
From East or West, from North or South,
I call to mind
The green of Sussex Downs.

From isles where icy moods,
Antarctic winds, whip up the sea—
Endanger life and ships; so bleak
It seems that Spring could never be—
I call to mind
The green of Kentish woods.

The jasmine scented dawns
Fade out the star-girt orient skies.
Exotic colours, flowers, drowse
The sense, like lovely women's eyes.
I still recall
The green of Surrey lawns.

The green of England's pleasant land,
The green that makes no cruel demand.

My Days in the Western Pacific: I

by DOUGLAS FREEGARD

ELEVEN years ago, as a somewhat elderly cadet, I was posted to the Solomon Islands. It took me nine years to get there, after serving on islands over 2,000 miles to the East and 1,000 miles to the South of the Solomons and still within the jurisdiction of the High Commissioner for the Western Pacific. This is not surprising if you consider that the High Commission stretches from Longitudes 155 East to 159 West and Latitudes 4 North to 21 South, includes ethnological groups varying from the naked Melanesian bushman of the high Santo hills to the statuesque Polynesians of the Ellice Islands and the robust Micronesian fishermen of the Gilberts, and contains an Anglo-French Condominium, a Protectorate and a Crown Colony as well as sharing joint administration of two islands with the United States of America. The fact that one of the two is inhabited only by sea birds and rats adds a touch of the bizarre which is not out of place in a territory which has attracted the Romantics from Hakluyt to Mitchiner and has in its time dealt in such exotic trades as sandlewood and shrunken skulls, whale oil and bêche de mer.

When I set out for the Solomons Her Majesty's Government had not yet decided that the time of embryo administrators was of sufficient value to warrant air travel. That first journey soon taught me the difference between war-time Europe and the post-war Pacific. My instructions were to report to Liverpool on a day in March and there to board a Blue Funnel ship for Sydney where I could expect further orders. These instructions did not relate that the ship was routed by way of the Cape of Good Hope with cargo for Dakar, the Cape, Fremantle, Adelaide and Melbourne as well as Sydney. By mid-May we reached Melbourne. I had played for the ship at soccer and cricket and learnt that a schooner was a measure of beer, but did not feel nearer my job. Having learnt in twelve years of soldiering the folly of assuming that silence always implies disinterest, a telegram was sent to Fiji, then the High Commissioner's headquarters, to say the ship was delayed by strikes and to ask for instructions. These were, to entrain for Sydney and there to board the trading vessel *Morinda* routed for the Solomons by Norfolk Island and the New Hebrides. As she did not leave for another fortnight my education in Australian geography continued its leisurely way.

The *Morinda*, of 1,400 tons and built in the '20's for Pacific trade, was a good introduction to the peculiarities of island life. Her master, the son of one of Australia's best water colourists and himself an exhibitor of oils in both Australia and the United States, was also an extra master and had been the chief navigational instructor of Australia's Coastal Command. The twenty odd passengers included planters, traders, tourists and the famous Doctor Fox of the Melanesian Mission, who had changed name and personality with a bush chief who by now lay buried under a head-stone bearing the Doctor's name. The islands were in sight.

Norfolk and Lord Howe Islands introduced me to the surf boat which was to disembark me, soak my luggage and deposit me in the surf many times in the next few years. Two weeks out from Sydney we entered the High Commission territory at Vila, the capital of the New Hebrides. Here a duty call on the Resident Commissioner earned me an excellent luncheon and, when it was discovered that I spoke French, an invitation to stop in the New Hebrides. A cable was sent to the High

Commissioner and twenty-four hours later I received instructions to disembark at Santo in the Northern New Hebrides and return to Vila. Although I did not know it then, the Solomons had retreated nine years into the future.

The administration in the New Hebrides has changed since I left in 1952 but my experiences there may still have some degree of relevance. In those days eight officers, including a Resident Commissioner, were responsible for the whole of the British administration, staffing the Secretariat, the police and four districts. After six months at Vila I found myself, then still a cadet, performing, or rather filling, the roles of Acting Assistant Resident, Commandant of Police, British Agent for two districts and British Judge *ad hoc* in the joint court all at the same time. The joint court, I should add, consisted, in principle, of a French judge, a British judge and a president appointed by the King of Spain.

It would be invidious as well as inaccurate to say that these concurrent duties were discharged with efficiency. A spell as DAA and QMG of a parachute Brigade is not generally accepted as the best preparation for civil administration. I can only claim for this stage of my career that it showed clearly the saving of correspondence inherent in a plurality of functions. Those who eventually filled these posts more effectively than I, no doubt suffered from *lacunae* in the records due to my reluctance to move from desk to desk exhorting myself to greater efforts.

In 1951 the staffing position became less straitened and I left the centre of Government to act as British Agent for the two Northern districts. Here, with a French colleague in each district, I ruled an empire stretching from latitudes 13 to 18 degrees south and containing some forty islands varying in size from Santo's three hundred miles coastline to Vao with one of three miles, and in population from Aoba's seven thousand to Maevo's three hundred. The parishioners varied from the bushmen of Malekula, who could, and frequently did, field some two hundred rifles when excited, to the Tangoans who shared their island peacefully with a theological college. My headquarters was on a pretty, if inconvenient seven acre island off the coast of Santo which I shared with one clerk, ten policemen and an average prison population of fifteen. Its inconvenience consisted of inaccessibility to the mainland if the wind was in the south-west, when fifteen foot rollers made the passage impassable in a twelve foot dinghy. Transport consisted of this dinghy, a twenty foot cabin launch in which to visit my French colleague eighteen miles down the coast, a thirty-two foot gaff rigged cutter for longer trips and an antiquated jeep of temperamental performance. My second colleague lived ninety miles away on another island. A married officer who hears of his posting to this island paradise, and whose wife doesn't enjoy a thirty-six mile shopping trip through a maze of reefs in a small boat, may be relieved to hear that the British Agency has now moved to a more civilised location.

The duties of the district agent in those days were more static than dynamic; lack of finance effectively precluded any ambitious schemes of economic development. We collected such small taxes as were levied, administered the law on a magisterial level, and attempted to discourage the more individualistic planters and traders from selling cheap liquor illegally at exhorbitant prices to a thirsty populace, and to encourage the locals to settle their social and economic differences in court rather than single combat. Many of them really enjoyed litigation, particularly if it involved the arbitrator in a hard and uncomfortable walk over rough country to examine the unmarked boundary separating properties which had not been cultivated in living memory and which could only be divined by the memory of the oldest inhabitants. Particular entertainment was provided if the district agent could be persuaded into reversing a predecessor's judgement, especially if the predecessor had been of the opposite nationality. This was not as difficult as might appear, since a lot of the records had been mislaid during the war.

Another sport of the local populace was to bring charges against a planter of the opposite nationality to that of the district agent, in the hope that patriotism would embroil the administration in strife. Since British Resortissants had to be tried before a British chairman of the Bench and French Resortissants before a French chairman, the possibilities of sport were almost inexhaustible.

I was fortunate in my colleagues, especially in the northernmost of my two districts, where my opposite number was not only a close personal friend, but also an administrator of many years' experience. Whenever it was physically possible we would tour together, toss for which of us should deal with any particular problem and record its solution on the spot. Where this was impossible we would work out our tours together and check previous decisions on both sides in the area to be toured. This entailed a good deal of paper work but could save endless misunderstanding and formal correspondence.

I used to enjoy sailing and hill climbing equally in those days and would spend approximately two weeks out of four away from home. This could be tiring as my cutter was crewed by policemen, most of whom came from the bush for some reason and were more at home on mountain ridges than on deck. I remember one gentleman who went over the side half a dozen times before he learnt the danger of standing up to a swinging boom. Fortunately for him he was a natural water-treader.

Day to day activities were enlivened from time to time by more spectacular occurrences in keeping with both the history and the geology of the group. A place possessing the world record for missionary martyrs, four active volcanoes and a site in the centre of the hurricane belt was not without opportunity for the unusual.

If the south could boast of Jonfrum, whose activities have been publicised by David Attenborough, in the north we could claim a very active volcano on Ambryn, the ebullient Amok of Malekula, who enjoyed burning down mission stations, a naked cult in the Santo hills and a very volatile population on South Pentecost.

During my two years stay in the north we had, by way of extra curricular activity, an eruption involving evacuation by boat of some 2,500 people, rapidly followed by a hurricane which killed over a hundred people and sank fourteen small boats. Not long after this my opposite number and I were called to Pentecost at short notice to deal with a blind man who had decided that he was God and convinced a fair part of the population that this deity required the forcible removal of all other religious sects. We caught up with this gentleman, after some of the most uncomfortable walking I can remember, which took us to places which had never seen a white man, and resolved the theological problem by having the supposed God operated on for cataract by a French surgeon. With the recovery of his sight he turned to more mundane pusuits.

Another eventful incident was the investigation of a singularly unpleasant double murder at the north of Santo. After completing our investigations, the motor of my vessel broke down on the way home. Fortunately, as we thought at the time, we had given a lift to an Indo-Chinese cook from the plantation where the event occurred. It was not until we eventually reached home, after being towed by canoes for some way, that I discovered that our passenger had infected me with amoebic dysentery. As my struggles to get the boat's motor going had given me a rupture, my memories of that particular episode are not happy. I cannot think of two more incompatible complaints. Luckily they occurred when I was already due for leave, after which I moved to the Gilbert and Ellice islands, about which I hope to write something later.

My Days in the Western Pacific : III

by DOUGLAS M. FREEGARD

I REACHED the Solomon Islands in November, 1958, over eight years after leaving Liverpool for the Protectorate, and with the experience of the New Hebrides and Gilberts behind me. Five years of coral atolls with a mean height of ten feet above sea level had not provided physical training for the high peaks of the Protectorate but the pleasure of working in the shadow of hills more than compensated for unready muscles. After a time the narrow surf-swept islands of the Colony, where the sky and sea overwhelm the land, induce a sense of remoteness from reality which must be reflected in reaction to every day events.

The first impression of the Protectorate was of size, of wide coastal plains, rolling foothills and peaks high enough to spend a good part of the time hidden in the clouds. The next was, in some sort, of homecoming; in the Gilberts and in the Ellice Islands the media of expression were either English, Gilbertese or Ellice; in the Solomons the most usual means of communication is still pidgin English once one is outside the capital and away from schools. Although there is a great deal to be said for the replacement of pidgin English there is still a selfish satisfaction in making oneself understood in Guadacanal or Malaita in a tongue learned in the New Hebrides and practised with Tahitians and Wallace Islanders, New Caledonians and natives of New Guinea. Different background patterns depending on earlier contacts with German or French speaking settlers make a very slight barrier between pidgin speakers from Papeete to Papua.

As one of the very few people still serving who have worked for any length of time in all three of the Western Pacific Territories I may perhaps be forgiven for dwelling shortly on the basic differences of the three administrations as they have struck a junior member of the administration. In the New Hebrides in my time the efforts of the administration were necessarily directed mainly to the maintenance of law and order. Commercial and economic development were largely in the hands of the trader and planter. This has changed over the last few years with an increased concentration of national funds on exploration and development of natural resources, but it had one very noticeable effect on the development of the indigenous New Hebridean. During my time there the price of copra was high by present-day standards. This had the effect of placing local labour at a premium, and at the same time creating among the locals a category of business men whose like I have not seen elsewhere in the Western Pacific, the really large scale local planter who would from time to time buy a European-run plantation from his own resources and work it without expatriate help. Competition was fierce, but my stay in the New Hebrides planted firmly in my mind the basic fact that the Melanesian is quite capable, given financial stimulus and competitive experience, of becoming a very shrewd and capable business man.

The Gilbert and Ellice Islands Colony presented a very different commercial picture. Since the war the Colony has possessed virtually no private enterprise. The only major exports, of phosphate and copra, are controlled by the British Phosphate Commission and the Colony Copra Board, each in its own way a "nationalised industry". Imports are almost entirely in the hands of the Colony Wholesale Society whose board is headed by and largely composed of Administrative Officers, and retail trade is carried on almost exclusively by co-operative societies whose Registrar is necessarily an Administrative Officer. Most of my readers will be

familiar with the advantages and disadvantages of such a system. Few would claim
for it the virtues of flexibility associated with free enterprise. Equally, few would
deny that without the introduction of this system after the devastations of the last
war the lot of the Colony would have been an unhappy one.

Both economically and politically I found my return to Melanesia from
Micronesia an exciting and stimulating experience. In the economic field the next
two years showed a very considerable advance in the post-war rehabilitation of
both expatriate and local coconut plantations in the Protectorate. With the assistance of Colonial Development and Welfare Funds and the co-operation of Levers,
a programme of agronomic research into the selection and propagation of high
yielding strains of nuts was well under way; real progress was being made with the
introduction of a second main economic crop, cocoa, which had already proved its
viability in similar climatic and soil conditions in the neighbouring territory of
Papua and New Guinea; a most interesting experiment had begun into the introduction of wet paddy and we were well on the way to the exploitation of the very
considerable timber resources of the Protectorate. One of the most heartening
indications of local interest in the improvement of both production and marketing
of copra was the increasing use being made by both local and expatriate farmers of
facilities offered by the Agricultural and Industrial Loans Board set up by the
Government with funds made available from War Reparations. No less heartening
was the regularity with which both expatriate and local borrowers were showing
their ability to service such loans as had been made available from this fund.
Politically the two years showed no less exciting progress. By the end of 1960 a
territory which before the war had possessed the most rudimentary elements of
local government had advanced to the stage of possessing its own Legislative
Assembly and Executive Council. The first meeting of the Legislative Council in
December, 1960, indicated a maturity of political thought among both expatriate
and Solomon Island members which was astonishing in so small and relatively
remote a community.

I was fortunate during these two years to have experience of both field work in
a District and financial work in the Secretariat. In the Districts the tempo of
local Government activity was rapidly increasing, with the realisation of the great
part to be played by the elected local councils in the furtherance of facilities for
education, public health and communications. At the centre the standing committee
of finance rapidly came to grips with the problems of financial priorities in a
limited economy.

It is appropriate to mention here the peculiar difficulties imposed on the
Solomons by communications. Apart from an excellent small artificial harbour at
the capital, Honiara, and small harbours at Levers' headquarters at Yandina in the
Russell Group and Gizo in the Western Solomons, both administration and commerce are dependent on a fleet of small vessels ranging from the local launches
used by villagers and plantations to centralise their crops and distribute supplies,
to 80/100 footers working between the main ports and the outlying centres. It will
be readily appreciated that the necessity for such small scale means of transport
throughout the territory presents a very real problem in terms of cost and economic
use.

For the administrator there are few things better calculated to hamper the
lucid exposition of policy in a language other than his own than the physical
nausea so often attendant on twenty-four hours of tumbling about on a small
vessel in the Pacific rollers. Nor is it easy to fill in the journey in these circumstances with preparation of papers. For the merchant or planter it could hardly

be claimed that the collection of one's crop from scattered plantings in small craft loaded by hand is the most economical way to put them on the market.

It is difficult for anyone used to working in territories whose communications by road and rail make it possible to exercise close supervision over large areas with a minimum of travelling time, to appreciate the logistical problems posed by the difficulty of access of the Pacific Islands. It is, however, one of the most cheering reflections on human nature that the attempt to solve these problems is one of the greatest attractions of administration in the Pacific. The pitting not only of one's brain but of one's physical resources against the physical barriers to progress imposed by nature has always exercised a peculiar fascination. I can imagine few jobs where such a struggle is carried on in a more lovely setting than that of the Pacific Islands. It has been claimed that the work of an administrator in this part of the world contains all the frustrations of the civil servant struggling with his problems in more modern surroundings, with the additional handicap of a climate which makes it essential to spend some months every two years recuperating in a temperate zone. How many civil servants in England on their way to a conference in the provinces would not appreciate the opportunity to catch a ten pound barracuda on the way, or who would not prefer to relax from committee work over a fresh coconut in the shade of a palm tree instead of a cup of office tea, and who would not feel a great satisfaction in attending the opening of a deep water wharf built by the communal effort of a group of villages spurred only by the realisation that by giving their labour voluntarily for this end they would secure a regular collection of their cash crop instead of relying on the sporadic visits of traders unwilling to risk their vessels off an open beach.

I hope I have not painted too glowing a picture of a part of the world whose very remoteness gives it an aura of romance, but eleven years of the Western Pacific have made me realise why it is that so many who have worked there are never completely at home anywhere else in the world.

AGONIES

Charge 5s. per line, as below, minimum 10s.   Cheques and postal orders to be sent to the Editor but made payable to the Chief Accountant, Colonial Office.

Parents troubled by the problem of finding a good English Preparatory School for their sons while themselves overseas are recommended to get in touch with the Reverend the Headmaster, Staveley Court Preparatory School, Eastbourne, where full charge is taken of boys from 6 to 14 at reasonable fees.   First class education and a genuinely home atmosphere. References given if required by parents of former pupils.

Switzerland.   Guests received by young couple in large, comfortable and ideally situated Chalêt in sunny Alpine valley 3,300 ft. above Montreux.   Wonderful view, walks and flowers, tennis, swimming, riding, fishing and climbing.   Winter sports and spring ski-ing. Ice-rink and ski-fields on doorstep with ski-lifts to 7,000 ft.   Special terms arranged for long visits.   Illustrated brochures on request.   C. B. Wilmot-Allistone, Chalêt Bon Accueil, Chateau-d'Oex.

For Sale.   Steel uniform cases pre-war.   Two (A. & N.) as new, three others in good condition.   All have mahogany battens.   Details Ardron, Cliff House, Sherborne, Dorset.

To Let.   For May, June and July, and from September, furnished cottage on the Solent at Gurnard, Cowes, Isle of Wight—4 bedrooms, ideal for children.   3½ guineas a week. Apply Box 23, *Corona*.

Nairn.   A few vacancies available for children, holidays included.   Roomy house with large garden near good schools and sea.   Suitable family home for children with parents overseas.   £14 a month inclusive.   Mr. and Mrs. Mactaggart, Grianach, Nairn.

Nairn.   Cottage, all elec., fully furn., incl. linen, 2 bed, sitting-room, kitchenette, bathroom, h. & c., mod. sanitation, near sea, golf course, bowling greens and tennis courts, to let from 8th Sept. to mid-Dec., 1951.   Mactaggart, Grianach, Nairn.

Wanted.   Administrative Officer's sword.   T. N. Rosser, Glenfield Crescent, Galashiels.

Furnished Flat To Let.   Reigate Hill.   May 10th to Dec. 31st.   2 double bed, 2 sitting, kitchen, bath, garage, phone.   6½ gns.   Odgers, Brockwell Gate, Tadworth, Surrey.

The Passing of the British Advisers in Malaya

by W. C. S. CORRY, C.B.E.

THE Residents have been the foundation-stones of British power in the Malay States, and the system of residential control introduced there over 80 years ago has been the model for 'indirect rule' in other dependencies, notably in Northern Nigeria.

In the middle of last century British administrators from their observation points in the British enclaves of Penang, Malacca and Singapore could see a state of feudal anarchy in the rest of the Malay Peninsula into which thousands of immigrant Chinese miners were swarming in a 'Tin Rush' comparable to the later rush for gold in the Klondyke. Fierce faction fights run by their secret societies tended to weaken the Malay Governments, and the Ruler of Perak—the State most deeply affected—turned to the British Government for help. He asked for a British officer to be sent to his Court on whose advice he would be guided in all matters save only those concerned with the Muslim religion and Malay custom. Mr. Birch, the first Resident appointed to Perak, attempted to do too much too quickly, and his fate was similar to that which overtook General Gordon some years later in Khartoum. But the residential system was established by the Treaty of Pangkor signed in January, 1874, and in due course Residents were appointed, in addition to Perak, to Selangor, Negri Sembilan and Pahang. These four States were then organised into the Federated Malay States at the turn of the century, with a central federal administration under a Resident-General, superimposed on their old local Governments. This was no doubt a wise and necessary administrative step in dealing with the phenomenal progress of Malaya as she emerged into the glare of the 'Rubber Age'.

There are many famous names among those of the early Residents. Sir Hugh Low was truly the father of modern Perak; Sir Frank Swettenham filled that role in Selangor. He became Governor of the Straits Settlements and retired early in this century to draw his pension for more years than he had served in the East! It is interesting to think that before he died at the great age of 96 he could look at himself as a young man in a group photograph taken on the island of Pangkor at the signing of the treaty 66 years earlier. Negri Sembilan still remembers the Honourable Martin Lister, and a few years later the great name of Sir Hugh Clifford first appears in the history of Pahang.

The key fact about the residential system was that it gave *de facto* control to the Resident, and so through him to the British Government, while at the same time it preserved unimpaired the identity of each Malay State and the sovereignty of its Ruler. It is important to remember a point often overlooked—that these States never became British Colonial territories. Their relationship to Great Britain was governed by treaties under which they were given our protection and the benefit of our administrative experience. There was in fact no cession of sovereignty to an alien Power, and the position in its fundamentals can be considered to be a temporary one—in which British tutelage could cease when the States were fit to stand on their own feet.

In fact, development took place at an astonishing pace and this created an urgent demand for the establishment of modern methods of government. A modern

Statute Book, once started, grew ever larger, and it was the Resident who became more and more the executive authority appointed under the law to administer its increasing complexity. He soon had a heavier burden than one man could carry, and his authority had to be delegated to assistants, and partially decentralised to the District Officers. As government in these States became more complex and differentiated, technical officers appeared—engineers, doctors, surveyors, geologists, foresters, agriculturists, and all the panoply of administration as practised in the modern world. Thus the Resident ceased to be an adviser; he became the *de facto* ruler of the State, with almost all the threads of power in his hands.

A new chapter in the system opened at the end of the first decade of this century when an international game of power-politics resulted in the transfer to Great Britain of Siamese suzerainty over the four Northern Malay States of Kedah, Perlis, Kelantan and Trengganu, which had had indigenous Governments of their own under shadowy Siamese control. They were not prepared to join the Federation and to contribute to federal revenue, though they expected help from federal sources and personnel for their governmental machines from the Straits Settlements and the Federation. The treaties between their Rulers and the British Crown were almost identical with the earlier treaties, and provided for British officers at each Court whose advice must be accepted by the local Government. These four came to be known as the Unfederated States. The British officers appointed to their Courts were styled 'British Advisers', and they remained, in fact, as true advisers without executive functions.

When we first intervened in the Malay States we found a desperately poor peasantry at the mercy of an unscrupulous and brutal aristocracy. The Sultans had no more control of their Chiefs than King Stephen had of his Barons, and the Government made up in tyrannical cruelty for what it lacked in efficiency.

The following story from Trengganu—a story which is barely 40 years old—gives a clear picture of what could happen in one of the more backward states in the second decade of the 20th century. J. L. Humphreys was the first British Adviser there, and one of his early meetings in Council with the Sultan and major Malay officials was concerned with a recommendation from the Malay judge for a sentence of death upon a Malay couple who had confessed to adultery. Malay judges in Trengganu at that time had only the power to impose sentences of imprisonment up to a maximum of seven years; death sentences were recommended, but were 'imposed' and confirmed by the Sultan in Council. In this case the accused were a man and woman of the Muslim faith, and as Trengganu's Criminal Code was the old Mohammedan Penal Law, the sentence for this offence was quite legally one of stoning to death. The British Adviser did not feel that this 'Old Testament' drama could be played out to its tragic end in the 20th century, and on his advice the Council ordered a retrial. Unfortunately the two principals again insisted cheerfully on pleading guilty. Finally the Council had to order the judge to refuse to accept a plea of guilty at a third trial, and as witnesses to the deed could not be found the accused were acquitted and discharged for lack of evidence, rather, perhaps, to their own disappointment—the disappointment of two actors whose desire to play highly tragic parts had been frustrated.

The last State to accept an Adviser was Johore, which had always been in a peculiar and rather privileged position. In close geographical proximity to the headquarters of British power in Singapore, it had tended to become an interpreter of the British Government to the other States. It has only had two Rulers in the past 80 years, both outstanding personalities who successfully adopted highly individualistic and independent lines of conduct. To emphasise the difference in status the officer sent to Johore was styled the 'General Adviser', and the omission of the word 'British' was punctuated by the omission of the Union Jack from its accustomed place beside the State flag at the Adviser's residence. Nevertheless the treaty with Johore was worded like the treaties with the other States; and the General Adviser's powers of giving advice were the same as those conferred upon the Residents and the British Advisers elsewhere.

Between the two wars there was considerable murmuring against the evergrowing powers of the central Government, and during his pro-consulship in the early 1930's Sir Cecil Clementi endeavoured to weaken the federal bonds of the Constitution and so induce all the States to combine in a loose federation in which their individualities would be clearly preserved. This was to anticipate events by more than ten years, and little came of Clementi's proposals at the time apart from an increase in the powers and status of the four Residents at the expense of the Chief Secretary, who in fact disappeared from the scene and whose place was taken by a Federal Secretary junior to the Residents. This reshuffle resulted merely in a serious weakening of the executive powers of the central Government with disastrous consequences in 1941 when the Japanese avalanche fell upon the country.

The concept of the Malayan Union proved abortive in the face of Malay nationalist opposition after the war, and in 1948 the post-war 'look' was established by the Federation of Malaya which included all the nine Malay States and the British Settlements of Penang and Malacca federated together under a strong central Government in Kuala Lumpur. Each of the nine States was to have a British Adviser who was to be truly an adviser and not an executive Minister; but the Sultans still agreed to rule on the advice of these officers in terms which have persisted since their forebears made their first agreements with Queen Victoria. The essential break with the past was that the Rulers were now in effect constitutional monarchs whose territories had almost similar written Constitutions.

In the early days of the Federation many British Advisers had little work to do. The Malay Premiers were at pains to show that they could run the State machine without asking for advice: the Adviser felt that it was his duty to stand on the side-lines without interfering; and in any case, most important administrative functions were in the hands of the federal authorities.

Then in June, 1948, the armed Communist rebellion broke out and it was not long before the British Advisers found themselves again in the thick of affairs. It began to be tacitly established in many States that the British Adviser should take charge of emergency measures in the war against Communist terrorism, thus leaving the State Premiers free for normal administrative duties. This was a sensible arrangement in that it gave the Advisers responsibility for something of overwhelming importance, albeit—it was hoped—of a temporary nature. The 'war' came to be run by the various State War Executive Committees and the British Advisers became chairmen or deputy chairmen of these bodies. It was they who in most cases were the unifying force in these committees, who maintained close co-operation between the Administration, the police and the military forces—all represented in these 'War Cabinets'. If the British Advisers had not been there to bear the initial burden of the emergency it is almost certain that the new and largely untried State Governments would have foundered under the strain and that there would have been no dearly-won breathing space for the architects of that future military success which now at last seems to be within the grasp of the Malayan authorities.

In the event, Malaya has proved to be a rock against which the angry surges of militant Communism have beaten in vain. She has thus been able to choose the path which leads to democratic self-government and to eschew the road to proletarian dictatorship. In this the British Advisers have played a full and worthy part, and it is to be hoped that this will not be forgotten by the people of the country.

The Constitution of 1948 will soon be superseded by a brand new one to be designed by Lord Reid and his Commission now at work in Kuala Lumpur. A few months ago Her Majesty's Government agreed with a representative delegation from Malaya that there was no reason to delay Malaya's advance towards self-government and independence within the Commonwealth, and the end of August, 1957, has been fixed as the date for the consummation of this result. In the meantime a majority of seats in the Federal Legislature and in many of the State Legislatures have become elective; an elected Federal Government is in power with an overwhelming majority behind it, and British authority and control is fading out of the picture. It is therefore no longer appropriate that British officers should have access to the ears of constitutional Princes who should now listen only to the advice of Ministers responsible to democratically chosen state Legislatures. So it has been decided that the British Advisers must disappear from the scene before next August and many posts are already vacant and will not be filled. Thus the succession of a noteworthy body of men will come to an end—a line of men who used their power in a responsible manner and, in giving unselfish service to Malaya, greatly helped to bring her into the comity of the modern world.

The head realises that all this is necessary and inevitable as part of the onward march of human affairs, even if the heart is not so easily comforted. It is pleasant to read of the tributes paid to the Residents and the British Advisers by speakers of all races and differing view points in the debate when the momentous decision was taken by the Federal Legislature. Let us hope that the great traditions established by the residential system will live on and prove an inspiration in good government to those who will now control the destinies of Malaya. We can hope that the nostalgic deliberations in the Chamber and the tear or two shed over the dying past were listened to with appreciation by the mighty shades of Low, Swettenham and Clifford.

The Corona Club

THE Annual Dinner of the Corona Club will be held this year on the 19th June at the Connaught Rooms at 7.15 for 7.45 p.m. The tickets are 35s. (inclusive of wines) each, and evening dress (tails or dinner jackets) with decorations will be worn. Members will receive notice of these arrangements by post and officers on leave who are not members will also be notified as far as possible.

Membership of the Club is open to all past and present members of the Government Service in overseas territories at present or formerly administered under the Colonial Office, and of the Colonial Office itself and the Office of the Crown Agents for Oversea Governments and Administrations. The annual subscription is 5s., which goes towards printing and other necessary expenses, any balance being devoted to keeping down the cost to members of the dinner. A payment of £2 2s. secures life membership.

The Chairman of the Club Committee is Sir Cosmo Parkinson, G.C.M.G., K.C.B., O.B.E., and the Hon. Sec., Mr. A. R. Thomas, C.M.G., Colonial Office, will welcome any enquiries about the Club and the dinner.

THE WOMEN'S CORONA SOCIETY

The Annual Evening Party of the Women's Corona Society will be held as usual on the same night as the (men's) Corona Club, and this year will take the form of a dinner to be held at the Connaught Rooms, Great Queen Street, W.C.2, at 7.15 for 7.45 p.m. It will, of course, be quite a separate function from that of the (men's) Corona Club.

Tickets are 30s. for members and 32s. 6d. for guests who are not members, and as members will have noted from the last Bulletin, those intending to be present are asked to apply for tickets to the Hospitality Secretary, Women's Corona Society, Colonial Office, Great Smith Street, S.W.1, by the 1st June 1958. Any other women connected with the Overseas Service who would like to be present, should apply for membership to the Organiser, Women's Corona Society, Colonial Office, Great Smith Street, S.W.1. The annual subscription is 10s.

The Administrative Officer Today : Barotseland

by A. F. B. GLENNIE, C.M.G.

(This article is the second of a number *Corona* hopes to publish from time to time illustrating the work done by Administrative Officers in the Overseas Service. As readers will have seen from the article on the work of a District Commissioner in a particular station in Tanganyika (p. 464, December, 1958, and p. 14, January, 1959), it is not intended to discuss administration generally but by recording personal experiences from a variety of places to build up a picture of the many differing duties and responsibilities still required from a branch of the Service which is particularly susceptible to change. It is hoped that these articles will answer the question sometimes heard in these times: "Just what does an Administrative Officer do nowadays?" They will be most effective if officers in *all* stages of their service write accounts of their work, and *Corona* will give special welcome to junior officers who send factual descriptions of their life and duties in their present stations.

The following article seeks to give a composite picture of the Resident Commissioner of Barotseland at his headquarters. The writer says that the Resident Commissioner's work and that of Provincial Commissioners elsewhere in Northern Rhodesia is generally similar, but Barotseland itself is unique in that it is in direct Treaty relationship with Great Britain and is officially styled a Protectorate within Northern Rhodesia. As a result the Resident acts more through his capacity as Political Adviser to the Paramount Chief than through direct action *vis à vis* the Chief and Native Authorities. . . . Ed.)

THERE is something to be gained from an early start before the heat slows up effort of brain and hand. Apart from the fresh greens and soft reds of the spring foliage the Barotse countryside is scorched a drab yellow; but the grass round the office is a rich contrast and already the sprinklers are at work. The District Assistant is there, tenderly examining the new rose pink Bougainvillea. A string of horses clops by to the stables from the morning ride.

Once at his desk the Resident Commissioner plunges fairly briskly into a heap of files which has materialised on it—during the night, it seems. The D.A. comes in with the diary and runs over the appointments. There is a meeting with the Paramount Chief: he will want to talk about the new water supply—best to see the Provincial Engineer first for a progress report. Some crocodile hunters are due to call; and the mail 'plane will set down an out-station District Commissioner who is coming for his medical examination prior to leave. He must be given lunch and a chance to unburden himself before returning to his Boma.

The files are first attacked and classified. The larger pile although bulky contains mainly routine matters and some of lesser urgency: more reading than action. There are debit notes for stores purchases by District Commissioners; the D.A. points out that an order for wheelbarrows has been charged to "Travelling on Duty", and the Resident notes on it that touring by such means is out of order! Returns of tax collected and of touring planned and carried out follow, and there is a resumé from a district in the plains, hard hit by floods, of the native food-stuffs position. The Provincial Veterinary Officer reports on the castration of young bulls and some opposition encountered from their owners. Out of the normal run is an enquiry originating from U.N.O. about the prevalence of narcotics. Small quantities of *dagga* are clandestinely cultivated in these parts and give it topical application.

In the smaller pile are to be found a couple of tour reports, with neat sketch maps made from a compass traverse, which will require careful reading and comment where necessary before they go in to the Secretary for Native Affairs; and a batch of criminal cases from the Magistrate of a Class III Court for review. The Provincial Education Officer comments pungently on the lack of a sense of vocation in some African teachers: one who had reported that he was sick and had closed the school for several days was, it turns out, absent on private affairs. The children had complained. From headquarters come instructions to give effect to a boundary agreement recently concluded with a neighbouring territory. There is news of an outbreak of smallpox along a labour route up which the infection has been carried, and the feasibility of wholesale vaccination is outlined.

Next comes a minute dealing with some rather delicate arrangements for meetings to be held by a religious sect whose followers have shown reluctance to accede the conventional courtesies to the Native Authority. There are items for the monthly meeting of the Provincial Development Team, a memorandum on early burning of the bush by the Forest Officer among them; and a report from the Area Team, the working party at present engaged in formulating a smallholding project, financed by the Native Treasury, in an attempt to establish rice as an economic crop. Criticism of the kitchen arrangements at a transit camp by the Labour Induna will be passed on to the Management and District Commissioner concerned for investigation.

A storekeeper who is also an honorary Game Warden writes of the discovery of the remains of a giraffe. These are Royal game and are jealously protected by the Paramount. The letter will be mentioned to him together with another from a hunter from the south who wishes to kill game with the object of manufacturing biltong, a valuable form of dried meat which sells like wildfire in the towns. At least he is honest in stating his intentions.

On a side table is laid a cold collation of Secretariat Circulars.

After an hour in which to digest some of this matter and draft a few replies, the visitors begin. The crocodile hunters, two cheerful young men out after profitable adventure in an era in which this is becoming unfashionable, are told where their section of the river runs and of the few rules which the Native Authority desire to be observed: chiefly the burial of the corpses to avoid pollution of the river. After the Engineer, with his perpetual hangover from bottle-necks in the transport line which delay the delivery of materials, comes the local District Commissioner and a young African who earnestly aspires to a clerical post. He proclaims his wish to serve "all my life" and is engaged as a learner.

The D.C. also brings the itinerary of a visitor from the "New World", a member of an exploratory group bent on "restoring", as someone said, "the bank balance of the Old." He is making a trip as the guest of the Government down the Zambesi River, which seems destined to play a dynamic role in the industrial future of the Federation of Rhodesia and Nyasaland. There are paddlers and barges to be arranged and many other details of equipment and commissariat to be put in hand. District Commissioners will pass him on in succession as he crosses their borders with as little interruption of their normal duties as possible.

But now a car drives up and much clapping and verbal salutation announce the arrival of the Paramount and his Councillors. They enter and are seated and a cup of tea warms the opening exchanges. Soon the meeting is deep in its agenda. Trading leases are ready for approval and cheques for signature. The question arises of mineral prospecting. The Chief does not view without a certain misgiving the possibility of an industrial area springing up in his rural retreat. Should Missions adhere to spheres of influence or should there be a policy of free-for-all ? Is the proposed appointment to the post of Education Induna (one of the Senior Councillors chosen to act in a liaison capacity between the Barotse Native Authority and the Government where educational matters are concerned) a really suitable one ? There are grounds to suppose that the selection may have been due rather to family connections than zeal for the cause of Education. All these form the kind of topic which presents itself for discussion. Today a new car for the Paramount is another—there can be little occasion for argument here: the workshops staff of the Public Works Department have reacted to the proposal with audible relief.

Some of the more debatable subjects have to be talked out at successive sessions with patient elucidation stage by stage and plenty of give and take. Now the education appointment is left to stew, for the time has gone, and after fixing a date for a return visit the Resident sees the party drive away.

By this time the morning 'plane has landed with the outstation D.C. The police bugle sounds for the luncheon break and afterwards correspondence is saved in a talk on the various matters the D.C. has brought with him—a cluster of disputes over land and fishing rights for example, and a tricky judicial inquiry which must be left to the incoming Magistrate. It concerns a case of sympathetic magic in which an African woman practitioner, allegedly treating a patient for a distressing complaint, has made incisions in her infant daughter with fatal results. It is particularly desirable that any charge brought shall succeed and the choice of charge must be scrupulously made: Crown Counsel's opinion is indicated.

The end of the Quarter is approaching and the Resident devotes the rest of his office day to planning the contents of the letter which will summarise the main course of Provincial events for the period. A rather featureless three months, he thinks, and yet on reflection what a fascinating landscape of variety and interest a backward glance evokes.

Finally, he signs the letters brought to him and goes home to tea and a look at *The Times* published only three days before. Then comes tennis or golf at the Club, a swim in the bathing pool or a potter in the garden.

As evening falls a few of the threads handled in the day will be drawn together for a time when guests arrive for a leisurely drink on the lawn before the Residency. There they may look over the wide plain which meets a sky already lighting up for a riotous display of colour and reflection. A scheme for a weekend fishing expedition is hatched. The all-engulfing floods have gone and the Zambesi with its tiger fish is once more confined within banks and can be reached by car.

When the guests depart night has come bringing the soft African silence with its many overtones, from far-off drum to tree frog in the garden, pulsing steadily on until they pass beyond immediate range of consciousness. The notes of Big Ben heralding the news on the radio are more insistent.

The Administrative Officer Today : Uganda

by K. V. ARROWSMITH

WE left the train at Tororo, just inside Uganda on our fourth wedding anniversary. We spent a few hours in Tororo Hotel before leaving by road for Gulu, the head-quarters both of the Northern Province and of Acholi District. We were excited to be at last in Uganda, to which for many months we had looked forward as the Promised Land; and as we drove towards our destination we wondered what the future was to hold in store, and whether everything would be very different to our time in Nigeria.

Gulu is about 250 miles by road to the north of Kampala and 70 miles by road to the south of Nimule on the Sudan-Uganda border. It has grown considerably since the end of the last war. The European population of about 150 consists almost entirely of Government officials and their families. The Government station is situated half a mile away from the bazaar area which has an Indian population of about 500. Also scattered in different parts of the township area live several thousand Africans. Within two or three miles of Gulu there are the Church Missionary Society and Roman Catholic Mission stations, a Roman Catholic secondary technical school and a Government secondary school.

In spite of the fact that Gulu is somewhat remote and has at present no electricity supply, living conditions are remarkably good. We have an attractive house and a pleasant garden. We have a mains water supply, running hot water in the bathroom, and a telephone—not yet connected, because a telephone system has only recently been installed in Gulu. We are left wonderfully undisturbed by insect life. Thanks to gauze screens protecting the windows hardly a mosquito, flying ant or sausage fly succeeds in penetrating into our house. Most of our day to day wants can be obtained in the bazaar. Fresh vegetables come twice weekly from Kenya; ham, bacon, sausages, kippers and so on can be bought on certain days each week, and just recently it has become possible to buy Walls ice cream. Meat, eggs, fruit and vegetables are available in the market; and a small African-run dairy supplies milk and sometimes cream. There is plenty of opportunity for playing games: among the Europeans golf is the most popular, and cricket, hockey, tennis and squash are also played. The Africans enjoy football and athletics. Some of the younger Indians play hockey, while the older men of an evening play cards on the pavement in the bazaar. In the Government station there is a small swimming pool and a flourishing club.

Acholi District comprises an area of 11,176 square miles. It is divided more or less into two halves by the Aswa river which joins the White Nile north of Nimule. In the main the countryside is flat, most of the district being about 3,500 feet above sea level. To the east there are some hills, the highest being the 7,603 foot Rom peak. To the north there are mountains along the Sudan border. Lomwaga on the border rises to a height of 8,649 feet. To the south-west the district is bordered by the Victoria and Albert Niles; it is in this area that the Murchison National Game Park is situated.

The district has an estimated population of about 275,000, the vast majority of the people being farmers. Cotton is the main economic crop. The average cotton farmer realises £20-£25 a year for his crop; and this comprises nearly all his cash income. In the neighbourhood of Gulu tobacco is grown. The value of the leaf grown in 1957 was about £12,500. The principal food crops cultivated are millet, simsim, groundnuts and sweet potatoes. Some farmers own a few cows, and the total cattle population is believed to be in the region of 70,000.

The District Commissioner, Acholi, and three or four Assistant District Commissioners live in Gulu. Kitgum, a town 65 miles to the north-east of Gulu, is a sub-district headquarters with an Assistant District Commissioner-in-charge and usually a second Assistant District Commissioner resident there. The offices of the Acholi District Council are situated in Gulu. This local Government body covers the whole of the District. The Chairman of the District Council is the holder of the office of "Lawirwodi" (the Head of the Chiefs). The District Council has several committees, among them the Finance, Works, Natural Resources and Health Committees. The District is divided into six counties. In charge of each is a Chief, known as a Rwot, who is an employee of the District Council, (the Rwot of one of the Counties went last summer to England on a six-week visit sponsored by the British Council; what seems to have made the greatest impression on him is a circus he saw in the north of England, and the Fire Brigade in Birkenhead). Counties are divided into Divisions, which average four to a County. A Chief, known as a Jago, who like a Rwot is also a District Council employee, is in charge of each Division. Each Rwot and Jago is Chairman of his County and Divisional Council respectively. Beneath the Jago there is the Mukungu ('Parish' Chief) and beneath the Mukungu there is the Won Paco ('Village' Chief).

During the past 16 months my activities have been fairly varied. Soon after arriving in Gulu I did the work of Township Executive Officer for two or three months. I was then second A.D.C. in Gulu for a couple of months. Since the beginning of 1958 I have been first A.D.C. In the middle of the year I had a temporary break for a month as A.D.C. in charge of Kitgum. Throughout the year, in addition to my other duties, I have had the job of making the arrangements in the District for the holding of the first direct Legislative Council elections, which took place in October*.

My time as Township Officer gave me a chance to find my feet and I began to learn Lwo, the language of Acholi. I had many duties connected with township sanitation and upkeep, planning proposals, applications for leases and allocation of quarters, milk supply problems and petrol pumps; but the thing which remains most firmly in my mind is the difficulty I had in getting a corpse buried on a Saturday afternoon!

Stationed in Gulu are officers of many Government departments. To help co-ordinate the work of departments in Acholi there is a body known as the Acholi District Team. The District Commissioner is the Chairman; and as Senior Assistant District Commissioner I am Secretary. Members include the Office Commanding Police, the District Agricultural Officer, the District Veterinary Officer, the District Community Development Officer, the District Medical Officer, the District Health Inspector, a representative of the Public Works Department and senior officers of the Acholi District Council. Meetings are held each month. A wide range of subjects of general interest is discussed. On glancing through the minute book I see that among others the following matters have been considered in recent months: the recording of talks for the Uganda Broadcasting Service, firewood supply, the prison farm, the siting of a police post and a water borehole drilling programme. Valuable practical work by a committee of the District Team

*See the writer's article *Symbols and Ballot Boxes*, Corona, April, 1959.

has been achieved during the past year in the shape of two or three agricultural demonstrations in different counties. The farm of a go-ahead farmer has been used to demonstrate cotton-spraying, cattle-ploughing, manuring and so on. The aim is to increase and improve agricultural production throughout the district. In order to improve housing and sanitation conditions in the district an annual health competition is held and a shield is awarded—earlier last year one of my colleagues spent two weeks on safari with the District Health Inspector judging compounds in all parts of Acholi.

The main function of us Administrative Officers is, as I see it, to advise, assist, and to some extent control the Acholi District Council in the discharge of its work. My dealings with the Council concern the 'Works' side of its affairs, and for a time I was concerned with the educational side as well. I work in close liaison with the Council's Engineer; we constantly meet in each other's offices; we both attend meetings of the Works Committee and prepare its agenda together; and periodically we go on safari together. A major preoccupation is roads, the maintenance of existing ones and the building of new ones. More than anything else roads open up the country; and although there are about 250 miles of P.W.D. maintained road and 600 miles of District Council maintained road there are still many people in Acholi who live far from the beaten track. In the past maintenance of all Council roads was by the sweat of the brow, and all too often I fear the brows of the road labourers sweated either not at all or not enough. A recent innovation has been for a mechanical maintenance unit to do maintenance on the more important roads. The unit comprises a traxcavator, a larger grader, a small grader and three tipper lorries. Roads mean bridges; three new ones have been built during the past year. One of these is a single span bridge, 100 feet wide. The Council built the two abutments, and a Nairobi firm erected the actual bridging.

'Works' also includes other types of building. During the past year or so one new Divisional headquarters in permanent materials has been built. Three more new Divisional headquarters are under construction. Two new Dispensaries have been built; and work on another is about to begin.

Inevitably rather more of my time is spent in Gulu than out of it. One of my jobs is to see that the District Office operates as efficiently as possible. To this end I try to ensure that staff come to the office on time (difficult in the case of some who live up to ten miles away), that correspondence is filed correctly and dealt with promptly, and that our expenditure votes are not overspent. Periodically I hold a staff meeting which clerks, interpreters and office boys attend.

As grade III Magistrate my colleagues and I from time to time undertake magisterial duties of a modest nature when the Resident Magistrate is on safari. There are persons to be remanded, search warrants to be signed, and sometimes minor cases to be heard. Some time ago I tried a man charged with having *Waragi* (a potent and illegal African drink) in his possession. He pleaded guilty; in my ignorance I imagined that the offence was much on a par with the Nigerian one of being in possession of illicit gin, which was not considered as being particularly reprehensible. It appeared that this was the accused's first offence, and I therefore merely cautioned and discharged him—much to the subsequent consternation of the O.C. Police, who thought he should have had at least six months!

About once a quarter my turn for prison visiting comes round; apart from that I find I have little or nothing to do with prisons or prisoners—very different from Eastern Nigeria where supervision of the local prison bulked large among the doings of the District Officer.

An essential part of an Administrative Officer's job here is the 'routine' safari, and as I write this I am out in a rest camp, 125 miles from Gulu. My wife and young son are at home, and I am alone here. In days gone by, when we went on tour, two 'boys', a refrigerator and a mass of furniture and camp kit accompanied us in a lorry. We no longer travel in this grand style; today I brought only an interpreter with me in my car. He has gone off to stay with a friend and I have prepared my own meal on a small oil stove . . . and have found that I have forgotten to bring any cooking fat or bread with me!

For these safaris I have one of the six Counties as my special preserve, and I meet if possible all District Council staff in the area. I meet and discuss affairs with the County and Divisional Councils. There may be cases on appeal from the local (African) courts to be dealt with and in any event I look through the court records to see that everything is satisfactory and that judgments have been complied with.

Applications for tax exemption are considered; the position with regard to tax collection is enquired into. During the cotton season a particular function is to visit cotton buying centres in order to obviate complaints and differences betwen Africans selling their cotton and Indians buying it. Always one tries to find time to visit water boreholes, dams, dispensaries, schools, leper-camps, trading centres and any other places of interest in the neighbourhood.

Apart from my duties as an A.D.C., living in Gulu—which compared with my former stations in Nigeria is a sizeable place—has involved me in other commitments. I am on the Committee of the Gulu (European) Club as tennis and squash member, and I am secretary of the Acholi (Inter-racial) Sports Club. I am church-warden of the local English 'church', a title I by no means merit in view of the fact that nearly all I have to do is to make sure that chairs are arranged in time in the Acholi Central Court building, which is what is used twice a month for a morning service—the wooden witness box serves the preacher as a pulpit. With others I have helped to organise a series of discussion group meetings on certain Sunday evenings, and also periodic social evenings attended by both Europeans and Africans. We ourselves frequently receive invitations to functions of one kind or another: during recent weeks we have been invited to a Solemn Requiem Mass for the late Pope, the opening of a new Mosque, the opening of three petrol filling stations and a tea party given in honour of the Assistant Commissioner for India.

We have also helped to entertain a variety of visitors, ranging from a distinguished lady London County Councillor (whose inspection of our local soda water bottling facilities was marked by the explosion of a bottle) to the American Consul from Kampala who had the experience of being in my car when all the leaves of a rear spring snapped. We have taken the British Ambassador to the Sudan and the wife of the G.O.C., East Africa, on picnics to our nearby 'ancient monument', Baker's Camp. During our election week we were visited by the Assistant Governor of Sudan's Equatoria Province and I took him round some of polling stations*.

Any misgivings we might have had 16 months ago as we were being driven towards Gulu were dispelled soon after our arrival by the extremely friendly reception we were given. The kindness and consideration shewn to us by our District Commissioner and so many others during our first days in Uganda made a great impression upon both my wife and me. In some ways conditions of life here differ vastly from those we knew in Nigeria, and in some respects I find differences in my duties as an Administrative Officer. But in spite of having moved from one side of Africa to the other, there is much that is familiar, and I am pleased to feel that in essence our work here is the same as that to which we had become used. We are very thankful that we were offered and accepted transfer to this delightful country.

The Administrative Officer Today : Northern Nigeria

by C. J. HANSON-SMITH

IT is extremely hard to give a short answer to the question: "How does a District Officer in charge of a Division spend his time ?" Even officers of other departments living in the same station may ask this question, picturing the average D.O. as someone harassed by mounds of files and always trying hard to escape from the office to 'bush'. There is an element of truth in this picture: the D.O. is continually striving to reduce office work and increase the time spent with the Native Authorities and in the Districts. In the North local government is done by the Native Authority, and the D.O. is there to advise, restrain and encourage. To appreciate the scope of his work, therefore, some idea of the Native Authority organisation is necessary—the D.O's first question on being posted to a new Division will probably be: "What is the local N.A. like ?", as its efficiency and co-operation will decide largely how his working days are to be spent.

A typical large Division is that of Kontagora in the Niger Province. There are two large Native Authority areas and one very small one, with a total population of 251,000. The Emirate of Kontagora that gives the Division its name is 9,132 square miles in extent but largely uninhabited, due to concentrated slave-raiding in the past. One area in the north, Zuru, was not affected, and the five chiefs who traditionally held sovereign rights have now become federated to form one viable Native Authority under a paramount chief. The third and smallest Native Authority is an historical relic, the Chief being closely related to the Emir of Kontagora and sharing with his 'big brother' the N.A. services. However, he is independent and rules with the help of a traditional council. In Kontagora the Emir-in-Council is the Native Authority; in Zuru the Chief-and-Council. Each Native Authority area is divided into Districts which in Kontagora are ruled by heads appointed by the Emir. Each District now has an instrumented Council which at the moment is hardly more than advisory, presided over by the District Head or Chief and meeting quarterly. In Kontagora members of the District Councils are elected to sit on the Native Authority Council which is the mainspring of the Native Authority. The D.O. is the constant adviser of the Councils, giving advice when asked for it and proffering it when he thinks there is need for it. The relationship between the D.O. and the Native Authority is a delicate one and calls for a mental approach on the part of the former quite different from that of one who administers directly.

The Kontagora Division is a convenient administrative unit shaped by the basic needs of communication and the telegraph. The D.O. has his house and 'pavilion' office in Kontagora while his Assistant District Officer lives in Zuru, 78 miles to the north. There is not always an A.D.O. posted to the Division which means that the D.O. runs it single-handed with the help of one clerk and his three messengers. The two main Native Authorities are entirely independent. Just over half a century ago their leaders were continually at war and the mutual feeling of distrust lingers on into the present. The D.O., therefore, must be completely impartial in his attitude towards the Native Authorities, hence the need for a 'pavilion' where he can be approached without hindrance by all with grievances imagined or otherwise. This miniature 'ivory tower' allows the often harassed D.O. to sit back and put the local problems into their proper, perhaps 'Divisional' perspective. It also allows him to note how fast the country really is changing. Papers, politicians and circulars proclaim the swift changes, but how difficult it is without detachment to anticipate how they will inevitably affect the local administration.

The D.O. now has no non-statutory 'executive' functions—as far as the N.A. is concerned he is their resident adviser and the local representative of the Regional Government. These basic responsibilities of the D.O. are apparent, but there are other powers vested in him by Statute or Ordinance that are not generally known.

District officers are invariably appointed as 3rd class magistrates and can hear cases within their limited jurisdiction that Native Courts are not empowered to hear. These are usually prosecutions outside Native Court jurisdiction, such as offences committed on the railways. In practice the District Officer fights shy of judicial work as there are professional Grade I Magistrates to undertake it. In Kontagora the only cases now taken are those involving prosecutions under the Wild Animals Preservation Ordinance, and occasionally those when Europeans are affected. Preliminary investigations in murder cases are now done by the professional magistrates, but as a magistrate a District Officer is also a coroner and there is usually an inquest to be performed each month—with some 200 lorries plying the roads in the Division every day there are usually at least two fatal accidents each month to be investigated. As a magistrate the D.O. can also certify lunatics, after medical advice has been taken, and order a juvenile offender to a remand home.

Apart from wielding his statutory magisterial powers, the D.O. has the very important task to perform of advising the native courts. In the case of the Grade C and D courts, of which there are 13 in the Division, the D.O. has the power to review any proceedings of these courts. This means that he can reverse or vary decisions made; set aside any conviction or order of the court; transfer the case to another court, or order a re-trial. In cases heard in the Grade A and B courts, he can advise the Resident to exercise his powers of review. The D.O. therefore has a chance of implementing the old rule of English Law that justice shall not only be done but shall also be seen to be done. In order to make an effective appraisal of the various court proceedings the reviewing officer must understand the rudiments of the Maliki law and Muslim court procedure, so one of the District Officer's duties is to learn about them. To learn Arabic is neither strictly necessary nor compulsory but a knowledge of it is a distinct advantage. Apart from his powers of review, the D.O. cannot himself hear appeals—there is an avenue of appeal through the grades of native courts which finally ends in the Muslim Court of Appeal or the High Court.

Powers vested in District Officers under Ordinances include inquiry into applications to sell liquor, and the issue of licences for the sale and storage of petrol; at times the District Officer may be seen poking about in dusty and pungent storage bins or near pumps, looking for the missing lightning conductor or fire-fighting equipment on which the results of a petrol application may depend.

The advice of the District Officer is most often required by the Native Authorities over matters affecting policies of the various Ministries. The Ministry concerned sends to each Native Authority, through the Resident and the D.O., a circular on a particular subject to which the attention of the Native Authority must be drawn. It could, for example, ask the N.A. to make an order under the N.A. Law for the control of public meetings and processions; advise on the system to be adopted for paying students attending courses at the various Government institutions; or simply to ask for the views of the Native Authority on the solution of some problem that concerns the Region as a whole. The language used in provincial and regional correspondence is English and, in circulars, this is not always easily understood by the few educated members of the Native Authority who speak

English. The D.O. is therefore in continual demand for interpreting, and suggesting the right answers to the questions posed. A feature of the N.A. system is the pronounced parochial attitude adopted by many Native Authorities—it is the District Officer, experienced in the ways of many of them, who must make them see beyond their proverbial noses.

The various representatives of the Ministries in the Province tour the N.A. areas as often as possible to keep an eye on their respective departments. But the D.O., being on the spot all the time, has the most important duty of liaison between them and the N.A. When an officer new to the Division arrives, it is the D.O. who must introduce him to the Council and in particular to the Councillor responsible for the N.A. department concerned. If, for instance, the roads engineer finds labour hard to obtain he can always ask the D.O. to approach the Emir or Chief on his behalf. Frequently a new arrival to the country will not understand Hausa, the *lingua franca* of the North, and the District Officer is therefore called upon to interpret for him in the Council. An understanding of Ministerial policies enables the D.O. to check on the work of the various N.A. officials while on his tours.

This leads on to a basic duty of the District Officer, whatever his seniority, that is becoming harder and harder to fufil—touring: of keeping in touch and in sympathy with the people. The accepted method of training, or rather breaking—in, newly joined cadets used to be to pack them off to 'bush' for several weeks at a time until they learnt the language and acquired the 'feel' of the country. Those who once experienced such treatment will often exclaim that these were the most memorable and enjoyable days of their Colonial career. Such halcyon days are now over but the D.O. must still spend some days of the month on tour in order to retain the 'feel' of his Division, to be accessible to all and to train the district administrations for greater responsibilities. Horses and bicycles as means of touring are now largely replaced by the kit-car although the mounted D.O., with his long line of attendant porters, is still to be seen during the rains in the more inaccessible corners of the Division. He usually only finds time to visit the District Headquarters of which all but four can be reached by motor throughout the year. Most of them have rest-houses—normally rectangular buildings of mud and thatch with the odd stick of warped furniture. At the Headquarters the touring officer meets the District Council and joins in discussions. He checks the various records to see whether the projects scheduled to be completed in any one financial year have, in fact, been attempted. Technical help may be required from the veterinary officer or the rural water supplies inspector, in which case the D.O. arranges for this on his return. The court books can also be perused although the routine duty of checking the cash can be left to the Councillor or Emir's representative who invariably accompanies the D.O. As much as possible the Districts must look to the central Native Authority for their development and for the righting of their wrongs—the touring D.O. cannot now be regarded as the panacea of all the ills that so often beset the 'backward' district.

During his tours the District Officer can perform the valuable task of inspecting the various N.A. institutions—the primary schools, the dispensaries and the veterinary clinics. The departmental officer cannot hope to visit all 'his' schools or clinics at frequent intervals but the D.O. can visit and at least see that the policies recommended by the Regional Government are put into some form of practice. Such visits are usually much welcomed by the Native Authority staff working in them—and the addition of one more name to their visitor's book is a great booster to local morale.

The *haraji* or poll tax, currently assessed at £2 per head in Kontagora, is collected by the District administrations after the Regional Government has approved the capitation rate. In each District there is a Tax Assessment Committee whose function it is to assess those with salaries or incomes greater than those of the average tax-payer. The annual incomes of these people are calculated and the tax is then assessed in accordance with a scale applicable to the whole province. The D.O. is appointed as the Chairman of each Committee but in practice his work is done by the District Head or Chief who is vice-chairman. Only when a person appeals against his assessment are the services of the Chairman required. Thus the D.O. has little direct responsibility for the assessment or collection of tax. The *jangali* or cattle tax is likewise collected by the district and village heads but the D.O. can himself take an active part in this collection should there be a serious shortfall in the amount collected. Indeed, the chasing of crafty Fulani tax-evaders on horse-back is the one form of direct administration in which the contemporary D.O. can occasionally indulge.

In a comparatively unsophisticated division like Kontagora there are only a few committees on which the D.O. is bound to sit. He is Chairman of the Local Education Committee which has the important duty of co-ordinating the work of the various Native Authority and voluntary agency schools. It also has to recommend any new school for the capital building and recurrent grants paid by the Government. Serving rather the same purpose is the Divisional Leprosy Committee, of which the D.O. is also Chairman, established for the effective co-ordination of Government, N.A. and Missionary leprosy work. At the headquarters of most large Divisions there is now found a Catering Rest House which is run by a Committee, again led by the D.O. and this responsibility can often prove to be very trying.

One major aspect of the D.O's work that has not yet been mentioned is that of financial supervision of the Native Authority accounts. Under directions imposed by the Regional Government the District Officer must perform in the Treasuries certain basic checks, the nature of which depend on how 'sound' the finances are. The D.O. in his daily dealings with the N.A. will find he is continually combating financial irresponsibility on the part of some officials that can, unchecked, wreck the smooth running of the N.A. machine.

The lesser duties of the D.O. are innumerable and often come as a complete surprise. Indeed, that is why administrative work is so fascinating. There is the entertaining, the hearing of complaints, the purveying of general information and the upkeep of Government buildings. Very recently one more duty has been added to that long list—that of training the African who will step into his shoes when the proper time comes. One might say that this task, although the latest on the list, is the one now demanding the most attention. The expatriate D.O., while being bound to do his best to make his own presence unnecessary, must at the same time train his successor to do all that he has done—and do it better.

The Administrative Officer Today : Northern Rhodesia

by J. M. WILLSON

[Earlier in this series of articles we said we hoped to get articles by junior as well as senior officers. We now publish an account of one such officer's earliest days in the Overseas Service.—Ed.]

I have lived and worked for only three years in Northern Rhodesia, so that this article is very much a collection of first impressions and first opinions, both of which will doubtless be changed by time. Moreover, it concerns only one district of the 40 or so which go to make up the Protectorate, and only one short period in the development of that district. However, one of my first impressions was that certain of a District Officer's activities are "time-hallowed", so to speak, so perhaps what is true of my 18 months in Lundazi District has a somewhat wider application.

Many people in England have only the sketchiest knowledge of the whereabouts of Northern Rhodesia, and still less of what goes on there. "Ah, let me see, that's Salisbury, isn't it ?" was the most common rejoinder of my explanation of three years absence from England, followed closely by "Farming, I suppose," or "Oh, you're one of those rich copper-miners we've read about." And let me confess at once that, up to the time of receiving my telegram of appointment from the Colonial Office, my knowledge did not amount to much more than this. My ideas of a District Officer's life in Africa were largely gathered from *Sanders of the River*, and my inclinations had been towards service in the Far East, mainly because Arthur Grimble influenced me more strongly than Edgar Wallace.

However, having successfully negotiated the 'Devonshire' Course at Cambridge, I embarked for Africa, accompanied by my wife and three-week old son. On reaching Cape Town I was informed by the Northern Rhodesia Government Agent that I had been posted to Lundazi, and he pointed out a rather isolated dot on the map. "Lots of game there," he said and left it at that. After four dusty days in the train we reached Lusaka, the capital of Northern Rhodesia, where one senior official on whom I called, hearing where I was bound for, asked me what guns I had brought with me, or was I buying them in Lusaka ? When he heard that not only had I no guns, but had never shot anything more animate than a target on an Army rifle range, he obviously considered my posting a wasteful mistake.

While in Lusaka we laid in a two-month stock of food to take with us, since Lundazi is 120 miles from any European shop, and 550 miles from the nearest big store. We also bought lamps and a paraffin burning refrigerator, since electricity was as far away as the shops.

The next leg of our journey was by 'plane from Lusaka to Fort Jameson, headquarters of the Eastern Province, in which Lundazi is situated. Here I met my Provincial Commissioner, bought all the things we had forgotten in Lusaka, and set off on the last stage of our 8,500 miles journey—120 miles in a Land-Rover to Lundazi.

My first view of my first African station was what appeared to be the towers of a Scottish baronial hall rising out of the rolling bush. This I very soon discovered

was the well-known Lundazi Castle Hotel, built by a previous District Commissioner whose architectural tastes were not orthodox Public Works Department.

Just beyond the hotel were the Government Offices—the Boma—and the
European and African staff houses, which together with some Indian stores, a 'bus
terminus and sundry other buildings, constituted the township of Lundazi. The
township is situated in the southern half of Lundazi district, an area of 12,000 square
miles, bounded on the east by Nyasaland and on the west by the Luangwa River
and the Muchinga Mountains. Geographically the district is divided into two distinct areas: the plateau running along the Nyasaland border, and the valley going
down to the Luangwa River. The population consisted of some 96,000 Africans, in
three main tribal groups, approximately 35 Europeans (members of the Overseas
Service, missionaries and mining prospectors) and about 20 Indians who ran
trading stores. The whole district, with the exception of the Boma area, is Native
Trust land or Native Reserve. The Boma was first built on the present site in 1908,
and one building, the prison, still survives from that time. Then there were only
two Europeans living there, the Native Commissioner as he was then called, and
his assistant. Today, besides the District Commissioner, District Officer, and
District Assistant, there are representatives of the Health and Posts Departments
of the Federal Government, and of the Game, Education, Co-operative and
Marketing, Public Works, Water Development and Veterinary Departments of
the territorial Government. Some of these departments have European representatives, others African.

After staying for two days with the District Commissioner we moved into our
own modern house, a far cry from the thatch and mud brick of former days. We had
to live on borrowed possessions apart from heavy furniture, as luggage takes six
weeks by goods train from Cape Town. On my first day at the Boma I met my first
Northern Rhodesian Africans, the various employees of the Provincial Administration—clerks, drivers, storemen and, of course, the District Messengers, hand-
picked men with an encyclopaedic knowledge of the district, selected for their
ability and initiative. The head messenger, who had been a messenger before I was
born, went by the prosaic name of Frank, but the others' names read like something
out of the Old Testament—Isaac, Daniel, Zacharia, Jeremiah and Hosea—a
reminder of the early influence of Church of Scotland missionaries in the district.

Later I settled down to read through the principal files, and the District Note
Book—a large volume, maintained by successive District Commissioners on all
points of interest concerning the District—and slowly gained an impression of the
work which is done by Administrative Officers, both in the office and, equally if
not more important, out in the district, touring the villages, talking to the people,
checking on roads, wells and gardens, explaining Government policy and how it
affected them.

I also began to meet the people of the district, who walked or cycled to the
Boma on their daily business—payers of taxes, or licences for guns, dogs and
bicycles; ex-askari or other pensioners drawing their allowances; and those who
just came with a *mulandu* (a word covering everything from a serious court case
to in-law trouble). I soon found that the Lundazi Africans were, in the main,
cheerful and happy people, with a keen sense of humour and high standards of
courtesy which are rigidly observed towards, and frequently misunderstood by
people of other races; one small example is their custom of holding out both hands
when receiving anything—not through greed, but to show you that nothing is
concealed in the other hand.

I soon had my first opportunity to get out into the district. This tour was not of the village-to-village type, but a sort of "Cook's tour" of the whole district, or as much as could be reached by road in a vanette. My wife and small son came with me, and we stayed overnight in small rest-houses set up at strategic points, mainly at Chiefs' headquarters. We covered 650 miles and met 11 out of the 17 Chiefs and hereditary councillors in the district. Of the remaining six, I had previously met four, and the other two lived on the far side of the Luangwa River, and were not accessible by road. We also saw, in the Luangwa valley, many different species of game, for the valley houses one of the biggest concentrations of wild life in Central Africa.

This tour was done at a time when all the roads in the district were open, but during and just after the rainy season all the valley roads are closed, as dry stream-beds turn into raging torrents overnight. At the end of the rains, road gangs go out to repair the ravages of weather and animals. Good communications are an essential pre-requisite of any development in Northern Rhodesia, but in the more remote areas it is a constant struggle against the forces of Nature. On one occasion we were cut off from the outside world, except for wireless communication, when the main north-south road was flooded on both sides of the Boma.

All our belongings now arrived from Cape Town, and I was able to do my first village tour properly equipped. After a day of preparation, assembling everything from tents to toothpaste, I set off in the 3-ton lorry, accompanied by messengers, cook, and the inevitable gang of hangers-on and lift scroungers, on the 100-mile journey north to the headquarters of a Native Authority—the 'local Government' of the Senga tribal area. This particular Authority had power to collect taxes and licences, raise financial levies, and with their revenue to build schools, roads and dispensaries. They produced their own estimates and kept their own accounts, which were checked each month by the District Commissioner or myself.

Our first camp site, near a river on the Chief's border, was the forerunner of many I was to see and use; a clearing had been made near the village, and three huts built, one for my dining-room-cum-office, one for the kitchen, and one for the messengers. Placed in the kitchen hut were several large pots of water and a heap of firewood, and waiting for us was the official ration of 25 carriers who would accompany me on my tour. Amid a babel of shouted orders the tent was erected and the gear unpacked; the cook lit a fire, made some tea and the tour had started. The next day I, the Chief, and our staffs cycled to all the villages within a certain radius of the camp, checked on the whereabouts of the inhabitants, entered details in the Tax Register, inspected the gardens, and had a meeting with the assembled villagers. Then we moved camp, visited the next group of villages, and so on for 14 days, when I bade farewell to the Chief, met the lorry again, and went back to the Boma. This, with variations in detail, was the pattern for all village tours, about which reports had to be written, which eventually found their way to the Secretary for Native Affairs in Lusaka.

There was always something of particular interest to be seen on each tour—irrigation schemes, improved farming, game-watching camps, cattle improvement work, educational development or the building of a school. I have already mentioned the messengers' names as indicative of missionary influence, and indeed Lundazi District had a strong missionary tradition. Church of Scotland missionaries had come over from Nyasaland at the turn of the century and for many years were alone in the field, converting the Africans, building schools and tending to the sick. Today their influence has waned and the mission stations have closed down; their schools have been handed over to the Government and their missionaries have gone back to Nyasaland. Their place has been taken by the Catholic White Fathers who have three mission stations in the district and have built, and administered, about 20 schools and a small hospital.

Apart from its permanent residents, Lundazi attracted many visitors—official ones such as the Governor, who came and presided at an 'Indaba' or meeting of chiefs; and unofficial ones whom we met at the hotel—big game hunters, big line shooters or people merely there for a rest and a change. The peace and remoteness proved a great attraction for many different people, and life was never dull for the residents.

I have mentioned that I started off in Africa with a wife and son, and this is indicative of a new trend, in that before and just after the war almost all District Officers did at least one tour as bachelors, whereas today a bachelor is the exception rather than the rule. I am wholeheartedly in favour of this, because, in my opinion, it is much easier to start a new life in a new country with the support and encouragement of a wife—whether it is in seeing that the cook gives you different meals each day, or in packing your touring kit (even if, as I did, you go on your first tour minus potatoes and a kettle), or generally in smoothing out all the rough edges of life in the bush!

After 18 months in Lundazi I was transferred to Mufulira, one of the mining towns on the Northern Rhodesia Copperbelt. Although I went in the same capacity, the work was entirely different. However, that is another story.

Near Hargeisa

by CORIN

Six camels, four Somalis, twenty sheep
Came quietly along the thorn tree glade
Then one of the Somalis happily
Shouted a song and his loud singing made

The summer woods more foreign than before.
A rainbow starling, red and blue and green,
Alighted on a thorn tree's slanting bole,
The fretted sunlight glancing on its sheen,

Two others dipped towards it and all three,
Like arrows of blue lightning, flashed away.
A dove billed softly, somewhere water splashed,
And children called to children in their play.

The group of nomads reached the river bed
Where not long since an angry spate had flowed,
A twisted tree lay wrecked upon the sand
And thirsty mud its curling segments showed.

The singing stopped. They crossed the sun-bright sand,
A pigeon flapped its noisy wings, and soon
More trees received them as they strode along
Towards Hargeisa in the golden noon.

The Administrative Officer Today: Fiji

by K. R. BAIN

THERE was a time when we came jauntily down the little gangway, still fresh complexioned after 13,000 miles of travel across the oceans of the world. We gazed for the first time on the fuzzy heads of the Fijian, the spindly legs of the Indian and the unexpected pallor of the European. From the sacks piled high in a nearby shed, we sniffed the sickly sweet smell of our first copra. As we reached the bottom of the gangway and stepped on to the soil of Fiji, we were greeted decorously in a language we had yet to learn. And then we were wafted off to lead and teach, we thought, when we ourselves had scarcely begun to learn. Today, things seem a bit different as we are ejected from the plush comfort of a Super Constellation into the passenger lounge at Fiji's international airport. More efficient, undoubtedly; less colourful perhaps, and certainly less stimulating to memorable first impressions.

Fashion in travel, as in advice to new Cadets, changes; and there are probably few who arrive today in their first Colony with quite the same approach to the new life as the veterans say used to be the case. And as there are new attitudes, so there are new conditions—more sophisticated and more complex—than those which used to be. Fiji is, of course, no exception in this changing world of administration—of boards and committees, meetings and conferences, of influence and suggestion, advice and compromise. The South Pacific may not make the world's headlines except in the glossier journals, but it is not the sinecure for the administrator, the welcoming haven for the beachcomber and the land of genial indolence which it may once have been misguidedly considered.

What, briefly, are some of the basic historical facts of Fiji? The Stone Age and cannibalism but a brief century away; the voluntary cession—after previous unsuccessful attempts—of the islands to Queen Victoria by the Chiefs of Fiji in 1874; the rule of the club replaced by that of law and justice; the indentured East Indian brought in first to work on the sugar estates and now grown to an energetic 55 per cent of a total population which approaches 400,000; the discovery of gold and the growing market for copra; the increasing impact of European settlement in the development of industry and communications; the emergence of Fijian prowess in rugby football, cricket and athletics, and, pre-eminently, their courage and skill as guerillas when pitted against the Japanese during the war and the Chinese Communists in Malaya.

In 1957, the Colony's administrative areas were re-defined and divided into four Divisions each under a Commissioner responsible through the Colonial Secretary to the Governor, for the administration of his Division. One of the important aspects of this is the Commissioner's position as head of the parallel Fijian administration in the Division. In the field of native local government, the seeds were sown almost immediately by Sir Arthur Gordon who arrived as the first Governor of Fiji in 1875. Gordon set about creating a system of indirect rule—later, so familiar in Africa—based on existing social patterns and established tradition. Those who were, by hereditary right, the principal Chiefs of the regions in question were recognized by the central Government and paid by it. From this humble beginning has developed in the course of time an almost completely self-contained system of Fijian local government, indeed a virtual *imperium in imperio*. The present statutory instrument is the 1945 Fijian Affairs Ordinance, whose architects were the then Governor, Sir Philip Mitchell, and his Secretary for Fijian Affairs, the late Ratu Sir Lala Sukuna. This Ordinance created a Fijian Affairs Board which stands, in a sense, as a committee of the Legislative Council and Council of Chiefs, beside a system of village, district, and provincial councils. The Board has its own Central Treasury controlling all Native Administration revenue and expenditure, including that of 14 Fijian provincial treasuries. Supported by an annual subvention from public funds, the Board assumes financial responsibility for the whole of the Fijian Administration.

The Indians of Fiji have no organised communal system comparable with that of the Fijians, but many serve on town and township boards and on Indian Advisory Committees which concern themselves with the welfare of Indian communities mostly in rural areas. Unlike the Fijian who still largely follows a tradition of village life, the Indian lives in scattered settlements on small holdings in the predominantly sugar-growing areas of the Colony. In the towns, he is the lawyer, the school teacher, the tailor, the bus driver and the clerk.

Now much of this the casual observer may superficially absorb from the small print in his tourist brochure or, less accurately, from the amiable chatter of his taxi driver. He learns nothing substantial of the Administrative Officer's life in the rain-soaked hills of the main islands, of his rôle in the councils he attends, or of the men and women of various races for whose well-being he is working. So let me give some random extracts from the diary I kept as a District Officer in the north-west of Fiji's main island.

". . . The Lautoka Indian Advisory Committee, of which I am chairman, met today. Discussions were necessarily parochial and ranged from the marriage age for Indian girls to feeder roads; from the iniquities of the Public Works Department to the problems of Indian destitutes . . ."

". . . By car and horse up the Sambeto valley to investigate a land dispute in a settlement of Punjabi cane-growers. I wonder whether the inability to agree on an apparently simple dispute is a characteristic of all 'primitive' people. It is certainly true that the village and Bedouin Arab is the most violent in verbal and often physical battle over what appears to us to be a triviality. The point is, of course, that it is not a triviality to him, but a matter which may affect the security of his everyday life."

"On through the hills to the lovely Fijian village of Nandele tucked snugly away among the hills. All the children of the school lined the track as we arrived and sang the National Anthem like mountain birds. Dressed in their white shirts and *sulus* (the Fijian knee-length skirt common to both men and women), they were an exciting and indeed touching sight for two hundred yards down each side of the winding track. What does this healthy devotion to a common flag and monarch have to do with "Imperialism" or "Colonialism" ? I talked about the Fijian Affairs Regulations and discussed the teething troubles of the new co-operative society with its committee. Then down to the valley again through moonlight and shadows . . ."

". . . Today being Saturday, I made my usual mid-day gaol inspection. This one was enlivened by a bearded white-robed Fijian (both attributes being in disharmony with practice) who was in for failure to pay his provincial rates and who steadfastly declined to put on prison garb. His reason when questioned: 'God has bidden me always to wear these garments and no others; and I may not change unless He tells me to.' In spite of my assurance of special personal dispensation from above, he stood his ground and so went into solitary confinement for a bit to permit his spiritual zeal to subside. He had, of course, an admirable biblical precedent for his conduct, the only thing found to be subsequently lacking being the earthquake . . ."

". . . A minor cane-cutting strike this morning complicated by the traditional antagonisms of two Fijian villages. The basis of the dispute was resentment felt by one village because the men of the second village had been absent from the joint cane-cutting gang until a few days before their own cane was due to be cut. Angry charges and counter-charges for two hours. Amid a feeling of general relief, agreement was at last reached, and work should begin again tomorrow after a break of three days . . . In the afternoon, to see progress in building a new Fijian school of which I am manager. Discovered by chance that the paint bought for the school has been quietly appropriated for brushing up the village church (on the grounds apparently that the church is at present the school and the existing school is the church). Later, in the office again, an unmarried part-European part-Fijian mother of a five-month old baby seeking maintenance under the Bastardy Ordinance. The putative father is a Muslim Indian; a relatively unusual case. The day ended with a Hindu school teacher who wished to sign the pledge before me and duly did so with appropriate solemnity . . ."

These and many other such events form the daily round—no one could properly call it routine—of the average District Officer in Fiji. I don't suppose they vary a great deal from the generality of experience in other Colonies where normal conditions of life prevail.

Then there are the tours of outlying islands—usually in company with a medical officer, health sister or a school inspector—which fall to the lot of the lucky ones (or for that matter, the unlucky ones if the sea is unkind to you). Here in the islands of Lau in the east and the Yasawas in the north-west is the nearest thing to the picture postcard South Sea Island legend. Life is more relaxed and a sense of the urgency of time has not yet cast its shadow heavily across the customary way of life: to the regret and frustration, it must be added, of the 'developer' and the tax-gatherer. A week, a fortnight, or a month can be spent in these islands—sitting at Fijian provincial council meetings, at Fijian courts, meeting the school committees and discussing with the Chiefs and elders the universal problems of village life—water, food, sanitation, good health and housing. Then, too, there are the hill villages of Fiji and they are some of its finest. To these you must go by car or punt, by horse or on foot, or a combination of all four.

The land mass of Fiji's 300 islands is 7,000 square miles but they lie scattered over 90,000 square miles of the Pacific Ocean. There is now an internal air service which has brought many of the islands closer than ever before; and it is now possible for the Administrative Officer of today to be present at the timeless ceremonies of customary Fijian life one day and to attend on the next a meeting in Suva's Government Buildings to consider the economic development programme for the district. The alternatives only a few years ago would have been a week's meandering journey each way by cutter, or several weeks of correspondence.

The evening social life of the Fijian village centres round the bowl of kava, that thirst-quenching brown liquid which refreshes the palate and loosens the tongue. It is at once the champagne and the *vin ordinaire* of the Pacific. No formal occasion can begin before the ceremonial libation has been duly consumed from polished half-coconut shells; and in the evening the lure of the kava bowl is roughly that of the English village pub. Around it gossip is exchanged and the fabric of domestic life dissected. Wit and song intermingle with wisdom and banter. And here it is in the village evenings that you are plunged willy-nilly into speaking your first hesitant Fijian, for not even the village schoolmaster will talk to you in English if it is suspected that you know five words of Fijian. Here, too, with formalities dropped and inspections over for the day, you learn what really makes village life tick; and find again and again what astute observers of human behaviour your parishioners are. When the bowl is at last empty, you are at liberty to retire to the comfort of a *bure* (the Fijian thatched house) which has been hospitably vacated for your use.

So far this article has discussed the Administrative Officer "in the country". It would not, as they say, be complete without brief mention of his counterpart sweating it out in the various reaches of the Secretariat—toying with his never-ending pile of files; trying to find answers, no doubt, to district problems he himself was once foolish enough to raise in another capacity; yearning, if his bent lies in that direction, for the day of his release from thraldom; keeping quiet, if it is not, in the hope that no one will notice how long it is since he last served in a district . . . *chacun à son goût.*

Notwithstanding all this, it is not exactly easy to define in precise terms the extent of the responsibilities and authority of the Administrative Officer in Fiji today. In the early years of Colonial settlement in New Zealand, there was a British Resident called James Busby who was known among the Maoris as "a man of war without guns". The present-day District Officer in Fiji is, in a sense, a modern Busby, for what he achieves is, I think, due more to his energy, integrity, persuasiveness and the confidence other people come to accord him personally than to any specific powers. He has to find his niche with the planter and the peasant, the technician and the lawyer, the company manager and the cane farmer. If he can become a man to whom all of these may feel disposed to turn—the Government's common denominator, as it were, in the district—then he will be doing his job in the polyglot society in which he is working today.

And what does this mean to the Fijian—those loyal, dignified and fearless people who voluntarily gave their lands and their trust to the protection of Queen Victoria 85 years ago ? This is how Ratu Sir Lala Sukuna, their eminent leader and chief who died in 1958, once summed it up:—

> "It is to the credit of the European community here that they have and hold the goodwill of the native race. It is an achievement of which they may justly be proud in these changing times of strikes and riots, of normality and reorganisation, of novelty and disorganisation. What the future holds for this country, none of us can tell. But of the past we can speak with certainty. In 1874 our fathers ceded their home to Great Britain. Casting our eyes over the world as it is today, we note that there are few places in the Empire where relations between governors and governed are better and more harmonious than in this Colony. Your predecessors—Governors and overseers, merchants and civil servants, planters and traders—have laid a sound foundation and on it they have started an edifice whose pillars are the humanities and common sense. To you, their successors, Fijians cry 'carry on'."

The Administrative Officer Today : West Indies

by A. F. GILES, M.B.E.

WEDNESDAY is half-day in St. Vincent. On Saturday we work full hours. Attempts have been made in the past to change this but they have so far failed. Saturday is market day: it was the old day when labourers from the estates came to town with their pay to spend, and their vegetables to sell; it was the day when traffickers brought in their sacks of "ground provisions" and a couple of goats and sheep, to load on schooners for shipment to Trinidad; it was the day when a man expected to dispose of his pig, or his stolen coconuts, fire a few rums with his cronies, and then go and do more difficult business in the afternoon with the store that gave him credit, or the Bank, or Government Office: and it is still therefore expected that all these be open and obliging for their Saturday afternoon customers.

And therefore today, as a Wednesday, was a half-day, and for once it was a real half-day because there was no bazaar or bridge to open ceremonially in the warm afternoon. The morning view from the steep front steps of Government House has changed little from what is shown in 19th century water colours: the Cathedral and the curving streets, the steep-sided crescent shaped bay; the island of Bequia filling the horizon ten miles off, crouched like a sleeping dragon; and the peaks of Canouan and Union Island strung out to the south. But instead of a couple of black and yellow frigates lying at anchor with bare spars, and a broad barquentine coming into the wind with sails set, as in the old prints, there was the green Canadian Saguiney steamer slowing into her anchorage, and the white Geest banana boat already loading, with her lighters alongside.

So I went down the marble steps and was driven to the office in the middle of the town. The first thing was to give instructions to have the Police Advance Proposals sorted out into the old, dreary order—Personal Emoluments, Other Charges, Special Expenditure and Public Works Extraordinary. For already next year's Budget is upon us, and if Finance Committee is no longer the somewhat irresponsible power it was, it is still up to the Administrator to get the Budget through the Executive Council, and to steer the Police proposals in particular. The Chief of Police will have to be sent for later to explain and expand his ideas, and he will cheerfully acknowledge that he has as usual been too greedy, but hoped that "the Admin." will do the best he can for the Force.

While Miss X got that file re-arranged, I was able to call up the Principal Assistant Secretary for Trade and Production whose Minister is (as I write) in London. He duly came in with a bundle of files under his arm and a smile on his face, and it was clear that he wanted to see me as much as I wanted to see him. Fortunately, our business coincided, and he went off with a brief for the other two Ministers, and left me with his bundle of files to add to another for the Financial Secretary about the new Windward Islands-United States Co-operative Fund.

It is now ten o'clock, so I ring the bell. The Government Secretary says that all the Members have not yet turned up, but would Your Honour put on your jacket and administer the Oaths of a temporary J.P. to the Chairman of the Layou Town

Board—the Oaths are duly administered to a large, shy young man and the latest news of Layou obtained.

The meeting of the Central Arrowroot Factory Advisory Committee then took place and lasted for just under two hours. The two Ministers remaining in the island had been specially asked to attend, and the depressing Accounts for the year 1957/58 were discussed, temporary management arrangements agreed, and the problems of future control analysed. After thanking the Members, I consulted for a time with the Financial Secretary as to the lines of a draft despatch to the Governor on the whole position, for onward transmission to the Secretary of State.

By then it was after midday, and I sat down and went through my In tray—mostly Establishment matters: how nice it is to be able to say "Yes", and how seldom it is possible.

But the draft Order Paper now produced for the next Legislative Council Meeting will need careful consideration—the election of a Fourth Elected Member to Executive Council might bring down the Government. And have the two Bills for First Reading been properly scrutinised? Rather dry, these Bills and as it is now one o'clock I feel a cold beer will be welcome—it is, I repeat, half-day in St. Vincent.

As midsummer means long light in all the northern hemisphere, it is still hot when we go down in the late afternoon to swim at the Aquatic Club. When we go in, there is a good opportunity to tackle the Minister for Communications who is having a drink with the Pilot of the Grumman amphibian 'plane of the Government Air Service. What is to be arranged about the experimental landing of a Dakota on our temporary strip (which we have just proudly completed alongside the new airfield under construction) and what were the results of the tests this afternoon—landing the amphibian on the temporary strip? "Is all right, Sir," says the Polish pilot. "He made the other planes look small," says the Minister in his deep growl, "and pulled up just over the main road line." "I bring in DC-3 first week next month," says the pilot, "but only 5,000 lbs. payload on temporary strip."

"Jolly good," I answer. "Well, I'll write officially to your General Manager"—and I jump into the sea before people start quoting more technical figures.

But at the shore end of the Club's jetty the Financial Secretary, the Superintendent of Agriculture, the Secretary of the Arrowroot Association and the Chairman of the Banana Association are deep in discourse. "You heard what happened, Sir?" "Well—I don't know that I did. But I know there was no strike." "There wasn't, Sir, but there b-y nearly was." "Tell me all about it." And so follow the tale, a tentative opinion, and a flat dive into the cool evening sea.

When I came out of the water the sun was touching Cane Garden Point and I talked to the Chairman of the Banana Association, who told me old stories of Flanders in 1915 and of the Frontier in the 20's; and to the Superintendent of Agriculture who told me of St. Vincent's last Agricultural Show in those same 20's when somebody stole the prize coconut. And while we talked and towelled ourselves, my wife was laughing with a batch of wives and St. Vincent's latest "Queen's Guide". So the sun went down under the blue-green Caribbean sea and we collected our dogs and drove home.

When we got home it was almost dark: the crickets were shrilling and the frogs were practising their Aristophanic chorus. While the day died we could look over the Botanic Gardens and the roofs of the town out to the shipping in the sheltered bay. Up on the ridge the light at the Fort had begun to flash.

The Government Secretary had sent up a Box containing what he considered urgent matters—a telegram from the Colonial Office giving advance approval to a

Colonial Development and Welfare Housing Scheme; an anonymous letter hinting at horrible goings on at Grand Hope estate; some pages of last month's Legislative Council Hansard to be checked; and an application for a licence to export a parrot. While I blotted my initials on the last minute I heard the wireless blare next door as my wife turned on 'Sports Round Up' from the B.B.C.—interesting to wonder where else in the world Administrative Officers thus tune in, and forget for a moment their public problems as they apply their minds to the Wimbledon upsets, prospects for the Varsity Match at Lords, the "Lions" latest injury, and the state of Ingmar Johannsen's right hand.

Here this Administrative Officer poured himself out a local rum, finished the air mail *Times* he began at breakfast, and waited for the 7 o'clock News: Foreign Ministers meeting, Canadian Seaway Plan, Chinese speech, Caribbean revolution—and the Crown Attorney rings up to ask if he could come up to discuss an urgent matter. I have time to spray and change before he drives up (amid a chorus of barking dogs) to discuss the need for enabling legislation before the end of this month for the Banana Industry. We stop our discussion for a moment to go through to the sitting-room and listen to the local news on the Windward Islands Broadcasting Service: Government Notices from the other islands; the Collector of Customs, St. Lucia, has gone on leave; a cyclist has been charged in Dominica with using obscene language to a policeman; Mr. Gairy has had an interview with the Governor in Grenada; and then the item we wanted to check, saying that the St. Vincent Government has made up its mind about the Report of the Commission of Inquiry into the Banana Industry. So we finish our discussion and the cheerful St. Kitts barrister makes his last rude, shrewd comment on the political situation and departs.

After dinner a Dominican cigar helps to focus the requirements of the week ahead. A speech to open 'Good Manners Week' must be tape recorded; something approaching a sermon must be prepared for the Methodist Annual Meeting; some jokes for the opening of the newly surfaced Leeward Highway must be polished; a few well chosen words to close the inaugural meeting of the Junior Chamber of Commerce must be considered; and there is the address to the Girls' High School on the Annual Speech Night.

Next week we must arrange a meeting with the Minister for Education and the Anglican Archdeacon, and try to keep the peace between two strong characters with strong principles; we must arrange a meeting between the Chairman of one of the Statutory Boards (who finds the 20th century moving too fast) and the Minister for Trade (who finds the 20th century moving too slowly); and without doubt we must arrange a meeting between the banana exporters and the two competing Trade Unions with the Labour Commissioner in the Chair. Like the Police, the Labour Department still comes under the aegis of the Administrator; when Labour is transferred to an Elected Minister, the Administrator will be formally relieved of one of his heaviest responsibilities, but will, I fancy, have to do a lot of back-seat driving.

When I first came to St. Vincent we were working the irresponsible but educative 'Committee System'; in 1956 the Constitution was changed and we inaugurated the 'Ministerial System' with three Elected Ministers; and by next year we shall have changed again to something approaching full internal self-government. And at each stage the Administrative Officer has his part to play, teaching a little and learning a lot. But tonight the moon is riding high, so let us forget politics and plan the next trip down the Grenadine Islands where the Administrator almost becomes a District Officer once again.

The Administrative Officer Today : Tanganyika

by M. B. DYSON

This is the second article from Tanganyika in this series, the first (*Corona*, December, 1958, and January, 1959) being by an officer of many years service about his work in a progressive district. The writer of the present article is still at the beginning of his service and he deals with his duties in a district which has suffered from under-administration in the past. The article well fulfils its purpose of describing the work required today from a junior officer in a district which still has much progress to make. For those who know (as does the Editor of this journal for the best of reasons) that in the area described the day of the 'one-man station' died hard a bare decade ago, the article will be welcome evidence—however nostalgic their personal memories—of considerable advance in a comparatively short time.

MY work as a District Officer is among the people of the third largest tribe in Tanganyika. They have the pleasantly simple name of Ha and there are about 300,000 of them in three districts, their country being called Buha. My district is Kibondo, lying east of the northern half of Lake Tanganyika and having a common boundary with the Belgian Trust Territory Ruanda-Urundi, from which large numbers of immigrants come into Buha. The people occupy themselves principally with the production of hides and skins, honey, salt, coffee and tobacco, the last two items under the guidance of the Government. They live primarily, however, on a subsistence economy and in their cattle-owning agrarianism are still practically untouched by the developments introduced by Western civilisation. The majority live in traditional bee-hive shaped grass huts, and the check-shirt and drainpipe trousers are a rarity outside the largest of the trading centres.

Kibondo is divided into two chiefdoms with 11 sub-chiefs; it has 31,000 African taxpayers (a population of about 110,000) who live in one-sixth of its total area, the remaining five-sixths being uninhabitable due to the prevalence of tsetse fly. The non-African population is confined, apart from Government officials, to missionaries and traders, and the problems of administration are basically the same as those of 30 years ago, except for the increase in paper work attached to the duties of all staff, and the supervision of the development schemes now in progress.

The administration of the district is in the hands of the District Commissioner assisted by a European staff consisting of a District Officer, a Settlement Officer (to deal with the ever-present tsetse problem), and a District Assistant concerned with buildings, roads, stores, bridges, and ancilliary matters, and there are also representatives of the Public Works, Agricultural, and Medical Departments, but these are directly responsible to their heads at Provincial headquarters.

The duties of the District Officer in Kibondo are spread over the finances of both central and local Government, court work (in his capacity as a magistrate), supervision of Local (African) Courts, organisation and running of the Minor Settlement Authority (not unlike a Rural District or Parish Council), supervising the work of Junior Service Officers in Departments which have no senior official on the station, and as often as possible in going on safari in the district.

Financial work plays a large part in the daily routine as the District Officer in Kibondo is, in the absence of a Revenue Officer, practically responsible for the supervision of the running of the Sub-Accountancy—the unit responsible for the receipt of Government revenue—and for the expenditure of Government funds. This is a wearisome but necessary task involving the checking of cash balances and statements of expenditure, the issue of licences of all kinds, answering treasury and audit queries, and checking through a multitude of ledgers, registers and returns. These duties take up a considerable amount of time each day if they are to be efficiently carried out, and there are times, notably when he has thousands of shilling pieces to count, when the District Officers feels more like a bank clerk!

In addition to central Government funds there are those of the Native Treasury to be cared for, and again the District Officer is required to exercise a practical tutelage over expenditure, the proper collection of revenue, and the physical checking of cash. These duties again involve hours of sitting at a desk checking over ledgers, receipts, payment vouchers, vote books, and specie. But here, behind the checking of an involved bank statement pasted crisply into the leaves of the main cash book, there is the fascination of dealing with a complete unit, and the continuous internal audit and attention to the work of the members of that unit have a visible reward in the development and the increase of efficiency of the Local (African) Authority. Throughout the district the officer will in the course of his touring be able to keep in touch with the work of this body through examining the accounts of the clerks posted to their different centres.

When the row of chattering clerks have left the office with their books in order, there remain the arrangements for the meetings of the Minor Settlement Authority and other local government bodies. In Kibondo the District Officer is the chairman of the Minor Settlement Authority and as such deals with health, housing, marketing, and the problems of community life; in detail this involves the allocation of land for urban housing schemes, the supervision of building on such land, the control of anti-malarial measures, and the provision of labour for burying corpses! Out in the District there are also local councils which, although meeting often without the presence of an Administrative Officer, always have plenty of matters to bring to him when he is on tour in the district; these often consist of matters such as a new roof for the clerk's house or a new latrine for the dispensary. Just as the arms of the Local Authority reach to every corner of the district, so the District Officer comes into daily contact with it at almost every point.

To the daily duties in Kibondo have to be added those connected with Departments which have no senior official on the station. Such are Prisons, Game, Police, Forests, and Education. The requirements of prison management are not arduous as the prison has a capacity for only 14 prisoners, but even they are capable of providing trouble—as when four of the inmates bored a hole to freedom through the crumbling walls not long ago. For the major part, however, one's work for these Departments is that of paymaster, and intermediary between the station representatives and their superior officers. The Police and Education staff are the only exceptions as the former often require active assistance by way of advice on legal points and prosecutions, and the latter call on us to assist in the assessment and collection of school fees; plaintive children and their parents who claim inability to pay the amounts assessed are a common sight in the office.

In Kibondo, where there is no resident magistrate, legal work falls on the Administration who hear some 200 cases a year. The work in this connection is not as tedious as might be expected for it is an old saying that murder and drunkenness are the main recreations of the Ha. Murder frequently takes the form of either poisoning or arson, and with this high proportion of serious crime the District Officer often finds himself sitting first as a Coroner and then as a Magistrate listening to lurid descriptions of "maggot infested spleens" and "charred remains". But legal work has its less exciting aspects in traffic cases, cases of failure to pay taxes, and the involved civil work which entails poring over the Indian Civil

Procedure Code in attempts to fathom the subtleties of attachments before judgement and applications for permission to defend suits.

When all these calls of bureaucracy have been either answered or shelved, the District Officer escapes from his enforced guardianship and leaves behind his eight a.m. to four-thirty p.m. desk life to emerge on safari into the district. In Kibondo the roads are comparatively good, but I did have two bridges collapse under my car during the recent rainy season. Struggles in bad places to insert logs and stones under mud-slipping wheels, with the help of a crowd of laughing and shouting peasant farmers, often provide a far more satisfactory means of assessing local feeling than the more official *barazas* and meetings. Most of the populated areas in Kibondo District are readily accessible by road, as the people are largely grouped in anti-sleeping sickness concentrations, and in the course of eight nights or so on safari in a month, the District Officer will visit on an average a third of the villages and local courts. There are, of course, objections to the use of road transport —did not a Provincial Commissioner once say: "The two greatest obstacles to the progress of Native Administration are the motor car and the timetable which hurry us through the country. I have spent years trying with very little success to convince my juniors that the human foot was not intended primarily to press an accelerator or the turf of a golf course!" But in these times when the tug-of-war between the demands of closer administration on the ground and the calls of the desk becomes increasingly consistent, the need is for rapidity of movement around the district.

So the District Officer goes back to his car and sweeps on to another *baraza*, dispensary, school, cattle dip and coffee nursery, to inspect and advise, to listen to complaints and to explain Government policies, to correct false impressions and to become better acquainted with the people, their desires, their ambitions, and their needs. For it is on safari that the strength of political development and pressure can be most truly measured among the less progressive Africans whose favours are still to be won by politicians.

On return from a week in the bush the District Officer in Kibondo takes up his social life again. The facilities for recreation are limited, but there is a nine-hole golf course which is capable of providing good exercise despite the winding fairways and uneven 'browns'. It is a tribute to the work of successive Government officials, and its grass is cropped daily by two sleepy donkeys which make a pretence of pulling a grass-cutter up and down its rolling slopes. It is one of the tasks of the District Officer to watch over the progress of the donkeys, and to see that they have their toe-nails cut as they suffer from some strange disease which leads them to have hooves rather similar to Dutch clogs! There is also a tennis court where we meet at week-ends for more vigorous exercise, after which we usually go to the 'club', a rest house into which has been built a bar. It is here that most of the gatherings for sundowners, buffet suppers, barbecues and dances are held as well as semi-official functions on a larger scale.

The District Officer, like all the other Government officials on the station, has a large concrete bungalow for himself and his family, on Government Hill, the highest spot in Kibondo itself. There is running water, but no electricity, and while this has some domestic drawbacks it effectively removes the scourge of the telephone. European food is almost unobtainable in Kibondo and has to be imported from the larger towns on the railway, 150 miles to the south, or purchased wholesale from the capital, Dar-es-Salaam, 800 miles away. The basic needs of paraffin, petrol, flour, sugar, salt, beer and cigarettes are obtainable at the local store in the market place, and safari does in addition bring in a welcome supply of eggs and, at times, chickens and fruit.

Home life includes gardening, which is profitable in such a high altitude, listening to the radio or gramophone, reading, and giving luncheon and dinner parties to neighbours and to people passing through the station on safari either on duty or on shooting holidays.

Kibondo is quiet, it is (to misquote) largely "Africa, red in tooth and claw", but for the District Officer it provides plenty of problems and plenty of hard work and humour, the work having a variety which is becoming rarer with the disappearance of bush stations such as those still found in Buha today.

Nightfall at Kampala

by JUNE HARRAP

As befits a twentieth century orchard of progress,
There pricks to sudden light some semblance of order,
Confused but tenuous pattern in the coming darkness,
As we approach Kampala's seven hills at nightfall.
Fast-spreading, countless oranges begin to shine
At harvest fruiting time, night time,
In homesteads, Western, African and Indian in design.
Now ripen the rows of luminous, green apples.
A few unnatural reds, the colour of some manufactured essence,
Flash on at sunset, but the sacrificial sun
Still leaves a light of love, all glory and magnificence,
That far outshines these night bright sequins.
Swiftly we pass beneath the modern, functional trees,
Along the new, macadam boulevard.
Above, the fruit lights illumine in a simple, geometric frieze
The warm descending, shielding, unyielding African night.
Then dark enfolds Uganda's endless hills; no history
Have these hills except the nebulous legends
Recurring since the ancient Alexandrian, Ptolemy,
Of the great White Moon Mountains and the sources of the Nile.
Darkness covers Uganda's forests and banana thickets,
Numberless lakes and wide papyrus swamps,
Darkness drops on the nearby mosque with minarets like egrets,
On the summit cathedral, architected native rose, Namirembe,
The Place of Peace, on the twin towered Rubaga,
The seven storeyed bank, the shops, the market
And the rush-enclosured palace. Nothing now we see bar
The disembodied lights from the old fort hill-top.

An Administrative Officer in Hong Kong

by I. M. LIGHTBODY

FOR an Administrative Officer four years in one post is a long stretch by Hong Kong standards, and I had just completed such a marathon posting. Today, the Establishment Office had decreed, an A.O. fresh from long leave would come to take over the post and so begin his first spell in the Colonial Secretariat.

As I got out of bed that morning and looked out to the islands to the south-west from the balcony of my flat on the Peak I hoped he would take kindly to it—most Administrative Officers prefer the greater freedom to be found in the outside departments, where there is much closer contact with the public. Perhaps the ideal arrangement is to do one or two hours in the outside departments and then to be brought into the Secretariat to learn what makes the whole machine tick; but the Administration has grown so much in Hong Kong over the last ten years that new entrants to the Administrative Service sometimes have to be posted straight into the Secretariat. This is a heavy demand to make on newcomers and it says a great deal for their capacities that it can be done, for they soon learn that they are expected to stand on their own feet as far as possible.

My own first posting, fourteen years ago, was to the Secretariat for Chinese Affairs where much of my time went on trying to settle Chinese family disputes. It was wonderful training in language and customs but often embarrassing for a bachelor, though my Chinese interpreter, a much-married man who knew most of the answers from years of experience in this job, was never at a loss for suggestions on even the most complex and stubborn cases. Looking back at the three years I spent in the SCA, I recall that my main feeling was one of complete wonderment that so many people of the coolie class, living on the edge of poverty, were yet able to afford such complicated family relationships.

But the SCA does far more than just settle family quarrels. There are three or four Administrative Officers in the Department and it deals with an enormous variety of work ranging from the operation of Chinese temples to liaison with the Kaifong movement (local residents' associations which do a great deal of welfare work in their own districts). It advises on effects of particular schemes on Chinese opinion, and it is kept very busy nowadays ensuring that the many development schemes afoot in Hong Kong are not forced through without due regard for any old villages in the areas of development. It is quite amazing how often these old villages prove to lie right on the one and only line for a main drainage scheme or some such improvement, and it is a slow business trying to put over a convincing case for changing a state of affairs that has been accepted for hundreds of years. The A.O. soon comes to realise the importance of good public relations and of keeping local people completely in the picture on any scheme that seems likely to affect them; there are always some trouble-makers who are agin' the Government and ready to distort its intentions.

As it happens, my successor's last post was in the SCA, so he brings a great deal of specialised knowledge with him to the Colonial Secretariat as well as a fresh approach to the problems of the Buildings and Lands section. He will have his own Registry and a team of two junior Administrative Officers and an Executive Officer to help him. When I took over this post in 1956 it was very much a one-man show, all papers, after being filed in my Registry, coming straight to me; but my successor will find that he has time, just occasionally, to pause and try to locate the wood among the dense mass of trees. The story is the same throughout the Government as every department struggles to cope with the increased volume of work. In contrast to the professional members of the Service such as lawyers and architects who join a department and spend the rest of their career in it, the Administrative Officer can look forward to a change of scene every few years (my own case of eight in four years may well be a record) and to a wide variety of administrative chores. This coming and going can, of course, be overdone and the public sometimes resent frequent changes of this sort. Things are complicated for the Establishment Office by losing A.Os. for up to nine months at a time every three or four years; new recruits have a shorter leave after two and a half years. However, the policy is now to leave A.Os. in a post for as long as possible, often a tour or more.

One of the attractions of the Administrative Service in Hong Kong is that so much responsibility is given at an early stage in one's career, and there is great scope for displaying initiative. Hong Kong is essentially civilised and not for the man who can thrive only in wide open spaces, but there are plenty of compensations for the somewhat restricted atmosphere and the lack of places nearby offering escape. Within an hour or two's drive from the built-up area is to be found some of the most beautiful scenery in the world and there is ample scope for rambling in the more remote parts of the New Territories on the Kowloon mainland. There is also a choice of fine swimming beaches very near the city, and for seagoing types there is an excellent yacht club in the harbour less than ten minutes drive from the city, provided the trip isn't attempted during the 5 p.m. exodus from town when the streets are jammed with slow-moving traffic. There is good golf and plenty of club life for those who like it, and even a Motor Sports Club and an Underwater Club for those who don't mind meeting an occasional shark or manta ray.

For many years the arts haven't found much appreciation in Hong Kong, but things have improved since the war and there is now a much wider cultural awareness, particularly in art and music. A new City Hall is being built on a reclaimed waterfront site to house a public library, art gallery and museum (facilities which Hong Kong sorely lacks) as well as a large concert hall which should help to entice large orchestras to Hong Kong. All this is largely a reflection of the great increase in the size and importance of Hong Kong's middle class, which received a boost from the influx of refugees from the new regime in China.

For those interested in food, Hong Kong provides lots of scope for experiment. Every type of Chinese provincial cooking is obtainable, as well as vegetarian food, cunningly disguised as meats and fowl. Snake is a popular delicacy and on one memorable occasion I ate bear's paw, brought all the way from North China; I was told it had to be cooked for a whole day.

Now off to the office. It is only a ten-minute drive down the Peak to the Central Government Offices (two imposing air-conditioned blocks), the first block housing the Colonial Secretariat and various departments. Within five minutes I had parked the car and taken the lift to my office on the sixth floor. Being in the same building as Public Works Department Headquarters is very convenient indeed as personal contact can be made much more easily with the department, and minute-writing kept down to a minimum—it's always a sign of good working relations when there is a free flow of visits between the Secretariat and departments. In any case, there is something unreal about lengthy minuting in such a close-knit government machine as Hong Kong's.

Land is the key to most current problems in Hong Kong, so my relief will find himself involved in almost every aspect of Hong Kong life, government and private. As he goes along he will learn a lot from the P.W.D. staff, who are always extremely patient and helpful in explaining their various technical mysteries to the administrator. He will gradually become as expert in these very specialised branches of administrative work as a layman can become, and he will be able to dispose of more and more problems at his own level without going "upstairs" for a decision.

In the old days Administrative Officers were found in a much wider variety of departments than is the case now; there was a time when the Director of Education and the Postmaster-General, for example, were senior A.Os., but now there is not one A.O. in either department. Despite increasing specialisation, however, quite a few departments are headed by A.Os.; they are of two types, firstly those where the intrinsic nature of the work makes an A.O. the ideal choice (e.g. Secretariat for Chinese Affairs, Labour Office, New Territories Administration), and secondly those which are being built up from scratch and may be taken over by specialists when the work has settled down to a regular rhythm (e.g. Civil Defence, Resettlement, Social Welfare). A recent development has been the posting of an Administrative Officer to the Police Headquarters (with the status of an Assistant Commissioner) to help with the enormous amount of purely administrative work in this large department. It is possible that this experiment will have to be repeated in other large departments sooner or later.

Medical Work in the Windward Islands

by A. D. LOW

THE medical newcomer in the West Indies is immediately impressed, not with the immensity of the medical problems, which are in fact small compared with other tropical countries, but by the size of the crowds which press around his office.

It is true that the crowds diminish to some extent as the months pass and the Medical Officer's newness ceases to attract the chronics in his parish, but the Windward Islander is as enthusiastic as the Briton for a virtually free National Health Service and consults his doctor for the most trivial complaints.

The new Medical Officer's main difficulty is accustoming himself first to the accent and jargon of the Islanders, and then to the interpretation of the expressions used to describe their symptoms. "Bad feelings" is an expression covering practically the entire range of disorders, both male and female, and as the sufferer is often unable to enlarge on this symptom, the doctor is left to his own interpretation.

The crowds, which usually number about two hundred of all shapes and sizes, are undisciplined, have no idea of queuing, and grow rather than diminish throughout the day. They have an insatiable interest in the activities of the doctor, so that the most intimate examination is likely to be interrupted by efforts to repel window-gazers. One M.O. is said to have been so infuriated by repeated and unsuccessful efforts to disperse his audience that he emptied a bucket of water over the foremost —and was later fined for assault.

In St. Vincent, where I work, I find that one has to be quite ruthless in deciding when to end the day's activities. This is normally determined by one's powers of endurance, and I remember almost crying with the pain of the stethoscope in my ears, after taking blood-pressures continuously in an ante-natal clinic for two or three hours.

Luckily, those who really want to get treatment come early in the day and the late-comers are just as happy to come again another day—so much the better, in fact, it is something to look forward to.

On the whole the islands are extraordinarily healthy, in spite of primitive sanitation and water supplies, which are explosive with possibilities. As a result of Community Development and Welfare grants the islands' hospitals have been modernised, but it is a constant struggle to prevent over-crowding and "double-bunking".

The World Health Organisation has conducted a number of 'campaigns' during the last few years against yaws and the yellow-fever mosquito, and now there is an environmental sanitation campaign to improve water supplies and sanitation in the rural areas. The danger of all these campaigns is that the populace is moved to great enthusiasm while the team is working but sinks back into lethargy again when it departs, so that the good work done during its presence tends to be wasted. For this reason the word 'campaign' is rigorously avoided nowadays and propaganda directed to a programme which suggests continuity of action.   During the present programme ten thousand latrine units will be provided over a five-year period and many springs and wells protected and it is hoped by these means to cut down the incidence of typhoid and the other bowel diseases.

Typhoid is always with us to a greater or lesser degree in scattered districts every year, but we are very lucky to have no amoebic dysentery and comparatively little bacillary. This is not to say that we have not got lots of diarrhoeas of different kinds, but bad cooking, and ill-directed drinking and dietary indiscretions probably contribute as much as infection. For many weeks all the children subsist almost entirely on mangoes, and after that on lightly toasted breadfruit so that the diet is not only ill-balanced but indigestible as well.

In St. Vincent malaria is not a problem for although there are a few anophele mosquitoes there is no infected blood for them to feed on and the disease has died out, but it is curious how the islands differ in this pattern of disease—both Dominica and Grenada have had a big problem in eradicating malaria though very close as the crow flies and apparently very similar to St. Vincent. One can hardly blame their French background unless the anopheles have hitherto unsuspected predilections! More research is required here.

Yaws is a most crippling disease which affected thousands until very recently, when a W.H.O. 'campaign' virtually wiped it out. I use the word 'campaign' advisedly here, for we did just what I warned against—we were lulled into a sense of false security and were caught out when the disease suddenly reappeared after a few months of complete freedom and swept through one isolated district like wildfire.

Luckily, yaws is easily cured by a single injection of penicillin, but everyone must be injected simultaneously in order to eliminate the focus of infection. At the time of our campaign someone with a chronic ulcer must have been missed out and the organism remained to reinfect a relation at a later date. Yaws is often referred to as venereal disease, but is in fact spread by direct contact and perhaps by tiny flies which emerge in the rainy season. Anyway, it is not difficult to see how easily it is spread when you see the crowded school benches packed with bare-legged and bare-footed children: one ulcer, and the thing is through the school in a flash. If not treated, the ulcer eats through flesh and bone and leads to terrible mutilation and deformity and has crippled hundreds in St. Vincent.

T.B. is another disease which we hope is on the way out though it has never been on the same scale as yaws. We get about thirty new cases every year, mostly young adults, who develop a very acute form of tuberculous broncho-pneumonia, breaking down probably as a result of bad housing or feeding. Nowadays they respond quickly to the 'wonder drugs' and return to their homes free from infection, but a few chronics are probably missed and continue to infect the children of the household, whom we are now trying to protect by B.C.G. vaccination, aiming mostly at the vulnerable adolescent school-leavers. It is the old granny with the chronic cough who so often looks after the children in a West Indian household who is the permanent focus of infection; until we can search them out with mass X-rays they are likely to remain a danger to all.

Leprosy is allied to T.B. in some way; we have only a few burnt-out cases now in St. Vincent, remaining in the beautifully situated leper-home. Some of the French islands, I believe, attribute their low incidence of T.B. to the prevalence of leprosy. Anyway, they are both now curable by the same kind of drug and will probably both die out in the near future.

The surgeon is kept busy on the women's side in the removal of fibroids, with ectopic pregnancies (he once had six of these in a single weekend), and by clean-sweeps for chronic gonorrhoeal pelvic sepsis, and on the men's side by road accidents. We don't get much cancer except for cancer of the cervix. Each M.O. has a district of about ten thousand patients, who attend at the clinic where there is a district nurse and a dispenser. He is kept pretty busy with the curative side of things, so the preventive side is left to the district Public Health Inspector and the nurse who visit the houses regularly and try to introduce some sort of hygiene into the homes and schools.

The M.O. has unlimited scope for midwifery, where so many girls of twenty have two or three children and the average size of a family is about eight or ten. The children give him all the experience in pediatrics he could want and a good deal that he would not want. There is a lot of malnutrition—as opposed to plain under-nutrition—though in families of ten on a wage of a few shillings a week, it is amazing how little there is of this. Even so, we have all too many shrivelled or bloated little pathetic bundles of humanity in the wards brought in too late for anything but a certificate. UNICEF milk is supplied to the thousands of children and also to pregnant and nursing mothers but cannot by itself fill the needs of the really indigent; the district nurse distributes the milk and holds ante-natal clinics and child-welfare clinics as part of her routine work.

By far the greatest cause of attendance in all sections of the community is worms, not necessarily recognised as such, but at the bottom of a host of minor troubles. Not all M.O's will agree on the frequency of worms but I take the view that it is impossible to make a diagnosis until the overlying symptomatology of worm infestation has been removed, and I worm almost automatically every patient from six months to eighty years old. After that I feel I can get at the patient. Adults often feel indignant at being wormed but they almost invariably admit to being all the better for it.

High blood pressure and diabetes are the two great diseases of adult life in the West Indies, for which there is no satisfactory explanation. The slow tempo and care-free life of the little islands would appear to reduce the chances of high pressure to nil; the West Indian, however, develops it even earlier than his American counterpart. The carbohydrate diet is probably at the bottom of both these troubles but I cannot help feeling that the ubiquitous worm may also have a say in the matter.

All in all, the life of a doctor in St. Vincent is not a great deal different to practice in the United Kingdom. He will get less tropical medicine than he expected; he will certainly not get rich on private practice but he will enjoy the good humour and gratitude of his patients even when he sinks under the weight of overwhelming numbers. And you can forgive them anything for the climate!

Eradication of Malaria in Cyprus

by M. AZIZ, C.B.E.

CYPRUS, like many other places in the Mediterranean, has been cursed by malaria for centuries. How much the armies of Richard I, King of England, suffered from this disease when he conquered Cyprus in 1191 we do not know. The need of money, as commonly recorded, might not be the only reason for the sale of the island. Perhaps he had found it to be too malarious.

Indeed, from records of various visitors there is no doubt that the history of malaria fevers in Cyprus has been long and tragic. The island was taken over by the British in 1878. The Government began distributing quinine, draining certain marshes and planting trees in and around towns, because both the army of occupation as well as the inhabitants suffered very severely from the disease.

In 1912 the Cyprus Government applied to the Secretary of State for expert advice in order to combat the menace. Sir Ronald Ross was sent to Cyprus in 1913 and found that twenty-five per cent. of the children he examined had enlargement of the spleen, a clear indication of the high incidence of malaria in the island. As a moustiquier and assistant to Sir Ronald Ross I toured the island with him and discussed future plans.

On his recommendation an anti-mosquito campaign was established. Marshes were drained and a special staff was trained to undertake mosquito control work. Conditions in many parts of the island gradually improved but there were still many villages highly malarious, as funds were not sufficient for an island-wide mosquito campaign. Extensive areas were, therefore, left uncontrolled and people from protected areas would suffer badly on leaving their homes. With any slight disorganization in the anti-malarial measures, or during abnormal years, malaria would become widespread and even assume epidemic proportions.

In 1935 the International Health Division of the Rockefeller Foundation sent Dr. Barber, one of their malariologists, to Cyprus and he found in certain villages up to seventy per cent. of the children with malaria parasites in their blood.

The eradication of *A. gambiae* in Brazil and the Nile valley encouraged us to think that the best way to redeem our island from malaria was to eradicate the *anopheles* vectors. It was, however, necessary to carry out first an experiment to test the possibility of such an undertaking. In 1946 an area of 500 square miles was selected and funds for this experimental work were provided under the Colonial Development and Welfare Scheme. Encouraged by the results obtained, it was considered that at an estimated cost of about £310,000 it would be possible to carry out an island-wide *anopheles* eradication scheme.

Although malaria was a serious public health and economic problem in certain parts of the island, there was no wide-spread epidemic as in Brazil and the Nile valley, and thus no call for drastic action by the press or the public as for a national emergency. It was purely a matter of changing the old system of " control " to a more effective direct attack on the vectors with the object of completely eliminating them. It was, therefore, necessary to carry out this work and incur expenditure within the framework of the normal financial and administrative procedure of the island. There was constant shortage of supplies. Essential items such as D.D.T., oil, sprayers and rubber boots were in short supply and at times not available. The task involved the eradication of all indigenous *anopheles* from the mountainous as well as the flat plains of an island 3,548 square miles in area. Marshes as well as all collections of water had to be reached and sprayed by hand as there were no aircraft, helicopters or boats at our disposal.

The population of Cyprus is estimated to be 450,000 out of which about 300,000 is rural, engaged in farming. The chief crops raised are wheat, barley, grapes, citrus, melons, carobs, olives, figs, etc. These crops are harvested at different months of the year in different areas and during the harvesting season the farmers, shepherds and often whole families spend the night away from their houses and often miles away from their villages. It was therefore doubtful whether adequate protection could be given to the people simply by spraying their houses. From records available it was known that persons living in the forest areas and away from any habitations suffered terribly from malaria.

The *anopheles* eradication service had certain advantages. Adequate data concerning the amount of malaria had been collected over a period of years and a staff of trained inspectors, who had been engaged on malaria control, was immediately available. The habits of the principal vectors were well known.

The eradication programme included: —

(*a*) A thorough spraying of all *anopheles* breeding places with 4-5 per cent. D.D.T. An ordinary spray pump of the slit gun type, modified to have a long handle, is used.

(*b*) Spraying of the marginal vegetation and scours along the sides of water-courses.

(*c*) A simultaneous spraying of all houses, cattle sheds, pig-sties, caves, rock-holes, tree-holes, etc., for the immediate knock-down of adults and not with a view to obtaining any residual effect.

(*d*) An intensive anti-adult campaign during the winter. D.D.T. sprayers and D.D.T. smoke generators were used.

(*e*) The interval between two larvicidal applications varied from two to three weeks and rarely weekly spraying was done.

For carrying out the spraying programme each district was divided into sections, each section into zones and each zone into blocks. Each block was further subdivided into twelve plots. Each block is under the charge of one D.D.T. man or, rarely, two. Several such blocks are constituted into a zone under a zone officer, several zones under a section officer and several sections under a district officer. In addition, at each level, skilled staff is provided whose sole business is to do larval and adult checking. Each block is combed by several teams and individuals, for both larvae and adults. Finding of one larva or adult of any species in a plot makes the whole block positive. There is a chief controlling officer at the headquarters with a team of independent checkers as well as laboratory staff for examining blood-slides, larvae and adults.

All species of *anopheles* in Cyprus are not frequenters of houses. Search and attack had to be made in caves, both natural and artificial, tombs, tree-trunks, fox-holes, etc. Checking for adult *anopheles* could not be limited to villages and other settlements but had to be extended over every part of the island. To approach some of the places needed courage and ingenuity on the part of those concerned, who had on certain occasions to be lowered by ropes to reach breeding places or treat sheltering places. The idea of applying residual insecticide alone would not solve the malaria problem in Cyprus because, as mentioned before, all *anopheles* do not necessarily enter habitations to obtain their blood meal.

The fact to be borne in mind is that the fight is waged against adversaries of various species with great varieties of habits, established over centuries throughout the island, and that the eradication staff is charged to discover the last breeding place and to find and destroy the last *anopheles* mosquito.

One cannot at present claim that the last *anopheles* on the island has been destroyed, yet weeks and months have elapsed when hundreds of skilled men have carried out searches daily for adults and larvae with very rarely positive findings recorded. Extensive areas formerly infested with *anopheles* and intensely malarious have been for months negative for any species of *anopheles*, although treatment of breeding places has ceased for periods ranging from two to three months. Not a single fresh case of malaria has been reported.

The effect of the campaign on the incidence of malaria has been remarkable, as will be noticed from the following table.

Year		No. of cases
1944 ⎱ Prior to eradication		7,686
1945 ⎰		5,908
1946		4,489
1947	Eradication	1,989
1948	period.	406
1949 up to the end of July.		71

None of the cases reported in 1949 was considered to be a fresh infection.

During the period 1944-1948 the spleen index among school children dropped from 32.4 per cent. to 10.6 per cent. and their blood parasite index from 51.9 per cent. to 1.3 per cent. The cost of the campaign from its commencement in 1946 up to the 15th July, 1949, was approximately 11s. per person, or 3s. per head of the population each year. No suppressive drugs have been issued. Indeed the need for quinine, which was formerly in great demand, has declined so much that big stocks remain in the hands of the importers.

As regards the effect of mosquito eradication on population figures, a recent report states: "An analysis of mortality statistics shows a significant reduction in the infant mortality rates and very slight improvement in the birth and death rates. It is not possible to compare the death rates before and after eradiation programme was instituted, by age groups, as the figures are not available."

It is, of course, wrong to assume that because mosquitoes cannot be discovered they cannot appear in places now apparently free. There is proof that infestation has taken place in areas regarded free, from within or from abroad; within by transport and slow moving animals and possibly by wind; from abroad they have been found on vessels and aircraft on arrival in Cyprus ports. It is, therefore, essential that a continuous and vigilant check be maintained and skilled staff be available to deal with any positive findings before the insects are allowed to re-establish themselves. A defeated and dispersed enemy becomes once more a formidable foe if the victors sleep.

Perversity

by F. J. M. PROUDE

Heat and Aden seem to be
Wedded in high humidity.
In September, June or May
Tourists—here but for a day—are heard to say:
THIS IS INTOLERABLE!

Then we who here do live and sweat
Dream deep of English cool and wet.
But how dissatisfied the mind,
How contrary, back home, to find ourselves unkind:
THIS IS INTOLERABLE!

A Doctor in the Falkland Islands

by F. HOWELL BROWN, M.B., Ch.B.

THE IMPECCABLY-DRESSED family doctor with his black homburg and stiff white collar is a far cry from his Falkland Island "camp" counterpart. Picture a farmer dressed for wet weather in gumboots and sea-boot socks and there you have him—not a strange picture because everyone working in the "camp"* dresses in like fashion.

The Falklands are a group of islands situated approximately 250 miles from the east coast of South America in 60° latitude south. There are two main islands—East and West—and over a hundred smaller ones, about a dozen of which are inhabited. They have an elemental, treeless beauty which typifies all island scenery, and for the most part are endless rolling stretches of dried-up looking white grass with rocky outcrops scattered here and there. Many people imagine them to be anywhere between the Outer Hebrides and the South Pacific and throughout my stay I received mail from one pharmaceutical firm *via* Falkland, Fife! They lie in the path of the "roaring forties" and the wind blows pretty constantly between ten and 30 knots; otherwise the climate is much the same as in Britain.

Sheep farming is the only island industry and the islanders, nearly all descendants of Britons, are English speaking. There is no colour or race problem. The population numbers 2,300 of whom 1,200 live in Stanley, the capital and only town, and the remainder are scattered around the islands in various farm settlements and outlying shepherd houses. There are properly built roads in Stanley but only clay and grass tracks in the "camp".

Medical services are provided by the Government and there is no private practice. For a very small yearly subscription a man and his family in the "camp" obtain full medical care paying only for hospital, operation and maternity care and treatment (an appendicectomy costs usually £5. 5s.). "Camp" people, old age pensioners and Government employees have completely free drug treatment and the remainder of the Stanley folk have to pay a little towards costs.

The islands are divided, medically speaking, into three regions. (1) Stanley and the North Camp, looked after by the Senior Medical Officer and another M.O., both working from Stanley, (2) Lafonia—the remainder of the East Island under the care of a M.O. at Darwin, the main farm of the Falkland Islands Company Ltd., and lastly (3) the West Falkland, the largest, territorially speaking but smallest in numbers of people, looked after by a doctor stationed at Fox Bay. I spent three years at Darwin and had about four months in Stanley in addition.

In Stanley there is a most up-to-date 32 bed hospital (the new Churchill wing was opened in 1953) with X-ray equipment and operating theatre to rival any hospital. There are single bedded private wards, twin bedded and multi-bedded wards and generally the hospital is full up. Unfortunately, as

---

* From *campo*, Span. countryside.

is widespread now, the geriatric problem is a big one and quite a large percentage of patients in the hospital are old folk who will remain there till the end of their days.

Surgeries (clinics) are held in the hospital daily and there are ante-natal, gynaecological and baby clinics in addition. The standard of maternity service is very high. All expectant mothers from the "camp" fly into Stanley for their confinements in the King Edward VII Memorial Hospital.

A dental surgeon in the hospital takes care of people's teeth and with the technician at present turns out a very high standard of gold and denture work. For a period of about 18 months while I was there, there was no dentist and the M.Os had to do whatever was necessary. The difficulty of getting dentists and doctors is a major and worrying problem at present.

At Darwin I had between five and six hundred people to look after, including a boarding school (for primary education) with about 50 pupils. By and large the people were healthy, young, active folk, who suffered from conditions similar to those of people in the United Kingdom, and the biggest problem in looking after them was getting to them. One gave a lot of advice by telephone, and by radio-telephony to outlying islands. The Darwin practice extended over an area of about 1,380 square miles and the various means of transport were aeroplane, land rover, horse and cutter boat in addition to shanks's pony. A brief description of transport problems is worthwhile, I think.

The Government Air Service started in the early 1950's primarily for medical use, and has at present two Beaver De Havilland float aircraft.* In emergencies the aeroplane based in Stanley flies out, picks up the doctor and takes him to another settlement. One big snag is that with high winds the aeroplane is unable to fly and one has to get to the patient by some other means. The other is that aircraft generally only land at settlements and so if one's patient is in an isolated shepherd's house, then another method of transport is needed. Sometimes, though, the aeroplane will land near an isolated house if it is on the seaboard—on one occasion I had ridden during the night to see a shepherd with a perforated stomach ulcer and telephoned the air service from his house to see if they could take him into hospital direct from there. The pilot landed the aeroplane and moored it in a small creek about one and a half miles from the house and then we carried the ten stone patient down to it on a stretcher over some very rough country—no joy walk! On another occasion we fixed up a large sledge pulled by a tractor as a stretcher for a 15 stone patient with acute appendicitis to take him into the nearby settlement to await the aeroplane. It was the most comfortable journey I ever made across country except that it was on a night in mid-winter and I was on the wrong side of the patient's blankets!

In 1960 a mass polio vaccination programme was started on the under 40's and the aeroplane proved of great value in getting round the different settlements in a hurry (the vaccine "goes off" if kept at ordinary temperatures for long). It also enabled the eye specialist who came out in 1959 to do a mass survey with treatment in a much quicker time than would have been possible otherwise. The pilots fly in medical emergencies if it is at all humanly possible and the aircraft service has revolutionised the whole medical

---

* See also *Rough Flying* by Michael Raymer, *Corona*, June, 1960 . . . Ed.

service, particularly for the doctor on the West who has many small islands under his care.

The second method of transport is by land rover and both camp doctors have these. They are only usable in summer when the land is dry and even then, with no hold-up, it takes about three hours to do 30 miles. It is unlikely from the expense point of view that a road system will be built in the near future and so the present inadequate tracks will have to be used for many more years yet. The land rover is a boon in that more equipment can be carried in greater comfort, but travelling single handed and getting out of bogholes of mud two or three feet deep can prove an arduous task.

Horse riding, the only method of transport until recently, is still the surest way of getting to a patient. One at least knows that one will be with the patient within a definite time. The horses are sturdy beasts and can carry on for a dozen hours or so at a steady pace of seven miles an hour. This way, of course, comes hard to someone who has never ridden before and I was always stiff after a long ride. I well remember riding from Fox Bay to Port Stephens during a holiday(!) on the West, in a head-on snow-storm for nine hours to see an acute appendicitis case.

Cutter boats are a necessity to take one to smaller islands if the aeroplane is unable to fly. They all have engines which function to greater or lesser degree and on one occasion we had to tack backwards and forwards for six hours, using sail, to get across a small stretch of water.

Tuberculosis was a big problem and in 1953-54 a survey of the islands was done by a German specialist—Chemotherapy with modern drugs like streptomycin, hospitalisation and constant check-ups have reduced it very much.

Communication with the Senior Medical Officer in Stanley was by telephone from Darwin on a multi-party line (doctors' conversations were always popular listening) and by radio telephone—even more public—from the West. Consequently, as happens in small communities, everyone knows everyone else's business and the doctor's is always most interesting! Everybody was always willing to give the doctor all possible help, and hospitality abounded in all quarters.

Between bouts of activity (and work from all quarters always came at the same time) life was quiet. There was shooting of duck and wild geese (very good eating); fishing for freshwater trout (the only free fishing of this type in the world), mullet and smelt; bird life abounded for amateur ornithologists and photography was very cheap. A healthy climate for children, a rent free house, free fuel and meat (a sheep a week for the family!), low income tax etc., all helped to make life in this southern-most Colony most interesting and enjoyable.

Tanganyika

THE SUKUMALAND DEVELOPMENT SCHEME

by JOHN T. PURVIS

AT the Cambridge conference in 1949 Mrs. Elspeth Huxley gave a very stimulating address which she called "Must Africa Starve ?"* and possibly a brief description of what is being done in Sukumaland in Tanganyika may be a useful contribution to that very pertinent problem.

Sukumaland is the name given to the country lying south of Lake Victoria and occupied mainly by Basukuma, with some Banyamwezi to the south and Bazinza to the west. Its total area is approximately eighteen thousand square miles, of which about nine thousand are occupied; two thousand at present lie within the Serengeti National Park, and the balance is unoccupied bushland, mostly infested with *tsetse* fly.

In the occupied part of Sukumaland there are now approximately one million people, who own two million head of cattle and a similar number of sheep and goats; in the more densely settled areas, surveys show densities of up to five hundred persons to the square mile. Stock are unevenly divided amongst individuals and their distribution throughout the area is dictated by available water supplies and grazing.

Sukumaland is semi-arid; the rainfall ranges from thirty to forty-five inches a year but the seasons are erratic and precipitation is usually in the form of tropical storms with consequent high run-off. The topography is gently undulating, with granite hills or kopjes near the lake. Drainage is mainly into Lake Victoria, except on the east where the flow is through the River Manonga system to the land-locked Lake Eyassi. None of the rivers of Sukumaland flow throughout the year. Soils derive chiefly from the granites and have proved to be reasonably stable and able to stand up, for long periods, to the burden of over-cultivation and over-stocking and to primitive methods of African husbandry. There is less spectacular gully erosion than in some other parts of Tanganyika but the more insidious sheet erosion naturally follows over-grazing, excessive trampling by stock in search of water, and flat cultivation on the tougher soils.

Sukumaland is often described as a "Cultivation Steppe," where increases of humans and stock, together with wasteful and destructive methods of husbandry demand a new approach and an overall plan for development and rehabilitation.

Officers of the Administration and technical departments have long been aware of the problem and dangers which inevitably arise with an increasing population and a steady decrease in land fertility, but it is only recently that federation of all the Sukuma Native Authorities covering the administrative districts of Shinyanga, Maswa, Kwimba and part of Mwanza made a concerted effort possible.

Federation of all the Native Authorities which now go to form Sukumaland was mooted by the Chiefs as far back as 1932; the idea was spontaneous but it made only a little progress during the periods of depression and war. A survey was made, chiefdom by chiefdom, by a Senior Administrative Officer in 1945, during which it was ascertained that all the fifty chiefdoms wished to form a Federation of the eight local federations which previously existed. The first full Federation meeting was held in October, 1946, and in order to expedite business an advisory council of fourteen Chiefs, representing the original federations, dealt with the agenda before the full council met.

The full Federal Council now sits bi-annually, preceded by sittings of the Advisory Council. A recent innovation has been the admission of so called

*See *Corona*, November, 1949, page 15.

"people's representatives" to the Federal Council in an attempt to make this governing body less autocratic, but, in the absence of any regular system of elections, it is yet too early to decide how far these "Bagunani" will prove to be independent of the influence of the Chiefs.

The new Federation naturally needed a headquarters and this was sited at Malya, on the Tabora-Mwanza railway, approximately at the centre of the area.

Various development plans for the whole of Tanganyika were being drawn up by the Government during the early war years against the time when money and staff would again be available to carry them into effect. A plan for the development and rehabilitation of Sukumaland gradually took shape as a result of the "Malcolm Report."

During the war years, the Government controlled the price to the producer of various kinds of agricultural produce such as cotton and coffee. The difference between the price paid to the producer and that realized for the produce on the open market was placed to the credit of the Agricultural Development Fund, and it is mainly from this source that finance for the scheme has been derived. An initial plan, estimated to cost about £230,000, grew, with further contributions from territorial housing and water development votes, until the approved expenditure finally amounted to £472,000 to be spent over a period of ten years beginning in 1946.

When the scheme was started it was agreed by Government that its detailed planning and execution should rest in the hands of a team specially selected for their experience and knowledge of the people and their land; this team was to consist of a Senior Administrative Officer as Co-ordinator, with technical officers seconded from the Departments of Agriculture, Forests, Veterinary and Water Development. The team came together in April, 1948; it is now housed at the Federation headquarters at Malya, where already quite a few buildings have grown up round a new four hundred and forty million gallon dam. These include the Council Hall and houses for Chiefs and subordinate African staff; offices, stores, and workshops; a dispensary and a village hall; African shops and a railway station.

The Chiefs do not reside permanently at Malya, but collect there for Advisory and Federal Council meetings twice a year. It is at these meetings that the members of the team present their progress reports, discuss plans with the Chiefs, offer advice, answer queries, or put forward formal requests for Native Authority Rules and Orders to enforce such things as improvements in methods of husbandry.

The team idea is something new in Tanganyika. It is in addition to, and does not replace, the ordinary district and departmental staffs, who carry on with their normal programme of propaganda and extension in the occupied areas. To avoid any departmentalism and foster team working, officers seconded to the scheme are divorced from departmental routine and direction and become answerable to the Provincial Council, but appeal on a matter of policy may be had through the appropriate Provincial departmental officer to the Head of Department.

The organisation also has its own subordinate staff consisting of Mechanics, Field Officers, Storekeeper, Office Superintendent Accountant, African Engineer, Clerks, Instructors, Forest Guards, Veterinary Guards, Lorry and Tractor Drivers, Dam Foremen, Road Foremen, Surveyors, Carpenters, Masons and Labourers.

Before the team came into being, the Provincial Agricultural Officer prepared a map of the whole of Sukumaland showing parish boundaries (where they existed), main roads, rivers, hill masses, bush edges marking the limit of settlement, and other details; this parish boundary map was supported by a soil map and a gazetteer showing the gross area of each parish in square miles, the number of people and stock in every parish and the density of each. In addition to this fundamental survey of the occupied lands, numerous other crop, stock, soil, water and population surveys have been taken from departmental records and made available to the team. The unoccupied lands present a much more difficult problem, as, in many cases, no detailed maps are available and often those which do exist have proved to be inaccurate and misleading.

At a very early stage it became clear that if there was to be any rehabilitation of the occupied lands, the development of new lands must proceed as quickly as possible in order to provide room for surplus population and stock; and the surplus stock is undoubtedly the more dangerous of the two.

It may well be asked why, in view of this over-stocking, the people have not moved to new lands of their own accord. The answer is that the undeveloped land is more or less waterless and is infested with *tsetse* fly, game and vermin; and that for many years indiscriminate penetration has been actively discouraged or forbidden because of a past history of sleeping sickness.

It is well known that desert-like conditions favour, up to a point, rapid increase in stock mainly because the incidence of tick-borne diseases such as East Coast fever is reduced. Records show that in spite of endemic rinderpest the cattle population of Sukumaland doubled itself between the years 1928 and 1948 and that the herds had multiplied to a point where the land could no longer support them. In the 1949-50 dry season severe drought caused the death of some 600,000 head of cattle and, although this alleviated the position for the time being, it did not provide any permanent solution, as experience has shown that the herds will have increased to their original size in a period of two or three years.

There always has been on the part of the cattle-owner a marked reluctance to move his stock into the long grass country, where ticks abound, until such time as these areas have been tamed by pioneer cultivators. In a bad season, however, stock owners are being forced more and more into the bush and *tsetse* country in an effort to save their cattle from death by starvation (e.g. the heavy mortality mentioned above), when losses amounted to thirty per cent of the livestock population in the more heavily stocked areas.

Over-grazing is responsible for most of the erosion so evident in the occupied country and in many areas the indigenous system of grazing reserves is disappearing under the constant pressure of hungry herds. When the land is kept so bare of cover, run-off, particularly at the beginning of the rainy season, becomes excessive, water ceases to penetrate the soil to any depth, the water table is seriously lowered and springs dry up.

A permanent solution of over-stocking can only come through education. For this purpose a stock farm of two thousand five hundred acres has been established at Malya where improved methods of animal husbandry and mixed farming can be demonstrated. The short-term policy must be the removal of the stock to new lands which, fortunately, are available. But there remains the immediate problem of so reducing the stock in the occupied country as to enable the rehabilitation of the pastures and the land generally to be undertaken; this cannot await the opening up of the new land, although nature has allowed a short breathing space as a result of the recent drought and the heavy losses.

The long-term policy towards solving the problem must be to change the attitude of the people towards their stock and this, unfortunately, has remained almost static during the last twenty years. Stock are the African's bank, his bride price, his barometer of affluence and social standing. Quantity and not quality is his aim and few, if any, look upon their herds as economic assets. True, sales have increased slightly on local auction markets since the war but until the African can be persuaded to regard stock as he would an economic crop, there must be provided some method of limiting his herds to numbers which bear some reasonable relation to the size of his grazing lands.

Culling of all unproductive and undesirable types of cattle has already been discussed as perhaps the only measure likely to produce results, but compulsion in this direction would hardly be popular with the influential cattle owners.

Progress has, however, been made recently in getting the agreement of the Chiefs and their people to a local rate for which stock will be the main standard of assessment, which will at least produce revenue, even if it has little effect on reducing numbers. This step forward may, we hope, prove to be a lesson in economics as related to livestock.

It is no exaggeration to say that, unless stock numbers are permanently controlled and fitted to the ability of the land to carry them, the development of Sukumaland will be so much waste of time and money, its rehabilitation an impossibility.

The policy of discouraging the movement of villages into the *tsetse* areas because of the danger of sleeping sickness could not be maintained during the war, owing to shortage of staff. The people began to move from areas of congestion and poor crop yields to new and fertile country. These movements are invariably started by adventurous pioneer agriculturists who have no stock or who leave their stock behind with relatives for an indefinite period. The development team has concentrated on these voluntary movements rather than on trying to initiate others, because it hopes, in this way, that the movement of adequate numbers of people, with their stock, can be maintained for some time by persuasion alone. The inducements offered will be better water supplies, adequate land to cultivate, higher yields per acre and adequate grazing for stock.

Water supplies have a very high priority in the development of the unoccupied country and the rehabilitation of the old. Machinery, in the shape of tractors, carryall scrapers, rippers and rollers, has now been provided by the Water Development Department, for the building of surface catchment dams in unpopulated areas and sites have now been found, surveyed and approved by the engineers, though the work has been much delayed owing to the difficulty of obtaining suitable units. It is proposed to build these dams, of about twenty million gallons capacity, every ten miles to avoid over-concentration of stock at any point.

Smaller mechanical units will be used, by themselves or in conjunction with manual labour, to improve water supplies in the occupied country in order to reduce the present excessive trampling caused by large herds moving to and from badly distributed water points. With manual labour only, approximately fifty small catchment works have been built or improved during the last two years.

In the new lands, as soon as a water point has been decided upon, the area is surveyed and mapped and soils examined ; woodland reserves, lines of communication and grazing reserves are investigated and planned, and, if possible, boundaries are arranged. It must be admitted that up to now this has been the theory rather than the practice because the people have always flocked to new water points in such numbers, before the work has even been completed, that the team finds itself behind rather than in front at almost every point. It is encouraging to know that the people will move willingly, but it is equally an embarrassment when they overrun the new areas to an extent guaranteed to produce deserts just as bad as those from which they have escaped. It is, however, hoped to catch up with this problem as soon as Field Officers are up to strength.

It has been agreed that three hundred taxpayers and their families form a convenient administrative unit or parish, and the aim of the team is to settle them at a density of one hundred persons to the square mile plus, say, two hundred and twenty-five units* of stock.

Most of the unoccupied country offers little in the shape of good forest ; the bulk is merely scrub, with varieties of acacia predominating, and it yields little fuel. Only in the western part of the area is there any well-wooded country. It is proposed to reserve, wherever possible, not less than ten per cent of the total area as forest reserve to provide fuel and building materials for the future. Reserves will be sited on all hilltops and on slopes which are considered too steep

*One stock unit equals one bovine or five sheep and goats.

for safe cultivation. Reservation in flatter country will be in blocks or belts, depending on the advice of *tsetse* experts on the local "fly" problem.

In the occupied country fuel is generally so scarce that much valuable cattle dung is used as fuel instead of being used to maintain fertility on the arable land. Plans have been drawn up for re-afforestation in these areas but suitable land is difficult to obtain. The Native Authorities are not at all enthusiastic, because they believe that trees encourage birds, which raid their crops, and in consequence the funds allocated for this work are meagre. They allow of little more than a series of pilot schemes designed to test out suitable varieties and methods of planting, management and utilization. There is no need to stress the importance of re-afforestation; adequate fuel to allow of the conservation of manure; tree cover to provide shade and shelter against aeolian erosion, and hillside protection against excessive run-off and gully formation are fundamental to rehabilitation.

There can be little improvement in the economic and social life of the Sukuma peasant if he remains tied to his hoe, and mechanisation plays a large part in the plans which have been agreed. Tractors, ploughs and rippers purchased by the Water Development Department, and augmented by other cultivation units included in the scheme, are to be used on experimental cultivation pilot schemes, when not being used on dam construction.

African peasant production is, at present, limited by acreage, type of soil, time of planting and the shortness of the season. Many of the tougher, cementing, but otherwise fertile soils are avoided by the African because of the inadequacy of his tools, with the result that the lighter lands are too frequently cropped and yields decline. Experiments were begun in the 1949-50 season on ripping and ploughing before the onset of the rains to ascertain costs, performance of machinery, and the reaction of the local cultivator. Effort has so far been directed to the initial breaking of new land or of those soils which are normally too hard to be tackled before the rains. It is thought that if, by the use of machinery, the African cultivator can plant an adequate acreage of food crops at the right moment, he will then be able and willing to pay more attention to his cash crops, also planted at a better time; this should further improve the yields and leave him more time for weeding, tie ridging and general care.

The Sukumaland team are collaborating with the Executive Officer of the Lake Province Increased Food and Cotton Production Scheme in which mechanisation also plays a large part.

It is yet too early to say just how this plan for mechanisation will develop, whether by family groups, village groups or full-scale co-operative societies. A few individuals may be able to afford units of their own but, in the main, group or collective farming would appear to offer the best prospects. It will allow of a more organised and orderly pattern of land utilization embracing strip farming on the contour, rotations and anti-erosion measures, communications and community of interest and ownership. There has been a marked tendency in recent years to individual "stake claiming" on common lands, which is at variance with Sukuma law and custom; group farming may well provide the corrective.

Malaya

THE TANJONG KARANG IRRIGATION SCHEME

by P. McNEE, B.Sc., M.I.C.E.

SINCE the Drainage and Irrigation Department came into being in 1932, it has completed schemes for the development of about 100,000 acres of new rice land in the Federation, and for the improvement of irrigation facilities on some 150,000 acres of existing rice land. One of the most successful schemes is the Tanjong Karang Irrigation Scheme for the conversion of 50,000 acres of useless jungle swamp to productive padi land.

The area covered by this scheme is situated on the West Coast of Malaya, and lies about fifty miles north of Port Swettenham. Lying between the Bernam and Selangor Rivers, the Tanjong Karang swamps cover an area of approximately 500 square miles. Historically, the swamps are of comparatively recent origin and consist of an immense mattress of water-logged vegetation, dead and dying, the surface of which is covered by recent growth of inferior swamp vegetation. The only drainage channel of any size is the Tinggi River, which rises on the eastern slopes of Bukit Balata and empties into the sea through a tidal creek near the village of Tanjong Karang, some eight miles north of Kuala Selangor. The mattress varies in thickness from a few feet near the coast to almost thirty feet at the eastern foothills. During the wet weather the Bernam overflows its banks and the mattress, acting like a huge sponge, absorbs the flood-waters and, later, slowly releases them through the coastal drains and the Tinggi River. As the water level in the swamp falls the mattress shrinks and the surface trees fall down, adding to the thickness of the mattress. New trees grow up on the surface of the mattress and this cycle, endlessly repeated, is responsible for the growth of the swamp.

The possibility of transforming these swamps into rice fields first attracted attention as early as 1895, when the Resident of Selangor, in emphasising the importance of irrigation to the native cultivators, made mention of the irrigation potentialities of the Tanjong Karang swamps. In 1924 a committee was appointed for the purpose of preparing a programme of work for the exploitation and development of this swamp area, but the committee decided, after one meeting, that the only manner in which anything could be learnt about the area was by thorough exploration. In 1933 the Department prepared a programme of surveys and investigations to ascertain the surface peat levels and the underlying clay levels in the area, to collect soil samples for analysis and to collect all the relevant hydraulic data on which to prepare a scheme. This programme took three years to complete. The importance of carrying out thoroughly the preliminary investigations and detailed surveys cannot be too strongly emphasised as economy in the design and maintenance of schemes, and the success of schemes will depend on the soundness and accuracy of these investigations.

The survey of the swamps was carried out under difficult and disagreeable conditions. Surveyors usually did a six months term in the swamps and labourers and *mandores* three months. At the end of these periods, the labourers and *mandores* were withdrawn for three months to recuperate. By this time, most of the personnel were suffering from tropical ulcers and ring-worm. Everyone was withdrawn to the coast or the rivers for four days each month for a rest. No clothing could be kept dry in the interior.

Survey was carried out by cutting a series of lanes through the swamp on compass bearings. The cutting gangs were followed by a survey party with levelling instruments. The surveyors determined the level of the top of the mattress and the level of the clay sub-soil. Camps were built at three miles intervals. The term "camp" is an euphemism ; it usually consisted of a series of crazy platforms constructed above water levels where stores and supplies could be kept and where men could sleep.

Surveys were completed in 1936 and the Tanjong Karang Irrigation Scheme was prepared for the development of a coastal strip, some three miles wide, parallel to the coast and about twenty-seven miles long, covering an area of 50,000 acres.

Though the Department was ready to start work on the Scheme in 1937, construction was postponed owing to lack of funds. After the outbreak of war in September 1939, the necessity for the increased local production of rice in Malaya became of paramount importance. Funds were then released and a start was made on the construction of the irrigation headworks and the canals and drains in the First Stage. At the end of 1941 construction work ceased because of the Japanese invasion. During the Japanese occupation the irrigation and drainage works were neglected and when the country was liberated in 1945, a large programme of rehabilitation work was necessary before new construction work could be started. Good progress has since been made and the scheme will be completed by the end of the year. The excavation of the drains and canals was done departmentally by ten dragline excavators, and one river dredger ; the construction of the reinforced concrete structures was carried out on contract by local contractors. The probable cost of the scheme on completion will be $3\frac{1}{2}$ million ($1=2s. 4d.).

The area of 50,000 acres covered by the scheme has been colonised by smallholders, by the grant to each of three acres of rice land within the area, and one acre for village land and cultivation of cash-crops outside the irrigated area. The area was fully colonised by the end of 1950, and from some of the earlier established lots excellent crops have already been obtained. From many lots yields of one ton of rice per acre have been reported. When the transformation of the area is completed and the padi planters firmly established, it is expected that the area will produce up to 35,000 tons of rice annually.

The area has been declared an irrigation area in accordance with the "Irrigation Areas Enactment" under which the irrigation engineers have power to control the distribution of the irrigation supply. In order to meet the cost of annual maintenance, a water rate of $5 per acre has been imposed in accordance with this Enactment.

The completion of an irrigation scheme according to plan is only the first step in the conversion of swamp jungle to productive padi land ; the colonisation of the area and the operation and maintenance of the scheme demand incessant attention. The colonisation and successful settlement of reclaimed land, inevitably a slow progress, is a problem calling for patience and perseverance, and to ensure systematic development, co-operation is essential between the Departments concerned.

Many varied and complex problems arise in the development and successful settlement of new padi areas ; problems such as the fixing of padi planting dates, provision of schools, mosques, dispensaries, provision of access paths, bridle-paths, road communications, size of padi lot and village lot, reservation of village land for padi planters, type of off-season crops to be grown, rice-mills, and so on. To deal with these various problems, experience has justified the formation of local Irrigation Advisory Committees. The principal function of these Committees is the co-ordination of the local effort, to ensure that the general policy as laid down by Government is followed, and that schemes are operated to the best advantage. The initial membership of such Committees generally consists of the District Officer, Drainage and Irrigation Engineer, Agricultural Officer, Colonisation Officer, Headman and two representatives from the colonists. As the area develops other local officers are co-opted to the Committees, e.g., Health Officer, Inspector of Schools, and Public Works Department Engineer. The formation of local committees of the planters is also encouraged, at which parochial matters, troubles and grievances of importance to the padi planters are discussed, and at which the padi planters' representatives can be briefed before attending the meetings of the local Irrigation Area Advisory Committee.

The conversion of a three-acre plot from jungle to productive padi land is a very arduous and difficult task for the settler. He leaves his friends and the amenities of his village, to eke out an uncomfortable existence and to endure vicissitudes and hardship in the initial years of opening up and developing his new padi plot. There are a number of factors which have a bearing on the successful colonisation of new padi areas, but chief credit must go to the settlers themselves. It is most essential, in the early days of opening up, that both the District Officer and the Drainage and Irrigation Engineer should take an active interest in the welfare of the settlers by visiting them in their temporary jungle houses and by assisting them whenever possible. It is no exaggeration to say that the enthusiasm, initiative and energy displayed by both these officers are the catalytic agents which transform schemes through the difficult stages from plans to first harvest.

At the end of 1950 it was estimated that the population in the Tanjong Karang area consisted of 16,000 small-holders, of whom 13,000 are Malays and the balance Chinese and Indians. The co-ordinated efforts of engineers and administrators have stimulated amongst the settlers a powerful ferment of activity—50,000 acres of land have been reclaimed, buildings erected, schools and mosques built, crops sown and harvested, and engineering works constructed on a large scale. Each community has played its part in the development of the area. There is an excellent spirit of co-operation amongst the settlers which has helped to build schools, mosques and rice-mills, and to organise the marketing of padi, eggs, poultry, dried fish, vegetables and copra which are exported in large quantities from the area. The success of the scheme has been achieved by the good will and co-operation of all concerned, and their reward must be the satisfaction that their efforts have been blessed by accomplishment.

Agriculture in Fiji

by C. HARVEY, C.B.E.

In 1954 the Fiji Department of Agriculture reached its half-century. As in the case of most Colonial Agricultural Departments its early start was on a modest scale, its principal function to provide specialist advice to plantation owners on pest and disease problems and to advise the administration on the general lines of agricultural development.

There was already at this time a well established sugar industry dominated by the Colonial Sugar Refining Company Limited, a company with large Australian interests which for many years past has operated all the five sugar mills in the Colony, transported the cane and marketed the sugar. At its own stations and laboratories in Australia and Fiji the company undertakes field experimentation and cane breeding. It also employs in Fiji a large staff of field officers who comprise an extension service for the benefit of the 12,000 or so mainly East Indian farmers who grow 98 per cent of the cane. More than a third of these, farming nearly half the total area cultivated to cane, are tenants of the company which, in addition to advice, also supplies fertilizers at cost, undertakes pest and disease control, provides portable line for transport of cane from the field, organises the cutting of cane and makes advances to farmers. It also operates what must be the only entirely free passenger train service in the world!

Thus, for historic as well as for practical reasons, the Fiji Department of Agriculture has no direct responsibilities for services to the most important agricultural industry in the Colony, though in recent years there has been increasingly close collaboration between departmental and company's officers in the field of animal husbandry, soil conservation and soil fertility.

Cane farming attracts most of the best Indian farmers and there is much competition for cane land when it becomes vacant. By and large the cane areas include much, though not all, of the best and largest blocks of farming land in the 'dry' (70 to 85 inches of rain) zones of the two principal islands. Disappointingly few Fijians are attracted to cane farming: the discipline imposed by the regular seasonal demands of a field crop does not appeal to them, nor does the independent one-man farm fit in with their still largely communal social economy.

The department thus finds itself chiefly responsible for agricultural services to the great majority of the Fijian people (who number some 155,000, just under half the total population), to those Indian farmers who are outside the cane districts and to the European farmers and planters whose interests are mainly in coco-nuts and livestock.

The principal agricultural industries apart from sugar (and the only other industries besides gold mining and tourism) are copra, bananas for export to New Zealand, and a wide range of products for the local market: rice, taro, cassava, yams, potatoes, tobacco, maize, pulses and the usual wide range of fruits and vegetables. A good start has been made in the establishment of a cocoa industry. The Colony produces most of its butter and a substantial proportion of its beef and pork.

There is, therefore, wide scope for the Agricultural Officer whether he is engaged on field investigational work on an experiment station or on extension duties among farmers and villagers, as well for the specialist in soils, crop sanitation or livestock production.

Most of the work of the department is directly concerned, as would be expected, with land utilisation—more particularly with soil conservation and the improvement of soil fertility. The total land area of the Colony, 7,040 square miles, is not small for the population of 350,000 when compared with some of the more thickly populated West Indian islands—the two largest of the Fiji Islands, Viti Levu and Vanua Levu, are approximately the same size as Jamaica and Trinidad respectively —but most of the interior is too rugged for cultivation and it has become increasingly evident that despite the great extent of sparsely occupied land—forest and reed-covered in the 'wet' zone and grass-covered in the 'dry' zone—there is no superfluity of arable land. What there is must be conserved and the best use made of it, especially in view of the rapidly increasing population.

This need for conservation and fertility improvement has been underlined by the reconnaissance soil survey carried out over the past few years under the direction of the New Zealand Soils Survey Division. All the larger islands are volcanic in origin, but recent (and therefore highly fertile) soils are confined to two of the smaller islands and the only extensive areas of good farming land are found where the many rivers and streams have deposited their alluvium as they break through the hills to the sea; and these are already in close occupation, often for cane, wherever drainage has not proved too difficult. For the most part the hill soils are badly leached and at best of only medium fertility; and in the more closely settled Indian farming settlements, especially on the margin of sugar mill districts, soil erosion has made serious inroads.

The department's soil conservation team has concentrated on awakening the interest of Indian farmers, particularly, in soil conservation methods and has achieved a great measure of success. Many hundreds of farmers have been converted to contour farming by a programme of farm demonstrations, displays of films and posters, and direct assistance by the conservation teams. In this work the department has been well supported by the Native Lands Trust Board, a statutory body whose most important function is the leasing of land which is surplus to the Fijian owners' needs in the immediate and near future. The Board is the largest landlord in the Colony and is thus in a good position to influence and, if necessary, to bring pressure to bear on its tenants to adopt better agricultural practices. More recently the Colonial Sugar Refining Company has added its considerable weight also to the soil conservation campaign in recommending the contour planting of cane.

Initially the emphasis in soil conservation work has been among Indian farmers rather than Fijians. All Indian farmers use the plough and for an increasing number the tractor is replacing the bullock; the arable land on their small farms is usually under regular cultivation; most of their larger settlements are on the 'dry' side of the islands where periods of several months without rain are not uncommon; and many of their crops—cane, tobacco, maize, potatoes—are row crops requiring regular inter-cultivation. All these factors are conducive to soil erosion. On the other hand, the Fijian villager, with few exceptions, does much of his cultivation by hand. In consequence he cultivates a smaller area but usually has much more land to choose from so that he can afford to rest his food garden under a long weed or bush fallow. Moreover, he favours permanent or relatively long term crops that give a good deal of cover to the soil such as cassava, taro, yams, bananas, breadfruit, coconuts, and seldom plants in straight lines, so that although the Fijian makes use of steeper slopes he maintains a better balance with the soil, and erosion on Fijian lands has not yet become an urgent problem. Nevertheless, this balance is achieved at least partly through being content with a lower level of production and as the Fijian villager develops from subsistence to farming for profit, soil conservation methods will become a 'must' for him.

Not even the alluvial soils can support good yields indefinitely unless the farmer makes some return to the soil. In the sugar industry the use of artificial fertilizers and lime has been practised for many years past. Outside the sugar industry and market gardens, however, the use of fertilizers has been virtually non-existent and the declining fertility of land long settled is witness to the need. The banana industry is a good example. There is a useful export to New Zealand and the banana is the chief money crop of the Fijians of Viti Levu, the main island, but whereas bananas were in the early years of the century grown on the lower alluvials, largely by Europeans under plantation conditions, production has been pushed back upriver and now comes from a great number of widely scattered small plots where pockets of virgin or long rested soil can be found. The place of bananas on the old lands has been taken by dairy pasture, rice and to some extent sugar cane, but the result to the banana industry has been the extension of lines of transport and communication with consequent liability to rough treatment and exposure of the fruit. This has increased the difficulties of marketing this highly perishable fruit and made the task of inspection and control much less efficient than it should be. Some concentration of banana growing is desirable and urgent, and for some years past the department has been seeking the right fertilizer and cultivation treatments to allow the re-establishment of banana planting closer to the roads and main rivers.

Land improvement is not solely a matter of applying fertilizer. Fiji's large Indian population is virtually self-supporting in rice, yet this crop is mainly grown as dry land rice, dependent on rainfall, and the yield is sometimes pitifully low. Under these conditions the use of fertilizers is a great help, but the bunding of fields and proper water control could either substantially increase total production or reduce the acreage required for self-sufficiency in rice. There is much potentially good land that is either not used at all or is used inefficiently because of poor drainage, and it is likely that increasing population will in the not too distant future make economically possible the reclamation of mangrove swamps for rice production.

But the most interesting problem in the Colony with which the Agricultural Officer is concerned—not, of course, the Agricultural Officer alone, though he has an important part of play—is to assist the Fijian villager to make the change from subsistence farmer to surplus farmer, a change that has started but which may take a long time. The Fijians account for half the total production of copra, and for almost all bananas for export, and they grow the bulk of their own food, but although they also make a substantial contribution to the general labour pool their production from the land is low in relation to their land and labour resources. Just what the incentive to change will prove to be, and how that change should be guided so that these generous and happy people do not lose in the change what is best in their social system, are problems that have yet to be solved.

Soil Erosion

THE PROBLEM IN JAMAICA

by W. C. LESTER-SMITH

THE main problem Jamaica is faced with today is that of a seriously degraded soil fertility, augmented by the absence of adequate measures for the conservation of natural resources. The direct causes have been the destruction, within barely two centuries, of much of Jamaica's most priceless asset—her forests; accompanied and followed by the production of bananas, coffee, ginger and yams, over large areas of comparatively steep land, on mono-cultural and conservationless systems of agriculture. These cultivations, originally, were largely confined to the more easily erodible shale, soft conglomerate and alluvial soils; and banana disease on the coastal areas gradually pushed this crop on to more critical slopes.

When these facts are placed in their proper perspective against the prevailing climatic and topographical features of the island, it is not surprising that they have left their mark on the social structure, mainly in health (malnutrition) and morale, of the population as a whole.

Jamaica is a very mountainous little island, roughly oval or fish-shaped in outline, about four times as long (east and west) as broad, and with a population of well over one and a quarter million increasing at the rate of about 20,000 a year. Its area is approximately 4,000 square miles or about half the size of Wales, but with elevations rising to twice the height of the Welsh mountains.

At a generous estimate there is, on the island, only ten per cent. of flat to gently sloping land, about three quarters of which is in permanent cultivation under sugar cane, coconuts, tobacco and livestock farming. Roughly half of the remaining area, nearly a million acres, consists of very steep to precipitous land, most of which should not be materially disturbed; about one tenth of this area is very rough and rocky karst-country. The greater part of the million acres should be under forest, as it was originally, instead of which less than half of it now has on it anything approaching forest growth.

The deforested steep land is utilised for poor grazing, coffee and citrus fruits on the shallower and rather pockety soils, and for the shifting cultivation of bananas, yams and ginger on the deeper soils. These are the areas which should be the guardians of the island's numerous small rivers and streams, many of which now only have a transitory flow. There are about twenty-five main rivers and at least twice that number of smaller streams, many of which have an extremely high hydraulic gradient, and none has been given throughout their course the necessary protection and reservation.

About two-thirds of the remaining area, nearly one million acres, is steep land with a gradient of from about 15 to 30 degrees. Obviously this land should not be used for any form of agriculture without maintained precautions to moderate soil and water movement and to build up fertility, bearing in mind the fact that there is generally a definite absence of any effective conservation measures on the land above.

The remaining one third, approximately half a million acres, has a more moderate slope, roughly from about 6 to 15 degrees. Much of this land should not be cultivated, particularly under arable crops, without safeguards that will satisfactorily promote and maintain fertility, including moisture conservation.

Some of these moderate slopes and limited parts of the flatter lands, particularly in the drier coastal areas, suffer periodically from wind erosion. Most of these areas grow such crops as tobacco, tomatoes and various vegetables during the one rainy season. Surface mulching in the form of thatching the land with grass or wild vegetation is practised, but because this is a dry area, supplies of mulching material are very limited. Practically nothing is done to establish suitable windbreak vegetation, chiefly on account of the fragmentary nature of the land holdings, the grudging of land-room and the fear of crop reduction from shade and root invasion.

Periodically, years of drought interspersed occasionally by short spells of heavy rain, hurricanes and less violent tropical storms, often mainly wind and frequent " northers " as they are locally termed, affect different parts of the island. Thus, as a result of drought, flood or wind, the Jamaican farmer's lot is frequently not a happy one. These events increase his indebtedness both to the land and to commercial enterprise; they also induce a feeling of insecurity and impermanence, which is frequently reflected in general outlook and the appearance of the holdings. These are factors which can tend to retard the development of a sense of individual responsibility and pride in well-doing.

It is the intensity of the rainfall and the consequent volume and rate of surface run-off water over localised areas of steep land with an inadequate mantle of vegetation, that are responsible for the most serious erosion and flood damage. In a twenty-four hour period falls of ten inches are not unusual; there are many records of falls of over twenty inches and one of over thirty. There is even a record of eleven inches in eighty minutes. The wettest area in the island has an annual mean of almost 240 inches, with a record high in 1931 of just over 335 inches. It will be evident, therefore, that the distribution of the rainfall favours erosion and flood damage, and reacts adversely, not only on the agriculture of the island but also on all the other communities.

Well over a million pounds has been spent on flood and storm damage repairs over the past twenty years, and expenditure on such works is largely recurrent. The expenditure of half this sum on effective conservation measures designed to control and reduce surface run-off, with the requisite degree of co-operation and co-ordination for their maintenance, should reduce recurrent expenditure on such repair works to very negligible proportions within a period of ten years. It should also materially assist in raising soil fertility and thus tend to promote a more stable environment and a healthier population.

Piecemeal efforts at natural resources conservation and the improvement of living standards are more costly in time and money; and time is an important factor at present, both as regards producing food and raising morale. Unemployment relief works now cost about one million pounds per decade, but only a negligible part is spent on work of a basically productive nature. The desirability of deflecting much of this labour into part-time parochial civil conservation units, officered and directed by the local representatives of the Agricultural Society, is worthy of careful consideration.

Until Jamaica has brought her soil fertility to considerably higher levels, and has done more to narrow the present wide gap between the local production and the import of nutritionally necessary food, her social reclamation should be based primarily on her soil. Food is a prior essential to industry, and in a primarily agricultural country production of the essential foods for home consumption can be of relatively greater importance than crops produced for export.

Group Farming in Kenya

by P. C. CHAMBERS, B.A., Dip.Agric.Cantab., A.I.C.T.A.

AT a Conference in 1947 the Agricultural Officers of Kenya passed the following resolution: —

"The policy of the Department for the Native Lands shall, in general, be based on encouraging co-operative effort and organisation rather than individual holdings. It is considered that only by co-operative action can the land be properly utilized, and the living standard of the people and the productivity of the land be raised and preserved. While this involves a change from the modern trend towards individualism, it is in accord with former indigenous methods of land usage and social custom."

In the Nyanza Province "co-operative action" has taken the form of "Planned Group Farming" and it is possible that a short account of this system, as accepted by the Provincial Team in February, 1948, might be of general interest.

Individualism, lack of planning and the fragmentation of holdings are as prevalent in this area as anywhere else in Africa, and we have been faced with all the usual difficulties in trying to bring order out of chaos. The boundaries of holdings usually run up and down slopes, rainfall is heavy and the first requirement for soil conservation is the building of drainage-type terraces and the treatment of land in drainage units. In these circumstances, some form of co-operative planning is inescapable, because contour strips and the drainage unit itself can take no account of the individual holding, but must be designed according to technical requirements. The Group Farm at once suggests itself as the most suitable means of co-ordination, and the basis of the Group Farm must be co-operation, because it is the only system by which interference with the individual's tenure of his holding can be avoided and at the same time the consent of the individual be obtained and an agreed farming policy. Contour strips, for instance, must be communally planned by all the members for the whole Group Farm and put to the same agreed uses; one for housing, another for bananas and others for fuel or timber plantations, permanent grazing and, in the flatter lands, for alternate husbandry (arable and grass leys) in accordance with an agreed rotation.

Permanent hedges and fences are allowed only round the perimeter of the Group Farm and on the contour, and all fences running up and down the hill must be moveable so that for arable courses of rotation implements may traverse all holdings. It might be thought that the quality of intelligent co-operation required for this degree of planning might be almost impossible to achieve among typical African peasants but, in fact, since the Group is composed of neighbouring cultivators, most of its members are usually relatives and they co-operate more readily than might be imagined. One virtue of the Group Farm system is that the obligations of co-operation are limited ; the individual must follow the agreed programme and obey the edicts of his group, but within those limits he is free to farm as he likes and to sell his crops how, where and when he pleases.

On the other hand, the Group Farm opens up wide co-operative possibilities and once the members have learned the benefits of communal planning and mutual confidence they are likely to become more and more receptive to any ideas, including new varieties of co-operation. They can, and in most cases should, register themselves as Co-operative Better Farming Societies.

A certain amount of precautionary legislation may be needed, such as a Local Authority rule to ensure that if land in a Group Farm passes under the control of an outsider he can, nevertheless, be compelled to obey the group-edicts, but this is not a system to be developed by Government Order. It is essentially a project which must depend mainly on the wholehearted support and initiative of the African. Right from the start, ideas and opinions should be drawn from him and not given to him by us.

Since the proposal for the development of Group Farms was approved early in 1948, the Africans of the Province have shown great interest in the idea. Already in the Central Nyanza district the Luo, a Nilotic tribe, have formed twenty-four groups with 540 members covering some 7,805 acres. No mechanical assistance has yet been possible, but most of the groups have made a good start with preparing drainage ways and terraces, applying manure, planting grass and closing grazing areas for recovery. The first group to be formed, that at Nyanera, which has seventy-seven members and 960 acres of land, has made most progress. They have said that they realise that not more than half of the land should be cultivated at any one time, and that they are willing to sign an agreed set of rules, and to pledge unlimited security in the event of their group receiving a loan for development. Land exchanges are taking place and all members are making manure. One, who has no stock, obtains manure from a neighbour in return for all his stover and assistance in making. Two strips have been planted with grass for leys this season.

In North Nyanza a start has been made with developing a group farm for trial and demonstration at the Agricultural Department Station at Bukura, and Government has provided funds for the development of a union of three groups at that station. This will provide facilities for investigating the agronomic, social and economic aspects of group farming, for testing mechanical equipment and for training specialists sent there for courses by the various groups. Several groups are already developing in the vicinity, and it is hoped that the system will radiate out from the station with the assistance of mechanical equipment based on it.

In South Nyanza a number of groups have been formed in the lake shore Luo locations, some of which will use land at present undeveloped. In the Kisii (Bantu) highlands one group is starting, and the Local Native Council and' a Location Advisory Council have recommended that an area of two hundred and fifty acres should be set apart for ten years for trial and demonstration of group farming.

In the Kericho district the Kipsigis (Nilohamitics), who until recently were pastoralists but are now over-cultivating their land for maize production, are showing great interest in the proposals. Their Local Native Council has provided two mechanical units, each with one Fordson and one Ferguson tractor with implements, fencing, and full assistance for ten group farms as a trial. Four of these group farms, totalling 1,180 acres with seventy-five members, have now been formed. Perimeter fencing has been completed, graded strips have been pegged and left under grass for terracing later, and some three hundred and fifty acres have been mechanically ploughed and cultivated. Rotations and strip usage have been agreed, and the requisite maize strips will now be undersown for grass leys. Cattle dips will follow, when the groups develop and show that they can control numbers and grazing for cattle improvement. It is interesting to record that one group has asked for a water ram and piped supply, for which it will pay.

In Kericho ownership, or right of user, of particular areas of land has not developed to the same extent as in the other districts, and one of the first functions of the group, when formed, is to apportion land to its members. This makes land utilization more simple, but may give rise to trouble within the group in the early stages. It does, however, test their mutual trust before development starts.

Numerous applications have been received from others interested in all four districts of the Province, and it is apparent that planned Group Farming is arousing considerable interest. The social aspects and economics of the system need study and the difficulties, in particular the rampant individualism that has developed in recent years, are appreciated, but it would appear that by virtue of its elasticity and capacity for gradual, guided development, the Group Farm has great possibilities.

Safari in the Rift

by R.O.H.

From far cloud cornice water ropes
    descend unmoving;
pull, and the frosted skylight lifts,
    the forests revealing,
blue in air and leopard-haunted,
    million eyed,
hunched expectant, ghosts of old gods
    in Saturday stadium.

White the dust that knifes my fingers,
    bright the wind that claws my face.
Fire and water leap and mingle
    in my helmet's carapace.
Stone and shingle start from ambush,
    thorn and aloe twitch and stab.
Lift the foot and you will anger
    snake and centipede and crab.

In hiss of sand and pebble's rattle,
    ears listening
to dim gongs of foam on rock
    and far singing;
red eyes, white mind attaining
    the unattainable,
the hanging water, the lotus fruit
    and citron blossom.

The New Forester

by C. SWABEY

WHEN I was first appointed to a Colonial territory the address of my house there was 18, Victoria Avenue: it was a tremendous let-down. In imagination I had seen the column of porters winding over the hills to my pioneering bush hut at Mbongo, Hausaland. Instead the tram dropped me among suburban villas in a large town.

In most developing countries there are always, I suppose, two more or less clearly defined phases, the period of creating order and then the developmental phase—it certainly applies to forest administration: the first stage is the period of mapping, of finding where the forests are, of protecting them from abuse, of settling forest boundaries, of building up and training local staff.

I imagine that for most foresters who have sought a career in Colonial territories it has been this phase that has appeared so attractive—the long trekking on foot over the plains and over the mountains, the camp fires in the evening, the surveying of new country, the gradual emergence of the settled forest boundaries, and the absence of red-tape and office routine. It is much more than a remote and romantic dream—it is a reality which existed in nearly every territory and which still exists in some, but surely and inevitably it is giving way to the next phase, that of development.

It is easy to be sentimental and nostalgic about these things and to deplore their passing, but the development phase is no less interesting, though in a different way. One can still have the thrill of accomplishment when the new forest roads bring a previously inaccessible forest into production, when a valuable young tree crop covers the scars of eroded and barren hillsides, when the managed forests turn out an increasing volume of timber for the use of man. But it means also that the forester must increasingly be a technician: as his work becomes more intensive, he has to call into play many more of the sciences which he met during his training and he has to master the use of the new tools which science is continually bringing to his aid. This, I think, is a stimulating challenge and the 'new forester', with his aerial photography, his statistical analysis, and his mechanical and chemical equipment need have no fear of lack of interest in his job.

Few developments have given the forester a tool of greater value and precision than aerial photography, but it is only in recent years that the full value of this has been exploited in many Colonial territories.

For many years the Colonial forester has used the contact prints of aerial photographs (A.P.) to help him in finding out the extent of his main forest areas and in roughly defining the boundaries between forest and grassland or scrub: but the techniques of constructing controlled print lay-downs as a basis for plotting forest-types and topography have, in general, lagged behind. The equipment for doing this is moderately expensive, the techniques have to be learnt and time must be available for using them, time which the average district forest officer rarely has to spare. With the reorganisation of the Photo Forestry Section at the Directorate of Overseas Surveys at Tolworth, it has been possible to provide the expert advice and assistance which was previously lacking, and a number of forest mapping sections have been established in Colonial territories using modern techniques of A.P. interpretation and plotting.

Although in tropical forests it is rarely possible to attempt estimations of timber volumes by A.P. alone, a combination of A.P. type mapping and ground enumeration enables the latter to be undertaken to known degrees of precision at a fraction of the cost previously possible.

This leads me to the use of modern statistically-based sampling techniques. It is obvious that to measure every tree in hundreds of square miles of forest, in order to find out how much timber is available, would be an unsupportably costly and time-consuming operation. Earlier techniques of regular sampling on a basis of 1%, 2%, 5%, etc., had the grave disadvantage that one never knew how precise the sample was—what in fact were the chances of sampling error. By the use of statistical methods, which we will not attempt to describe here, it is possible to define the limits of sampling error—for example, it enables one to say that a certain forest contains 125,000 tons of timber plus or minus 15% within a 95% probability: in other words the chances that the actual timber found will lie within those limits are 95 : 100.

When it comes to establishing industries based on these sampling figures, the importance of precision in volume estimations is obviously very great.

The application of statistically designed experimental methods in silvicultural and other forest research has also lagged behind in many territories: I suppose that there are no Colonies which are not littered with abortive and inconclusive forest experiments. Often the deficiencies of experimental design have delayed indefinitely the emergence of significant results from years of carefully recorded measurement. Nowadays, there are well-recognised criteria of experimental layout and analysis which enable us to determine the significance of our research results: this has a bearing on even the simplest of field trials.

In the more intensive management of forests there are many applications of modern chemical development: this is particularly so in the field of insecticides and fungicides, while the use of artificial fertilisers and even trace-element applications are finding a place in routine field work. A particularly interesting development is the use of the so-called hormone arboricides in the removal of weed trees in tropical forests. In most natural tropical forests there are a high proportion of stems of no commercial value: these must be removed to permit the development of more valuable stems. To fell them is extremely expensive as well as causing damage to the young economic trees around them. For many years foresters have been using arsenical preparations applied to frill-girdles cut into the bark of the unwanted trees. In many areas the use of these highly toxic poisons is ruled out for reasons of human safety, while cutting frills in heavily buttressed trees is a laborious process. The use of the compounds 24D and 245T in a diesel-oil solution applied as a basal spray overcomes both of these difficulties and is proving most successful in some tropical forests.

Considerable progress is being made in the field of mechanisation: with improving standards of living, the old concepts of the cheapness of tropical labour are becoming increasingly mythical. Parallel with this have been the development of less unreliable mechanical equipment and the gradual emergence of an artisan class: although it would be idle to pretend that mechanical maintenance has yet achieved high standards in many Colonies, it is now possible to replace some of the more wasteful applications of hand labour by the machine.

The development of the light 4-wheel drive vehicle has in many places been able to tide over the period between the virtual disappearance of the foot safari and the development of all weather roads: this is particularly so in the case of ground reconnaisance and forest enumerations. The tractor and bulldozer also are increasingly used in the construction and maintenance of forest roads, while firebreaks and external reserve boundaries are not infrequently maintained by tractor.

Power pumps for water supplies to forest nurseries and buildings are taking the place of the strings of water carriers.

In some territories Forest Departments operate their own V.H.F. radio or telephone systems, while there are possibilities in the use of electrified fencing to control game damage.

A promising field of development lies in forest genetics in the tropics—a field in which the forester has lagged far behind the agriculturist and the horticulturist. Increasing attention is being given to scientific seed selection, to ensuring that it is only the best trees in the crop that become the parents of the next generation. It is believed that production of timber can be greatly improved in this way.

Parallel with intensification of forest management along these and similar lines is the development of local staff training facilities. With a trained subordinate staff, at any rate a proportion of routine forestry operations should be taken off the shoulders of the professional foresters, enabling them to intensify their scientific work.

The scene is changing indeed, but there need be no more cause for regret in the functional changes of the 'new forester' than in his altered sartorial ideas. Who now wears the drill breeches and the puttees of my own days in Trinidad in the 20's ? Who but the bald, perhaps, and the be-spectacled in the rains, think of a topee or a double terai ? But I wonder, if I was still in Jamaica, doing much of my work on horse-back in the mountains as I used to do, if I should by now have evolved a footwear which would come easily out of the stirrup when I fell off ?

Contributors to this Issue

J. F. R. HILL, after long service in Tanganyika's Administration and as Member of Communications and Works in that country, also served in the Bahamas. C. SWABEY is Secretary of State's Forestry Adviser after 25 years in the Colonial Service, his last post being Chief Conservator of Forests in Uganda. P. J. GREENWAY continues his East African story, and SIR ARTHUR KIRBY, also writes of East Africa; he is now Commissioner in London and was formerly General Manager of East African Railways and Harbours. SUSAN LESTER is a London journalist. SIR JAMES HARFORD and JOAN GIBSON are new contributors. The former recently retired from the Governorship of St. Helena, after service in Nigeria, the West Indies and Mauritius; the latter has a husband in Uganda's Administrative Service, four children, and is in charge of an electoral office. MARY GOODWIN who writes from the Capital School, Kaduna, Northern Nigeria, is also new to *Corona*, but MICHAEL TAAFFE and R. J. A. W. LEVER need no fresh introduction. MARGARET ROSS, FRANCES DRUMMOND and SYLVIA SMEE did the drawings on pages 370, 388 and 397 respectively. The main illustrations are by courtesy of EAST AFRICAN RAILWAYS AND HARBOURS.

Veterinary Services in Nyasaland

by D. E. FAULKNER

ON the map Nyasaland seems a small country compared with the other East and Central African territories but it is some 500 miles long and although averaging about 70 miles in width, its topography is so broken and varied that communications are difficult. A large part of the area within its borders consists of the waters of Lake Nyasa, while it possesses a human population getting on for 3,000,000 which is greater than the populations of either Southern or Northern Rhodesia. Its resources are limited, its economy largely depending on a subsistence form of peasant agriculture and the marketing of a small number of plantation crops grown in the southern parts of the country.

Livestock occupies a relatively unimportant place in the agricultural industry. In relation to the human population numbers are small and many of the peasant holdings have no cattle on them at all. In spite, however, of the intense pressure to meet the needs of the rapidly expanding human population, cattle continue to increase, if slowly, while the other classes of stock such as sheep, goats, pigs and poultry either remain relatively stable or else fluctuate somewhat from year to year.

The organization of veterinary services in the territory is along lines familiar in other Colonial territories. As a Department of the Government, with its headquarters at Zomba, Provincial and District Veterinary, Livestock and Assistant Livestock Officers function through the country as members of the Provincial and District Teams. These officers maintain the field services provided for the prevention and control of animal diseases, the giving of advice on animal health, husbandry and production problems of all kinds and other ancillary services such as the distribution of improved stock and the administration of the livestock subsidies and bounties scheme. In addition, the Department maintains Livestock Improvement Centres in each of the three Provinces and a Poultry Centre, a Veterinary Laboratory and a Livestock Quarantine Station and Holding Ground which, although all are situated in the southern part of the country, operate on a territorial basis.

Much of the work of the Department is similar to the work carried out in other territories but there are a number of features in Nyasaland which are not generally encountered elsewhere and a brief description of them may be of interest.

One of the most important features of the work in Nyasaland is the relatively extensive cover afforded by the system of dipping tanks against the tick-borne diseases which are by far the greatest single cause of ill-health and low productivity in the stock population. Compared with the systems of dipping built up in South Africa and Southern Rhodesia, dipping in Nyasaland is far from being unique but for other territories in Africa the system has a number of interesting features.

During recent years great efforts have been made by the Department with Colonial Development and Welfare funds to complete the coverage over the whole of the cattle areas of the country and to this end a large number of prefabricated, mass produced, steel tanks in sections, assembled and installed on site, have been used.

Dipping is often looked upon as an end in itself and of course the control of ticks and the tick-borne diseases (such as East Coast fever), where these assume the importance that they do in Nyasaland, is of considerable economic value. In Nyasaland, however, the control of ticks and the tick-borne diseases is considered as only a part (although an important part) of the contribution to livestock improvement which a system of dipping can make in underdeveloped areas. In the first place, the demarcated dipping tank area is an important veterinary administrative unit because stationed at each dipping tank is a Veterinary Assistant whose job it is to know what goes on in his area. He can report at once to his District headquarters if assistance is needed; he knows all the stock owners whom he advises and helps during regular visits to their farms and holdings; he regularly inspects the stock each week on dipping days and he provides the information for the compilation of the annual stock census. While these are, of course, important functions, the dipping tank and its Veterinary Assistant serve also as the centre for all the animal husbandry activities of the area. At many dipping tanks in Nyasaland demonstration units have been created at which African owners can see in use simple, but improved, types of buildings and handling facilities for their stock, and these provide them with models which they can reproduce on their own holdings. In one area supplying the Blantyre market with milk, for example, a small demonstration milking shed at the dipping tank has led to its adoption by many of the milk producers in the area with a consequent great improvement in the standards of milk hygiene maintained.

At the dipping tank demonstration centres small numbers of indigenous live-stock are also maintained under simple but improved conditions, and their feeding, management and care provide a continuous demonstration to the local stock owners. Frequently included in each small group of animals are bulls, or other male breeding stock, bred at the Departmental Livestock Improvement Centres and issued to the dipping tanks for communal use by the local stock owners.

The poultry development scheme has been a most encouraging feature of the Department's animal production activities, as will be mentioned later, but it is at the dipping tanks that the young birds produced under the scheme are held for short periods after delivery from the Centre, while distribution is taking place. In some areas the dipping tanks provide centres for the purchase, collection, prepara-tion and despatch of hides and skins, and now that the Cold Storage Commission is taking over the marketing of hides and skins throughout the territory, this is likely to become an increasingly common practice.

The value of the dipping tank as a rural centre for all animal health, husbandry and production activities can therefore readily be appreciated.

Before describing one or two of the Department's other livestock improvement and production projects mention should be made of the rabies control scheme. Rabies during recent years has increasingly assumed more dangerous proportions, and it became necessary to take drastic action without, however, laying too heavy a financial burden on the Government. Accordingly, a Rabies Control Unit was formed composed of a number of dog inoculation and dog destruction teams. These teams began work, after very thorough preparation, in the Central Province where the incidence of the disease had been high. A system of mass immunization of village dogs, followed up by intensive campaigns for the destruction of all unimmunized dogs, was started. A fee to cover the cost of the vaccine only was charged to each dog owner. At the end of the first year's operations the results were so encouraging that further teams were created to operate in the Southern Province and, given the same degree of co-operation from the dog owners in the future, it is expected that, even under the difficult conditions of the African rural areas, the disease will have been reduced to negligible proportions within four to five years.

Nyasaland is one of the few territories where there is no private veterinary practice of any kind; not because this would not be welcomed but because, generally speaking, the more valuable stock are too widespread to attract private practi-tioners. To meet this situation the Department has evolved a scheme under which

Government Veterinary Officers carry out the duties of private veterinary surgeons. Fees are charged to the public as in a normal private practice but, in this case, on Government accounts. At the end of each month the Government Officer concerned is permitted to claim back from the Government not only his mileage, but a proportion of the fees, in compensation for the extra hours on duty necessitated by the calls coming in at all hours of the day or night. This has been found to be the most economical system which, under local conditions, could be devised, since the farmers obtain a constant and reliable service—if Government officers were not permitted to undertake practice during the course of their other duties additional staff would be required. Also, individual officers have an incentive to attend patients at any hour of the day or night and the Government benefits in that not only is it able to maintain a reasonably economic service but it quickly becomes aware, at an early stage, of any abnormal health problems occurring on the farms or among the stock brought to the clinics.

Mention has already been made of the Livestock Improvement Centres in each of the Provinces and the Central Poultry Centre maintained by the Department. In the former case these perform several functions. In the first place they carry herds and flocks of indigenous livestock, the maintenance of which provide much valuable information on the characteristics and requirements of these largely, as yet, unknown classes of stock. Improvement in productivity of the different types is making encouraging progress. In the Southern Province where most of the European farming population resides, small herds of the two main milk breeds found in the area, namely the Jersey and Friesian, are also maintained for purposes of comparing the economic productive ability of these two breeds under tropical conditions and of evolving suitable methods of management and feeding for them.

From all the herds and flocks in the Centres breeding stock are distributed to the farmers—either to individuals or, in the case of the dipping tanks, for communal use.

At the Livestock Improvement Centres are also maintained African Training Centres where future recruits to the staff of the Department as Veterinary Assistants and Animal Husbandry Instructors receive one or two year practical courses while working on the Livestock Improvement Centres. In addition, farmers, teachers, village headmen, members of Local Native Councils and others are given short courses of varying duration. The training of African staff is, of course, of vital importance to the Government's work in the field, and while standards of training are gradually being raised, a look out is constantly kept for suitable candidates who can be sent home to Britain with scholarships or bursaries to enable them to take their full qualifications in veterinary service and animal or dairy husbandry.

The Poultry Centre and poultry development scheme has developed rapidly during the past three years. Although fish from the lake provide a valuable source of protein to the population adjacent to Lake Nyasa over much of the country, the human population is greatly deficient in this important element of diet. Owing to the density of the human population and to the lack of economic incentives to stock owners, increased production from cattle and other classes of stock can only be a slow and difficult business, but poultry are in a different category altogether. Although the Centre now meets a large part of the demand for day-old chicks and hatching eggs, it has concentrated its production mainly on six to eight-week old birds for distribution and sale throughout the rural areas. After considerable experience it has been found that at this age the young birds have their best chance of adapting themselves successfully to the conditions found in these areas. It has also been found that of all the commoner breeds of poultry the Black Australorp has adapted itself better to the conditions than any other.

The poultry scheme has won the support of the whole population and is undoubtedly meeting a great need. Newcastle's disease periodically decimates flocks over large areas in the African rural areas; with the resources of the Centre now available they can quickly be repopulated with birds. Supplies of eggs and table birds for local market needs have greatly increased and, in fact, for short periods supplies are embarrassingly abundant. The scheme itself is almost self-contained because all birds and eggs are sold at prices which, although reasonable, just about meet the costs of the scheme. For conditions in underdeveloped areas such as those found in Nyasaland, the encouragement and development of the poultry industry is undoubtedly one of the most effective and economical ways of contributing towards an improved diet and a higher standard of living.

Finally, mention must be made of the Cold Storage Commission in Nyasaland which recently began operations. Whatever competition in the slaughter-stock and hides and skins trade may do in other areas, where supplies are relatively more plentiful and conditions less difficult than in Nyasaland, it has been clear, for some time, that material progress could only be made in developing the industry if all the various production branches of the industry could be closely integrated under a single direction. While limited funds for capital development precluded the setting up of a public utility body such as the Meat Commission in Kenya, the presence of the Cold Storage Commission has given Nyasaland the benefits of a large scale (but non-profit making) organization with ample resources behind it to enable it to undertake various developments within the territory (including a modern abattoir and cold storage plant) which can only be to the benefit of the economy. In every branch of its work the Commission will be working in the closest co-operation with the Department but this also can only be to the mutual benefit of both.

This article has been concerned with the Nyasaland veterinary services, but it would be well to emphasise that animal health, husbandry and industry are all parts of an agricultural industry on the well being of which the people of Nyasaland almost entirely depend for their welfare and livelihood. One of the most important objects, therefore, of the Department's work is to co-operate in every possible way with the Agricultural Department in promoting more efficient agricultural methods and use of the land so as to raise general productivity and thus the standard of living.

Locusts

by B. P. UVAROV, C.M.G., D.Sc.

LOCUSTS occupy a unique position amongst agricultural pests of tropical countries, by virtue of two salient points in their biology. The first is the irregular periodicity of their visitations which, in the past has been a potent factor against continuity of anti-locust work; the second is the vast migrations of swarms, which make the problem of their control practically insoluble within a single territory. The practice of locust control in the past consisted in rapid improvisation of various measures for the defence of standing crops whenever an invasion occurred, and every territory was concerned only with saving its own crops. Local and temporary successes were frequently achieved by these means, but the locust problem continued to exist and to grow in importance. It was believed in the past, without any supporting evidence, that locusts could thrive only in undeveloped countries and that they would be ousted by advancing civilisation. It has now been recognised, however, that the reverse is more frequently true and that the locust and grasshopper problem is largely man-made. Cultivation in many cases provides conditions specially favourable for these insects, while the expansion of cultivated areas makes it more likely that wandering locust swarms will destroy valuable crops instead of wild vegetation.

During the last twenty years, great advances have been made in the study of locusts and in their control. In the present article, it is not intended to summarise this scientific progress, but rather to describe how the present knowledge is being used as the basis of a rational approach to the solution of the locust problem.

The approach can be along several lines. Firstly, it is necessary to think how the modern technique can help in the direct defence of crops against invading swarms. The basis of defence, in practically all countries, is a legal obligation on every citizen to kill locusts on his land; and the duty of administrators is to see that this is done. When the technique of locust killing consisted in beating them with branches, driving them into hastily dug trenches, burning and so on, administrators, policemen or village headmen had to exercise their imagination and energy to organise anti-locust operations by the usually unwilling population. This may have been unavoidable, but was clearly a policy of desparation. Apart from inefficiency, it involved wastage of labour on an astronomical scale.

At present, synthetic insecticides are available which are not dangerous to man and domestic animals, but kill locusts when applied in very small doses by special machinery requiring only a small number of skilled operatives, instead of vast crowds of compulsory labour. Mechanisation of anti-locust operations is making rapid progress, and it requires a thorough revision of the organisation of control. It is obviously unreasonable to expect an administrator to be an expert entomologist as well as a skilled mechanic; and it would be unfair to continue to hold him responsible for anti-locust operations in his area, when conducted by experts. Nor is there longer any sense left in the legal obligation on everybody to control locusts on their lands, since they have no adequate means of doing so. This abnormal situation has been resolved in the Union of South Africa by recent legislation making locust control a duty of the central Government, the only legal obligation on owners or users of land being to report the appearance of locusts. In the past, this duty was often evaded, since a report would automatically involve the obedient citizen in further trouble and expense; under the new system, a farmer reporting locusts can only benefit from having done so, as they will be dealt with by experts. Similar action in revising archiac anti-locust laws is long overdue in other countries and territories.

Even fully mechanised locust control cannot achieve its objective, unless it is organised on a scale determined by the infestation. In the case of a highly mobile insect like the locust it would serve little purpose if an all-out effort were made in one district, while the next one offered a safe refuge to swarms; it is not enough to kill locusts where they constitute an immediate danger to crops, and they must be sought out wherever they breed, and destroyed before they have had any chance to cause damage. In other words, defensive tactics should give way to offensive, and the campaign should be based on a single plan for the whole country. Indeed, the campaign plans, in most cases, have to be even wider and extend to several countries, since international boundaries offer no obstacle to locust swarms. The need for co-operation in anti-locust measures on an international scale is beginning to be realised, though in practice there are many obstacles to overcome, which are mostly political in character and bear little relation to locust control, apart from making it less efficient and more difficult.

Planning of anti-locust campaigns became possible only recently, as a result of many years of careful study of the seasonal movements of swarms, which made it possible to forecast developments in the situation. A fully planned campaign was carried out in the Middle East and Eastern Africa during 1941-1946, when a plague of the Desert locust threatened crops in a vast region, from India to the Sudan and Tanganyika Territory. The campaign was directed by experts, and involved the use of troops on a considerable scale, with motorised transport, radio communications and so on. It was a costly undertaking, the total expenditure being estimated at some £6 million, but the results were striking since it was the first time in history that a plague of the Desert locust, which has periodically devastated those countries since Biblical times, had passed with only minor local losses of crops. A feature of the campaign was that the major operations took place almost exclusively in the areas most remote from cultivation —in the Arabian desert, and the vast plains of Somalia and northern Kenya, for example. The principle of planned defence on distant approaches fully proved its value.

The Desert locust, against which that campaign was waged, is only one of the three different species of locusts which used to devastate tropical Africa. The African Migratory locust swarmed over the whole of West and East Africa, down to the Rhodesias and the Union of South Africa, during a period lasting from 1929 to 1939; and swarms of the Red Locust roamed over the southern half of the continent for some seventeen years, from 1928 to 1945. As the plagues of these two locusts partly coincided in time, many territories were subject to continuous visitations by swarms and the damage done by them ran into millions. In drier parts of Africa, such as Kenya and northern Tanganyika, swarms of the Desert locust were also present during the early part of the same period.

Since 1929, investigations on the locust problem have been conducted by the many Governments of African territories, and a notable practical achievement was the discovery that locust plagues, which may overrun a continent, start from small beginnings. It was definitely established that the last great invasion of the Migratory locust commenced with a few swarms which appeared in about the year 1927 in the flood plains of the river Niger, near Timbuktu, in the French Sudan; it required only five years for the plague to spread across the continent to the Anglo-Egyptian Sudan, Eritrea and Ethiopia, and further south through East Africa, the Belgian Congo and Portuguese territories. Similarly, it was found that the first swarms of the Red locust appeared at about the same time in the marshy valley of Lake Rukwa in southern Tanganyika, and in a few years their progeny spread far and wide.

This discovery made it possible to envisage an entirely new, and more radical, approach to the locust problem. It appeared that, by establishing a close watch on the areas where the first swarms can arise, an early warning of the impending trouble could be obtained, and by suppressing the original swarms, which are known to be small and not too numerous, effective prevention of a plague could be achieved. This theory has been subjected to test in the case of two locust species. The Governments subject to invasions by their swarms have agreed to establish and to maintain permanent anti-locust organisations in the " outbreak areas " of the Red and the Migratory locust. Field staffs of these international organisations are continually patrolling the outbreak areas, destroying every small concentration of locusts they can discover. The International Red Locust Control Organisation had a severe test in 1947 when some swarms, formed in the outbreak area, escaped control and spread to other parts of Tanganyika and the Belgian Ruanda-Urundi. An extensive campaign was organised and the swarms which got out of hand were completely suppressed. Thus, a threatening plague was successfully prevented and central and southern Africa saved from a long period of devastation.

A similar spectacular success of the new anti-locust policy was achieved in 1949 by the organisation set up by the French Government, with the financial support of Belgium and Great Britain, to watch the outbreak area of Migratory locust on the river Niger. After two years of favourable weather, in spring 1949 some hundreds of small concentrations of locusts were discovered and promptly exterminated. No swarms escaped, and an imminent plague of the Migratory locust was brought to a premature end.

These successes with the Red and the Migratory locust have made it possible to hope that similar preventive measures may be applied to the Desert locust. However, this is an infinitely more difficult problem, because the outbreak areas of that locust are as yet imperfectly known and they are scattered widely —on the coastal plains of the Red Sea and the Persian Gulf, in the Sahara and in the Indo-Pakistan deserts. Apart from the geographical difficulties, there are so many countries involved that it appears almost hopeless to reach a working agreement between them in order to establish a preventive service, which must be rather large if it is to be effective. Nevertheless, an attempt towards prevention of plagues of this locust has been made by the East Africa High Commission, which has established a Desert Locust Survey, based on Nairobi, whose mobile teams work in close co-operation with similar teams mounted by the Governments of Egypt, Anglo-Egyptian Sudan, Iran, Pakistan and India. This co-ordinated international effort at preventing a new Desert locust plague had hardly a chance to be properly organised before it had to face a very critical situation.

After a quiet interval of three years, when swarms were absent, in the winter of 1948-49 exceptional rains fell in the inaccessible deserts of Eastern Arabia and this favoured locust breeding. Some small swarms emerged from the desert and appeared in Aden in the summer of 1949, but soon dispersed. Other locusts, presumably from the same source, reached desert areas of Pakistan and India, where considerable swarms were formed after the 1949 monsoon breeding. By winter, these swarms had moved to Baluchistan and the coasts of the Persian Gulf, where breeding is expected to occur in the spring of 1950. On the other hand, scattered locusts from Aden have been crossing the Red Sea and are now breeding on a serious scale in British Somaliland. Anti-locust measures are being taken in the Persian Gulf area by joint mobile teams of British and Pakistan experts, with material support from Iran and India. In Somaliland energetic efforts are being made, in order not to allow the invasion to develop, by experts of the Desert Locust Survey. The Desert Locust Survey has other mobile teams watching the situation in Eritrea, Saudi Arabia, Yemen and Aden, but the areas involved are so vast and difficult that the outcome of the battle is in the balance. Should all efforts to stave off the invasion fail, the swarms can be expected to spread to Somalia, Kenya, Tanganyika and Uganda during this or next year, and agricultural production in these countries will be gravely threatened. At the other end, in Pakistan and India, serious breeding during the 1950 monsoon is a foregone conclusion and very energetic measures will be required to protect the crops.

Obviously, the present effort cannot be relaxed. Even if the new plague cannot be prevented from spreading, a continual battle against swarms breeding in desert areas will result in a reduction of the enemy forces available for the invasion of agricultural countries. The great war-time anti-locust campaigns achieved that objective, and there is no doubt that crops in Africa, the Middle East and the Indian sub-continent can be saved again. The only condition is not to be content with half-measures; the cost of full-scale anti-locust campaigns may be high, but no amount of money saved by economies in locust control, could buy enough food to replace the crops that would be eaten by the locust hordes.

Taking a long-range view, the present plague of the Desert locust may have a salutary effect. There are still many countries subject to periodical devastations by that locust, which prefer to remain " neutral " until they are actually invaded. The idea of co-operating, in their own interests, with the countries already attempting to prevent plagues still needs to be brought home to them, and a few invading swarms may have a great propaganda value.

Education in Montserrat

by T. E. RYAN, M.B.E.

RISING majestically in the sea 27 miles south-west of Antigua in the Leewards is Montserrat, 32½ square miles in area and the smallest unit of the West Indies Federation. It was discovered by Columbus and thus named from its close resemblance to a mountain in Spain where lies the monastery in which Ignatius Loyola originated the idea of founding the Society of Jesus.

Colonised in 1632 by Irish settlers from the adventurers under Sir Thomas Warner in St. Kitts, the island is often referred to as the 'Emerald Isle' or 'Shamrock in the West Indies'. So great was the Irish impact that the names of many places and people remain Irish, and the people, who are exceptionally hospitable, friendly and entertaining, still speak with a distinct Irish brogue. Volcanic in origin Montserrat is picturesque and fascinating and can hardly be surpassed in tropical beauty, vegetation and amazing scenery.

Like most of the West Indian islands, at the time of discovery Montserrat was rich in natural resources. A plantation economy which persisted until the first quarter of this century was at the core of the social and economic life of the people. With the coming of mechanised methods of agriculture, the setting up of central factories and the highly increasing competition in the markets of the world the geographical and physical conditions of Montserrat presented a formidable challenge. Sugar, then the cash crop, had to be replaced by sea island cotton which flourished and enhanced the economy of the island until its recent decline in the world's market.

Quite obviously, this created grave problems for and placed heavy responsibilities on the leaders as well as on the people generally. There was no alternative but for them "to give their brains a racking," "pull up their bootstraps" and "dip down their buckets where they were" if they were to survive and remain an honest, hardworking and progressive people. Admittedly, development involved a radical change of economic and social policy and further economic development depended then, and still largely depends, on capital assistance from outside.

Many schemes and projects, heavily financed by Colonial Development and Welfare grants and loans, provided among other things for the introduction of cash crops, soil conservation and improved methods of agriculture, animal husbandry, land settlement etc. Progress in these areas of development together with the recent establishment of an efficient tomato paste factory, the expansion of the electricity services, the provision along modern lines of adequate hotel accommodation and the lively interest which is being evinced by investors from abroad have brightened prospects for the future and quickened hopes for a better way of life.

But what has this preamble to do with education ? Irrelevant as it may appear to be, it is nonetheless inseparable from it. Education, in the period briefly reviewed above, was more academic than functional. It was not designed to meet the needs of the West Indian community nor to foster and promote a sense of good citizenship. After all, education can be a solvent of social stratification; it makes achievement rather than origin the main measure of merit. It should go hand in hand with economic development; it is best seen and understood against a social and economic background. It is the foundation upon which development superstructure can safely be made. Educated people are better able to understand, appreciate, interpret and apply plans and schemes designed for improvement.

This conception has led, within recent years, to revolutionary thinking, and consequently, to revision, reorientation and expansion of the education system. It has been realised, as never before, that every man and every woman has a right to knowledge, to an education appropriate to his or her ability and to a decent way of life in order that he or she may live fully and exercise their rights and responsibilities in a democracy by being able to judge the issues at stake in as unbiased a fashion as possible, and become worthy and useful members of the community.

It was Lincoln who said, "If we know where we are and whither we are tending, we can best plan what to do and how to do it." It might be advisable at this point to state that the administration of education in Montserrat, with its 3,500 schoolchildren in a population of 11,000, presents problems which cannot be lightly brushed aside. The acute shortage of qualified teachers and youth leaders, the inadequacy of facilities, the insufficiency of money and the like are questions for which, undoubtedly, answers must be found. They demand vision, determination and courage, a clear purpose, initiative, resourcefulness and, at times, humility. They call for an ability to work, when expedient, from within and not from above, for the art of blending the efforts of everyone concerned to produce the desired results. An approach which has proved most helpful is to operate through, and with the assistance of, the Parent-teacher associations, the Teachers' Union, the Head and Specialist-teachers conference and voluntary organisations.

Except for the efforts undertaken by the Roman Catholic and the Seventh Day Adventist Churches, formal education is Government controlled. Full responsibility for education was assumed by the Government in 1945 when the schools were taken over from the churches.

The education policy, in the main, is directed towards:-

(a) providing a general education in the basic subjects for all children as well as school places sufficient to accommodate them. Many schools are housed in buildings rented from the church authorities. These buildings, designed years ago, are one-roomed, inadequate in space and other amenities, and not easily adaptable to the modern approach to teaching. There is, however, a government building scheme and, although it is being implemented very gradually, the buildings already finished provide classrooms and facilities convenient for and conducive to effective teaching;

(b) making facilities available for practical courses in wood and metal work, handicraft, housecraft, needlework and rural science;

(c) more secondary education and an increasing number of scholarships;

(d) establishment of modern secondary schools in which, among other subjects, commercial courses will be taught;

(e) increasing school libraries;

(f) promotion of extra-curricular activities such as inter-school visits and educational tours, games and sports competition, school clubs and Savings Unions;

(g) training of teachers;

(h) youth work and adult education.

Elementary education is free for all children between the ages of five and 15 years. So great is the urge and the desire for education that it has not been necessary, within the past 30 years or so, to enforce the compulsory education law. The schools are co-educational and equal opportunites are made available to boys and girls. Approximately 98 per cent of the children of school age are enrolled in the schools and the daily average attandance over a long period of years has been in the region of 89 to 92 per cent.

Children walk to school. During the mid-morning recess they are given, free of charge, a snack consisting of a glass of milk and yeast biscuits. They have to make their own arrangements for lunch and those who are unable to return home, due to distance, take it with them to school.

In youth work the fullest co-operation between voluntary organisations and the Education Department has been found essential to any plan for improvement. Basically, the aim is to stimulate, guide and help young people, through leisure time interests and purposeful activities to acquire and strengthen those attributes which are so vital to a good, useful and worthy life and, at the same time, eliminate the tendency to undesirable habits. In accordance with the needs and social development of young people, the programmes permit the greatest possible variety, flexibility and informality.

As regards adult education, experience has proved that success depends largely on a survey of the needs and aspirations of the people. It must grow out of their instincts and interests. Seeking their views prior to making decisions has been most valuable, the result of which has been reflected in the co-operative spirit, the helpful and constructive approach which spells progress.

Courses in adult education are not necessarily arranged for examination purposes but with a view to improving the material well-being of the people, to quicken interests and widen experience, to create an attitude of mind which influences the way men think, to strengthen family relations and to make life and work meaningful. Drama, music, open forums and discussions, lectures, debates, radio talks and practical work are valuable features of the programme.

The publication of a quarterly bulletin, the education half-hour broadcast over Radio Montserrat every Wednesday evening and the mobile cinema are channels which contribute in no small measure to the success of the work.

Education Officer in Sierra Leone

by C. L. HOLDEN

I am not sure of the exact strength of the members of the Overseas Service who are employed in the Education Services of the various Colonies. It must be fairly large. But I am sure that most of those who joined the Service had little idea of what it would really be like. Of course I dare say most of us read beforehand the literature available, recent annual reports of the Colony concerned and so on; but the reality, I found, was different; at least, it was in my own Colony, Sierra Leone.

The main reason was variety—not only of people but of work. It was not only that work might be new educationally—Classics men doing methods of infant teaching, for example—but some of it was right outside the newcomer's interpretation of 'educational', as when one finds oneself an administrator at headquarters in charge of finance.

This sounds dignified, and the amount of money, on paper, that one has to account for, is rather terrifying. The job falls into several sections. There are the yearly budgets from each school, institution and office to get in in time, to be reduced to reasonable proportions, and submitted to the Director. The subsequent battles with the financial authorities are interesting because they give one an insight into policy—an insight sometimes denied to other educational officers.

Then there is the wearing job of dealing with matters of salaries and allowances: it is really extraordinary how almost every officer has occasion to query the Department about his salary, or deductions for rent or for car allowances or something of that kind! These queries are sometimes made none too politely, and the administrator at headquarters gets good training in the development of tact and the answer that turneth away wrath.

Such an officer, of course, seldom travels, does not see schools, and may find a ready answer to the complaints of others in reminding them of his own banishment from 'pure' education—he longs, he says, to be in the classroom; he would delight in cramming pupils for the School Certificate, or to be in the field.

However, this administrative job is not without excitement; financial crises do occur; major ones to do with the country's development, and minor ones when someone over-spends or mixes up his allocations. And it's not unpleasant to talk about hundreds of thousands—but beware of the temptation to tell the man at the other end of the 'phone that he'll have to manage with ten thousand, and not twenty—and then bang down your receiver.

Another job away from the classroom—though nearer to it—is that of the District or Provincial Education Officer, whose work is mainly inspectorial. He goes from one village school to another, rarely able to spend as much time as he would like at each, but he does get to know *people*—villagers, the headmen, and Chiefs. He has battles with the weather and the roads; he has frequently the pleasure of opening new schools; he has also intimate contact with the various missionary authorities who do so much for education in Sierra Leone. It is a good job, for it gives him the chance to become known and respected as a person in authority, and he is in a better position to gather experience than many others. He acquires, too, a pride (if not the reality) in feeling that his area is the most alert educationally.

Variety and activity fill the Provincial and District Education Officer's life. There is also comedy. He frequently has to teach the teachers themselves how to spell, or to persuade headmasters that work on a farm is not really what is meant by nature study. Sometimes he must explain that a boy who is 14 one year can hardly become 11 the next, just because the Department has made an alteration in age grouping.

Domestically, life is sometimes a little restricted, for his station will be small, electricity may be intermittent, supplies of European food not always regular, but this is so much a part of the pattern of life up country and so readily accepted, that although it may be grumbled against, it is not a serious complaint. Social life on these small stations can be most intimate and friendly, and one has direct access to the local heads of the other departments—police, law, medical and public works— and there are always people visiting from the capital and central Government.

Your appointment as an Education Officer may bring you to a Teacher's Training College, of which there are several in Sierra Leone. They are concerned with the training of primary school teachers, and inevitably, perhaps, the standards of the colleges are lower than their title would suggest to an outsider, but very important work is being done there, and even more remains to be done. The colleges are residential, and are rather isolated, but there is the feeling of belonging to a place of great opportunity. Many of your colleagues will be African, and the physical isolation of the place plus the comparative length of one's stay roots one in the country—you feel you are really with Africa here.

You may feel the isolation at first, and you should take all your own books and records, but there are many compensations: fresh vegetables and meat from a college farm; excellent chances to learn about the local flora and fauna; village crafts and village customs to be studied, the local languages to be discovered and learnt.

Most of my time recently has been spent in a secondary school in Freetown. I suppose in many ways it is identical with secondary school life in England. We have our school certificate examinations at ordinary and advanced levels. Our Sixth form work is flourishing. We have specialist teachers. We have games, hobbies, and much inter-school rivalry. Being in the capital there are all sorts of modern facilities. We are a world apart in our school, and yet at the centre of things. Our boys broadcast over the national radio; they write plays for it. They take part in the local theatrical productions. They write short stories for the local papers—all this, of course, under encouragement, and it is our privilege to provide this encouragement. It all makes for a full life.

My own work now is the teaching of English to the Sixth Form Arts and Science sides, and to the Fifth forms. I spend a great deal of time on examinations, not only the school terminal ones and the two public ones for School Certificate and Higher School, but in the school holidays—a misleading term to the would-be Educational Officer, for we are still then employed. I also take part in the national Common Entrance examination to Secondary schools. Our numbers, of course, are microscopic compared with England, but last year we had over 5,000 pupils taking one examination. I did not mark all their papers, but the statistical analysis and professional report was quite a labour, though it was one I enjoyed.

One of the modern things that has struck Sierra Leone is the Quiz, either on the radio or in a public place. This is not really a thing I liked at first, but I have done it so often now I would be at a loss without it, and I find preparing the quizzes improves at least my own general knowledge. Most satisfying is, however, the purely professional work in teaching English to African boys. To the newcomer the standard at first seems low, but against that impression one has to set the fact that our best boys do get, like the best boys in English schools, to universities, and do well there. Probably the major part of my time and effort is given to the best boys, but I am equally concerned with the average boy. Here I can only record a problem, and not its solution. The initial difficulty is the physical absence of books, magazines, and newspapers from the lives of the boys. The second difficulty is the home background of many boys who either come from impoverished village homes or equally impoverished town homes. A third factor is the mental turmoil caused by growing political self-consciousness, and a fourth is the tremendous wish of the boys to get to the top at once without climbing any of the rungs of the ladder. The professional problem basically is to explain the meanings of words when the words are lacking, and to clarify meanings when analogies are not there. It is made the more intriguing by the survival in Sierra Leone, or at least among the English-educated Africans in Sierra Leone, of a Victorian woolliness of expression as the model of good English; and it is perplexed by the persistence and indeed rapid growth of an English patois which is their home tongue, not without its own charm, but not acceptable to the English teacher or examiner.

Yes, as an Education Officer in Sierra Leone you may be called on to do many different jobs, all good and useful, and not merely interesting but exciting, too.

Lessons from Mass Education in the Gold Coast

by PETER DU SAUTOY

MASS education deals with simple things and simple people, but it has never been simple to define. To begin with it has many titles, such as fundamental education, social development or community development. It is interesting, however, to note that in the Gold Coast, a country which has been one of the pioneers in mass education in its modern sense, "mass education" has now become a vernacular word, and it would be impossible to use any other title for it in the rural areas which it is primarily designed to serve. This is important. Mass education has a predominantly rural bias. It is aimed at the villager rather than the townsman, although certain mass education techniques are of very great value to the social worker in the towns. It aims at acting as an extension service for all types of education in improved living conditions in the rural areas; it seeks to show the villager how, by his own efforts, and with the small resources at his disposal, he can live under better material conditions and can also be a better citizen. All means of inducing people who are living in primitive conditions to improve themselves fall within the scope of mass education. The teaching of literacy is only one of the uses of mass education, but it is an important one. Not only can one get new ideas across to people who can read and write, but also the fact that they have found reading and writing to be not nearly so difficult as they had imagined increases their self respect and stimulates them to further improvement in other spheres. Mass education must be practical and it must be closely linked to the life and thought of the people. They must be led step by step, and induced to see both their own needs and how they can meet them by their own efforts without lavish expenditure of money. For instance, the mass education worker must not only be able to show villagers the need for an improved type of latrine, he must also be able to show them how this can be constructed. He must not only be able to deliver a stimulating address, he must also be able to show on the spot what can actually be done to improve conditions. An adult is not like a child, who can be compelled to attend classes by his parents. He must actually see that he is making progress, and that he achieves some concrete result from the time he has spent. Otherwise he will no longer continue. From this arises some of the apparent flamboyance and superficiality of the mass education technique—the apparent rapidity of the results, the presentation of badges, medals and certificates, the singing of mass education songs and the dancing, the bands and the cinema shows. But although instruction must be made attractive and speedy results must always be shown, it is in the continuing improvement by the villagers that the worth of the mass education worker is really tested, and, beneath all the flamboyance, there must always be a solid foundation of advance preparation and hard painstaking work to sustain, as well as to stimulate, interest.

It has often been said that mass education is not new. Many government officers from all the various government services have devoted much of their time to village extension work. But it is the first time that there has been a separate service with special techniques and specially trained staff to put across new ideas on rural welfare. Other departments are concerned only with certain aspects: the mass education service is concerned with all aspects of rural welfare.

Much attention is paid in the Gold Coast to voluntary service. The mass education staff is there to stimulate, to give technical advice, to show the way, and to organise, but it cannot do everything itself. There is not the personnel, nor the money. Therefore, it is essential to enlist the full support of the village notables, the village teachers, storekeepers and clerks, and, above all, the women. It has been said that if one educates a woman one educates a family, and it is in the family that most progress can be made in improving material and spiritual conditions. In the Gold Coast it is the voluntary leaders, organised and trained by the Department of Social Welfare and Community Development, who do the actual instruction in mass literacy, and who lead the work on simple village construction projects. They are unpaid, but their work is recognised by the award of special badges and certificates at imposing public ceremonies. Mass education is useless without the co-operation of the people—it must not impose ideas from above, but it must bring them up from below. If the people prefer a latrine to a water supply, and both are needed, the people's wishes should be observed.

It is desirable that mass education should be regarded as a new and national service, which all can support, even though it owes much to the work of past officials. It can thus be untainted with any criticism which may have been levelled, justly or unjustly, against all the other older established branches of the Government. The staff can be drawn from other services; indeed, it is desirable that they should be. They should be mature people of experience and enthusiasm, but with a hard head in addition to a soft heart. They should be good at collaborating with other officials, at talking man to man and woman to woman with adults in a style which village people can understand. They must live among the people and know them and their problems. They should never discourage, but they should guide misdirected enthusiasm tactfully into useful channels. It has been found in the Gold Coast in recruiting staff that an aptitude for formal education or training as a school teacher is not enough. Special training is needed for persons in mass education and much early training has to be forgotten, but any person of mature or sympathetic outlook, able and ready to improvise, can pick up the technique easily enough.

In the same way as special training for staff is needed, a special service is also required. Mass education finds formal education an uneasy bedfellow; and while it can be of the greatest value to the District Officer in assisting him with the social improvement of his district, if it is officially attached to the Administration there is not only the danger of its becoming involved in politics, and thus possibly losing the unanimous support of the people, but also of its not getting the full attention it needs. In the Gold Coast the mass education service, when it first started in 1948, was made a part of the Department of Social Welfare (which itself was a very young department) under the Ministry of Education and Social Welfare. Mass education *is* social welfare in its broadest sense. It fits into such a department perfectly. The problems of the towns with detribalised and mixed societies need special handling, more on the lines of welfare work in Europe, but in the countryside mass education provides the real social welfare. The identity of the two has been recognised in the Gold Coast, where mass education is a part of the welfare service, and in the Colonial Office, where mass education is dealt with by the Social Development section.

As so much depends in mass education on the new and unexpected, its budget should be flexible. The staff must be adequate and well paid. Without a contented staff it is hard to inspire others. Sufficient funds must be provided for proper equipment, but mass education is not expensive, since it depends so much on self help. It should have its own direction and be permitted to experiment. It must also have the wholehearted support of the other departments of Government. A certain suspicion on the part of other specialised departments of the educational efforts of the "amateur" intruding in their special field is inevitable at first, but when the mass education service has proved its value by results it will be found that the request for extension services from other departments may actually be more than the mass education service can cope with. This must never be forgotten: the mass education service is there not only to initiate improvement schemes on its own, but to put across to village people ideas for improvement by special techniques which the professional agriculturalist, veterinary officer or doctor can never be expected to learn.

Mass education is complementary to local government and, in the end, may well be conducted by the local authorities. At the moment, however, it is dealing with a much smaller unit, that of the village, and by instilling a sense of citizenship at the village level will persuade people to think in terms of the larger local government unit. Mass education must work closely with the established local government authority where it exists. It must at no time appear to be a rival supported by the vast weight of the central government prestige and funds. By close collaboration on the part of the mass education staff with local authorities in time the influence of mass education will rise from the level of the village unit to the higher level of the local authority unit.

As has been said above, the success of mass education will be judged on its continuance. There is, however, always a grave danger that too much will depend on the personality of one man and that when he is removed the work will collapse. The only way to prevent this is to build up an efficient decentralised organisation that will carry on when individuals depart. Continuous attention must be paid to staff training to provide the leading officials of the organisation of the future and to provide a base of capable trained staff at the lowest level. At the same time the training must be practical and must never allow the officer to forget that he must deal with villagers on their own level. Care must be taken to move gradually and not to overload the organisation from the beginning. In the Gold Coast the country is divided into seven mass education regions based on language and tribal groupings and there are four Rural Training Centres for training staff and voluntary leaders. Considerable latitude is given to the regional officers of the department in view of the need for different techniques and for tackling different problems in different parts of the country. Within each region a hierarchy of staff has been built up, with each man knowing his area and sphere of influence, and with mobile teams for special work, such as work among women. There are periodical conferences of senior staff at headquarters to plan for the future and to ensure as much uniformity as is possible between the regions. Administration has been centralised and standardised at the same time as the professional work has been decentralised, in an endeavour to assist the regional officers in their inevitable administrative functions and to give them more time for their field work. However unorthodox and informal a service, discipline and organisation are essential if it is to last; a sound mass education service, which may start with the inspired efforts of a few individuals, cannot be built up without it. Individuals may depart but the policy and the service will continue.

These are some of the lessons learnt in the Gold Coast, and they may be of value elsewhere. For those wanting further information about mass education in the Gold Coast, the Department of Social Welfare and Community Development, P.O. Box 778, Accra, Gold Coast, will always be willing to supply it.

Community Development in Udi

(Contributed from Nigeria)

II

W HAT might be called Community Development proper, as opposed in any way to Mass Education, started something like this. The people of Ogwofia decided to raise a village fund and they announced this to Major E. E. G. Haig, the Registrar of Co-operative Societies, on one of his visits. He suggested that they should decide to work their palm bush on a co-operative basis. They could not do that as some of the trees belonged to individuals, but they thought that some communally owned machines for processing the fruit would be a good idea and the profits from them might go into the village fund. They were helped to obtain a hand oil-press and a nut-cracking machine, for the use of which all comers paid one penny—a halfpenny to the labourers who worked them and a halfpenny to the village fund. After this a Co-operative Consumers' Shop was suggested and at once volunteers set to work to collect stones and other building materials. They themselves paid for the cement and for the services of the Native Administration bricklayer and carpenter. The District Officer was able to provide the corrugated iron at half-price, so the total cost was £38, plus voluntary labour, to build the first Co-operative Consumers' Shop in Nigeria.

At the same time the village had decided to build a Reading Room, and as at that time there was a Government fund for such work a grant of £80 was made to cover the cost of materials. The women then thought they would like their own Maternity Home. They were told there was nothing they could not have if they were ready to work to build it and provide the funds to run it, so they said they also wanted a Dispensary. Now the cost of a Dispensary would have been about £300 and the cost of a Dispensary Attendant would have been about £100 but the Native Administration just did not have that amount of money. So the people suggested they might have a room in which medicines and things could be stored, then the Dispenser from Udi (eight miles away) could cycle down to them at regular intervals. This was contrary to existing official practice, but, when put to the Senior Medical Officer in Enugu, it was approved the very next day. Cement, sawn timber and shingles for roofing were sent to the village and a Sub-Dispensary was finished by the end of the month.

Work then started on a Maternity Home, but this took several months to build and taxed the resources of the village heavily. It cost them £160 in the end. On this occasion the adult women agreed to a tax of half-a-crown which became the membership fee for the Maternity Unit, as it is now officially called, and the Co-operative Shop paid over its profits, about £65, towards the cost of the building. From Native Administration funds came the cost of the corrugated iron for the roof and the cement for the building. Later, with a little more assistance from Native Administration funds for cement, a 3,000 gallon water tank was added.

These were the beginnings of Community Development. Model latrines, and an incinerator, houses for chickens and an attempt to improve the local breed of fowls were all completed. The Women's Co-operative bought a sewing machine and citrus trees were planted at the village centre. Elders from other villages were encouraged to visit Ogwofia but it was not until 1945 that they started to copy it, yet by 1947 well over thirty communities in the Division had started their own plans for village development. At Mbabu, for instance, in a space of twelve months, they built a motor road ten miles long, bridging two rivers. The material for the bridges, each of three spans, was provided by the Native Administration, but all the work on road and bridges was done voluntarily. They have completed a Maternity Unit and started a Reading Room, and asked for permission to build

1. A young Nigerian woman.

2. LEFT. A Fulani milk maid.

3. BELOW. A Northern Rhodesian chief and his wife.

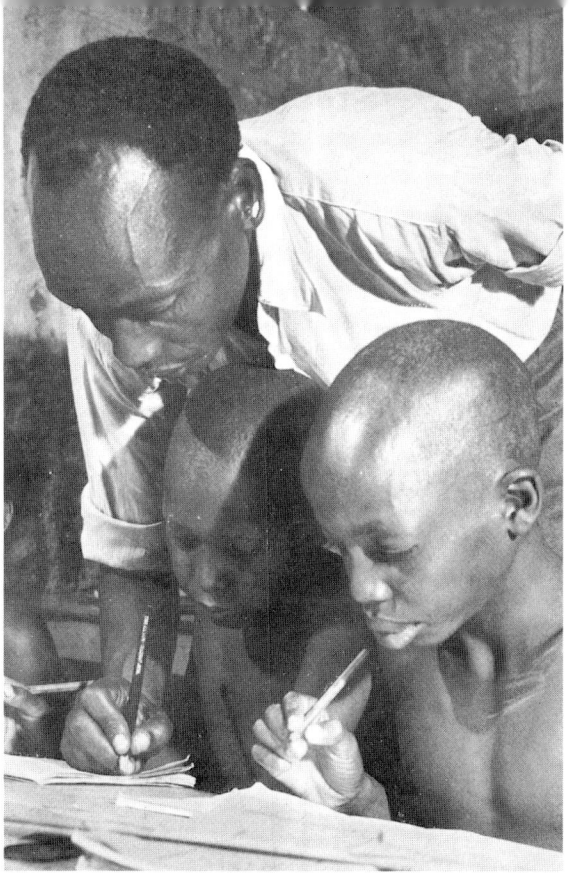

4. Attentive pupils and their teacher in Kenya

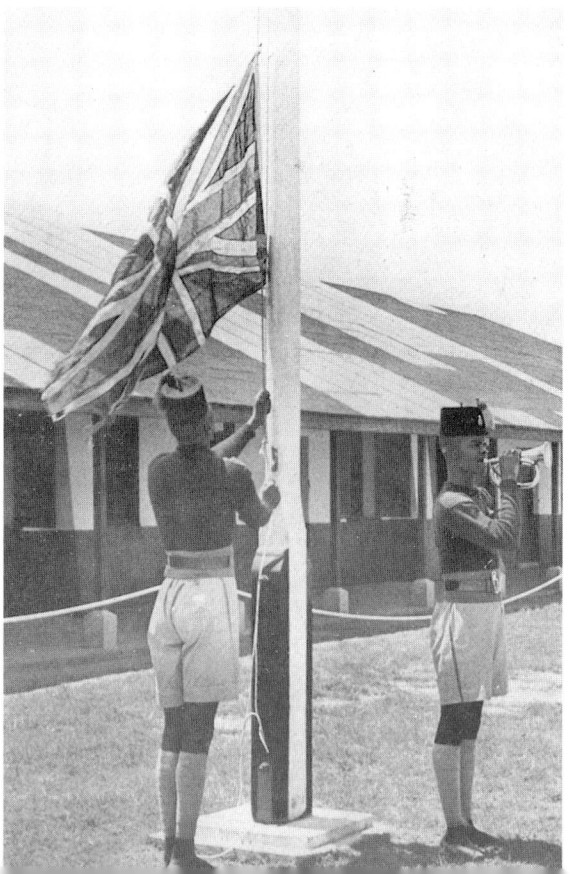

5. Sunset: a Colonial tradition

6. LEFT. A Kenyan warrior.

7. BELOW. Time for coffee in Zanzibar.

8. ABOVE. Funeral ceremony in Nyasaland.

9. RIGHT. Picking tea in Mauritius.

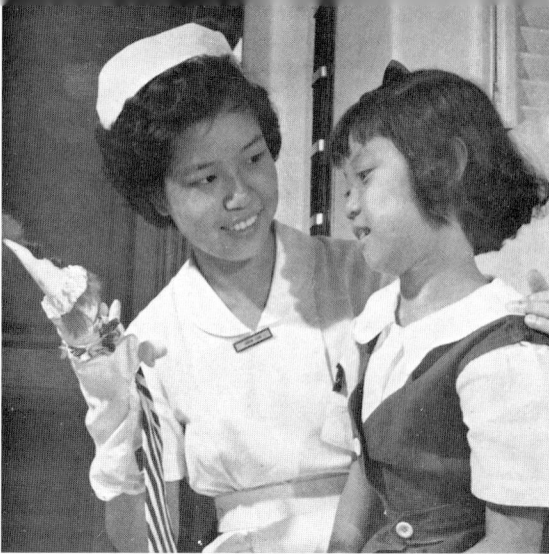

10. 'Honestly, it won't hurt'.

11. Hong Kong street scene.

12. Market scene, Malaya.

13. A mosque in Malaya.

14. Building a house in Fiji.

15. In a Sarawak longhouse.

16. Portrait of a woman, North Borneo.

a Co-operative Shop as well as for the services of a surveyor to help them with the layout of a cleared space, where they intend to rebuild the village.

Community Development does not follow a set pattern. The people themselves decide what they want, when they will start, and their choice is governed by the relative urgencies of the things they need. For instance at Alfa there was a very meagre water supply, which meant that some people had to stay up all night to catch the thin trickle of water in the dry season. The first thing the village did was to build a cement catchment with a pipe to run off the water into a tank so as to avoid waste. Then the Nkanu people decided to build a village for their lepers. It was designed for 120 people but it was filled within a year and in eighteen months several additions were made, such as a village hall and a four-bed hospital. The cost of materials for the former was provided in part from the Public Relations Department and the Native Administration. At Ugbawaka the people started off first with a new market, with proper stalls rightly spaced out. The only rule in guiding a community in its development plans is: what do they want most? If they want it sufficiently to do the work voluntarily and provide the greater part of the cost, then they are encouraged to go ahead.

The most noticeable effect is that now the District Officer is, for the first time in the history of the Division, able to attend quite large meetings of women. They come as calm gatherings and not as agitators or hysterical mobs pushed forward by male malcontents. The experiment has not created a community spirit: that was there all the time. It has, however, called forth that spirit and created a sense of civic pride. Ogwofia, for example, has for itself invented three songs about its achievements and a flag, half blue and half white, with an arrow going from the " darkness " to the " light."

Unlike Missionary activities Mass Literacy and Community Development do not divide a village community, for of themselves they are bound to introduce a new social activity and bring together the people of the whole village of all ages and sexes. But, more than that, the villages which are engaged on such campaigns are more contented internally and do not have the time for picking quarrels about land, for example. Moreover they have a greater confidence in Government. They infer from the help they are receiving from the Administrative and other Officers on the spot that Government is " trying "—that is, that Government really does want to help. Generally speaking the Ibo is not unreasonable in his demands on Government and if assistance is given he greatly appreciates it, even if he fails to get exactly what it is he wants.

There is one theory about Mass Education which maintains that once the people are able to read and write they will at once undertake to improve their own conditions. While on leave Mr. Chadwick sought information at the Colonial Department of the Institute of Education of London University about other experiments, but he was unable to find a single one in which there had been an improvement in the standards of living of a people as an automatic result of Mass Literacy schemes being introduced.

Considering the extent to which the work at Udi had grown out of the Mass Literacy campaign, Mr. Chadwick found that such campaigns had the effect of giving villages a new social activity, which brought together the people of all ages and both sexes and of widely different religions and views; but although it had assisted, Mass Literacy had nevertheless not been the cause of Community Development. This has grown naturally out of the labours of Administrative Officers, who had the assistance of a few Departmental Officers and a few Missionaries—it has been grafted on to, but was not a function, of Native Administration: it was a logical extension of the Administration.

But Mass Literacy was important. It had the result of removing the feeling of inferiority felt by the illiterate towards the intelligentsia—the newly literate acquired a greater self-confidence and an enhanced self-respect. Once a campaign was well under way the people generally realised that, if they were prepared to make the effort, it was within the ability of everyone of them to become literate: there was no insoluble mystery about literacy, even to the " bushman." In gaining this new confidence a community set to work with a greater will to do for itself what it saw or heard had been done elsewhere. Centrally provided amenities are all very well, but it is the village-built and owned amenity which creates a proper pride in the ability and achievement of the community.

One aspect of the work of Administration is to promote the growth of social services. With the funds at its disposal the Government can only do this at the Provincial or Divisional level. The Native Administrations can do this only at the Divisional—or, at most, a Clan level. For example, the Abaja Clan could maintain only two Dispensaries for 150,000 people living in an area of approximately 1,000 square miles. But Mass Education on the Udi model brings such amenities right within the village fence. In a report on a recent visit to Nigeria Miss M. Green admitted the need for large scale developments, which would take years to build up and need much money from outside sources, but she went on to make an urgent plea for something more " homely " (her own word) to be undertaken at once. Udi is doing just that.

Another important point is that the restrictions and controls which apply to Native Administration funds do not apply to village funds raised by the people voluntarily. Consequently village developments based on such funds are more fluid than normal development work. The people can choose to have what they want when they want it, and as fast as they care to work for it. That means they get quick results, and quick results are what the primitive villager likes to see. Decisions to start a project can be taken one day and it can be started on the next without reference to any authority other than public opinion in the village, so Community Development (as Mr. Chadwick prefers to call the Udi type of Mass Education) not only brings Administration right inside the family circle, it makes administration and development intensely " alive," affecting everyone in the village as no form of centralised administration ever can. This running of their own development plan is most attractive to villagers and it is not necessary to base it on any form of Mass Education or Mass Literacy: in fact there are some villages in Udi Division which started their own development plans without the introduction of any official campaign.

It is because Community Development does on a " homely " scale what Government is trying to do on a Provincial scale that Mr. Chadwick has called work on the Udi model an extension of the Administration. So much has been achieved without any special " development teams " or " ten year plans," and at no cost to Government—though certain small grants, mostly from Native Administration funds, have been made for the supply of materials such as cement and corrugated iron sheets for buildings, things which the people could not have obtained for themselves. The basis of the whole scheme—the *sine qua non*—is sound administration, which has its roots in the work of Administrative Officers over a period of many years and that is why, perhaps, it is necessary for it to be done by Administrative Officers now, rather than by any technical Department—even that of Education.

Finally, Udi seems to show that Mass Literacy by itself, no matter how well supported by text books or other expensive items, will not give rise to Community Development. Primitive people learn by observation and experience and not from mere statements, however learned, whether written or oral. On the other hand Mass Literacy, whether it precedes or follows, does help in Community Development as it gives the people self-confidence that their communities can improve their standards of living by co-operative effort.

But there is also one other most important point: there must be leadership, and that leadership should preferably come from the District Officer in charge of the Division. To be successful in this he must first of all win the confidence of the people—personality and personal contact are most important, and it is necessary to remember that this sort of confidence does not come from a mere reputation for impartiality or fairness, or mere approachability. The District Officer must himself first of all make the approach to his people, and in this connection it is sound technique to find out what the community most desires and get them to build it before putting to them ideas for more important schemes. Once their pet scheme has been granted, the people will more readily think their District Officer is out to help them in providing things for their well-being, and to confirm this view it is necessary for him to co-ordinate all the forces at his command—particularly those of the local intelligentsia and the Tribal Unions.

Community Development in Kenya

by TOM ASKWITH

THERE has in the past been all too little understanding of the work of the Social Welfare Organisation in Kenya. This may be largely due to the very title itself. To those who served with the armed forces in the last war, it conjured up visions of recreation rooms and football matches, beer canteens and concerts. To those who have been connected with factories and large estates a similar interpretation would be called to mind. These people, and rightly so, questioned how such enjoyments could be provided for the millions inhabiting the African areas and what justification there was for an organisation to be formed for the purpose.

But the functions of the organisation, and of the Community Development Officers (serving under the District Commissioners) who until recently were known as District Welfare Officers, are very different indeed. It is true that they administer community centres which have been built largely from the funds contributed by the local community, where games are played and concerts and dances organised; but at the same time these centres are nuclei for the dissemination of information regarding the development and government of this country of Kenya and of the dim world beyond; they are at the same time bases for the African Welfare Workers paid by the African District Councillors.

But it is the work that goes on outside the centres which is the justification for the building up of an organisation which now consists of nine Community Development Officers and some fifty African Welfare Workers.

These Officers are members of the Provincial Administration and under the immediate control of District Commissioners. They are at the same time members of the District Teams, those co-ordinating bodies of officials and unofficials who plan the development programmes of the areas concerned. Their principle task is to act as liaison or public relations officers for the teams and as "follow-up" men once schemes have been put into operation. Some examples of how it works may help to illustrate the chain of events. The examples are actual projects which have taken place in recent months. Particulars of some have already been published.

There was the tree-planting campaign in Muputi in Machakos District, initiated to try to restore the country to some of its erstwhile luxuriance. The District Team put the Community Development Officer in charge of the education of the people regarding the value of windbreaks and plantations to retain the moisture in the soil and reduce the dessicating power of the wind. The inhabitants were suspicious and conservative, they attributed the increasing desert conditions to reduced rainfall and thought that mere man could not put things right. After a campaign in which modern educational methods such as the cinema, news sheet and poster, and the ancient ones of discussion and teaching were used incessantly, the people were won round. On the appointed day, with almost a religious fervour, they embarked on their vast voluntary effort to plant half a million trees. Nature, in symbolic fashion, encouraged their enterprise by sending rain that night.

Again, there was the stock improvement campaign in Kajulu, a small location near Kisumu. The number of inferior beasts to be found in this location is remarkable, and the grazing is poor and limited. The people again saw little point in castrating their bulls and bull calves; when the District Commissioner first announced the District Team's proposals, they were in fact actively opposed. The Community Development Officer was, as in Machakos, given the job of changing their attitude. He had a week in which to do it and he brought in the cinema van, the public address equipment, the wireless set, the news sheet, posters, pamphlets and his own personality. At the end of that time the District Commissioner decided to send out his teams of workers under the Agricultural Officer, the Veterinary Officer, and the District Officer, and see what happened.

On the first day they were almost inundated with stock owners driving in their bulls for castration. They dealt with 150 in the day and by the end of the campaign 644 had been castrated.

Other examples could be quoted where the people have been persuaded to cut firebreaks to protect forests, to build community centres and schools, and carry out other communal and voluntary works, but these will suffice.

On the other hand, many instances will be called to mind where eminently worthwhile schemes have been brought to naught by a lack of appreciation of their desirability by the people concerned. Would these have been successful if a campaign from the human aspect had been conducted in the first place?

Apart from the work in connection with special projects the Community Development Officer has a full life. He must be constantly on *safari* in his district, getting to know the people, their language and customs, their problems and needs. He is not liable to transfer from district to district, and so is in a favourable position to do this.

Among his other activities is that which is concerned with youth, possibly the most problematic section of the community in some areas. The difficulty lies with the young man, often little more than a boy, who leaves the primary school and goes to seek clerical employment in the towns. Apart from manual work, which he is disinclined to accept, this is all he is qualified for. In the vast majority of cases he is unsuccessful in his search as the number of vacancies is few. He then resorts to drifting round the towns, living with friends, often getting into debt, sometimes resorting to crime, eventually driven to return home penniless, disgruntled and embittered; unable to understand that the little education he has received will not qualify him for a well paid job; unable to realise that he can be of more value in living among his own people and improving methods of cultivation or starting at the bottom in a more humble form of employment and working his way up.

To assist this type of youth in finding his feet and turn him into a useful member of society, the Community Development Officer in Fort Hall, where the problem appears perhaps in its most acute form, is planning Youth Camps on the lines of the Duke of York's Camps in England and the Y.M.C.A. camps during the years of depression. He has managed to persuade groups of these young men to give their labour voluntarily in the reafforestation of bare hillsides and in building community centres, and is now planning to build workshops where they can learn a trade.

Sport is another outlet, the value of which is sometimes insufficiently appreciated, except by those who have had experience of its value. It must be remembered that before the advent of the European the place of the youth in society was assured. Having graduated in the initiation ceremonies, he automatically entered the warrior age-grade. He had a purpose in life, his task was the protection of the home and the seizing of cattle from neighbouring tribes to swell the clan's herds. He had to keep himself physically fit for this purpose and he was an object of admiration when he returned home from a successful foray; when he was unsuccessful he often died in battle. The only substitute he now has is a somewhat uninspiring journey in search of employment with, if he is fortunate, a return home with sufficient money to give presents to parents and friends, and to dress himself in finery. There is, however, an opening for the footballer or the athlete to become a hero, and for this reason, and in order to develop the manly virtues, competitions of various kinds are fostered in all districts. We find that the Nyanza tribes excel at football and also show great enthusiasm for canoe racing; the pastoralists excel at athletics, those in Central

Province, though not so athletically inclined, are becoming keener on sport year by year, and many have reached the front rank.

Other organisations such as the Boy Scouts are given every encouragement and there can be few movements which have a greater appeal among Africans or a greater value.   Most Community Development Officers take an active interest and some are Area Commissioners.

One of the principal duties of Community Development Officers, however, is that of District Information Officer.   It is probable that in the near future each of them will be provided with his own travelling cinema unit ; at present there are only sufficient units for them to work on a Provincial basis, which means that they can have little educational value, owing to the short time for which they can be made available in any one area.   All community centres, however, have their own film-strip projectors even now, and it is the centre which is used as the principal focus of information ; its library, newspapers, posters, charts and the like make it possible to teach those who are willing to learn something more of their country, its problems and the steps being taken to solve them.   But this is not enough and Jeanes School, the centre for Community Development in the Colony, has to make its contribution.   In a recent article in *Corona* I described some of the work now being done at the School and need only recapitulate briefly here.

Apart from students on long courses, a number of adults such as Chiefs, African District Councillors, Welfare Workers, male and female, Probation Assistants and the like attend short courses.   They are taught how to carry out their various jobs, but at the same time are given a concentrated series of lectures on matters concerning the Colony which every citizen should know if he is to be a loyal and useful member of society.   The methods employed are similar to those adopted at Ashridge in England.   The subjects include the history of Kenya from slavery and barbarism to its present stage of economic and social development ;   the history of the growth of our economic system from that of subsistence to one of industry ;   the methods of taxation adopted by Central and Local Government, showing how the wealthier individuals help to finance the services of the poorer sections ;   the importance of the family and home ;   the form of government that has grown up in the Colony and how it works ;   basic principles of agriculture, veterinary science and hygiene ;   and many other subjects such as co-operative societies, the probation system and the like.   To supplement the lectures, instruction is given through films and visits to places of importance around Nairobi, such as factories, trade schools, farms and public institutions.

To enable those attending these courses to pass on what they have learned, however, they are all provided with copies of the lectures given, and if present plans go through, they will shortly be published.   They will then be available for much wider distribution in Teacher Training and other departmental schools. They will also be available for District Courses organised at schools in the holidays for leading Africans in the area, though such courses will naturally have a more local bias.   In this way, it is hoped to extend the scope of Fundamental Education with, it is hoped, a better appreciation among responsible Africans of Government's achievements and plans for the future.   In this way it is hoped to engender a spirit of co-operation, to enable greater strides to be taken in future, unhindered by the detractions of ill wishers and disgruntled malcontents.   Knowledge is an essential ingredient of the useful citizen and Africans are thirsting to acquire it and thus understand the meaning of this strange modern world.

Before concluding, a word must be said of that most important aspect of Community Development which is concerned with the training of women.   No general improvement in the standards of the ordinary African home, of the upbringing of the children to become decent citizens, of the methods of agriculture, and so on, can be achieved unless the mothers are given appropriate training.

Africans in Kenya are, perhaps not unnaturally, unconvinced of the value of normal education for girls, but they are in no two minds regarding that of practical domestic training. Jeanes School is starting such courses, which have for long been given to the wives of those attending the school; other centres at Kericho and Kisumu will follow suit. Centres in the African areas already exist but will be expanded and staff engaged to supervise them. In this way it is hoped to achieve a general improvement in the standard of living in the course of time.

The training of women up to the present time has been principally in connection with village crafts. This will not be abandoned, though it will take its proper place in the general domestic training scheme. At the same time the Rural Industries Officer, who is a member of the Social Welfare Organisation, will continue to develop rural crafts, to preserve those that are tending to die out and to foster others which can be of economic value to African craftsmen. A very considerable secondary industry is growing up in the production of carvings, soapstone ware, basket and leather-work, and we may look to a considerable expansion in the future.

Community Development is becoming an important part of the machinery of government. Its preoccupation is with the individual; its task the solution of the human problem. As the technical departments deal with the material problems of development, so does this organisation deal with the psychological ones. How fruitless it would be were new methods of agriculture or animal husbandry to be discovered by the research organisations, and their adoption resisted by the people whom they were intended to benefit, simply through suspicion and lack of understanding. New methods must constantly be evolved to avoid so great a tragedy.

Bridging the Gulf

by JOHN MOFFETT

A WRITER in *Corona* recently described how he thought the specialist Community Development Officer could assist the District Officer today. He pointed out how the process of disengagement involved in modern Colonial administration brought about "a profound modification of a human relationship", between the District Officer and the people, and suggested that this was comparable, viewed from the psychological angle, to the relationship between parent and child. In this situation, the specialist Community Development Officer could effect the "transference" of feeling more easily than the District Officer.

I feel that this argument (thus very briefly summarised) may already be out-dated, for whatever may have been the case in the past, the relationship is not the same today. The purpose of this article is to try to show that it has indeed changed and to make suggestions as to how the changed situation may be met. I agree with Mr. McMullen that the Community Development Officer has a useful function to perform and can indeed be of the greatest assistance to a District Commissioner, although our reasons for thinking so may differ. In what follows, although I hope that much may be of more general application, I am dealing mainly with the situation as I knew it in Tanganyika.

With the best will in the world a District Commissioner today, with few exceptions, finds it impossible to keep in as close touch with the people of his district as he would like. The main reason is that the nature of his work has changed and that he now has so much office work to do that it is just not possible, for example, to spend weeks on safari. Governments have been well aware of the difficulty for some time and steps have been taken to relieve a District Commissioner of as much as possible—thus Revenue Officers, District Assistants and Magistrates have taken many of the more time-consuming duties off his shoulders. But the hard fact which has to be faced is that even with such assistance a District Commissioner still cannot find the time to spend long periods away from his office or to deal in detail with the "human relations" side of his job. Whereas in former days he could set off on leisurely foot safaris, with all the opportunities these gave for frequent informal contact with all sorts of people, now he finds himself hurrying from one formal meeting to another by car, a figure often rather remote from the common people. No one bewails this more than the District Commissioner himself, but he feels impotent to do anything about it, although conscious that his impression on the local people may be only fleeting before he is succeeded by another. It would be a very salutary experience for us all, and especially for the younger officers, if one of the older and more intelligent Chiefs could be got to record his impressions, outspoken and unexpurgated, of the series of occupants of the big chair in the District Office. It is likely, indeed almost certain, that he would remember some of the old hands far better than those who have occupied the chair of recent years.

While we are trying to look at things from the receiving end, let us remember some of the changes which have taken place in the life of the ordinary peasant. He now has much more to interest him, and more to think and talk about than formerly. Not so long ago the activities of the District Commissioner were news: I doubt if they often are now—and of course there are now far more Government officials than there used to be; the D.C. may be one among dozens.

Nor is the D.C's position as the chief local representative of the Government strengthened *vis à vis* the people if local politicians foster the idea (as they have done on occasions) that at any moment he will cease to be a vital factor in government.

In these circumstances there is a danger of antipathy, or at least of apathy, always a widespread characteristic among many peasants, and both are conducive to the opening of a gulf between the people and the District Commissioner. Attempts to bridge it by providing District Commissioners with additional staff and relieving them of some of their burdens have failed—new burdens have taken the place of the old. In this situation some new approach is called for.

This new approach can be made by the Community Development Officer. His job is specifically to bridge the gulf, not by any Maskelyne-ish stunts but by the proven, patient methods which have been arrived at after much trial and error by community development workers throughout the world.

One would think that at least the general principles of community development were now widely known and understood, but it is regrettably true that there is still an astonishing degree of ignorance of the subject outside those circles directly concerned with it. This was clear at the C.C.T.A. conference at Tananarive,† where some of the delegates, including those from British dependencies, obviously had little idea of what the term implied. In Tanganyika I have frequently been astonished at the ignorance, at all levels, both of what is implied by the term 'community development' and of what has been done in other countries. There is still a tendency to look upon community development as a 'frill' and to think that its main concern is with community centres or womens' clubs ("just places to natter in").

Now it would be difficult to exaggerate the importance of community development in present circumstances. Here we have a means, not only of bridging the gulf, but of bringing about lasting results of permanent value. A splendid tool is to hand, but is little used through ignorance of its value. Yet there is nothing 'frilly', or outlandish, or pseudo-scientific, or difficult about the community development concept. It is in fact only common sense applied to a special situation.

Let us watch a Community Development Officer in action (there is an excellent description in *Progress in Pare* by H. Mason in *Corona*, June, 1952). While he is still a stranger not much attention is going to be paid to what he does or says, so his first task is to establish friendly relations with the people he wants to influence. To do this he must go and live right among them, and it may well be necessary at first to cut down his contacts with the District Office to a minimum. It may take time, and ingenuity, to make an entrée, but he must be prepared to wait and use any opportunity which presents itself. Mason, working among the Meru in Tanganyika, did it by showing films to school children; and the attraction of the moving picture gradually brought in the adults.

Next, the Community Development Officer will spend a considerable amount of further time in getting to know as much as possible about the people; their way of life, language, customs; their natural leaders; their wants, hopes and aspirations. Once he knows who their real leaders are (and these may not necessarily be the ones paid by the local authority), and what their wants are, he will be in a position to stimulate them to take action to satisfy those wants. This will often best be achieved by merely throwing out a suggestion in a somewhat offhand manner and waiting for it to come back again in the form: "We've been thinking that we might do such-and-such a thing if you could help us" (as though the idea had originated with them—which of course is just what one hopes for). Unless the want expressed is wildly impracticable (which is unlikely) the people should be helped to satisfy it. It may not appear to the outsider to be the most urgent need, but that is beside the point. The important thing is that the people are now prepared to take action to help themselves and they should be given every encouragement to do so, and given assistance with those things which they cannot provide for themselves—for example, cement for culverts on a new road.

When the people have carried out this first project they will have a feeling of considerable satisfaction in their achievement, will have gained self-confidence and will have accepted the Community Development Officer as a friend. He can then go on to stimulate them to take further action to satisfy other needs—needs whose existence they would probably have refused to admit at first. The really crucial point in all this is, of course, that the people have taken action *themselves*, they have done the work because *they* wanted to. It may have taken a long time, but once they are convinced of its value and do it of their own volition there is not likely to be much falling back. We are all only too familiar with cases where, when the pressure has been removed, the new practice has been at once abandoned, showing clearly that the people's hearts were never in it.

At this stage, if the Community Development Officer has been properly trained, he will gradually withdraw himself. He should be the catalyst, the stimulator, the producer of ideas, the guide, but not the friend that sticketh closer than a brother. His task, having got the people working on their own initiative and standing firmly on their own feet, is to make himself dispensable and to fade out of the picture. It will be seen that the whole process is an exercise in persuasion, with a raising of the standard of living as the ulterior motive. It is often forgotten that this is something which cannot be done for people but which they must do themselves.

Now I have no doubt that it will be generally agreed that these methods are greatly preferable to those so often used in the past, and much more likely to produce results. Indeed, it is evident that the days of 'benevolent compulsion' are gone for ever and that only persuasion is now possible. How to persuade is what a Community Development Officer learns to do. He has thus, in my view and in the opinion of all those who have seen for themselves the results which he can achieve, a vital, indeed an indispensable rôle to play in modern Colonial administration. In fact, if one followed the argument to its logical conclusion one would say that every District Commissioner should have a Community Development Officer on his staff.

How practicable is this in the hard light of available finance? Finance depends on productivity, and in Tanganyika, for example, a priority list was prepared shortly before I left with some 30 schemes for productivity increases to raise funds, in this case for expansion in education. The total was an imposing figure which, if realized, would go a long way towards improving the general economic position of the territory. But extra productivity means extra work, and that depends on the willing co-operation of the people.

Obviously that can be achieved only if one goes the right way about it. It is my contention that the community development approach is the right way, indeed the only way in present circumstances. One must turn, as is being done more and more in other parts of the world, to Community Development Officers for help. But what if there is only a handful of them? Does this mean that nothing can be done until many more have been taken on by the department? Must the implementation of increased productivity plans await their recruitment?

There is, I suggest, a way out of the difficulty—by the secondment to the department of officers specially selected from other departments for their sympathetic attitude towards the local people and their willingness to learn the principles and techniques of the community development approach. As has been pointed out, part of a Community Development Officer's task is gradually to withdraw himself once he has fulfilled his mission and stimulated action, and this would make possible secondments for short periods only. It would also make it possible to consider the secondment of non-officials—at first sight a somewhat revolutionary idea, but missionaries, for example, have been engaged in this way in Uganda and Sarawak and I see no reason why other non-officials also should not be able to assist, provided they have the right outlook and are adequately trained.

The main limitation on numbers will doubtless be that of finance, but my argument is that Community Development Officers are a direct means of improving a country's finances through increased productivity and that by spending a few thousand pounds on them a return measured in millions can be looked for.

For both 'professionals' and seconded officers training will be of the very greatest importance if they are to be successful in their work. Such training will enable them to see, for example, how a special project of increased productivity can best be linked with a general programme of development, in which literacy, women's clubs, health measures, and other activities may all be included, the whole being based on, and growing out of, the people's own expressed needs. Also the terms and conditions of work, for seconded officers as for 'professionals', must be attractive if they are to do a worth-while job. That they are already doing so is without doubt. Their rôle is not so much to transfer to themselves the filial feelings which the people once had for the District Commissioner, as to help him with the human relations aspect of his work and, in doing so, to set the people on the path of self-help, the surest road to lasting economic and social development.

For Your Leave

APRIL TO JUNE

Music and Arts: Stratford-on-Avon, Shakespeare Season of Plays (*Mar.–Oct.*); Hove, Royal Academy 1954 Selection (*Mar.* 26–*Apr.* 23); Royal Scottish Academy, Edinburgh Annual Exhibition of Painting, Sculpture and Architecture (*Apr.* 22–*Sept.*); Pitlochry, Pitlochry Festival Theatre (*May* 7–*Oct.* 1 (prov.)); Bath, Bath Assembly (*May* 8–21); Glyndebourne, Festival Opera (*early Jun.–late Jul.*); Aldeburgh, Festival of Music and the Arts (*Jun.* 18–26 (prov.)).

Shows: Agricultural Shows: Balmoral, 88th Royal Ulster (*May* 25–28); Launceston, Bath and West and Southern Counties (*Jun.* 1–4); Worcester, Three Counties (*Jun.* 14–16); Costessey, Royal Norfolk (*Jun.* 29, 30); Birmingham, National Trades and Homelife Exhibition (*Mar.* 30–*Apr.* 23); London and Birmingham, British Industries Fair (*May* 2–13); Windsor, Royal Windsor Horse Show (*May* 12–14); Windsor, Olympic Horse Trials (*May* 19–21 (prov.)); Royal Hospital Grounds, Chelsea Flower Show (*May* 25–27); Earls Court, Royal Tournament (*Jun.* 1–18); Grosvenor House, Antique Dealers' Fair (*Jun.* 8–23); Horse Guards Parade, Trooping the Colour (*Jun.* 9); Richmond, Royal Horse Show (*Jun.* 9–11).

Rugby Football: Wembley, Rugby League Cup Final (*Apr.* 30).

Racing: Epsom, Derby (*May* 25), Oaks (*May* 27); Ascot, Royal Ascot (*June* 14–17).

Table Tennis: Wembley, England Open Championships (*Mar.* 29–*Apr.* 2).

Association Football: Wembley, England v. Scotland (*Apr.* 2); Wembley, F.A. Amateur Cup Final (*Apr.* 16); Wembley, England v. Wales (Schoolboys' International) (*Apr.* 23); Wembley, F.A. Cup Final (*May* 7).

Golf: Ganton, Spalding Professional Tournament (*Apr.* 20–22); Ganton, English Amateur Championship (*Apr.* 25–30); Royal Portrush, British Ladies Golf Championship (*May* 16–20); St. Andrews, Walker Cup—Britain v. U.S.A. (*May* 20, 21); Royal Lytham and St. Annes, Amateur Championship (*May* 30–*Jun.* 4).

Cricket: Nottingham, 1st Test Match, England v. South Africa (*Jun.* 9–11, 13, 14); Lords, 2nd Test Match, England v. South Africa (*June* 23–25, 27, 28).

Rifle Shooting: Bisley, National Small Bore Meeting (*Jun.* 25–*Jul.* 2).

Motor Cycle Racing: Isle of Man, International T.T. Motor Cycle Racing (*Jun.* 6, 8, 10).

Cycle Racing: Isle of Man, International T.T. Bicycle Races (*Jun.* 21–23).

Tennis: Wimbledon, All England Lawn Tennis Championships (*Jun.* 30–*Jul.* 2).

Henley Royal Regatta: (*June* 29–*Jul.* 2 (prov.)).

Co-operation Advances

by B. J. SURRIDGE, C.M.G., O.B.E.

An invitation to write an article in *Corona* should be welcomed. It should be easy to dash off 2,000 words or so on a subject with which the writer has been closely connected for quite a long time. The facts are there and the latest statistics supplied by hard pressed Registrars of Co-operative Societies should speak for themselves. But when the time comes to consider what would interest the readers of *Corona*, many of whom spend much of their working time reading reports and sometimes writing them, niggling doubts and fears begin to arise. The man or woman devoted to a single purpose can be such a bore! In this account of co-operation in the Colonies I have sought to keep figures to the minimum consistent with showing the scope of the work, and to avoid any suggestion of a 'message'.

In an article on Co-operation in *Corona* in June, 1949, it was considered desirable and necessary to define a co-operative society. There is no need for a definition now. The co-operative society is a feature of the landscape in many parts of most territories. In paragraph 56 of the 1954 Swynnerton plan to intensify the development of African agriculture in Kenya it is stated: "It is most important to establish a strong co-operative organisation to weld the very large numbers of small producers into a corporate body—co-operative organisations are also desirable for educating people in running their own affairs to train and pick out leaders and to raise funds through shares, commissions or levies for the operation of the business affairs of members. . . ."

When Mr. Swynnerton prepared his plan he was Assistant Director of Agriculture in Kenya. He was in no way connected with co-operative organisations, and so this extract is valuable to show an attitude towards Co-operation which, ten years or so ago, was a rarity except among those who professed and called themselves co-operators.

Over these years there has been a gradual—possibly in some territories rather too gradual—realisation that a co-operative society is not necessarily "The Co-op", that the organisation of a society need not upset relations between local authorities and their people, and that social and political as well as economic conditions can be improved through the medium of co-operative societies.

In 1945 there were 1,885 societies in ten territories with 266,000 members, paid up share capital of just under £1,000,000 and reserves of £410,000. In 1954 in 26 territories there were 8,626 societies with just over 1,000,000 members, out of an estimated total population of 82,000,000 and it may be assumed that in one out of every 16 households there is one member of a co-operative society. Six thousand seven hundred of these societies are mainly concerned with thrift and credit, and marketing and processing. Few societies have a large membership, the average being 105 members, and they operate mainly at the village level.

The prerequisites for consumer co-operatives, namely sufficient capital, skilled management and cash trading, implying a regular weekly income, are rarely to be found. Credit is usually obtainable from shopkeepers and, except in times of shortage, there is strong competition. Many of these factors are not fully appreciated by those with experience of co-operatives in urban areas in Europe.

The total paid up share capital of all societies amounted in 1954 to £5,000,000, or around £5 for each member, deposits to £5,000,000 and reserves to £3,800,000.

Of these reserves Tanganyika and Cyprus with 196,000 and 130,000 members respectively account for nearly £2,000,000 or just over £6 per member. The average in the other territories is just under £3 per member. The value of produce marketed was £39,000,000. The loan operations of societies totalled £9,600,000 of which £2,000,000 were lent by societies in Cyprus, £2,000,000 in the Federation of Malaya and £1,600,000 in Kenya. Loans repaid amounted to £7,400,000.

The advices contained in the Secretary of State's despatches of March and April, 1946, for a proper legal framework in the form of a Co-operative Ordinance and Rules for the appointment of a Registrar of Co-operative Societies assisted by a staff of the necessary quality and strength, have been generally accepted. There are now Registrars in all the territories of major importance. No Registrar would agree that the strength of his staff was sufficient, and only the most optimistic that they were all of the necessary quality.

In numbers the staffs of Co-operative Departments have grown considerably. To some extent a modification of Parkinson's Law, formulated in the *Economist* early in 1956, has tended to operate in that as societies increase in number more staff is required to supervise them and with more staff more societies come up for registration. A recent examination of estimates of revenue and expenditure in the territories shows that in all the territories there are 32 Registrars, 162 Deputy and Assistant Registrars and 809 other Co-operative Officers. In addition to the Registrar in each territory there are in East Africa 57 Co-operative Officers of senior grades and 259 of junior grades; in West Africa 61 senior and 360 junior; in Central Africa 23 and 59; in the Far East 11 and 116 and in all other territories ten and 115.

In most territories the head office of the Co-operative Department is now recognisable as an office belonging to any well established government department. This was not always so. One Registrar at the start of his co-operative career was allotted a room in the Secretariat and told to organise societies. Another, more fortunate, was allowed a two roomed flat, a clerk and a downstairs garage which later became the first office of the Co-operative Central Bank. Another, on first appointment, had to establish himself in a store previously used by the Agricultural Department for inorganic fertilisers and insecticides, the smell of which remained to remind him of his duty towards the farming community.

Strickland in a contribution to the International Labour Review in 1938 summarised his long experience of co-operation in Asian countries by stating that the training of staffs of Co-operative Departments had often been neglected: "The ignorant have been sent to lead the ignorant, the blind to guide the blind and the result has naturally been disastrous". That lesson has been heeded.

Since 1947-48 over 120 Co-operative Officers and employees of Co-operative Unions from various territories have passed through the nine months Overseas Training Course at the Co-operative College at Stanford Hall, Loughborough. Many of them have received promotion to the post of Assistant Registrar. One has become the Registrar in the territory where he is serving. At the East African School of Co-operation near Nairobi, during the past four years there have been two five month courses yearly for junior Co-operative Officers and employees of co-operative societies. In Uganda special training courses are organised at the Community Development training centre in Entebbe and in the Northern Region of Nigeria at the School of Administration in Zaria. The Co-operative College in the Federation of Malaya opened its doors in November and similar colleges are due to be opened shortly both in the Western Region of Nigeria and in Tanganyika. Elsewhere one of the first tasks for Co-operative Departments has been to train the trainers, i.e. the staff.

With the aid of funds provided under the Colonial Development and Welfare Acts, two training courses, of two months each, for senior staff in Africa, have been held, one at Moshi in Tanganyika and the other at Kabete in Kenya. During these courses visits have been paid to co-operative organisations in nearby territories. It is expected that in 1957 a similar course will be held in West Africa. And every year for a week in July in the pleasant surroundings of the Overseas Services Club at Oxford there is a gathering of Registrars and Assistant Registrars on leave in the United Kingdom where co-operative questions of general interest are discussed— not without refreshment. One lesson learnt at these gatherings is that the other man has his problems too. For the Co-operative Officer is still in some territories the new boy—a young Assistant District Officer in Africa, asking a Chief why his rest house had not been supplied with firewood and water, is said to have been told that only a Co-operative Officer was expected. He has to learn how to make his own way, and sometimes it is a lonely way, especially when something goes wrong with the society he has cherished as an example to others—when the swan has turned into a goose. It was laid down in the despatches of 1946 that one of the most important qualifications for a Co-operative Officer is "the ability to survive discouragement".

In the Federation of Malaya during the height of the terrorist campaign the staff of the Co-operative Department moved freely in the countryside except when military operations were in progress. In Cyprus the disturbed political conditions have not had any serious effect on co-operative societies and the staff of the Co-operative Department have carried on business as usual. Committees and secretaries of societies in mixed Greek and Turkish villages are reported to have taken action to stop outbursts of communal violence. For in many villages in Cyprus most of the members of the village council are also members of the village co-operative society and they have learnt to work together as friends in economic matters. It has been reported—not from co-operative sources—that the orderliness in the election of the first Paramount Chief of the Chagga tribe on Mount Kilimanjaro in Tanganyika some few years ago was due in part at least to the fact that the people had been accustomed to meet, discuss and vote at the general meeting of the societies which compose the Kilimanjaro Native Co-operative Union and at meetings of the Union itself. In the despatches mentioned earlier the belief was expressed that ". . . above all a practical training in the working of democratic processes are all encouraged by the association of the people in co-operative societies."

People who have studied the development of co-operative societies in the United Kingdom or Denmark, for example, often ask how far it is possible to reconcile sponsorship of societies by a government department, as part of government policy, with the idea, basic to co-operation, of self-help. The belief is expressed that co-operative societies can and should emerge from the people themselves. It is expected that leaders will arise out of the earth fully armed to spread the idea of co-operation and to organise efficient societies far and wide.

In countries where the standard of general education was high, such as in Denmark, where the Elementary Education Act of 1814 made it compulsory for all persons to send their children to school from 6-14 years of age, or where public spirited citizens such as Raiffeison in Germany, Sir Horace Plunkett in Ireland, and Ludlow and Vansittart Neale in the United Kingdom, were forthcoming, it has been possible for co-operative societies to develop with little or no sponsorship and assistance from the Government.

And yet as recently as in 1944, in the Province of Saskatchewan in Canada, it was found necessary to introduce "an act respecting the Department of Co-operation and Co-operative Development to provide for the establishment and duties of the Department under the Minister for Co-operation and Co-operative Development". The duties and powers, in addition to registration and approval of bylaws, include encouragement and assistance in the organisation of co-operative enterprise, inspection and examination of the affairs of co-operative bodies, collection of statistics, and dissemination of information. In the U.S.A. a credit union is defined as a co-operative association for thrift and for creating a source of credit, and under the Federal Credit Union Act of the U.S.A., 1934-52, the Director of the Bureau of Federal Credit Unions performs many of the functions of Registrars of Co-operative Societies in India, Ceylon and in British oversea territories. Sponsorship, guidance and assistance from the Government are found to be necessary in at least one of the Provinces in Canada and in India and Ceylon.

Territory wide Co-operative Unions on the lines of the Co-operative Union in the United Kingdom are being established and are beginning to operate in a number of territories. Some co-operative education is now being done by the staff of these Unions, a news-letter is being published and some supervisory work is being done. As a body representative of all aspects of co-operative activity, the Union is able to convey to the appropriate Minister the views of members of Co-operative Societies on any of government policies which may affect them. Equally the Union can bring its influence to bear on the Registrar in any decisions of policy which have to be made in the Co-operative Department. It is early to prophesy on the future of these Unions. Much will depend on how far they appear to be effective in the eyes of their member societies and on that will depend the amount of financial support which they will receive from their members. For while local marketing or processing unions are actually seen at work by the individual members of societies, and the operations of co-operative banking unions are understood and appreciated, it is difficult for the small farmer member of a remote village society to appreciate the need to contribute to the upkeep of a territory wide Co-operative Union. It seems that until funds are readily forthcoming, the growth of power and authority for this type of Union is not likely to be rapid—nowhere near as rapid as the growth of the primary societies and of the local unions.

It may be asked whether, with the growth of power and authority, territory wide Co-operative Unions will follow the example of the co-operative movement in the United Kingdom and enter the political field. At present the legislation, based on a Model Ordinance sent out by the Colonial Office in 1946 or, earlier, on the India Act of 1912, does not permit any contribution from co-operative funds to the funds of any political party, with the result that neutrality in politics has been observed. Unless the Government of a territory as a matter of policy deliberately sets out to undermine the co-operative movement, it is probable that this neutrality will continue to be observed, especially as now one of the Ministers usually has co-operation as one of his responsibilities. But it must be confessed that the existence of a Minister for Co-operation in the Gold Coast did not prevent the formation, under government auspices and with capital provided by the Government, of a strong rival company to the Co-operatives for credit and the marketing of cocoa.

Colonial Trade Unions

SOME GROWING PAINS

by A. H. COUZENS

AMONG the more important imports into the colonies must be placed ideas: by way of newspapers, radio, literature, schools, students returned from abroad, foreign missions and agencies. New, strange and oddly attractive ideas are spreading rapidly and widely through communities not yet very well equipped to receive and appreciate them. How can patient tutelage keep pace with impatient desire? It is not my purpose here to examine this problem in its wider aspects of administration and government, but to point to a few of the ways in which it becomes manifest in the management of enterprises in which large labour forces are employed.

The late Lord Passfield, better known as Sidney Webb, when Secretary of State in 1930, evinced a particular interest in the development of trade unionism in the colonies. Since that time, this development has been encouraged, with varying degrees of energy and enthusiasm, as a matter of policy. The legislation introduced in pursuance of this policy has been designed to give properly constituted unions a status before the law, to establish their rights and to protect their members. The English trade union law, which was developed by a long and often painful advance, marked significantly in 1824 by the repeal of the Combination Act and in 1871 by the enactment of the Trade Union Act, has been used as the basis for the colonial drafts. The latter, however, all contain a provision which is inconsistent both with the historical development and the spirit of the model, namely a provision for compulsory registration.

The effect of this, although it may not be immediately apparent, is great and is considerably intensified by the relevant circumstance that the trade union movement, under the protection of this legislation, has not been strengthened and refined by any struggle for right and principle but has had benefits freely bestowed upon it. In the result, there is a tendency on the part of all concerned to identify the formal registration of a trade union with its recognition as a bargaining agent. There is a tendency on the part of unions and of union members to emphasise their rights and overlook their responsibilities. Perhaps most serious, there is a tendency amongst union members not to appreciate that they themselves comprise the union. Rather they imagine the union as a small group of officials whose business it is, fortified by subscriptions which might more appropriately be paid occasionally into an " action fund " than regularly to the union's treasurer, to engage in a campaign, constant even if varying in intensity, for ever higher wages.

This analysis is over-simplified and could not be justified in relation to all of the unions but it gives an indication of the source of many of the difficulties faced by employers and by serious and sincere trade unionists in the present stage of development. It accounts for the comparatively large numbers of paid union officials; for the prevalence of the " company " type of trade union; for such things as a reference in the report of a recent commission of inquiry to " the duty of ensuring that the *promoters* of a trade union will properly discharge their responsibilities to their members "; for the all too common irregularity in the payment of subscriptions, and for the doubts which often exist as to whether demands spring from the needs and aspirations of the union members or from the anxiety of the union officials to justify their tenure of office.

The idea of community of interest is obviously not an innovation in tribal communities, and tribes and tribal unions have for centuries existed by acceptance of the principle. What is new is the extension of the idea beyond, or even across, the family, the tribe or the tribal union on the basis of the interests shared by and peculiar to persons engaged in wage-earning. There may thus be a disruptive as well as a unifying tendency.

There are limits to the efficacy of tutelage and precept in this matter, and limits to what can be learned without experience. It is natural, therefore, that colonial workers and their trade unions should make mistakes and, sometimes, serious mistakes of a nature not to be anticipated solely by reference to the history of the progress, in very different circumstances, of the British trade union movement. Employers in the colonies do not need to be told how troublesome and expensive these mistakes can be, but it will bear repeating that they do not all as yet appear fully to appreciate to what extent the mistakes may be prevented, or lessened in ill-effect, by close attention to the question of good labour management.

There is one particular matter, arising largely out of the present state of colonial labour organisation, that could be regarded as a direct challenge to good management. The workers are for the most part illiterate and so understandably tend to choose union officials, not from among themselves but from clerks and other persons able to express themselves in reasonable English and in writing. This, together with the general conception of unionism described earlier, leads to a lack of identity between the workers and the union executives, the latter becoming spokesmen rather than representatives. Consequently, it is by no means certain that an agreement with the " union " will always be acceptable to the majority of the members and negotiations are often hampered by the frequent necessity of reference back. In other cases, the negotiations revolve in futility around a fixed point or cease summarily because the spokesmen have not the authority or, maybe, the courage to abandon a declared position. This is a state of affairs requiring, on the part of the employer, understanding, sympathy and patience and firm rejection of the sometimes not unnatural desire for a " show-down." Employers do not invariably appreciate or satisfy this requirement.

In this way it happens that there is little opportunity or encouragement for the development of a spirit of compromise and, frequently, no real efforts are made to reach a settlement otherwise than by force. Each side maintains its original stand and, rather than yield a little, forgoes the inestimable advantage of a settlement by agreement, perhaps involving the third-party intervention of a Government Labour Officer or demanding arbitration or formal inquiry.

The normal way of life over large areas of most colonies is subsistence farming and the proportion of regular wage-earners is very small. Outside a few main towns many workers are employed reasonably near their families and their earnings may be regarded as an addition to the family resources. Wages, however attractive, thus have not the same essential importance as in an industrial community. Consequently, colonial workers may often be more easily persuaded than workers from communities depending entirely upon wages to use the strike as a means of argument and, having struck, do not have the compulsion of economic necessity to return to work, to make demands on union funds, or even to seek a speedy settlement. A strike took place recently in a large tropical plantation and continued for some weeks. Thousands of the workers returned to their homes to await results, others lived on food grown on or near the plantation, and a small number took advantage of the willingness of the local petty traders to supply goods on credit. When a settlement was eventually reached, a considerable time elapsed before the labour force could be fully reassembled and full production resumed.

Among people to whom regular employment and wage-earning is a novel way of life the considerations on which the conditions of employment are determined are almost beyond understanding. This fact, together with the effects of tribal traditions and practices concerning chiefs and headmen, leads workers to regard individual members of the management as personally responsible for conditions which are unpleasing. Lists of grievances often include demands for the removal of Smith or of Jones, or may even be condensed to a simple " Brown must go," if the unfortunate Brown has been the channel for the conveyance of all of the management's decisions. In a case, as sometimes happens, where Brown, in addition, has not the knack of getting on with people, the resulting situation is very difficult and perhaps may be eased only by Brown's departure.

Another important factor among those which lead to such cries as " Brown must go," is the effect upon inter-racial relationships of the increasing part played by indigenous peoples in the management of activities, including governmental activities, in their countries. The extent of this participation and the rate of its increase vary considerably between the territories concerned, but in the West African colonies, for example, the " Africanisation " of the civil service is a systematic operation pressed forward as an important measure of government policy. It would seem that the speed of the operation is not generally appreciated and that among the colonial peoples themselves, or such of them as are articulate, there is certainly no general appreciation of the difficulties involved. It might have been expected that this process, carried out steadily and in good faith, would be a source of satisfaction to the public in general and to the African employees of Governments in particular. In some degree it is so, but it is not unnatural that the very existence of the policy, the wider vistas and the greater opportunities it discloses, the hopes and aspirations it engenders, should cause a restlessness which is much more noticeable. Vacancies left by European officers in the service of Governments and, less frequently, of managements are closely scrutinized, desired and sought after. Extravagant claims are often made on the strength of modest attainments and, on occasion, extravagant allegations are made concerning the failings, real or imagined, of individual European officers. Events of the past are responsible for the fact that most senior posts in the colonies in Government, commerce and industry are at present occupied by Europeans. When trade union officials, for example, sit down to argue a case they almost always see, on the other side of the table, Europeans. The reactions, in the circumstances, are natural and therefore understandable: with understanding, it should be possible by tact and patience to dispel the suspicion and mistrust. In any event the effort must be made, and constantly made.

Considerable attention is paid in modern enterprises and development schemes to the training of workers. There is much to be done. There is a great shortage of skill and an even greater shortage of that combination of skill, experience and character which is the basic requirement of a foreman. There appears to be a need for the making of particular efforts to develop foremanship among workers. The foreman occupies a position of great importance everywhere, but nowhere is he of greater significance in industrial relations than in a colony. As elsewhere, it is not enough that he should have a certain seniority and a certain skill as a craftsman: he should have natural authority and a degree of formal authority accorded him: he must have a facility in gaining confidence and an ability to settle minor grievances promptly and with manifest justice. These qualities may be brought out and strengthened in suitable workmen by extended training and encouragement. Foremen so produced would very considerably assist colonial development schemes and industries and would do much to improve their labour relationships.

It would not be difficult to enlarge upon the problems already outlined or to add observations on other labour matters not touched upon. My present purpose will, however, have been achieved if what has been written is enough to awaken interest in a field of endeavour in which there are many opportunities for good and useful work. The difficulties are not to be underrated; neither is the urgent need for their being overcome.

The Public Works Department in North Borneo

by L. JACKSON

"Borneo ? Well, I suppose you will have plenty of money to spend with all that oil around ?" That is the usual reaction to the statement that one comes from that part of the world. Unfortunately, North Borneo is not rolling in oil, for though it is about, it has not yet been found in commercial quantities. The Colony is therefore dependent upon its agricultural and forestry produce for its livelihood.

The Colony is the size of Ireland and largely undeveloped, with practically no internal communications, so that the majority of its population live around the coasts, dependent until recently upon the sea for its contacts with its neighbours. The scope for development is therefore great, but it has been necessary first to repair the ravages of war. North Borneo suffered from the effects of the Australian counter-offensive against the Japanese and most of the towns were flattened in the process. The task—and the opportunity—for the Public Works Department was tremendous. In some ten years of struggle, in the face of shortages of staff, labour and materials, the towns have been substantially rebuilt and the Colony is now moving forward into new development. Such was the picture before me when I was offered the post of Director in 1957.

Flying out to take up my duties, my first touch down in the Colony was at the principal airport on Labuan Island. Taxiing up to the terminal building the first thing to be seen was a Skymaster aeroplane with its belly on the ground and one wheel of its undercarriage well and truly down in the 'hardstanding'. The P.W.D. engineer was engaged in trying to lift the 'plane out—not very successfully. Life looked like being promising, particularly as the runway at Jesselton, the capital, was known to have failed the previous year. In fact, one or other of these airports has been engaging my attention ever since.

Arrived at my headquarters I was soon advised that in addition to the airports, there were problems concerning water supply, irrigation, roads and harbours—and also that the department as a whole had recently been the subject of an investigation and the report thereon was awaiting attention. In all, it looked like being a busy time.

The first thing, obviously, was to have a look at the country. This in itself was a new experience for my previous service had been in Colonies which could be motored around in a matter of hours. The first item on the itinerary was a ten-day trip on the coastal steamer from Jesselton to Tawau and back. So much for the stories of roughing it on tour that one hears of: this was First Class comfort. However, the next trip was up the railway into the interior which was less than comfortable, and the return by air in an ancient 'Rapide' flying through cloud over the mountains, was most uncomfortable. My first impression was of a vast country covered with trees and rivers, yet the two shortages first brought to notice were of water and timber. They both seemed to be in the right place at the wrong time—or *vice versa*.

Since that first trip, travel has mostly been by air. Having acquired some 'Twin Pioneers', the internal air services have been much improved, and it is now possible to get to most places quickly, and at reasonably short notice—that is, to all places that a Director might have the time to visit, but the Divisional Engineers still find it necessary to make trips by river, pony, or even on foot to reach the more outlying parts of their domain. As so few Europeans have been seen in these areas, the hospitality of the local people is still rather formidable and one needs the constitution of an ox to cope with it. One of the trials of any P.W.D. officer on tour, and even more so of a Director, is the very natural attempt of others to put in a word for their own pet schemes. But this often includes some little extras to their own house or office. One early request to me was for some redecoration in a house in special colours. The offer of 'P.W.D. Buff' was not very well received! Nevertheless, showing the flag of the department is an extremely worth while occupation, particularly in a country which had no experience of an established P.W.D.

The Divisions themselves vary greatly, from a small area such as the capital town of Jesselton, to a very large area of mostly undeveloped country comprising a whole Administrative Residency. In the former the work is practically that of a municipal engineer, responsible for the upkeep of modern roads, water supply, sewerage and buildings—with, of course, the doubtful advantage of having the Director on his doorstep all the time. In the latter there used to be a glorious feeling of isolation when it was five days away by the weekly boat, but those concerned are not so sure they like the ease with which the Headquarters staff are now able to hop on an aeroplane at a moment's notice.

Borneo is a challenging country. Although it has so far produced no mineral wealth it has revealed large areas of land suitable for agricultural development. But this land is situated in the jungle far from existing roads, so that early expansion of the road system is called for. Even a skeleton network to cover the Colony would require some 750 miles of new roads. It is hoped to make a start on this task in the immediate future, by the employment of two construction units each aiming at about one mile of new road a month. As there are no maps of much of the area, and the steep hillsides are covered with dense jungle even to the summits, prospecting an alignment is no sinecure. As regards the construction, in the present state of development of the Colony, quantity must come before quality at least as far as running surface is concerned. Alignment follows the need for future development, but surfacing must wait the growth of traffic. One reason for this decision lies in the shortage of stone and consequent expense of providing it. But it still poses a major problem to build a road on a clay soil in a wet climate which will not be impassable to traffic for days or weeks at a time.

To overcome some of these difficulties, we have a Soils Laboratory which controls the foundation work on roads, runways and structures. Recently established, its first full scale operation was in connection with the Jesselton Airport. As a direct result of soil examinations and testing, not only did they achieve economies of nearly 20 per cent in the cost of construction, but the consistency of the finished work was much improved. This laboratory is under the control of an Executive Engineer with an all-Asian staff, many of whom have been trained in the laboratory, which deals also with concrete control and materials testing. Some of its first concrete testing was concerned with the new waterworks structures in Jesselton.

Waterworks in the various townships provide many problems. It might justifiably be thought from a study of climatic data that water supply would not be difficult. But in fact every town in the Colony has its water supply difficulties, and almost every town's problem is different.

In Jesselton the new supply was to have been ready before the end of 1957, but as so often happens it was behind schedule just when a dry winter turned up. The usual heavy rains of October and November did not appear and by December the small storage reservoir of the existing waterworks was getting very low. An emergency was declared and every available engineer diverted to help in the erection of a temporary scheme which made use of part of the new works trunk main, a new intake from the river using such pumps as could be brought at short notice, and a cross connection to the old works *via* an open stream course. In three weeks the work was completed, just in time, for still no rain had fallen and the reservoir was almost empty. In fact, by somewhat restricting the supply to the town, we were able to gain on the falling reservoir and survive the drought without further alarms—this in a country where it is supposed to rain two days out of three all the year round. Coming as I did from Aden, I had imagined rainless weeks would be a thing of the past, yet there was hardly a drop of rain in five months. So much for average statistics.

The new supply was gradually brought into use during the summer of 1958 and had been in operation for about a year when two of the staff died rather suddenly. This upset the local staff, who raised a petition for action to pacify the 'spirits'. On checking with the District Officer, it was confirmed that the indigenous employees would only go about the works at night in threes, but that the slaughter of a water buffalo, accompanied by a formal opening celebration, would meet the case. So one Saturday afternoon the Director, in the presence of the Resident and District Officer, pressed a starter button, made a small speech and, having provided a supply of the local brew, returned to his golf happy in the knowledge that the 'spirits' were now at rest.

Water supply is also a problem on the island of Labuan. Having a good harbour, a thriving little town has grown up here, and the island also boasts the only runway suitable for the large aeroplanes. Yet it is short of water and almost completely lacking in building stone. Ironically enough, boring in the likeliest spot for water revealed oil in sufficient quantities to spoil the water, but not enough to be productive for the oil drillers. In place of stone much use is made of coral. It is used for the foundations of roads and as an aggregate for concrete. It has also been used on runways, even on the latest at Jesselton. But the engineers were very worried about their time schedule when they tried to put it through the stone crusher, for when slightly damp it churned up inside the jaws like toffee, only spilling out one small stone at a time. However, some experiments with different jaw settings soon produced a more satisfactory result and the use of the coral made a worthwhile saving in expenditure.

These are only some of the activities of the Department, which has a strength of some 60 technical, 30 professional and 40 clerical and accounting officers and has branches dealing with roads, airports and harbours; water, drainage and irrigation; architecture; and mechanical and electrical services. These branches all operate from headquarters under the direction of an Assistant Director, while a second A.D.P.W. co-ordinates the work of the Divisional engineers.

Working in undeveloped countries at this time requires all that is best of modern engineering practice on the one hand, together with a capacity for improvisation under primitive conditions on the other. From a concrete framed five-story block of flats in the capital, one may have to turn to a consideration of a one-room timber framed school in the interior; from a dual carriage-way urban road to a bridle path in the jungle; from 2,000,000 gallons per day water supply to 200 gallons per day. That is a challenge. It is also a wonderful opportunity: and on top of all that North Borneo is an extremely peaceful and pleasant country to work in.

Mechanical Engineer, P.W.D.

by HUMPHREY TRACY, A.M.I.Mech.E.

IT was with some trepidation that I took over the mechanical workshops at Accra. Arriving in the Gold Coast at the end of the Second World War, knowing nothing of Africa or her peoples, I was starting from scratch with a vengeance. Looking back, however, I am extremely grateful for this experience.

The Workshops at Accra are not particularly large, though they became fairly well equipped, but, owing to the lack of other facilities in the Colony, they assumed a great importance. They employed about 100 men of varying degrees of skill, and it was to them that mechanical problems of every kind were brought; lorries, rollers, power station plant, printing presses, all came under our care.

My introduction to West African Engineering practice came with a request that I should inspect two small boilers at Korle Bu, the big African hospital that lay by a somewhat odiferous lagoon outside Accra. One glance at these boilers was enough for me, and I condemned them, to the great delight of the electricity authorities, who were eager to install a pair of electrical boilers of their own.

The workshops at that time were doing much work for the power station, which was being extended, and making the overhead gear for the power line to Achimota College. In addition, we were remetalling bearings in a race against time, to keep the necessary number of generators in service. The margin of load was so small in the evening that a Station Engineer used to stand by on the switchboard ready to reduce the load. Tired of always cutting out the poor parts of the town, he broke the switch for Government House. I never heard the sequel.

The waterworks also kept us busy; Weija, with its magnificent views of river and sea, is a delightful place, but not when one is called out to repair machinery in the middle of the night, as happened on several occasions.

The lighthouse, too, gave a certain amount of trouble; an over-zealous assistant keeper did several hundreds of pounds worth of damage to the lens, when cleaning it. The lighthouse was exceedingly uncomfortable during the earth tremors which occurred from time to time, and which always necessitated repairs. The occasion which sticks in my mind is that on which the revolving light became a fixed light, to the dismay of the sea-going folk.

Accra is a busy port, and it follows that work in ships occasionally took place. This meant a trip in a surf-boat propelled by 12 paddlers, who kept time to the strokes of a drum, and steered by an oar. One was lifted into the boat by a sturdy Krooman, and the whole seat was hoisted by the ship's derrick at the end of the journey. I ought to point out that before the completion of Takoradi Harbour, all immigrants and not a few motor cars came into the Colony in this way.

The opening of official safes was a frequent duty, necessitating the utmost care to protect the contents. In one such case, after hours of work, the safe was found to contain a single key labelled "Officers' Latrine."

In our work, accidents were fairly common. We had one fatal accident, when an African was caught in the pulley shaft. His funeral, attended only by a handful of workmen, was one of the most pathetic sights I have ever seen.

Quite a considerable time was spent in the survey of river craft on the river Volta. The headquarters of the ferry company were at Ada at the mouth of the river, an otherwise derelict port, surrounded by thousands of coconut palms. Here under an enormous kapok tree, once used for securing slaves, they repair the launches and pontoons that make up the fleet. Sometimes I would visit the vessels *in situ*, which meant a journey of perhaps 300 miles by car. On such trips I would see plenty of game, and would stay in the rest houses provided.

The rapid expansion of the Public Works Department and its equipment thrust a big burden on the workshops, which spent a lot of time assembling new rollers, and repairing the large fleet of tractors and graders, originally intended for the rehabilitation of Europe. A sudden demand for ferries started us ship-building, and we built a number of pontoons in the workshop yard. These were transported a distance of 400 miles by road.

I have often been asked my opinion of West Africans as workers. Taking into account their lack of experience and mechanical background, they do remarkably well. They are some of the most adaptable people in the world, and willing to work all night, provided they are allowed to go at their own pace. Above all they are loyal and just. A good master gets his reward.

The Public Works Department in the Gambia

by R. H. ARNOLD

THE sensation of landing on the steel plate runways of Yundum Airport and the first sight of the timber hut serving as the terminal building give an impression that the Gambia is a remote corner of the Commonwealth. However, the fairly comfortable lounge and modern bar, together with the helpful customs and other officials, result in a pleasant entry to the country before being quickly driven the fifteen miles to Bathurst.

In the modern hotel we meet our seagoing colleagues who have steamed up the estuary to Government Wharf where a crane is fighting a continual battle against the silting of the sand. Unfortunately the battle ceased for a time after the operator leaned too far forward, putting himself and crane over the edge of the wharf.

We now realise that Bathurst, which is the capital and only large town in the country, is situated at the end of a sand spit in the middle of the river. It would appear that the future of this sand spit is also the subject of a fight as the sea is trying desperately hard to wash it away while the Public Works Department meets all onslaughts with calculated defensive moves. The latest attempt at a break through was at a point three miles from Bathurst where the high water mark moved forward twenty feet in one day, to come within twenty feet of the edge of the road. A temporary rock breastwork was smartly put into place and the permanent work of building eleven timber groynes was done in only six weeks by the efficient use of a 19 R.B. excavator (fitted with pile driving attachment), a water jetting pump and by the co-operation and help of all concerned.

Further towards the mainland the sand spit is cut by the eight hundred feet wide Oyster Creek and it is here that there have been some anxious moments during the past years. In the autumn of 1959 one pier of the bridge was seen to be sinking gradually, together with the water main which was attached thereto. This was causing some consternation and the temperamental sea, the tide and the strong current did their best to delay remedial work. Despite these effects a system of timber piles and strutting was completed to provide a temporary support to the pier. Meanwhile work had been started on the construction of a new bridge of pre-stressed concrete beams supported on tubular piles of eight-inch diameter but misfortune set in for a time. Two of the piles split during driving, the second one involving the loss of the five-ton driving hammer which stuck underground in the tube and refused to move. Later on the workers were beset by a strange illness thought to arise from a nearby groundnut decorticating mill. However, after the ceremonial killing of a black bull the bridge was completed without further serious mishap.

Passing over the bridge, we cross through rice fields to meet the road from Fajara (where a number of Government quarters are situated overlooking the Atlantic Ocean). Turning eastwards we travel parallel to the river and then pass the airport which is managed by a private Company for the Controller of Civil Aviation (*alias* Director of Public Works) and which also houses his Meteorological Section. Driving on another seven miles to Brikama, we have time to take a look at the flat countryside, with its miles of bush type vegetation plus the addition of high grass in the rainy season (June to October) and interspersed with palm trees and occasional woods. The sandy soil provides the Gambian with his annual crop of groundnuts which is cultivated entirely by hand although the Government is now introducing a system of ox ploughing to help the farmers. His transport is also becoming mechanised and this is taxing the capabilities of the roads which, up to this point, consist of gravel with three coats of bitumen sprayed on to lay the dust and to keep out the rain. It is almost impossible, however, to keep the gravel perfectly dry as the ground water table is high, so that the roads are often saturated and as a consequence are subject to rapid deterioration.

This threat is met in two ways, firstly by the introduction of a higher standard of maintenance which is slowly being attained without additional funds by the use of mechanisation and by concentrating the maintenance personnel into a small number of gangs for ease of supervision. The second method is to reconstruct the roads by using a stabilising agent in the gravel, but as this is relatively expensive it can only be carried out where traffic is sufficiently heavy and a start is being made in the main streets of Bathurst.

The roads beyond Brikama deteriorate into sand tracks, their greatest use being to give an indication of direction, but at the same time they do their best to shake the landrover to pieces. We see, however, that Gambia has its equivalent of the British motorway programme and that new gravel roads are being constructed by bulldozers, graders, mechanical loaders, trucks, rollers and tractors, and although they do not have a bitumen surface the volume of traffic is very low so that the roads will be adequate to attain the object of improving the communications of the country as quickly as possible. The programme is also being pushed ahead by the local contractors who construct a quarter of a mile of road at a time, using local labour and transport, while a mixture of mechanisation and contractors is being used to build spur roads leading to the numerous river wharves.

The construction and maintenance of these wharves is another responsibility of the Public Works Department and since the river is the present main traffic artery, there is a hue and cry every time one is put out of commission. These wharves are constructed from rhun palm, which is a hard fibrous type of timber, and the difficulties encountered in this work range from the problems of obtaining and transporting by land and river the necessary rhun palms from remote situations, and countering the effects of heavy seas in the lower reaches of the river and flooding in the upper regions.

Another feature of the river is the numerous ferries which carry people, materials, transport, stores and cattle, etc., across the river at various points. No amount of precautions can make these perfectly safe, especially for persons like the one who drove his truck at speed down the ferry ramp when the ferry did not happen to be there. On the whole, however, the problems of constructing reinforced concrete ramps in the swamps adjacent to the river are being overcome as soon as funds are made available.

The river is also used for washing, but the vast majority of people obtain all their water from the local village well which is usually a crude, unlined hole in the ground with water of doubtful quality drawn up with the aid of a bucket on a rope. There are, however, the villages which have already benefited from the Government's well-sinking project and they have a well which is properly sited by an expert and is constructed with a concrete lining. Sometimes these wells also have a pump, but in all cases a plentiful supply of clean uncontaminated water is available throughout the whole year.

At the same time, a scheme is being carried out to improve the supply of water to Bathurst whose citizens are fortunate enough to enjoy the advantages of a mains supply. When the scheme is completed, water will be obtained from a number of boreholes mostly on the mainland. One borehole, 1,150 feet deep, has been drilled in Bathurst but this yields a somewhat brackish supply which also contains an excessive quantity of fluorine. At present this water is mixed with the purer water from the mainland boreholes, in such proportions that the resulting product is palatable. At the same time, plans are being made to install a small pilot de-fluoridation plant to investigate the feasibility of reducing the fluorine content of the Bathurst deep borehole water, so that greater use can be made of this source of supply.

Following the course of the water services, we take a look at some of the Government buildings including Government House (undergoing much needed modernisation), the Secretariat (a substantially built building which used to house the army headquarters garrison, including horses, in bygone days), old Public Courts and rambling offices, Government quarters of varied designs and also a number of new buildings such as the Electricity and Marine Headquarters, three storey flats and modern schools. One of the main maintenance problems is to counter the effect of white ants and this is being achieved by the use of metal doors, windows, purlins etc. But most of the older buildings have timber roofs which, if not attacked by the ants, are infested with bats producing an unpleasant odour. This latter problem is still being investigated and much difficulty is being en-countered in reconciling the advice against pitched roofs on the grounds of bat infestation and the advice against flat concrete roofs in the tropics on the grounds of difficulty with expansion and waterproofing.

It is time now to turn to the Public Works Department headquarters, situated in Bathurst and occupying an old Royal Air Force seaplane base. It is here that we see the things which keep the Department ticking along. The Motor Transport and Plant Section occupies a seaplane hangar and carries out complete overhauls on the three hundred vehicles and items of plant to fit them for further long and arduous service. Another hangar is used as a main store for up to £175,000 worth of goods and acts as a wholesale and retail warehouse to ensure a ready supply of every conceivable item used on works, vehicles repairs, etc. Yet another of these invaluable hangars houses the woodworking shop in which carpenters, joiners and machinists manufacture all furniture and built-in fitments for buildings, along with sheet piles for coast protection works, shuttering for concrete work and all other necessary timber items.

In the old but cool timber offices, we find the Accounts Section and Cost Branches which manage to balance the books, the Engineers, Architect, Building Surveyor and the Directorate and Clerical Staffs. We have an expatriate staff of about twenty-five, senior Gambian staff number about fifteen, and our total staff, with the above, comes to approximately nine hundred and fifty. Our daily paid labour strength is around seventeen hundred. These are the people, and this is the organisation which are now slipping into gear for the colourful task of preparing decorations and pavilions and applying the spit and polish to the buildings and roads of the town in readiness for the eagerly anticipated Royal Visit which it is hoped will now take place in 1961.

Architect in Hong Kong

by J. C. CHARTER

WHEN, shortly before the war, I was interviewed in London for an architectural appointment in the Public Works Department of Hong Kong, I was asked: "Are you familiar with the design of reinforced concrete buildings ?" and I replied hopefully: "Yes, a little".

I gathered at the interview that reasonably up-to-date standards of construction were used in the Colony, that such things as lifts were unknown and that I should not be required to deal with mud huts. I was subsequently informed by an aunt who had sojourned there a short while that the summers were very sticky but that the winters were delightful, and cool enough to enable women to don their fur coats; also, that the island of Hong Kong was separated from the mainland by the harbour, and that it was surmounted by a beautiful peak. So I set sail with a picture in my mind's eye of a small island crowned with a conical peak, adjacent to the flat main land which stretched into the blue distance.

How different was the reality. I shall always remember my astonishment and delight on first steaming up the beautiful harbour with ships at anchor, junks and sampans plying, and launches and ferries scurrying in all directions. Here was no solitary peak and flat land, but the grandeur of hills and mountains coming to the water's edge, with buildings crowding onto the narrow coastal shelf of the island, clambering up the steep slopes and spreading over the mainland peninsula of Kowloon.

What of the buildings themselves? I confess to great disappointment at my first sight of the uninspiring, mainly four-storeyed reinforced concrete structures with gaunt balconies, that stretched along a considerable length of the island's waterfront. Later I was to discover at the farther end a very pleasant array of gable-ended godowns (warehouses), all with their gables facing seaward. Because land is so scarce in Hong Kong, many of these, alas, are being replaced by taller buildings, a fate that sooner or later befalls most of the older buildings in the Colony.

Here are the conditions and the challenge that Hong Kong offers an architect: a beautiful setting that can be marred by unsightly development; a climate that alternates between a hot and humid summer and a cool and dry winter, with the effects that these conditions have on the design of buildings and the subsequent behaviour of building materials; some of the highest population densities in the world, together with very hilly terrain and a severe shortage of building sites; reasonable availability, by importation, of building materials; and a large pool of skilled and semi-skilled labour.

Granite is the one building material which is available locally in large quantities. Locally manufactured building materials and components include bricks; light-weight building blocks and slabs; cement; various metal products including some windows, doors and drainage ware; plywood with a variety of attractive veneers; and some paints and distempers. Most other building materials are imported free from Britain and elsewhere, and include structural steel, timber, sanitary goods and hardware, electrical fittings, ceramics and glass, and all kinds of mechanical equipment. Building construction in Hong Kong does not differ appreciably from that in Britain though, for structural purposes in permanent buildings, timber has largely given way to steel and concrete, because of the danger of white ants and of fungal attack. It is used a lot, however, in interior fittings and finishings. Buildings in Hong Kong are designed chiefly to meet the needs of a hot and humid climate and, in this connection, the use of air-conditioning is becoming increasingly popular.

Today, in the Colony, the use of reinforced concrete for building is almost universal, and to this extent building methods are more limited than in the West, and architectural design is correspondingly more circumscribed. Even in the two hundred feet high buildings that are now sprouting in the city centres steel framing is rarely used, largely on account of costs and the difficulty of ensuring that it arrives at the right time. Building techniques are also more limited than in the West, but this again is due more to economic factors than to lack of building skills: for instance, shortage of storage space and the plentiful supply of cheap and good labour discourage contractors from investing in very much mechanical equipment; and concrete mixers, hoists and vibrators, together with pumps and, occasionally, pneumatic drills and a circular saw, are about all the mechanical plant that one meets on a building site. Crazy looking bamboo scaffolding still cages most buildings as they climb laboriously skyward.

On my first arrival at the Architectural Office of the P.W.D., I found myself a member of a staff of eleven architects and one quantity surveyor, together with European clerks of works, and Chinese draughtsmen, foremen and clerical staff; there were no structural engineers. Then, as now, the minimum qualification for an architect was Associateship of the R.I.B.A., or equivalent.

My first job was the design and construction of a four bay fire station with three floors of single and married firemen's quarters above. Because of the gathering war clouds, I was required to design the reinforced concrete frame in such a way that in the event of enemy bombardment the first floor would withstand the collapse of the upper floors, in the hope that the fire appliances would not be wrecked. How I thumbed through my text book, wishing that I knew a little more about the subject! As, later, I watched the building grow, my anxiety about its structural worthiness gave place to a fear that it would sink below ground level, weighed down by the sheer mass of the steel reinforcing rods. However, I am glad to report that the building is still standing, and above ground. That was twenty years ago: in those days the architect designed the building, prepared the working drawings, wrote the specification, had a go at the estimate, supervised the construction and certified payments to the contractors—in fact, he did the lot; and there were few experts whom he could contact by picking up his telephone.

Things are different now: the same office has an all-in establishment of twenty-two architects and twenty assistant architects with about half the corresponding numbers of quantity surveyors and structural engineers, and a small section of electrical engineers (many of whom, in all the professions, are Chinese), together with a large number of draughtsmen, outdoor and clerical staff. The work now is more streamlined and specialised, each section dealing with its own part of the work but combining in the overall production of buildings. One section of the office deals with the maintenance of all Government buildings, which now number over 1,000 of all shapes and sizes and are scattered over the 391 square miles which comprise the mainland and islands of Hong Kong, though the majority are to be found on Hong Kong Island and the Kowloon Peninsula.

The Architectural Office is one of nine sub-departments of the Public Works Department which deal with buildings, roads, drainage, port works, water supplies, land surveys, planning and development, and Government electrical and mechanical plant, and are linked by a Headquarters staff under the Director of Public Works. The Architectural Office is responsible for the design and construction of nearly all Government buildings: at least, it used to be so, though in recent years, in spite of an increased staff, it has been unable to keep pace with the ever increasing demand for new buildings, and many private architects are now commissioned to undertake Government building projects.

What of the scope of a Government architect's work? Since the office deals with all types of Government buildings, the scope is very wide indeed. It is true that we do not build cinemas and restaurants, though a new City Hall project includes a concert hall for 1,540 and a small theatre, together with a banqueting hall, public library, and a small art gallery and museum. We do not build churches, though a scheme for a large crematorium, now on the drawing board, includes a Chinese pavilion, a Hindu pavilion and a Christian chapel, with an adjacent Garden of Remembrance. We build many schools (primary schools for 1,350 children are now becoming standard) and other educational buildings; police stations, prisons, post offices, parks and playgrounds; markets, magistracies and multi-storey car parks; fire stations, flats, flatted factories and a pharmacy; also, many office buildings, and medical buildings including clinics. One large scheme in the New Territories is for a 1,000 bed mental hospital with staff quarters, which will be a small village in itself. The biggest single building that has been handled in the office is the new 1,320 bed general hospital with adjacent staff quarters, to which Her Majesty the Queen has graciously permitted her name to be given, and for which H.R.H. the Duke of Edinburgh laid the foundation stone during his recent visit to the Colony. In view of the specialised nature of the building, Messrs. Easton and Robertson of London were commissioned to plan the hospital, the subsequent detailing and preparation of working drawings being the work of the Architectural Office. When completed, it is thought the hospital will be among the largest and best equipped in the British Commonwealth.

Resettlement housing at present forms an important section of the work in the office. The large influx of refugees to the Colony resulted in the rapid spread of insanitary and inflammable squatter settlements, cheek by jowl with urban development, and posed a problem which the Government has been actively tackling within the limited resources of the Colony. The Public Works Department in collaboration with the Resettlement Department and others has embarked on extensive resettlement housing projects which involve large scale site formation, often in rocky terrain; the entraining of streams; provision of road, drainage and water supplies; and the construction of blocks of resettlement housing and flatted factories, frequently on piled foundations. The population of rehoused squatters now amounts to 215,000 and the aim is to step up construction to provide rehousing at the ultimate rate of 100,000 persons per year. This last figure represents about three per cent of the total population of the Colony, so, in spite of the minimum accommodation provided, it is no small undertaking.

The pace of building in Hong Kong is now tremendous. Because of the high proportion of urban development and the variety of buildings required by an urban community, the work of a Government architect is very varied and interesting, and it has to be carried out at high pressure—or so the architect and his colleagues think.

I forgot to mention that the inevitable public latrine also falls to our lot; but no public houses—no pubs at all!

News of Your Friends

BIRTHS. Brown. On the 13th March 1956, to Priscilla (*née* Day) and David Brown, Agricultural Officer, Moshi, Tanganyika—a son (Alexander Edmund Llewellyn).
Campbell. On the 10th April 1956, at Nairobi, to Jacqueline, wife of Colin Campbell, Colonial Administrative Service—a son.
Geare. On the 15th December 1955, at Kuala Lumpur, Malaya, to Fern (*née* King), wife of John Geare, Malayan Civil Service—a daughter.
Hennessy. On the 23rd February 1956, at Mokhotlong, Basutoland, to Patricia (*née* Unwin), wife of J. P. I. Hennessy, District Commissioner, Mokhotlong—a daughter (Susan Margaret).
Lawrence. On the 9th April 1956, at the War Memorial Hospital, Nakuru, Kenya, to Renée, wife of Henry Patrick Lawrence, Colonial Police Service—a daughter.
Moore. On the 11th April 1956, at Westminster Hospital, to Joy, wife of Gerald Moore, University College, Ibadan—a daughter.
Tilney. On the 5th April 1956, at Dar-es-Salaam, to Rosalind (*née* de Renzy-Martin), wife of C. E. Tilney—a son.

ENGAGEMENTS. Mitchell : Thacker. The engagement is announced between Charles Robin Wingate Mitchell (Nigera Police), elder son of Mr. and Mrs. O. W. Mitchell, of 1, Henshelwood Terrace, Newcastle-upon-Tyne 2, and Anne Marie, only daughter of the late Flying Officer W. L. Thacker, R.A.F., and Mrs. M. Thacker, of Upper Beeding, West Sussex.

MARRIAGES. Simpson : Duthy. On the 15th March 1956, at Nairobi, A. B. Simpson, of Her Majesty's Oversea Service, to Barbara Lois, elder daughter of the late Mr. and Mrs. C. W. Duthy, of Makuyu.
Webb : Chatterton. On the 7th April 1956, at St. Mary's Parish Church, Horncastle, Lincolnshire, George Hannam Webb, of the Administration, Kenya, to Josephine Chatterton, of Horncastle.

DEATH. Sircom. On the 27th March 1956, at Eastbourne, Harold Sebastian Sircom, M.A., B.E.M., Malayan Civil Service (retired), aged 77.

We also regret to report the deaths of the following serving officers:

Weton. On the 7th April 1956, in Accra, V. J. Weton, Soil Scientist, Agricultural Department, W. Reg., Nigeria.
Wilson. On the 10th April 1956, peacefully in Accra, Sir Mark Wilson, Chief Justice, Gold Coast.

PROMOTIONS AND TRANSFERS (*From April List*)

Accountancy: BEDINGFIELD, S. G. (N. Rhodesia), Acct., Gde. I, Kenya.
Administration: AINSWORTH, T. M. (Nigeria), Admin. Off., Sarawak. ARTEMIS, H. C. (Admin. Off., Cl. I), Sen. Admin. Off., Cyprus. BARTON, P. T. (Admin. Off., Cl. III), Admin. Off., Cl. II, E. Reg., Nigeria. BELL, J. B. (Admin. Off., Cl. III), Admin. Off., Cl. II, N. Reg., Nigeria. BROWNING, R. F. (Federation of Nigeria), Admin. Off., Cl. II, Cyprus. CAMBRIDGE, T. C. (Warden), Sen. Warden, Tobago. CARTER, W. S. (Admin. Off., Cl. II), Admin. Off., Cl. I, E. Reg., Nigeria. CHRISTIAN, J. (Admin. Off., Cl. III), Princ. Asst. Sec., E. Reg., Nigeria. COLLINS, D. (Admin. Off., Cl. II), Admin. Off., Cl. I, Fiji. CORNISH, V. L. (Admin. Off., Cl. III), Admin. Off., Cl. II, N. Reg., Nigeria. DUTTON, A. H. (Asst. Ch. Sec.), F.S., Aden. EDWARDS, C. R. E. D. (Sec., Public Serv. Commiss.), Asst. Sec., Barbados. FISH, J. M. B. B. (Admin. Off., Cl. III), Admin. Off., Cl. II, N. Reg., Nigeria. GIBBS, J. P. P. (Admin. Off., Cl. III), Asst. F.S., N. Reg., Nigeria. GRELL, E. H. A. (St. Kitts, Leeward Is.), Asst. Sec., Min. of Lab., Jamaica. GUISE, C. A. L. (Admin. Off., Cl. III), Sec. to Premier, E. Reg., Nigeria. GUNN, I. G. (Admin. Off., Cl. I), Admin. Off., Staff Gde., N. Reg., Nigeria. GUNNING, O. P. (Admin. Off., Cl. I), Admin. Off., Staff Gde., E. Reg., Nigeria. HALL, C. J. (Estab. Off.), Sen. Estab. Off., Uganda. IKPEME, T. W. (Asst. Sec.), Sec. to Public Serv. Commiss., E. Reg., Nigeria. KING, W. S. (Admin. Off., Cl. III), Admin. Off., Cl. II, E. Reg., Nigeria. LAWRENCE, T. W. (Admin. Off., Cl. III), Admin. Off., Cl. II, E. Reg., Nigeria. LETCHWORTH, T. E. (Admin. Off., Cl. I), Admin. Off., Staff Gde., N. Reg., Nigeria. MACBRIDE, D. F. H. (Admin. Off., Cl. I), Admin. Off., Staff Gde., N. Reg., Nigeria. McCLINTOCK, N. C. (Admin. Off., Cl. III), Admin. Off., Cl. II, N. Reg., Nigeria. MALCOLM, P. C. (D.C.), P.C., Sierra Leone. MICHIE, C. W. (Admin.

Town Planning Problems in West Africa

by A. E. S. ALCOCK

(continued)

TOWN planning should be the planning and the control of the use of all land in a town for the social, economic and aesthetic needs of its citizens. Control can only bring development into line with the plan when change of use is desired by the citizens either individually or collectively and by their ability to pay for and carry out the changes. It is therefore directly related to the desire of its citizens for a better town and to the economy of the times.

It is the lack of appreciation of the fundamental fact that towns are living growths made up of human beings who must be willing to co-operate and who must possess the ways and means to improve their towns that has led to so many past mistakes in planning. Town planning cannot be imposed by a central authority but a central authority can materially assist where the local desire for town planning exists. Imposition by a central authority of forms of planning developed outside Africa on West African towns will not succeed. Study of the ways of life of the people in their own environment must be made and new forms produced which will bring spaciousness, convenience and amenity within the reach of the people.

The past has given us out of date grid-iron layouts, rigid and early American in character, laid out with almost complete indifference not only to social requirements but to topographical ones as well. One lesson which can be learnt from these early layouts is that order can be uglier and duller than the most haphazard growth, and that therefore we should try to preserve individuality where we can ; or try to produce it by including diversity in our planning technique.

The other lesson which can be learnt is that order can be uneconomical. It can create many superfluous streets and lanes, the cost of making up and upkeep of which can be met neither by the frontagers nor by the local authorities. It can encourage soil erosion by ignoring topography, leaving problems that are beyond the economic resources of the local authorities to solve.

Our fundamental observations in West Africa seem to show us that a properly developed town with its well-built structures, made roads, electric light and piped water supply, shops, cinemas and varied social amenities is a phenomenon in the surrounding countryside. Outside it the villages have mud buildings, unmade roads, no electric light nor piped water supply, few shops, no cinemas and primitive social amenities. Village life has an entirely different character from town life. In times of economic prosperity, therefore, the populations of towns grow fast while villages are depleted of their inhabitants.

It is, however, a characteristic of West Africa that in hard times the people tend to leave the towns in favour of the villages where living is so much cheaper and food is more plentiful. Thus the fluctuation of town population becomes a factor to be taken into account in our planning.

Despite the fact that the villages are generally poorly served with those things considered essential to civilised life, their social structure is a happier one than is that of the towns. In the villages the family system and the traditional way of life retain their influence on the closely-knit community, satisfying its social needs and keeping up the standard of morality and behaviour. In the towns, on the other hand, the breakdown of the family system and the mixing of peoples of many different kinds has led to such social problems as crime and juvenile delinquency. Until active steps are taken to build up cultural and social activities, so that the mixture of people can meet in common satisfying interest, no social cohesion, which will replace the loss of family ties and stabilise the community, can be formed.

The climate of West Africa is such that many of the normal activities of daily life can be carried on in the open air.   These include cooking and eating, bathing, washing clothes, taking leisure in the day time and so on, as well as the practice of many trades, such as fitting, carpentry and sandal making.   Thus space is more important than buildings, and economy of space by adding height to buildings is not possible when there are no original buildings on which to add height.   The predominance of open-air over indoor activity leads to the use of towns by more people than can be suitably accommodated in the buildings, resulting in nightly overcrowding of sleeping rooms and much sleeping on verandahs, in markets and under temporary shelters.   It is probable that population figures are more closely related to areas of land than to areas of floor space.

We ought therefore to concentrate our planning on those things which bring relief to people living in overcrowded conditions.   Housing is the first essential and planning for residential use a first priority.   Planning for residential use must take into account the daily needs of the community.   To plan barren wildernesses of suburbs without providing for these needs is to nullify the good effects of housing.   It is sometimes said that as houses are needed so badly all effort should be concentrated on their erection and other things such as schools and community, welfare and health centres, and even shops, should be left till later.   If there is a long period between erection of the first houses and providing other things required for the welfare of the community, then serious harm can be done to the nascent social structure of the area.   Good housing management in the most liberal sense and good social welfare services are essential and ought to be developed parallel with the erection of houses.

The making up and keeping clear of footpaths for pedestrians, who are by far the most common users of streets in African towns, and the provision of shelters and seats on small open spaces and so on, are often neglected matters, which, if attended to by the local authorities, could bring much relief to the ordinary townsman, and enhance the general appearance of the streets.

It is said that when two Englishmen meet they start a club and when two Irishmen meet they start a fight.   It may equally be said that when two Africans meet they start a market.   The habit of petty trading is universal, and yet, beyond the inadequate provision of some markets, little is done to provide the petty trader with facilities to help him to carry on his trade.   In consequence he uses the footpaths in the streets, forcing pedestrians into the carriageways, causing obstruction, injury and loss of life.   Originality in design might deal with this problem.   Street corners could be set back whenever possible and petty traders allowed to use the extra space provided.   Footpaths could be made wider at some points, providing bays for petty traders.   Street markets are ancient institutions and their use under municipal control can pay well in the fees charged by the local authority.   This control can take several forms.   Certain streets, for example, can be closed to vehicular traffic on certain days, or during certain hours, and used as markets for wares of certain classes.   Whatever the measures, active interest by the municipality and the use of imagination in tackling the problem is necessary.   Too often a policy of *laissez faire* is adopted towards the street trading problem, while disproportionate attention is given to the creation of monumental public buildings, and to lucrative activities, such as bus services.

The central market is one of the problems of town planning in West Africa. Its magnetic effect on sellers and buyers alike paralyses all attempts to establish a number of smaller markets each more conveniently situated for use by people living in the different residential areas.   The reason for this may be found in the system of trading in West Africa where goods are sold through a chain of middlemen, or more often middlewomen.   The goods often reach the consumer via the petty trader, who sits in a strategic position by the roadside.

To bring the market problem to solution, street trading in residential areas might be prohibited and the sellers concentrated in small market-places by local authority control.   This would have a snowball effect, if properly organised, because the concentration of the buyers would attract more sellers.   In all West African towns the sale of food and other daily essential commodities by sellers, sitting along the local main street at small movable stalls lighted by candles in the evenings after dark, is a feature of social life.   Local residents stroll along the street between the sellers, meeting each other, gossiping and enjoying the relaxation of the end of the day.   If the evening sellers were concentrated in an open space, if possible lit by street lamps, next to the small market and close to the places of social activity, where people could stroll in the evening and meet their friends without the interference of street traffic, the total effect would be to build up a lively centre, which would grow naturally and create a feeling of local unity and cohesion.

All these town planning problems need handling with imagination and understanding and with a desire to do those many small things which will improve the life of the people, rather than to do fewer bigger things in "major capital works" which would demolish houses and deprive people of their homes.

Veneers of fine buildings, wide boulevards and grandiose civic centres may deceive visitors, but the true worth of towns lies only in the conditions under which the majority of their citizens spend their lives.

Sarawak's Posts and Telegraphs

by R. KIRKWOOD, M.B.E.

SARAWAK (47,500 square miles) lies along the north-west coast of the island of Borneo and is approximately 400 miles east of Singapore. She has for neighbours Indonesian Borneo to the east and south, the British territory of North Borneo in the north-east and the State of Brunei to the north. Her coastline is washed by the South China Sea. The territory is entirely tropical, and the multi-racial community of approximately 655,000 consists of Dayaks, Chinese, Malays, Indians and Europeans.

Land near the coast is undulating and rises by degrees to mountains over 7,000 feet in height. Innumerable rivers flow from these and are, in the absence of a territorial road system, the highways of Sarawak.

Communications are vital in this fast developing territory and recent years have seen major development in projects for new roads and airfields. The postal and telecommunication services have been called upon to keep pace with general developments.

For administrative convenience Sarawak is divided into five divisions with five major towns as divisional headquarters—Kuching, Simanggang, Sibu, Miri and Limbang.

The Posts and Telegraph Department with its headquarters office in Kuching, the capital, is responsible for the running and development of postal and tele-communications services in Sarawak. The Department is under the control of a Postmaster-General assisted by a Deputy Postmaster-General, an Assistant Controller of Posts and Telegraphs and headquarters staff. In each of the Divisions there are resident Assistant Controllers who are responsible for the efficient running of postal services and radio and telephone communications in their particular regions.

Senior staff number 12 and the total number of Departmental officers in the various other grades is 519, of whom 312 are engaged in telecommunications work and 207 in postal duties.

The first Post Office in Sarawak was opened on the 1st March, 1869, at Kuching. Today there are 40 Post Offices throughout the territory.

The sea mail between Kuching and Singapore relies mainly on one ship each week in both directions, as it has for many years. There are also direct services between Singapore, Sibu and Miri. Immediately prior to the war the usual Kuching mail consisted of about 75 bags; today this number has increased fourfold despite the fact that a large and increasing amount of correspondence is carried by air.

To the outstations, mail is distributed by small ships and launches which run to reasonable schedules.

In 1952 there were two aeroplanes weekly in each direction between Singapore and Sarawak stopping at Sibu and Kuching. Today there are aeroplanes in both directions daily, sometimes twice a day. Feeder services are now in operation to six airfields other than Kuching and Sibu.

The use of air services for carriage of first class mail is exploited fully. A separate bag is closed for each stopping place on the main and feeder air routes.

At the main towns of Kuching, Sibu and Miri sorting and delivery arrangements for mail are satisfactory but the great increase in the volume of mail handled and the number of transport services for which mails have to be prepared requires the constant development of organisation and methods. There are mail deliveries at these towns and Private Box and Counter Delivery facilities also exist.

In the smaller places a visit to the Post Office and enquiry as to whether there is any mail for the person named secures delivery. This arrangement is very informal but is as effective as possible when it is remembered that mail may be addressed to persons several days journey from the nearest Post Office.

Wherever it is reasonably possible to do so, it is the general policy to take postal services to the public. To this end letter boxes for posting are provided and stamp vendors are licensed, but there are still many small villages in Sarawak without Post Offices. There are others where Post Offices exist but they can hardly be justified by the volume of business done. Usually in these places postal work is undertaken by Treasury or Administrative Service staff.

Development of Postal Agencies along orthodox lines at small villages is rendered difficult as, in general, it is not always possible to find Agents with a sufficient knowledge of English or accounting. Development of a postal service restricted to ordinary mail collection and delivery through the agency of local Headmen and citizens of prominent standing has provided a useful arrangement which is being extended.

The Department is responsible for the operation of a Savings Bank in Sarawak which is of considerable use, providing services in many remote places where no other secure means of depositing money exists. A new Ordinance and Regulations became effective on the 1st January, 1957, and an entirely new system of centralised machine accounting was introduced.

Since 1952 the number of Savings Bank accounts has increased from 5,424 to 8,122 and at the end of 1958 depositors had $3,581,039 to their credit.

The telegraph system in 1952 was composed entirely of low power radio equipment operated by hand keyed Morse Code. All equipment was old and difficult to maintain, and it was decided not to renew the system but to plan for the services to be incorporated in a telephone network.

The general plan was to introduce teleprinters instead of Morse keying between the large towns and to use word dictation on the telephone system between the large towns and their outstations.

There was no telephone system in Sarawak in the accepted sense. There were very small, very old, inadequate manual exchanges in the main towns but there were no Trunks and Junctions.

Development of the telephone system divided itself into three compartments, Automatic Telephone Exchanges with underground cable systems for connexion to individual telephones within a small area, a Junction System for interconnecting these main exchanges to outstations within 30 or 40 miles radius and a Trunk System for connecting the main Exchanges throughout Sarawak.

Development along these lines is proceeding and brief details of the telecommunications network as it now exists in Sarawak are as follows:—

The three largest towns—Kuching, Sibu and Miri—are equipped with automatic telephone exchanges and associated underground cable systems. The exchanges are of the latest design; Kuching is equipped for 2,000 lines, Sibu for 600 and Miri for 300. Each exchange has adequate manual board positions which operate as trunk and junction switchboards and are used for other duties.

Simanggang and Limbang are equipped with central battery exchanges which also incorporate trunk and junction termination. At other places in the territory central battery or magneto exchanges have been newly installed and are connected by junctions to the main exchanges.

The gradual replacement of the outstation manual exchanges by small automatic exchanges is planned and some are already on order. Main automatic exchanges will be extended as required and plans are already in hand to extend Sibu Exchange to 1,200 lines this year. The demand for telephones is greatly stimulated by the provision of junctions for connection to places outside the main exchange telephone systems.

Sarawak has not got the roads and railways usually found in other countries, and the provision of landline and cables for long distance telephone connections is an impossibility on practical and economic considerations, but VHF radio has provided a suitable medium of communication which, although restricted in range, serves to cover the 30 or 40 miles required by Sarawak conditions.

Standard VHF radio stations using about 10 watts of radio power and directional aerials mounted on masts 100 feet high have been installed at 60 stations. These stations work into main VHF radio stations at Divisional headquarters, mostly directly but in some cases it has been necessary for technical reasons to use intermediate stations.

For full utilisation of the telephone exchanges and junctions already described it is necessary to enable any subscriber in Sarawak to speak with any other subscriber in the territory and eventually to any country in the world. The immediate requirement for this is to provide a trunk telephone system linking Divisional headquarters.

The distance between Kuching and Sibu is 120 miles and between Sibu and Miri 200 miles, and the orthodox methods of providing circuits over such distances by VHF radio would be to use repeaters at intervals of 30 or 40 miles or to operate from stations on high mountains. But the mountains of Sarawak are not reasonably accessible for servicing of equipment and staffing. Also inhabited villages between the main towns are irregularly spaced and are generally not accessible.

It was, therefore, decided to make every effort to avoid repeater stations as far as possible and to conduct a survey to determine what could be done with VHF on long distances in Sarawak.

As a result of this survey an initial VHF trunk system has been planned and implemented, using towers 150 feet high and available stations. The system as expected has given some serviceable results and has provided design information for a final scheme now being carried out. This scheme involves towers 300 and 250 feet in height and highly directional aerial arrays.

Telecommunications development has not lagged. Teleprinters are replacing Morse circuits and further progress is anticipated in the provision of Voice Frequency Telegraph Systems.

At present the Department is setting up equipment for a Kuching/Singapore circuit, using Independent Sideband technique which will carry speech circuits and a channelled telegraph system.

In 1952 trunk telephone facilities were practically nil. Today the telephone network handles 46,000 trunk calls monthly and from this figure it is possible to gauge the impact which the development of telecommunications has had on trade and commerce in Sarawak.

A Geologist in British Guiana

by J. H. BATESON

I am back again in civilisation after another mapping trip in the interior, so let me tell you a little of how we geologists occupy our time here in British Guiana.

Primarily the chief function of any Geological Survey is economic and that of British Guiana is no exception. All our work is aimed at the discovery of economic minerals or materials for specific uses such as road metal, building stone, etc. After the initial discovery of a deposit and an assessment of the quantity available it is then up to the industrialist and economist to organise its exploitation.

In predominantly forested territories, such as British Guiana of which 85 per cent is covered by tropical rain forest, a map of the geology is necessary before large scale exploration can be reasonably attempted. This is the task which we in British Guiana are tackling at present—to produce an accurate geological map of the 87,000 square miles of the Colony; quite a large task.

The Guianese climate allows two dry seasons each year, approximately from February to May and again from August to November. It is during these periods that we leave our headquarters in Georgetown for the interior. The wet seasons are spent in town writing up the reports of our dry seasons' work. About a month before an expedition leaves Georgetown the organisation starts—it takes just about this length of time to ensure that all the necessary arrangements are completed.

Each geologist is personally responsible for the recruiting of the necessary labour force, obtaining sufficient rations and all the equipment. Experience in British Guiana has shown that the Amerindians, tough, energetic people with an extremely good knowledge of the forest, are the best labour force for our needs and without them our work would be impossible.

Usually the geologist is aided in the routine—and often tiresome—tasks of getting an expedition organised by an assistant on whom falls the unenviable duty of filling in numerous forms and ration orders. Eventually from the mounds of forms and letters there emerges a fully organised expedition ready to set off once more for the interior. A D-day is chosen and arrangements are made for the rendezvous of men, supplies, equipment and (one hopes), the geologist. Georgetown is exchanged for the four or five hundred square miles of hills and vales—all thickly mantled by forest—which are to be our home for the next twelve weeks or so.

The location of the area to be studied determines the method used in the transporting of men and equipment. Since British Guiana boasts many navigable rivers, these often are used; but in a few areas road or air transport is used instead. The majority of the surveying done in any area is, however, carried out on foot, the geologist walking over as much of the area as possible. The one exception to this being the completely water-borne traverse of a river system.

No matter by what method the area is reached, all types of expedition require a base camp, from which to operate and to serve as a main store for rations and equipment. The task of building such a camp probably takes about a week or ten days to complete, after which the party is ready to begin its task of mapping.

Since many areas of British Guiana are unmapped we often start our work without any knowledge of the area at all. In some areas we may, however, be more fortunate and obtain some information from earlier work. Armed with what information can be obtained, the next step is to plan the broad outlines of the mapping programme with a view to covering as much of the area as possible in the allotted time. Each individual geologist has, of course, his own methods of attacking the problems of a new area—methods which are liable to modification by local conditions. The terrain of the area, mountainous, undulating or flat and the type of bush through which the lines and trails are cut, are all factors that tend to limit the effective range of a surveying party. River surveys, likewise, are affected by obstructions in the river course—rapids, falls and shallows; all take time to negotiate.

As a preliminary to the party moving away from the area of the base camp numbers of surveying lines are cut. These it is hoped will give an indication of the grain of the country and thus enable future operations to be planned. Very often small streams are useful in this way since they invariably lead towards the higher ground and often they have rock outcrops in their courses.

Each of the lines cut is surveyed by simple but reasonably accurate methods and plotted on the base map. It usually requires a team of three or four Amerindians, using cutlasses, to cut such a line; a distance of three or four miles is usually covered in a day. To ensure that the line proceeds in the required direction each cutting party is accompanied by a 'compass-man', who constantly checks and re-checks the direction. It is not unusual for the chief cutter—the 'line-leader'—to be the compass-man. The cut line is then measured into sections, each one-tenth of a mile long, often by using a cyclometer gauge or in more difficult country by accurate pacing. A slashed and numbered tree marks the end of each of the tallies, as the sections are called. These tallies are important to the geologist as they enable the observations of topography and geology to be put more accurately on the map. Aneroid barometer readings are taken regularly along the lines and the heights determined by reference to the diurnal graph of barometric changes kept at base camp.

It is hoped that solid rock will be found on each line but unfortunately this isn't always the case. When rocks are found, out comes the notebook and copious notes are made and a large specimen is collected for further study in Georgetown.

When sufficient lines have been cut away from the base, the work has to be extended further afield, which involves the establishment of smaller temporary camps. Existing surveying lines, suitably widened, can usually be used as droghing trails along which all the necessary food and supplies are carried by the Amerindians. Although the amount of material to be transported is cut to the minimum, the men often carry weights of over one hundred pounds. In some cases where the distances involved are great a small party of men may be permanently employed carrying food from the base camp to the most advanced parties.

After a period of about ten weeks surveying a geologist may have used a dozen or more camps and surveyed two hundred miles of line. Camps and lines are plotted on the map, thus building up a network for the topographical and geological observations. During the trip prospection is undertaken at the most likely places; sands and gravels are washed and the heavy residues collected for more detailed work in Georgetown.

Having successfully covered the area, the geologist for a short while becomes an administrator. He pays off all the labourers and returns them to their homes, packs up the equipment and with it returns to Georgetown. Here the pen replaces the hammer and the microscope the prospector's sieve. Thin sections of the rocks are examined and bit by bit the geological pattern of the area becomes apparent and eventually a map and report is produced. Thus the first chapter in geological research is ended—the results of which it is hoped will provide some of the necessary stepping stones to future discoveries and knowledge.

This then is briefly the work of a geologist in British Guiana, an interesting and varied work encountering all kinds of situation and made all the more exciting by the uncertainty of what is to be found along the next line or around the next bend.

Tembo

by RUTH BULMAN

She stands with terrible patience
    Locked in dim dreams,
Then lumbers with the others, linked at trunk and tail,
    Slowly around the ring.
She waltzes, bows, bereft of dignity
Twice-nightly amidst pleased applause;
Well fed, well groomed, but dead save that her giant heart
Still beats, still aches with cold bewilderment
And puzzling shadows linger in her mind,
    A sudden sight, a sound of Africa.
Perhaps she has forgotten why the surge of loss
    Swells in her belly; or perhaps she roams the scorching plain,
Remembers where the lion eats his kill
With innocent and bloody jaws thrust deep in flesh.
Perhaps the wild, harsh smells come faintly now, distilled in pain
And knowledge that these scents long-gone
Are now out-scented by this stink of Adam
    Who has lost his innocence.

And do the clouding lenses of her eyes
Record the lost days of the gold and green,
When great and sloping shapes moved slow
    Towards the rains ?

Meteorology in Mauritius

by EDWIN G. DAVY

(*concluded*)

THE headquarters of the Mauritius Meteorological Service is situated on the western side of the central plateau in a pleasant climate at 1,400 feet with temperatures not often outside the range of 65° to 85°F. and a well distributed rainfall of about 80 inches. The climatological, finance, equipment and upper air sections are housed there with the usual headquarters services. The close attention to maritime interests is emphasised by the accommodation in a wing of the headquarters building of the Mauritius ship-to-shore wireless station. During cyclonic periods the hurricane warning centre at headquarters is a favourite place of call for local sugar estate employees and for Government officials and businessmen on their daily journey from their residences on the plateau to their offices in Port Louis. The release of large hydrogen filled balloons from the Upper Air Stations is a perpetual source of interest to passers-by in the early morning hours.

The uses of the Royal Alfred Observatory in the northern plain have continuously decreased until now only the geo-magnetic station remains among the buildings badly damaged by the recent cyclones. The decay had already started in the 1920's when it was found necessary to open a small office on the healthier site of the present headquarters. The invasion of malaria over all the low-lying parts of Mauritius has caused frequent illness and quite a few deaths at Pamplemousses especially among those who did night duties. The proximity of the Armed Forces and radio stations, and better road and telephone communications and the general development of the central plateau all pushed the old Observatory into greater isolation in an area abandoned by the residents of earlier days.

The assumption by the local Government of the responsibilities of meteorological services at the aerodrome held by the Royal Naval Air Service and the Royal Air Force until 1947 had to mean the end of the old Observatory as a 24-hour observing station. New accommodation at the headquarters and more suitable observing stations in the north have almost completely replaced the usefulness of a station which was one of the prides of Mauritius at the beginning of the century.

It is also the air traffic at Plaisance and the common use of radio communication which have so much changed the structure of the Department generally. Three world air lines regularly use the trunk routes through Mauritius and several civil and military aeroplanes come on special missions. Air France terminates its twice or thrice weekly trunk route from Paris to the Indian Ocean at Mauritius. Quantas Empire Airways and South African Airways regularly fly the long hauls from Johannesburg through Mauritius and Cocos Keeling to Perth, Australia. The two thousand miles and more of open space between Mauritius and Cocos may still provide the longest regular scheduled flight operated in the world; certainly it represents one of the dullest flights for a passenger and one of the more difficult for the weather forecaster and the navigator. The pre-war activities have nevertheless been considerably expanded. The collection and distribution of observations from and to ships over a large part of the south-western part of the Indian Ocean have been made more regular and frequent; the forecasters and tropical cyclone warnings service to ships have been extended, using present-day facilities to provide an up-to-date service. The network of climatological stations is probably as dense for the country as a whole as any in the world but so is the population, and the irregular topography causes quite a variety of climates over a small area. There is one rainfall station for every three square miles. Rainfall maps recently drawn up show that while annual rainfall averages 200 inches in the forest area at 2,000 feet above sea level, it is as low as 35 inches only ten miles away, near the western coast where crops can only be grown under irrigation. Climatological studies have to be made for aerial survey for a new road, for new power stations and crops, for developing secondary industries and always, continuously, for the sugar cane plantations on which the very life of the Colony of Mauritius at present depends.

Such is the day-to-day work of a meteorologist in Mauritius and in spite of the south-east trade winds the normal weather of the area is not so monotonous as might be imagined. But the focus of attention in Mauritius in 1960 was the hurricanes, the disastrous wiping away of fourteen years' growth of luxuriant vegetation and fourteen years of relative prosperity for the sugar industry and the Colony as a whole. During 1959 there was not a single hour in the year in which the wind averaged over 18 miles per hour. In 1960 hurricane winds tore twice across the island for hours decreasing the sugar crops to 40 per cent of normal expectations, blocking every road, breaking down every overhead telephone and electric power line and destroying dozens of churches and tens of thousands of homes.

From both a professional and personal point of view one such experience for a meteorologist is probably worth a life time of back-room service and study. The knowledge that 600,000 inhabitants locally and administrators, bankers and insurers in many parts of the world are waiting for what he alone can say about the coming danger, and the rare experience of seeing the much-described sequence of events as the centre of a very severe tropical cyclone moves over him, are not easily forgotten.

When the first warning for cyclone 'Carol' was issued on Thursday, 24th February, the public still had unhappy memories, only six-weeks old, of cyclone 'Alix'. The Meteorologists Class I warning, that there was one chance in six that Mauritius would suffer damage in the next few days, was sufficient to set all the island thinking about precautions and the majority actually taking some action. The class of warning was gradually stepped up by the Meteorological Department until on Saturday afternoon the final Class IV warning was issued with a statement that gusts might exceed 120 miles per hour—higher than had ever before been recorded in Mauritius—before dawn on Saturday. Steadily during Saturday evening human activities in Mauritius slowed down almost to a halt as nature took over. Roads became obstructed, telephones went dead, high voltage cables flashed and all electric power was cut off.

Throughout the night wind increased fitfully and rain, which totalled 25 inches within 48 hours, increased and moved more in a horizontal direction rather than falling vertically. On Sunday morning there were none of the callers to talk to the forecaster still at his chart after almost continuous duty over three days and nights. Bulletins on progress of the storm were only of interest now and could be distributed only on a few underground telephone and radio-telephone links to the cyclone emergency centre and to the broadcasting station for the benefit of the few owners of battery-operated sets. Nobody could move outside in this howling mass of air and rain rushing at speeds from 118 to 160 miles per hour over the whole island. Then, while this was at its fiercest outside the meteorological office, the Commissioner of Police kept his promise—he rang up to say that outside *his* office only twelve miles away there was no wind, no rain—just hot tropical sunshine. Half an hour later, as the calm central area or "eye" of the storm started to move over the meteorological headquarters, the wind fell and a candle was lit in the garden, while twenty miles away in every direction the wind continued its furious circular chase at hurricane speeds.

This was a large "eye", forty miles in diameter, made to measure, almost, so that at one time every part of the island was in calm, sunny weather. But all knew that this was only a temporary respite in which refugees could move to shelter or the more fortunate householders could patch up their partly broken dwellings before the hurricane winds came again from the exactly opposite direction. One of the most memorable things was the symphony of hammering which sounded on every home throughout Mauritius in the otherwise deadly quiet lull of three hours. During the hurricane winds before and after the calm, the noise was frightening. Above the roar of the wind and rain, the crashing of trees and roofs was hardly audible and many left their place of refuge to find that major parts of their houses had completely disappeared.

Within a year of the greatest cyclone the Colony and its meteorologists had to face the worst mid-summer drought on record. In four months from November to February the rainfall in the main catchment area was only eighteen inches whereas only four days in the two cyclones of last year gave forty inches.

The climate even in a sub-tropical island is far from monotonous and until the day that man can control the weather his dependence upon it and his studies of nature's ways must be continous. The daily forecasting, too, for ships, aircraft and any future means of transport is unlikely to be diminished in importance as long as the motto of Mauritius correctly remains: *Stella Clavisque Maris Indici.*

Dealing with Ships in Hong Kong

by W. R. K. COLLINGS, I.S.O.

IT is difficult to do full justice to the organisation, work and special problems of our Marine Department without going to great length, but an appreciation will be obtained by reference to the latest Departmental Report which shows a year's total of 97,453 vessels of all classes, of 32,641,842 nett tons, entering and clearing the port. These vessels loaded and discharged 7,472,335 tons of cargo and landed and embarked 2,614,927 passengers. In addition to the Department's work in this connection, 7,611 visits were made by officers of the ship survey sub-department in respect of surveys on vessels of divers nationalities.

The importance of Hong Kong from a ship-owing aspect and as a port of registry can also be appreciated by noting that at the end of 1958 there were 473 ships of a total of 503,130 nett tons registered at Hong Kong. All this movement of ships, cargoes, passengers, surveys and registration in one way or another comes within the scope of the Hong Kong Merchant Shipping Ordinance or International Conventions for the Safety of Life at Sea which, besides Port Administration, it is the function of the Marine Department to deal with.

The organisation of the Department is unique in that all the facilities for conducting ships' business, i.e., entry and clearance, dangerous goods, licensing, mercantile marine office, registry, emigration, port medical officer, ship and radio surveys, examination of Masters, Mates and Engineers, and Marine Court are all housed in one building.

In the administration of the port the Director of Marine is assisted by two important bodies, namely the Port Committee and the Port Executive Committee comprising representatives of shipping firms, Foreign and Chinese Chamber of Commerce, the Government, the Army and the Navy. The Port Committee consider and advise on the long view problems of the port and the Port Executive Committee on its day to day problems.

The day to day work of the Department is under the control of an Assistant Director of Marine (Port Control) and an Assistant Director of Marine (Ship Surveys). The former is responsible to the Director for the safe administration of the port and covers entries and clearances, buoyage, lighthouses, communications, pilotage, wreck removal, dangerous goods, licensing, ferry services, mercantile marine office and crews and maintenance of 133 Government owned vessels. The latter deals with and advises the Director on the application of the Safety Requirements of all International Conventions for the Safety of Life at Sea, the Merchant Shipping Acts and local Shipping Ordinances in respect of all vessels entering or clearing the port.

Under the Assistant Director of Marine (Port Control) there are four Senior Marine Officers and seven Marine Officers all holding Master Mariners Certificates of Competency for ocean-going ships.

Under the Assistant Director of Marine (Ship Surveys), or Safety Division of the Department, there are three Senior Surveyors of Ships at the head respectively of the Nautical, Naval Architectural and Engineering branches, and 11 Surveyors of Ships. All these officers are highly qualified in their own particular profession and are also required to complete a special course of instruction under the Ministry of Transport and Civil Aviation in the United Kingdom. This ensures that all surveys of British and foreign ships carried out by these officers applying International Conventions for the Safety of Life at Sea, are to the standard required by the Ministry of Transport and Civil Aviation and thus all Hong Kong Certificates issued have wide world validity.

The expansion of the Ship Survey branch goes back to 1925 when two passenger ships were built by the Hong Kong and Whampoa Dock Co., Ltd. for the Australia/ Japan run and registered at the port of Hong Kong. When the Australian authorities became aware that these vessels were to be issued with Hong Kong passenger certificates they said that they would not recognise these certificates on the grounds that they (the authorities) were not satisfied the vessels were up to the safety standards required for passenger vessels on international voyages. As a result of this the Hong Kong Government requested the Board of Trade to send out one of its senior surveyors to examine the composition of the Ship Surveys Department and to make recommendations that, if carried out, would ensure that surveys and certificates issued would have world wide validity. This was done and resulted in additional surveyors being appointed covering all three branches of ship construction and operation, namely nautical, naval architectural and engineering, and this naturally brought about a stricter application of the rules. The tale goes that the small, hard pressed staff of those days rushed from one ship to another with barely enough time to get into boiler suits and instead of a testing hammer an umbrella, normally used for protection against sun or rain, was used to test the soundness of ships' plates and life boat hulls—indeed, the saying that some old ships held together by rust and force of habit was in many cases more fact than fiction.

Before the war most of the China coastwise ships were engaged in the unberthed passenger or coolie trades between China ports, Hong Kong and the Straits Settlements. These were called 'Simla Ships' so named from the Simla Conference which met at Simla, in India, in 1931, to consider safety standards for these ships which were built primarily for carriage of cargo but also carried large numbers of unberthed Chinese emigrants in the between-decks and on the weather deck. In some cases these ships measured up for as many as 2,000 souls and the provision of sufficient life jackets was always a problem. It was not uncommon for life jackets to be shifted from one ship just completing a survey to another just commencing. The problem of ensuring that jackets were adequate was made more difficult by the unberthed passengers stealing the kapok from those so filled and substituting rags. This resulted in this type of life jacket being disallowed, except for crew and cabin passengers, and only cork being permitted for the unberthed passengers.

A favourite trick of life jacket manufacturers in those early days was to produce what we used to call a 'pot pie' jacket. This was done by pegging together pieces of cork in the shape of two pie dishes; the inside cavity thus formed was then filled with cork sweepings from the floor.

Looking back over the pre-war years when the unberthed passenger trade was really flourishing, one cannot forget the worries that the cabbage season brought. Cabbages were carried in large baskets and shipped in great quantities to Singapore, and as they were stowed on the weather deck they were often found greatly to restrict the airing space required for the between-deck passengers, not to mention restricting passageways and access to life boats, life rafts and emergency steering gear. There were often long drawn out arguments between the Surveyor and the ship's compradore to get sufficient baskets off-loaded before clearance could be granted. I often used to wonder how the passengers managed to tolerate the smell of being perpetually in a pickle factory—but there, that is life in China: a voyage with a deck cargo of cabbages, large jars of pickles and pigs on the after well deck, a hot sun and a following breeze is something one will not hurriedly forget.

Problems arising from a brisk unberthed passenger trade and inadequate staff diminished in the course of a few years after the last war. The unberthed passenger trade practically ceased to exist, additional staff was recruited to fill unfortunate losses due to the war, and the problems of port administration and surveys became similar to those of any large modern port. There were two main exceptions, however, one concerning mechanisation of local primitive type vessels and the other arising from the increase in ships registered at the port of Hong Kong.

With the terrific increase in Hong Kong's population, the demand for fish, which forms a large part of the Chinese diet, resulted in a rapid mechanisation of a large number of primitive types of fishing vessels. These vessels when in port, and particularly when taking shelter from a threatening typhoon, lie up in one or another of the few Typhoon Shelters which are situated within the port of Victoria or Waters of the Colony. They moor close to one another, forming a locked mass of junks with a forest of masts and rigging, and the possibility of a fire spreading with devastating effect became a worry to the Department, the Fire Brigade and the Marine Police, and consequently propulsion by petrol or semi-diesel engines was prohibited. In these types of vessels cooking is done over an open 'chatty' fire on the deck and it needs no imagination to visualise what could happen by careless filling of a petrol tank or an accumulation of petrol vapour due to a leak, should one of the numerous members of a family on board upset the 'chatty'. Constant vigilance was required to enforce the regulation against petrol propulsion and also that which required keeping on board sufficient life saving appliances and fire extinguishers in good condition. The Marine Court presided over daily by one of the two Assistant Directors, who are appointed Marine Magistrates in addition to their normal professional duties, deals with these and other offences against the Marine Ordinance. These officers have acquired over many years of service a sound knowledge of the problems besetting the local population, who are gradually beginning to appreciate that the purpose behind it all is the safety of life afloat among a population where the value of life is not high.

A ship manned by Chinese crew requires about 30 per cent more hands than when the crew is European. In post war years there has been a large transfer to Hong Kong registry of ocean going ships employing Chinese crews and this has resulted in the existing crew accommodation and life saving appliances in these ships being taxed to their utmost. Ship owners were allowed all possible reasonable and practicable concessions so as to keep vessels operating, and the drafting of regulations concerning crew space in ships based on Hong Kong and manned by Chinese crews was discussed with all interested parties as a prelude to making rules. The overcrowding to which the Chinese are generally used ashore, combined with national habits and custom, often resulted in a *maskee* (don't care) attitude both from shipowners and the crews themselves, but the matter has been earnestly pressed forward and is now reaching completion. Life saving appliances in these ships have been brought into line with international standards which are applied to all foreign going ships operating in and out of the port. It is strange that those who go down to the sea in ships are often the least concerned with the adequacy of the life saving appliances on board.

These and other local problems give the Hong Kong Marine Department many tasks of complexity and interest. But it is perhaps the international character of the work that is its greatest stimulus. With ships of so many nations passing through Hong Kong, we cannot know monotony.

A Keeper of the Peace

by HARRY CONWAY, O.B.E.

"THE PREVENTION and detection of crime, and the maintenance of public security"—that was how our duties were defined in the Palestine Police. It proved to be an accurate definition applicable to the Colonial Police Service as a whole.

I went to Palestine in a squad of a dozen recruits. At the Jerusalem training school we underwent an intensive three months course in P.T., police duties, law, musketry, foot and arms drill, colloquial Arabic and first aid. As the basis for our lectures we were issued with a comprehensive manual containing not only what we had to know about such essentials as powers of arrest and search without warrant, and when we would be justified in using firearms, but also a summary of the more important ordinances, and a chapter on the constitution of the Force and the structure of district administration. Around this book, these lectures and the sweat of squad drill on a dusty white square our training revolved, supervised by the commandant and his staff.

Although our training was semi-military it was made clear to us that in our daily duties we would be alone and would have to act on our own initiative. Emphasis was placed upon the importance of crime prevention, but half-way through our course we had practical experience of the maintenance of public security—an aspect of policing which, paradoxically enough, was to assume ever greater importance as territories moved towards independence.

At that time passions were inflamed by the influx of Jewish immigrants, legal and illegal, then fleeing from Nazi persecution, and the Arabs decided to hold a protest demonstration in Jaffa. It was prohibited but the prohibition was defied and we went to Jaffa as part of reinforcements. In the riot that occurred we made baton charges in an effort to disperse a turbulent mob. Then the mounted police came in and finally an armed party. A few rounds of controlled fire aimed at the knees of ringleaders speedily dispersed the rioters, patrols were put out and peace gradually restored.

Life in the Palestine Police was varied. There were frontier outposts to be manned and isolated Jewish settlements to be guarded. There was plain clothes work in the cities. There were port and marine duties, including coastal patrols, to check illegal immigration and arms smuggling; and there were mounted patrols in rural areas and camelry patrols into the Negev desert. I had a year on foot patrol duties. Night patrols were best because instead of being alone we paired off with Arab constables, and this helped the learning of Arabic and the acquisition of local knowledge. There followed a spell in the investigation branch of a Jerusalem police station. The investigation of crime was done by Arab detectives, my duties being confined to records and fingerprinting, but this routine was enlivened by our searches of strange but unromantic places in our quest for criminals, arms, drugs and stolen property.

All police work in Palestine was complicated by the Arab-Jewish conflict. Everything we did had a political repercussion and the problems that arose had to be considered with this in mind. The pattern of work changed drastically during the Arab and Jewish rebellions. The Force was increased and more troops were brought into the country. Police and Army co-ordinated their efforts to counter gang warfare in the hills, ambushes on the roads, terrorism in the towns and villages and sabotage everywhere.

The British police idea is that the force behind the police is public opinion. It usually is in the United Kingdom, though it has to be fostered and sustained by goodwill on all sides. In the Colonial sphere, when extreme nationalism aggravated unrest and caused emergencies, the police enjoyed no such support. The articulate and influential section of the public was antagonistic to the Government and therefore to its agents of law and order. Moderates, feeling helpless or bewildered, rarely opposed extremists but allowed themselves to be intimidated and manipulated by them. Opinion as reflected, for instance, in the vernacular Press was hostile to the police.

A Force which has the opinion of a temperate public behind it will rarely have recourse to arms in the execution of its duties. Colonial police forces are armed and given a measure of military training to enable them to deal with riots and other grave outbursts of violence—though by far the greater part of their duties is performed unarmed. Behind the police stand H.M. Forces ready to step in and restore order should civil strife get beyond police control. Colonial police have therefore to function in close co-operation with them, though it is not often that H.M. Forces have to be used in this way.

After Palestine I served in the Windward Islands where the routine of work was done in tranquillity. Included within our Province were such extraneous duties as prison administration, fire brigade, immigration and certain measures of poor relief. There were interesting and agreeable interludes of liaison work with U.S. Forces at certain air and naval stations, but in due course I welcomed a transfer to Aden.

Initially my duties there included passport control but soon I was back on the more stimulating activities of divisional police work, with a number of busy police stations to look after. There were patrol systems to be worked out in as varied a way as possible, both to relieve their tedium by day and to defeat the wiles of criminals by night. There was the policing of a very busy port to attend to. There were parades, kit inspections and interviews to be held, defaulters to be dealt with, courts to be attended, canteens to be supervised and sports to be arranged. The investigation of crime and traffic accidents and the scrutiny of case files occupied much time. There were lectures to be given so that personnel could be prepared for their proficiency examinations, the passing of which meant an increase in salary. Police were responsible for the safe custody of prisoners before their remand to prison pending trial or bail, and also for the custody of found property and court exhibits. The numerous registers maintained by station staff had to be regularly checked. Armouries had to be inspected to see that the police arms in them were being properly kept, and that firearms and daggers deposited temporarily by Arabs entering Aden from the Yemen or the Protectorate were labelled and ready for return to them when they left.

Arab reaction to events in Palestine caused periods of racial tension which eventually erupted into serious anti-Jewish rioting. After that many Jews went to Israel and agitators turned their attention to Indian and Somali immigration and to the political exploitation of incipient labour unrest in the port and the oil refinery. Strikes followed and for many months demanded unremitting vigilance by the police who had to exercise patience, tact and firmness in preventing clashes between pickets and strike-breakers, in protecting property from the attacks of hooligans and in moving on and dispersing crowds of discontented people.

Service in the Special Branch gave me a new experience. Special Branches in Colonial forces are a post-war development made necessary by the growth of subversive activity, whether communist or nationalist, of a sort to threaten public security and disrupt or undermine constitutional government. Police work overseas was never as straightforward as I had observed it to be in the United Kingdom. In the Special Branch it was even less so. I learned, for instance, that there were occasions when too rigid enforcement of the law might jeopardise the public security which it was the duty of the police to maintain. There was always force available to restore order should it be broken, but was it not better to prevent a breach and take suitable action at a more propitious time? Sometimes it was.

The policing of political meetings, when tempers were exacerbated and excitement high, posed delicate problems which could be assessed accurately only when there was relevant information about them; but strong precautions were always necessary. In times of political tension or strife caused by subversive activity a Commissioner can use his Force to best advantage only when he has adequate information on which to act. The Special Branch had to supply it, and did so in conjunction with other branches of the Force, with the help of the man on the beat and by using its own "sources" among the public.

Colonial Police Forces managed more often than not to maintain law and order even in critically difficult circumstances. Perhaps more people than we realised saw and appreciated that the rule of law which they represented led towards justice and conciliation. It was possible to mistake timidity for public indifference. What the police had to contend with was a vociferous but not unimportant minority whose leaders had to be reckoned with, and understood.

Colonial Police Forces have changed as much as the territories they serve. There is a more careful selection of recruits, with greater attention to their character, physique and standard of education. Most Forces now have their own training schools where a more thorough instruction is given in a wider range of subjects than in the past. There are periodical refresher and promotion courses, and at stations a curriculum of instruction to ensure the required standard of efficiency, knowledge and turnout. There are arrangements nowadays for advanced training overseas. Selected inspectors attend courses for junior officers at the Metropolitan Police College, Hendon; and officers of the rank of Assistant Superintendent and above may be sent to the Police College at Bramshill in Hampshire for courses, with British police, in police administration. In addition selected personnel have the benefit of specialist instruction in the United Kingdom in traffic control, forensic medicine, photography, criminal records, fingerprinting and prosecution procedure.

Keepers of the Peace in Sierra Leone

by W. G. SYER, C.B.E.

M Y feelings were somewhat mixed when in July, 1951, a few days after returning to Lagos from leave and having completed unpacking thirty-odd loads, I was offered the appointment of Commissioner of Police in Sierra Leone. I had always thought that Freetown looked very attractive from the mail boat when passing through, and even three weeks there in the transit camp in 1943 awaiting onward passage to Lagos had not entirely disillusioned me. I had also been told by a former Governor (not of Sierra Leone) that it was not the best of places in which to serve, though his advice was not so mildly expressed.

On accepting the appointment I was told by a senior officer that the principal objective was to get the Police into the Protectorate. I was somewhat surprised that there should be no Police in such a large area—it is rather large, even though it looks so small on the map—and wondered how the process of law enforcement could work with any degree of efficiency. I was even more astonished, when shortly after my arrival in Freetown I discovered the question of policing the Protectorate was most controversial. Obviously it was important that toes should not be trodden on by a new boy—even toes that had trodden nowhere else but the United Kingdom and Sierra Leone in the course of duty.

I found that the Sierra Leone Police Force policed only the area around Free-town, which is known as the Colony, and the Force consisted of some twenty officers and about seven hundred men. It is one of the oldest, if not the oldest Police Force in what, until recently, has been known as British Africa, being constituted as the Sierra Leone Police Force in the Royal Gazette of the 27th October, 1894. But this was by no means the beginning of the Force. There were five Constables as long ago as 1808 after Great Britain took over the government of the Colony. It was not until 1836, however, that Sierra Leone followed London's example and formed a Police Force consisting of an Inspector, three Sub-Inspectors and sixty Constables. In those days Sierra Leone moved smartly with the times in matters of security.

The Protectorate was proclaimed in 1896 and a Court Messenger Force was formed in 1903 for purposes of law enforcement and other duties. This Force was legally constituted in 1907, but it was not until 1948 that arrangements were made for some Court Messengers to receive training at the Police Training School. The Police-trained Court Messengers were later officered by Police Officers who were seconded from the Police Force. The remaining Court Messengers served in Districts under District Commissioners and assisted them in their duties, particularly their law enforcement and magisterial duties.

No Colonial Police Force is adequately provided for without a problem affecting internal security. This may seem an over emphatic statement but history has, alas, shown on so many occasions that there has often been a tendency in Colonies to economise on security, sometimes until it is too late. When I was in transit in Freetown in 1943 I, like many other young men, and some older, occasionally had a drink in the somewhat notorious City Hotel. Brazilian beer of doubtful quality at 7s. 6d. a bottle was available, I remember, as well as Crystal Gin, a product of South Africa, of painful memories for some. But it was at the City Hotel that I first heard of the illicit diamond trade, and there appeared afterwards of course that dreadful (in my view) book *The Heart of the Matter* by Graham Greene. I therefore asked one of my officers if there was still any I.D.B. in Sierra Leone. He supposed there was but that nobody had ever done much about it as only nominal fines were inflicted and anyway the illicit mining and source of the illicit diamonds was in the "Protectorate"—the great beyond in the minds of many in Freetown including, of course, the Police who were not allowed there without a pass from the Secretariat. In the course of discussions at a higher level outside the Police Force I gathered that there was no need for alarm—of course the odd diamond was lost, but that one had to expect. I was satisfied we had our problem.

The C.I.D. consisted of three rooms and ran a Special Branch as a side line. After Nigeria it all seemed very small and, I suspected, inadequate. I gave instructions to the C.I.D. that illicit diamonds were to be number one target and that no effort was to be spared to unearth the truth.

I visited the Sierra Leone Selection Trust diamond mine at Yengema in Kono District shortly after taking up my appointment and saw one of my officers who was seconded to the Court Messenger Force and was in command of about forty supernumerary Court Messengers. None of them was trained in Police duties, and all were illiterate. I could not help but share the anxieties of the Manager of the mine on the question of security. Subsequently the Company appealed for more satisfactory protection and in 1952 the first detachment of the Sierra Leone Police Force to be stationed in the Protectorate was formed in Kono.

Meanwhile the C.I.D. had been successful and had caught two Lebanese with several hundred diamonds in their possession. They were convicted, sentenced to terms of imprisonment and ordered to be deported, but the deportation orders were subsequently rescinded (one of these individuals later became one of the biggest men in a game in which it is difficult for the Police to score points). In 1952 the world's record seizure of over 6,000 carats, worth nearly £250,000 was made by the C.I.D. and it was then fully appreciated that the illicit diamond problem was one of tremendous proportions and that interested international eyes were upon Sierra Leone. It was clear that Sierra Leone had been losing diamonds wholesale for years—it was no new problem.

The new formation of the Force at Yengema had proved extremely efficient and successful. The Police had not usurped the authority of the Tribal Authorities and Native Courts as was feared by so many people. Efficient and effective law enforcement had not proved disagreeable to the Chiefs and people. On the contrary, the people decided they wanted the Police Force throughout the country, and at the Protectorate Assembly at Bo in 1953, the Paramount Chiefs expressed their appreciation of the services of the Force in Kono District, and said they wanted the police throughout the Protectorate at once. This was strongly supported by the Sierra Leone People's Party, the party in power. As a Protectorate Assembly had passed a resolution saying that they did not want the Police in the Protectorate as recently as 1951, this was a major change of heart. The Police Ordinance was applied to the Protectorate on the 1st September, 1954, and the Court Messenger Force was disbanded at midnight on the 31st August. The task of planning the policing for the first time of an area about the size of England was an engaging one, and also very original. About one hundred and fifty suitable men of the six hundred Court Messengers were absorbed into the Police Force. The intake of recruits for the Force was stepped up from fifty a year to four hundred and the standard of training was happily improved rather than reduced, which so often happens on these occasions. A great deal of improvisation was necessary, especially as far as buildings were concerned—we started almost from scratch. The strength of the Police in Freetown was reduced to a minimum in order to provide officers and men for the new Divisions and Districts.

In February, 1955, just over five months after the 'take over', the most violent riots that Freetown had experienced for nearly thirty years broke out, and sporadic disturbances of a minor nature occurred in several places in the Protectorate. The Police in Freetown were one hundred under strength as a result of the expansion and very few had had any experience of a rough house, though fortunately they had received plenty of training and this saved the situation, but not without military aid. One European Assistant Superintendent was beaten to death. The malicious damage to essential services was expertly done, which was then unusual in Africa. After three days of violence and after a Bren gun had been used, the riots ended. I drove round the city with the Governor and he estimated that the damage would be hundreds of thousands of pounds, but the miserable array of looted and burned shops, overturned cars, and torn up roads and railway lines was fortunately not as expensive as it looked. I was very proud of the way in which all ranks had done their duty, and Sir John Shaw's Commission of Enquiry into the riots were kind enough to include the following remarks in their report:

"Responsibility for the consequences, fatal and otherwise of these savage riots rests with those who instigated, organised and participated in them; it does not rest with the Police to whom the law-abiding citizens of Freetown owe a debt of gratitude."

After this test the Force settled down to continue the consolidation of its increased responsibilities, but towards the end of 1955 serious anti-tax and anti-Chief riots broke out in the Northern and South Western Provinces, and operations were needed over a very large area of the country. Villages and towns were badly damaged and a number of people were killed; three policemen lost their lives. The difficulties of the Police were increased considerably because of lack of local knowledge owing to their recent arrival in the Protectorate. The riots were eventually suppressed but not before a great deal of damage was done, and lives lost as the result of the activities of marauding gangs. Military aid was not required but it certainly would have been if the Police Force had not been deployed in the Protectorate and, though still under strength, had not been larger than it had been a year previously.

Towards the end of 1956 widespread illicit mining of diamonds was taking place in the South Eastern Province and 'Operation Parasite' was launched to remove about fifty thousand African foreigners from Kono District. In 1957 they were back again, having drifted over the frontier and 'Operation Digger' was set in motion to clear the area again, this time with limited military aid. But Kono, with its vast diamond deposits and political intrigue, was no easy nut to crack and at regular intervals it occupied much of our attention and resources and hit the headlines in the world press. There are now five hundred Police in the area and I have no doubt that the original detachment was posted there in 1952 in the nick of time.

Policing North Borneo

by J. B. ATKINSON, C.B.E.

NORTH BORNEO used to have an entirely undeserved reputation for being a wild country. It was, in fact, before the war a quiet and peaceful backwater which seemed to be completely divorced from the stresses and strains of the outside world. In those happy days it was governed by the British North Borneo (Chartered) Company which in its early days had been forced to raise an Armed Constabulary in order to pacify the territory. This was in 1882, and the Force had an entire strength of three British Officers and 153 men, consisting of Sikhs, Dyaks from Sarawak, Malays and, strangely, Somalis. The Somalis were found generally to be unsuitable for service in the country and their numbers dwindled quickly. The Armed Constabulary was at this time armed with Snider rifles and seven pounder guns, some of which were still serving as saluting guns when I joined the Force in 1929. In its early days the Constabulary spent much of its time on punitive expeditions in difficult country with practically no roads. The establishment had been increased to five Officers and 419 other ranks by 1891 and to five Officers and 595 other ranks in 1901. By this time the territory had settled down to a peaceful existence broken only by the Murut Rundum rebellion of 1915 and the Japanese occupation from 1942 to 1945.

In the days just before the second world war the establishment of the Armed Constabulary was five British Officers and 550 other ranks. The Dusuns, Bajaus, Bruneis and Muruts of North Borneo by this time formed the greater part of the strength but there was still a number of Sikhs and Hazaras serving. There were twenty police stations, a Headquarters and Depot at Jesselton and a Divisional Headquarters at Sandakan. There was also a Constabulary Reserve, first formed in 1916, in which men who had served not less than one agreement in the Force could enlist. This Reserve is still in existence and numbers now slightly more than 200 men. All serving men were housed in barracks at their stations, a policy which is still followed, although the provision of suitable accommodation for an increasing number of married policemen is giving cause for concern.

In the 1930's crime incidence was comparatively small. There were occasional marauding raids made by natives of the Southern Philippines upon isolated shops, but few vehicles used the small mileage of roads and generally speaking the Constabulary can be said to have had few real problems to face. It was organised and trained to meet the requirements of the time and service in its ranks was popular. Indeed, the number of men applying for enlistment was almost an embarrassment. There is still no difficulty about recruiting although the educational standards have been raised considerably since pre-war days.

The Dusuns and Muruts are delightful people, with good manners and a sturdy sense of independence with consequent absence of subservience. They are most amenable to discipline while preserving their natural fund of good humour. Their ability to cope with difficult situations is best illustrated by the action of the Murut sergeant, in an outstation, who was prosecuting a Dusun for theft before the local Assistant District Officer who had a very bad impediment in his speech. The trial had taken some time and the sergeant knew that the Sessions Judge was waiting to hear a murder trial in the same court. The magistrate had obviously written out a lengthy judgment which the sergeant realised he would take some time to deliver. As the magistrate began to read what he had written the sergeant slipped on to the Bench and looked over his shoulder to see what sentence had been given.

He then announced to the court "six months", stepped down, saluted the magistrate and marched his prisoner smartly down to the cells before the astonished magistrate could utter a word of protest.

That these people are courageous, albeit sometimes in a foolhardy manner, was shown by the Dusun corporal who was out on a patrol looking for an armed and desperate escaped prisoner. The two came unexpectedly face to face on a bend in the bridle path. The corporal quickly unslung his rifle and ordered the escapee to drop his parang. The prisoner refused and instead invited the corporal to show that he was a man by putting aside his rifle and fighting parang to parang. This he did and it was eventually a much cut up Corporal who marched an even more cut up, but satisfied, prisoner into the nearest police station, quite a number of miles away, later that day. It is pleasant to record that this corporal's son is now serving in the Force, one of many sons of former members so serving.

But the peaceful existence of North Borneo was abruptly and drastically brought to an end in January, 1942, by the arrival of the Japanese army, which remained in occupation of the territory until September, 1945, a period of immense hardship for all the inhabitants. At this difficult time the men of the Constabulary, of all races, showed the most steadfast loyalty and devotion in dealing with a situation for which they had not been prepared. I recall with pride and much humbleness, the acts of courage in assisting not only their own officers but all Europeans in adversity. They did much to assist allied prisoners of war who were brought to the territory by the Japanese from Singapore. No less than fifty-eight men lost their lives, most of them being executed, and fourteen were awarded the King's Medal for Courage in the Cause of Freedom. Naturally most of those who could do so left the Japanese controlled Force and returned to their villages. Many joined the guerilla bands raised by Allied officers who entered North Borneo early in 1945 by parachute or submarine.

The Occupation left North Borneo a particularly devastated country; nor were the means of rehabilitation readily at hand. As far as the Constabulary was concerned it had to face a lamentable lack of suitable accommodation, a shortage of uniform and equipment other than excellent Australian slouch hats, blankets and army boots; poor communications and a rice ration which could hardly be expected to keep an active man fit. One cannot but feel admiration for men who left villages where rice was plentiful to return to duty. Rehabilitation in such circumstances seemed at first to be a hopeless task. Although men were prepared to enlist there were too few officers to train them, all records had been destroyed, to find accommodation was extremely difficult, new uniforms appeared in small parcels and had to be issued immediately to make up the most glaring shortages, and new tasks seemed to be allotted to the force daily. However, gradually matters improved, new officers appeared, new buildings were erected, many of only a temporary nature, uniforms and equipment arrived in quantity—even full dress—and the Band was resurrected. The public also became more contented as more food, clothing, vehicles, building materials and machinery were imported.

North Borneo became the newest Crown Colony in July, 1946, and in 1949 the Force changed its title from Armed Constabulary (it seems to have been the last Force to hold this title) to become the North Borneo Police Force.

By the time the Police Force assumed its new title the general rehabilitation of the Colony was progressing most satisfactorily, and development was becoming the factor uppermost in the mind of the Government and public alike. But the development of the Police Force was not due to the problems created in an increasingly prosperous territory alone; much more was it occasioned by events elsewhere. The emergency in Malaya, the success of the Communists in China, the activities of marauding bands of pirates from the Southern Philippines and events in Indonesia have each contributed something necessitating changes in the establishment, organisation and structure of the Force.

The Force has had an emergency unit trained to some extent in jungle work since 1927 and in consequence this unit was available to assist the Malayan Police in 1948. It was then expanded to an establishment of five platoons and its equipment and training improved to enable it to be used immediately to deal competently with any armed threat to the Colony's security. The Special Branch was increased in size and reorganised to give more effective coverage to possible subversive activities. A Marine Branch had to be organised, trained and equipped with suitable vessels to enable it to curb the activities of pirates. The Muslim inhabitants of the islands of the Southern Philippines are a rapacious, fearless and ruthless people who, after the war, found themselves in possession of an apparently limitless supply of arms, mostly automatic, and ammunition. The advent of large outboard motors for use in their sailing craft gave them a mobility far in excess of anything they could achieve before the war. Prosperity in North Borneo meant that small communities would possess riches enough to excite the cupidity of such people. They have, in consequence, varied a piratical life on the high seas with peaceful trading visits to these North Borneo communities followed by carefully planned armed raids. An extensive police patrol system undoubtedly reduces the number of raids but it cannot, without the expenditure of much more money and the use of many more men and craft, provide a long coast line with complete immunity.

The normal problems caused by the ever increasing development of the Colony were met by increasing the C.I.D. establishment and providing this important department of the Force with the latest equipment, and by improving communications. Service in the radio branch is popular and the manner in which its trainees learn English is little short of phenomenal.

In recent years the Police Force has taken over the Immigration Department and has built up a Road Transport Department. It also has to deal with fire prevention and fire fighting, film censorship, control and licencing of firearems and theatres and, with the exception of the Central Prison, the administration of all the prisons in the Colony. It cannot be said that its officers lack variety in their daily work!

North Borneo can never hope to be a place of utter peace and quietness again and it is no longer the backwater it was. But it is still comparatively peaceful as compared with neighbouring territories and it is to be hoped that with the help of its Police Force it will remain so.

The Work of the
Police Force in Hong Kong

by W. P. MORGAN, D.F.M.

THE HONG KONG Government Annual Report of 1956 took as its theme 'A Problem of People', a problem posed by a densely populated area which almost overnight doubled in population and at the same time was deprived of its traditional means of livelihood. It is a continuing problem that has taxed the ingenuity of the Government for the past twelve years and one with which the Police Force is intimately concerned.

The total area of the Colony is only 398 square miles, of which 336 is virtually useless mountainside and marshland. Of the 62 square miles of habitable territory 50 are devoted to agriculture, leaving 12 square miles into which are compressed the main residential, recreational, industrial, commercial and ancillary requirements of a population approaching 3,250,000. Over 80 per cent. of the population lives and works in this small area which is roughly divided into two flat strips of land facing each other across the mile wide harbour. The remaining 20 per cent., mostly farmers and fisherfolk, is scattered about the remote country villages and among the 235 small islands which lie within our territorial boundaries.

We are concerned therefore with two basic types of policing, one geared to a large densely populated city, the other serving a widely dispersed rural community. This division of duties is dictated both by physical and cultural considerations. The rural area, known as the New Territories, was leased from China in 1898 and many of the inhabitants live in small village communities following the ancient methods and customs of their forefathers. To these people the police officer is not simply a guardian of the law, he is a representative of the Government and his counsel is often sought in civil and domestic matters. It is essential that the police officer understands local community life and problems and for that reason we try to recruit some of our constables from the villages and communities that they will later serve.

In the New Territories, too, is the 22 mile long land boundary with mainland China. Patrolling of the immediate border area is a purely police responsibility. Two main control points along the border, one rail and one road, permit the passage of authorised persons and commodities. To prevent unauthorised traffic across the border a series of small police posts are located on high ground overlooking the frontier and from these a 24-hour watch is maintained, searchlights being used at night to illuminate the area. Police foot patrols cover the ground between the posts and the border, while mobile patrols cover the roadways leading down to the main urban areas.

There is no way of knowing precisely how many persons enter the Colony illegally each month. Only a small percentage use the land route; most smuggle themselves in on fishing junks, for our 400-mile coastline and multiplicity of islands provide many convenient points for disembarkation.

Much responsibility for the detection of illegal immigration, and other forms of contraband, falls on the Marine Division of the Police Force. On this section of the Force also devolve the duties connected with policing a fishing fleet of over 10,000 motorised and sailing junks; a floating population of 140,000; and normal watch and ward in one of the world's busiest harbours. Craft ranging from special shallow draught launches to deep sea vessels which patrol for 72 hours before returning to base, form our fleet. Close radio communication is maintained with headquarters, and radar allows searches and patrols to be carried out by night as well as day. Many crew members are recruited from the local fishing population and have an intimate knowledge of local waters, but first and foremost they are trained police officers and carry out shore patrols on inhabited islands and at isolated coastal villages. Smuggling of gold, narcotics, dutiable wines, spirits, and tobacco into the Colony is also encountered by the Marine Police, although the main responsibility for the suppression of smuggling is vested in the Preventive Service of the Commerce and Industry Department.

Until recent years, in addition to the normal difficulties of dealing with crime, the Police Force frequently experienced a special obstacle caused by an inherent reluctance of many Chinese, who constitute over 99 per cent. of the population of Hong Kong, to involve themselves in any way with the forces of Law and Order, or for that matter, with any Government organisation. The reasons for this are historical. In times past the soldier, policeman and official were not regarded by the average Chinese as servants of the public or persons from whom assistance and counsel might be sought. Indeed, the traditional concept of officialdom was of a cruel, rapacious élite, appointed to oppress the people and to make their already miserable lot more burdensome. These ideas from the past centuries of China's history have been slow to die and have to a certain extent carried over into the 20th century. The Hong Kong Government has done much in recent years with the help of the local Kai Fong* and other welfare associations to eradicate the traces of this inborn prejudice. The results have been gradual but encouraging and in the Force, for instance, we have noticed that an increasing number of people come to Police stations not merely to report crime but to seek advice generally.

Another associated trait which for many years has been peculiar to Chinese residents of Hong Kong is the feeling that Hong Kong is a place of transitional or temporary abode where a living can be made. Except in the case of a comparatively very small number of locally born families, people never allowed their ties with Hong Kong to become very close and always looked upon their towns and villages on the mainland of China as "home". Since the second World War this tendency has been changing and today many families feel they have a permanent stake in Hong Kong and that their roots are here. These two evolutionary changes in Hong Kong's society are doing much to get rid of that traditional sense of non-involvement with the Government and the forces of Law and Order.

In certain respects a small, densely populated area provides many advantages, from a law enforcement point of view, over a large thinly populated area. Effective central control can be established, communications are rapid, scenes of incidents can be quickly reached, specialist services are more readily available, and full beat coverage provided with the minimum

---

* District welfare association; the literal meaning of Kai Fong is "neighbourhood".

number of men. In the main urban area we have exploited these advantages to the full.

Colony Police Headquarters are located on Hong Kong Island and here are concentrated the main administrative and specialist sections of the Force. Day-to-day control and administration are delegated to three District, or Command Headquarters, one on Hong Kong Island, one in Kowloon, and one in the New Territories. The Commands are sub-divided into Divisions each working from a main police station and one or more subsidiary stations. Each Command has its own radio network for routine communications but in times of emergency they are incorporated into the main control room at Colony Headquarters which also transmit all matters of general interest *via* radio or teleprinter. Commands also have their own Emergency Units, squads of highly trained men capable of taking all necessary initial action at any incident. They constantly patrol the streets in radio equipped cars and, in conjunction with a 999 telephone system, ensure that police can be at the scene of an incident within two to five minutes. Theoretically, therefore, we are in an excellent position for crime prevention and detection in the urban area, dealing with a tightly packed community where few crimes can be committed except in the presence of several witnesses.

But it would be somewhat misleading to leave the description of policing Hong Kong at this point. Despite the gradual overcoming of traditional suspicion of the Government, old habits die hard and there is still a reluctance on the part of many people to involve themselves in court as witnesses. But the main reason nowadays is economic. A large percentage of our labour force is employed on a daily-paid basis and a day in court means the loss of a day's wages which can result in actual hardship for the witness and his family. To avoid court attendance, a witness to a crime has been known stoutly to deny all knowledge of it even when it can be proved he was present when the crime was committed. For the same reason an escaping criminal may take refuge in a building in the hope of not being denounced by the inhabitants. This attitude hampers enquiries and results in the Criminal Investigation Department's spending a disproportionate amount of time locating witnesses to crime. It is not so much deliberate non-co-operation as unconscious rejection of anything that might interfere with the earning of the daily wage.

Despite extensive low-cost housing schemes set up by the Government in the last decade, accommodation for many is a mere matter of shelter from the elements and a space to sleep. Tenements are sub-divided into cubicles, and double and triple bunks are erected in the passageways, each bunk being the 'home' of a family. In such grossly overcrowded conditions, over 2,000 people to the acre in some areas, peace and privacy are out of the question. In the hot summer months especially, the squalor and incessant noise build up pressures which often explode into violent attacks, those concerned using any weapon at hand.

Narcotics also pose a serious problem in Hong Kong. Our Narcotics Branch seizes millions of dollars worth of drugs each year but the profits to be made are so high that the operators accept these losses as a normal business risk. Imported into the Colony, raw opium is prepared for smoking and heroin is manufactured. These products are then sold on the local market or exported overseas. To combat the traffic our narcotics laws have been revised and very heavy prison sentences can now be given to dealers in these commodities. On the other hand, mere penal sanctions against addicts are now giving way to medical treatment and rehabilitation.

The Triad Societies also influence our crime pattern but their influence is continually decreasing. Once a tremendously powerful and greatly feared group of secret societies, they took a leading part in organised crime and kept a tight grip on a large portion of the population through various protection rackets and control of labour. From late 1956 to 1960 a vigorous drive against the local societies resulted in the majority of important leaders being imprisoned or deported. Without leaders the organisation crumbled and Triad activity nowadays is largely restricted to individual members or small gangs of up to twelve persons. The names of these societies still evoke some measure of fear among the more ignorant members of the community. Advantage is still taken of this fact by petty thugs who collect protection money from the less enlightened members of the community.

We have our fair share of depredations on property, open windows and doors dictated by a warm climate providing a ready means of access. The actual number of professional breakers is small, many offences being committed by opportunists. This, plus the ease of access, makes it exceedingly difficult to detect offenders through the criminal record system known as 'Modus Operandi'. Violence is quite often resorted to in order to achieve escape but the use of firearms in the commission of crime has dropped remarkably over the last few years. At one time it was comparatively easy for an offender to escape from the Colony by land to mainland China or by sea to the neighbouring Portuguese Colony of Macau. All countries have long since tightened up their immigration controls and now escape requires careful planning with chances of success not very high. In this connection we are indebted to the high degree of co-operation extended by the authorities in Macau.

The tourist trade is now one of our largest activities (over 210,000 visitors in 1961) and the Colony is also a recreational centre for British and foreign servicemen. Bent on bargains and a good time, the holidaymaker is a tempting target for our professional pickpockets and unscrupulous traders. We have, too, our fair share of international criminals, mainly connected with commercial frauds and the smuggling of narcotics and gold. Close liason is maintained with Interpol and the exchange of information with this organisation has led to a number of important arrests.

Road traffic is a problem in all large cities and here, as elsewhere, it generates much criticism, and some small praise, of the Police Force. Our situation is aggravated by the shortage of land in the Colony which makes it impossible to provide adequate parking and garage space for the over 53,000 vehicles which crowd our 500 miles of roadway.

This short article is intended to give a brief outline of our main problems set against a teeming and gradually changing community. The Chinese people are basically a law-abiding, tolerant and industrious race, able to bear poverty without rancour and grateful for the opportunities and stability offered by the Colony. Apart from minor lapses, it is estimated that the bulk of our crime is committed by no more than 2,000-3,000 hard-core elements, not all Chinese, representing less than .1 per cent. of the total population. Indeed, comparatively speaking, crime is kept at a remarkably low level and from 1956 it has decreased progressively. It is a privilege to serve this community and to serve with their compatriots who make up the bulk of the Hong Kong Police Force.

African Evening

by JUNE HARRAP

The watchful evening waits
With amber sky,
Like a stealthy lion's eye,
And tawny fields that limply lie
Across the rounded haunch of hill.
Far away
The grey
Veils of rain trail
To touch the pale
Land with smoky wisps from a high
Cloud palisade.
Through its gates
Marauding night will
Swiftly raid,
Then spring to devour
In this pregnant, fateful hour
All the calm light
And busy rationality
Of the day's worn work.
Then wild night
Will magnificently stalk
With flexing feline walk
And mane of dark
His ancient monarchy.
Hills that huddle in servility
Will sound with eerie bark
Of scavenging jackals
And nightbirds' thrilling calls.

"Taxi! Colonial Office, please." "Is that the Foreign Office, sir?"
"Certainly not." "Never heard of it—sorry, sir."
"Great Smith Street." "Oh—a queer place to be, sir."
  —Reported by a recent visitor to the 'Corona' Office.

Police Progress in the West Indies

by W. A. ORRETT, C.B.E.

THE British Colonies in the Caribbean area stretch in a rough arc from British Honduras in Central America to British Guiana in South America, and the arc takes in, in the Caribbean Sea, the island of Jamaica with its dependency of the Cayman Islands, then several hundred miles eastwards is the Leeward Islands group comprising the British Virgin Islands and the islands of Anguilla, St. Kitts, Nevis, Antigua, Barbuda, Redonda and Montserrat; continuing southerly come the Windward Islands consisting of Dominica, St. Lucia, St. Vincent and Grenada; to the east lies the island of Barbados and nearest to the South American continent are the islands of Tobago and Trinidad. Including the two mainland colonies, they cover between them a total area of 99,688 square miles, being about 11,000 square miles larger than that of Great Britain with a population of 3,133,000. The inhabitants are mainly of African descent whose ancestors were brought there in the old slave days, the only other large racial group being about half a million East Indians descended from immigrants from India, who came to work on the estates, with a sprinkling of Chinese and Portuguese from Madeira.

The area is policed by the British Honduras police, the Jamaica police, the Leeward Islands police (a unified force covering the group with headquarters in Antigua), the four small separate forces of the Windward Islands, the Barbados police, the Trinidad and Tobago police and the British Guiana police. At the end of the first half of the present century the establishment of the police forces was 124 Officers, and 5,132 Inspectors, Non-Commissioned Officers and Constables; of this total the three largest forces, Jamaica, Trinidad and Tobago, and British Guiana had between them 97 Officers and 4,475 other ranks, Barbados had 8 Officers and 593 other ranks, the Leeward Islands 6 Officers and 281 other ranks, whilst British Honduras and the Windward Islands accounted for the balance.

Despite the fact that the Colonies are separated by sea from each other, and some very widely, the police pattern has on the whole been similar, and the story of the early start of two forces, Jamaica in the North Caribbean and British Guiana in the South, will form the picture for the others. Although there had been earlier legislation in both Colonies, which set up an elementary police system under the Magistrates, it was not until 1835, six years after the formation of the London Metropolitan Police, that Jamaica passed an Act to establish a Colony force consisting of an Inspector-General, 24 Inspectors and Sub-Inspectors, 70 Sergeants, and 700 Privates, the Act removing the control of the police from the Magistrates and placing the force under the Inspector-General. British Guiana followed in 1839, when an Ordinance on similar lines was passed bringing into being a force of an Inspector-General, 3 Inspectors, 17 Sergeants and 105 Privates. The Jamaica Force was very short lived, as the Inspector-General, falling foul of the Magistrates shortly after the formation, had his post abolished, with the police becoming separate units under the parish Magistrates, and it was not until 1866 that it was re-organised as one force and modelled on the Royal Irish Constabulary with a retired Army Officer in command. The British Guiana police, however, has continued as a Colony unit from its formation, although during its first fifty years it functioned as a civilian force under civilian officers, keeping such weapons as it had in armouries and unissued. Their original instructions, which have since formed the basis of police administration in the Caribbean, are of interest, namely that the Inspector-General should be in direct communication with the Executive, with the Inspectors receiving orders from the Inspector-General and communicating to him all matters concerning the police force, for the information of the Executive, when necessary.

There was considerable illiteracy at first amongst the rank and file, and as comparatively recently as 1884 the records of one force show that of 607 other ranks, 107 could not read or write. This stage of affairs, however, had been remedied by the end of the century, and for some considerable time since a high standard has been required from applicants wishing to join the forces, and nowadays many are in possession of a School Certificate or equivalent evidence of an education above the average. A good sample of the general advancement and of the type of man enlisted in recent years can be found in the case of four constables of the British Guiana police, who were granted leave to join the Royal Air Force during the last war. Three of these men earned their wings and were commissioned before the end of hostilities, two of them being demobilised with the rank of Flight-Lieutenant. It may have been through lack of sufficiently well-educated men to fill the higher non-commissioned ranks, or it may have been to increase police efficiency, that in the early 1880's the system started of recruiting members of the Royal Irish Constabulary as Sergeants and Sergeants-Major, which system only ended after the 1914–18 War. The example of these well-trained men had an excellent effect on the lower ranks, and many of them during the years rose to officer rank, with some reaching the higher posts.

The big change in the Southern Caribbean, which term includes all the forces except Jamaica and British Honduras, came in 1889 following on a decision to remove the military units that had been stationed for many years in this area. These plans included changing the Police from civilian forces, equipped with a certain amount of weapons, into semi-military forces to form with the Militia or Volunteer units the Local Defence Force; the Inspector-General being given the additional post of Commandant, and all other police officers, except in British Guiana, where it was confined to the Inspector-General, being gazetted to local military rank. In several forces, serving or retired military officers were appointed as Inspectors-General, with other military officers as Staff Officers or Adjutant, and army non-commissioned officers were brought out as drill, musketry, and later on as riding instructors. The system of placing military officers in command was not generally continued although such appointments occurred from time to time until as late as 1924, but the original system of having the Staff Officer commanding the Police Depot or Training School and bringing out army instructors remained in some forces until after the outbreak of the last war. A considerable advance was made with the formations of Depots and systematic instruction of recruits and from the beginning the organisation was based on the Royal Irish Constabulary, the recruits being trained in squad, company and baton drill and in musketry; the link continued, as, until the disbandment of the Royal Irish Constabulary after the First World War, Caribbean police officers on appointment went for their initial training to the Royal Irish Constabulary Depot, Dublin, and the first regulations and disciplinary codes were taken from those of the Irish force and a considerable portion has still been retained. Equally, Army traditions have played a big part in developing the *esprit-de-corps*, loyalty, and excellent relationships between officers and men, which are the outstanding features of the West Indian Police. As the years went by police subjects came more and more to the forefront of training, with Police Officers and Non-Commissioned Officers in charge, and during the last fifteen years riot drill and mob fighting have largely superseded military instruction.

The laws, the courts and the legal procedure are based on those obtaining in England and from the first there has been the same system of beats and patrols. Auxiliary forces were established by legislation as early as 1849, the personnel being chosen from persons of good character in the districts or selected employees on the estates; these men are appointed by the Inspector-General, or Commissioner as his title now is, and are under his control and have full police authority when called out for duty or when required to investigate or deal with any offence. Some of the large oilfield and bauxite companies have in recent years made use of these auxiliaries by forming trained units of them into watchmen forces, but they still remain under the supervision of the regular police. The last development has been the formation, by separate legislation, of Special Reserve Police who, like the English forces, are uniformed and trained bodies and have proved themselves valuable assets, when called out for duty.

To-day nearly all the forces have motor launches for sea and river patrol, motor bicycles, cars and lorries, some equipped with wireless and all manned by police personnel, fully trained to handle them and effect repairs. British Guiana, Trinidad and Barbados have efficient Mounted Branches, excellent in crowd control; their mounted sports and musical rides are largely attended by the public, British Guiana specialising in acrobatic and trick-riding performances. Jamaica, Trinidad and Barbados have for some years had Women Police sections, which British Guiana has also recently started. Some forces during the past twenty-five years have laid stress on first-aid training for the recruit from his early stages and encouraging the trained ranks to keep themselves efficient by passing the annual tests; two forces in particular have been most favourably reported on by Chief Commissioners of the St. John Ambulance Brigade, who have visited the colonies, and a number of officers and other ranks have been honoured by awards of insignia of the Order of St. John of Jerusalem.

The big forces have experienced and skilful detectives and well-established Criminal Investigation Departments capable of dealing with every type of crime, but the West Indies, although the first named system was started early in this century, did drop behind in building up efficient Finger Print and Modus Operandi Bureaux, and in the development of wireless systems; it is only recently that generally the former two have been brought up to date, and as regards the latter, Trinidad alone can at present claim an adequate system with trained personnel. It is of interest, in connection with the delay in taking advantage of these modern improvements, to see it stated in the last annual report of Her Majesty's Inspectors of Constabularies that "whilst an efficient C.I.D., crime patrols, wireless, forensic science laboratories, are all indispensable aids, the basic duty of preventing and detecting crime, still rests fundamentally upon the shoulders of the uniformed branch."

On the personnel side police federations have been established by law and are fulfilling a useful purpose. Encouragement has always been given to the development of games and most forces have sports clubs; the police hold prominent places in local athletics, with their cricket, football and hockey teams able to compete on a level with the best in the Colony. Several forces have police magazines, the bulk of many well-written articles coming from the pens of the rank and file, some have literary and debating societies, one has a male voice choir that is in great demand, and the Trinidad and British Guiana police have established scholarship schemes, the funds being subscribed voluntarily by the members of the forces, which have enabled many of their children to obtain a free education at the best schools.

The small forces of the Leeward and Windward Islands have not advanced as far as the others. Lack of finance has prevented progress, both in police efficiency and in improvements in salary conditions, barrack accommodation and married quarters. No adequate training system has been devised and these forces look to the Trinidad police, which have always been most helpful, for instructional and specialist courses, and for reinforcement in times of trouble.

The last stage of progress has been to extend further the avenues of promotion. Up to about ten years ago only Warrant or Non-Commissioned Officers who came from the Royal Irish Constabulary or the British Army were regarded as eligible for promotion to Officer rank, but this rank has been since opened to locally enlisted personnel, and already some of those promoted have reached the grade of Superintendent, and every recruit now joining can feel that it is possible for him to reach the highest positions. As recruitment of Cadet Officers from the United Kingdom has practically ceased and there has been a considerable falling off of local applicants of the right type for direct appointment as Assistant Superintendents, it would seem that the keeping up of the traditions and standards of the forces lies in the future with the men who started their police careers as recruit constables.

Since the end of the last war, there has been a powerful school of thought, mainly outside of the Caribbean forces, which advocates a change over from the Royal Irish Constabulary system to one more closely following that of the British police. The Jamaica police have recently been reorganised somewhat on these lines, and in view of the fact that gazetted officers have now for some years been attending courses at the Police College, Cadet Officers being trained with the British forces, and non-gazetted officers taking courses under the Metropolitan Police at Hendon, the signs point to the ultimate progress taking the forces back to the civilian stage they started at over a century ago.

(*Particulars of early start of the Jamaica Police from "The Colonial Police" by Sir Charles Jeffries, K.C.M.G., O.B.E.—Author's note.*)

A Magistrate among the Seals

by J. W. MATTHEW

"SKOL!" said Bogan, the Norwegian captain of the seal catcher, raising his glass one evening as we sat in his cabin after I had produced a second bottle of whisky, the existence of which he had not suspected. "Mr. Magistrate, you can come again next year, too. Whisky every night, that is good!". I was out with him on the last sealing trip of the season, which so far as South Georgia is concerned, lasts eight to ten weeks in our springtime—September, October, and maybe, a few days in November. By then the lower slopes of the island are mostly free of snow and the days are lengthening fast. South Georgia, a Dependency of the Falkland Islands, lies about 1,200 miles east of Cape Horn, and 800 from the Falklands themselves. It is about 100 miles in length and is a mass of mountains running up to 10,000 feet in height, divided on their lower slopes by glaciers, many of which end precipitously in the sea. There is no Gulf Stream in these seas; on the contrary, there is a steady north easterly set from the Antarctic.

It is in September that the bull elephant seals (*Mirounga Leonina* to the biologists) begin to haul out on the beaches after many months continuously at sea, where they have grown fat on the abundant shrimp-like fish known as 'kril' and on squid. They choose pitches along the beaches and then set about collecting themselves harems as soon as the cows begin to come ashore. This is not achieved without numerous battles between the bulls, which may be as much as twenty feet in length and weigh well over two tons. At the time of hauling out, they have an enveloping blanket of blubber, some five inches thick, which provides insulation against the cold and a supply of energy. This is what the sealers are after. It yields, on the average, about six hundredweights of oil per seal.

It was not long after Captain Cook's visit in 1775 that sealing began at South Georgia. Many lucrative voyages in search of both fur seals and elephant seals were made from London, England, and such ports as New Bedford and Nantucket in the U.S.A. By the 1820's seals had been reduced to negligible numbers. For the last fifty years, however, sealing has been under licence from the Government of the Falkland Islands. At present, permission to take 6,000 adult bull elephant seals is granted annually to a company registered in Argentina. The result of the conservancy policy appears to be a small increase in numbers—certainly no diminution.

It was one of my jobs as Administrative Officer and Magistrate, South Georgia, to watch the application of that policy. Thus it was that I came to be sitting in the skipper's little cabin that evening, having a noggin as we lay at anchor in a remote fjord after a long day's sealing. His ship was *Dias*, once *Viola* of Hull, built in 1906 as a trawler for the northern fisheries but converted later for southern whaling, and later still for sealing.

At first light, before five o'clock, the boats had gone in shore from where we had lain at anchor the previous night. The large bulls had been driven down to the sea edge, shot and flensed and the blankets of blubber towed away to the sealing ship. This business is carried out humanely and with considerable skill. The bulls have to be singled out sometimes from several hundred cows and pups and driven slowly to the sea edge. The flensers stand there in the edge of the sea, well covered in oilskins, frequently jostled by blocks of ice and nipped by a cold wind or snow. But they press on cheerfully, with their gory task, the sea running red the while. At about half past seven, the pram, a Norwegian type surf boat, handled by a

Norwegian boatman, born, I fancy, with a pair of oars in his hands, is deftly pulled in through the surf. The shore party leaps aboard and are backed off as quickly as possible. The motor boat takes the pram in tow and away they go, along with some remaining blankets of seal blubber, back to the ship and hot coffee and breakfast. If the weather remains reasonable the boats are inshore again after breakfast. When a beach has been worked out for the day the boats are hoisted and the crew enjoy a spell in the forward mess while the ship moves along the coast to another beach or bay.

They are a colourful lot, these sealers, who come year after year to South Georgia from Buenos Aires and Montevideo. They speak together in Spanish but include plenty of Slav-sounding and Norwegian words and expressions in their conversation. Miguel Zalek, the gunner of *Dias*, an Argentino now, but born in Poland, is remarkable for his lively conversation and his facility of eating with knife or fork in either hand, it being apparently immaterial which takes which. For a mid-morning snack he and his friends will wander off into the tussock grass, collect two or three fresh penguin eggs, if there are any about, and down them at a gulp—raw. Each to his own taste! The driver, who drives the seals to the water's edge, is, I suppose, about fifty-five or more. He smokes a cigarette held elegantly in a long cigarette holder all the time, be it tossing about in the boat going inshore or going about his somewhat dangerous business ashore. One of the flensers is a little old man, born somewhere on the Eastern shores of the Baltic. He has a large bulbous nose, a twinkling eye and a general appearance of being one of Snow White's Dwarfs released from diamond mining duties. Yet another is a gentleman with a slightly greying imperial beard, who is always neatly turned out and who carries himself with an air. He might be taken for the Spanish Ambassador to the Court of St. James on a fishing holiday in his oilskins.

As the boatload sets off for the beaches, the weather-worn face of the skipper, surmounted by a fur-lined cap of leather with earflaps either tied under his chin or folded up in a horned Viking effect, peers over the edge of the bridge. He is taking in the beach where the seals can be seen lying, the boats going inshore, how his anchor is holding, and the look of the weather. Already he has looked at the barometer a good many times, watching always for changes, and has listened to the weather forecast from the Government Meteorological Office at King Edward Point. These sealing skippers' knowledge of the coast of South Georgia is without rival; it is handed down from one to another and recorded only in their heads—from Admiralty charts vital information is frequently absent or is recorded inaccurately. Their skill in piloting their ships around the rock-strewn coasts of South Georgia, frequently in snow squalls and gales of great force and among ice of all sorts, is great. I once stood beside Captain Hauge of *Albatros*, another sealing vessel, as he took her through the passage known as Bird Sound at the north-west end of the island. This is a narrow, very inaccurately charted passage with dangerous rocks in it. We entered it with a strong gale and swell from astern of us. The ship was not easy to control in a following sea. There were large pieces of ice about, some afloat, some grounded. Hauge himself took the wheel—the only time that I saw him do it at sea—and we came through without hurry or fuss. He has some forty years' experience of this sort of work at such widely different places as Kamchatka on the Bering Sea, Kerguelen Island and the Antarctic. To him it was all in the day's work, but to an outsider it was a splendid piece of seamanship to watch.

Living conditions aboard the sealing ships are a trifle rough. On the second day that I was out in *Dias*, the skipper saw me with the galley bucket getting a jet of steam into some cold water for a wash, so he kindly lent me his personal bucket which he kept in his cabin, explaining that he would not be needing it for several days. Food is plentiful and good, and the pay is attractive, too; but for this, crews for these ships would not be able to be found.

Apart from sealing, the other and much more important industry at South Georgia is whaling, which goes on during the six summer months of the year. This industry, by contrast, has modern and often very expensive machinery both ashore and afloat. It includes the floating docks for repairing catchers, a freezing plant of the most modern design and capable of freezing and storing 3,000 tons of whale meat for the British market; also wireless, radar and asdic equipment and repair facilities and staff. Some two to three million pounds worth of whale products are exported annually from South Georgia—mostly whale oil, meat and bone meal. Old by-products such as whale bone and ambergris have largely given way to new ones such as meat extract and frozen meat.

There are three Companies which whale from South Georgia. They are Argentine, Norwegian and British, the last named having much the largest whaling interests. Some of the twenty whale catchers used are converted wartime corvettes, some are of modern construction, with diesel engines. The great majority of those concerned in the pursuit of the whale from South Georgia are Norwegians, many of whom have been in the business for several generations. It is a hard but well paid occupation. A good gunner can make several thousand pounds sterling a year and quite a number of young Norwegians spend a season or two whaling in order to save sufficient money to put themselves through university or technical school.

It was my job to see that the Colonial Laws concerning whaling, which nowadays conform with the International Whaling Regulations, were being obeyed and to watch their application. To one used to frequent evasion of both the law and payment of taxes in a large tropical Dependency, the Norwegian punctiliousness in such matters was a pleasant relief. As Magistrate, my duties by no stretch of the imagination, could be called arduous. Most of the cases heard were concerned with the smuggling of pure alcohol, known as 'Puro', from Buenos Aires for barter in South Georgia against cigarettes for smuggling back into Buenos Aires and sale at a clear profit of some four to five pounds on a litre of 'Puro'. South Georgia's whaling stations are dry, so the business has its attractions!

I am also Postmaster, and the whaling season has its effect on our mails, which are a bit of a problem, for although there are usually about twenty-five mails in and out each year, they tend to be concentrated round the beginning and end of the whaling season. It is no uncommon thing to be without mail for a couple of months or more in mid-season and mid-winter. The Post Office was first opened there in 1909. The Postmaster receives many requests from philatelists and numerous are the different modes of address. I recall a courteous Frenchman who addressed me as "The Honourable, The Postmaster General, South Georgia". Another wrote simply, "The Base Leader, The Cave, South Georgia."

It is in its geographical position that South Georgia has a peculiar interest. One day there may be geological finds of economic importance made in the hinterland of the Weddel Sea area of Western Antarctica, or possibly there may be other reasons for going there. Then South Georgia will be in a unique position to provide a selection of anchorages and harbours which never freeze and which could be used for collecting shipping and storing materials not far from the ice edge in preparation for the short summer season which follows the break-up of the pack ice each year. It is also worth remembering that in a world not infrequently under the threat of the outbreak of atomic warfare, only one bomb on the Panama Canal and another on the Suez is needed to make Cape Horn and the Cape of Good Hope main shipping routes of vital importance to the countries ranged round the North Atlantic. South Georgia's fjords, divided by high mountains, are not to be despised as places to base and refit ships involved in patrolling and protecting those sea routes. For such a purpose the Falkland Islands, although they lie nearer Cape Horn, are low-lying and so are open to observation and afford little protection.

So far it has been the search, first for the seal, then for the whale, which has brought men to South Georgia, the seas around which are so prolific in food for animals, birds and fish. No one, except, I believe, the Japanese recently, has found a way of exploiting successfully the huge quantity of cod-like fish that abound in these waters. So, for the time being, South Georgia continues to ride the frequent and violent storms of the sub-Antarctic, its great snow-clad peaks proud and majestic like the masts and sails of a full rigged ship pressing on through the storm without fear and revealing its destination to no man. But there would be no harm done if the owners knew a bit more about their vessel and if the helmsman were to be lashed more securely to the wheel lest some unexpected sea sweeps up and he is carried overboard before anyone realises quite what has happened.

The Zanzibar Prison Service

by P. H. HAMILTON BAYLY

WHEN I took over control of the Zanzibar Prison Service in August, 1956, I found it to be very much a Cinderella. Although completely separated from the Police Force for some years, it was still held to be the poor relation, and had lagged behind in a great many ways. Salary scales were similar to equivalent ranks in the Police, but there the similarity ended.

One of the first things to be done was to boost staff morale. In a uniformed service one of the most effective methods to do this is to give the men a uniform that they can be proud of. The uniforms in use were drab, out of date and uncomfortable, and an immediate change was necessary. The Government proved to be most sympathetic towards the inevitable increase in the Uniform Vote to enable changes to be made, and as soon as supplies could be obtained the bare feet, tall tarbush and long-sleeved, sloppy tunics gave way to boots, dark green puttees, smart helmets with a dark green puggaree, and short sleeved bush shirts. Brass buttons were replaced by chrome, and cap badges, which had not existed before, were worn in place of the individual numbers.

The result of the new uniforms was quite surprising. On the first Saturday morning parade after their issue I received a request from the men for permission to march through the town to show themselves off. The men started to take pride in their Service and applications for enlistment trebled in a week.

The Zanzibar Service is small, the total number of all ranks being 98. This consists of the Prison Commissioner (the only expatriate), Chief Prison Officer (Goanese), four Intermediate Officers (in fact clerical staff), one Senior Chief Warder and three Chief Warders, 82 N.C.O's and Warders and four Trade Instructors. There are two permanent Wardresses for the Women's Prison. The majority of the subordinate staff are from the mainland, some from as far afield as Nyasaland. Efforts are being made to encourage local applicants for the few vacancies, but the quality of those who apply seldom reaches the standard required, educationally and physically.

Staff housing at the Central Prison has been greatly improved in the last three years by the addition of four blocks of four quarters in each, modern and comfortable and fitted with electricity. A canteen, run by a contractor, has now been in use for three years and a small canteen fund built up, from which grants are made for staff celebrations at the Moslem and Christian festivals, and on other special occasions.

I think it can now be said that the staff are satisfied and contented and the number of applicants for enlistment runs into double figures every month.

The Prison population of the Protectorate is very small compared with neighbouring territories. The daily average in prison for the past three years is about 350. Serious crime is comparatively rare and the majority of inmates are committed for minor offences and for short terms of up to six months. The figures for recidivism are high, but this is due to a large number of habitual petty offenders who are constantly in and out. Several of these are for being drunk and disorderly or for breach of the liquor Decree. In a Moslem country these are serious offences.

Among the first receptions I had to interview on taking over were three men sentenced to one month for "Propelling a *hamali* cart* at more than walking pace". The thought struck me that if this was considered a crime worthy of a prison sentence, life in Zanzibar must be very pleasant indeed. It was not until I started walking about in the narrow streets of the old stone town that I appreciated that a *hamali* cart could be a very lethal weapon if "propelled at more than walking pace", as they have no brakes and in many places can only just squeeze through the streets.

The numbers of the real old lag type of prisoners, the bane of every Prison Officer's life, are comparatively few. There are seldom more than twenty to twenty-five of this type confined at any one time. They are never at large for very long, and the number and variety of their offences in the course of their criminal careers is surprising. This type, the perpetual trouble makers, do not get much support except from their own kind, but they have an insidious way of getting themselves into all the key points in the prison from where they can work all the usual rackets, unless they are closely watched. The staff get to know them all too well, and there is a tendency to allow them considerable scope, which has to be constantly checked.

Dealing with the really troublesome prisoner presents many difficulties in a small Service such as that of Zanzibar. In a larger organisation cliques and gangs can be split by transfers to other establishments, but no such means are available to us. It is a question of trying to keep one jump ahead of them, and of coming down heavily when any particular racket is exposed.

There are six establishments in Zanzibar and Pemba besides the Central Prison. These consist of four prison camps on Zanzibar Island and one prison and one camp in Pemba.

In Zanzibar, two camps—Langoni and Kinu-cha-Moshi—are farms for the production of food crops for prison consumption. An average of one hundred prisoners are employed on the land growing rice, sweet potatoes, casava and other crops, under the general direction of an Agricultural Officer from the nearby Agricultural Station at Kizimbani.

Two camps at Kichwele and Pangeni are in the forest reserve area and the labour is at the disposal of the Forest Officer for re-afforestation work. The daily average here is about fifty.

All the camps are well sited and most attractive in appearance. The two in the forest reserve would make very pleasant week-end holiday camps as they are on high ground and always nice and cool.

In Pemba there is a small local prison at Wete, which takes all receptions from the local courts, but retains only those with up to six months sentences. The rest are transferred to Zanzibar by the weekly service carried out by H.H. Ships (vessels of His Highness the Sultan of Zanzibar). The camp is at Chake Chake, and is of a temporary nature only. The work of the occupants of this camp is clearing the mangrove growth from the dhow channel to Chake Chake, and the bay itself. This is very hard and rather unpleasant work, as the men have to work in the mud and sand at low tide, digging out and removing the mangrove trees and roots. There are never any volunteers for transfer to this camp.

---

*Hamali (Swahili) = carrier. The long, low carts for moving goods have been a common sight in East African towns for generations, though now giving way to lorries—in streets which lorries can use.—Ed.

Selection for transfer to the prison camps in Zanzibar is based entirely on good behaviour. Short sentence men go out quite early in their sentences, whereas those with longer sentences are kept in the Central Prison until we are satisfied that they will behave themselves. The camps are all minimum security, with no fences or perimeters, and the men are only locked up at night. Supervision is also of the minimum, but the work done is of a high standard, and discipline good.

Two years ago all the camps and the two prisons were fitted with radio sets, and the local news and programmes are heard by all who wish to listen. The sports commentaries are very popular. Special concessions are granted for the men to remain out longer when any particular football match is being broadcast.

In 1959 football became very popular at the Central Prison and the camps in Zanzibar. By arrangement with a nearby school, the prison has the use of their sports field on three days each week, in return for which we keep the grass cut. This made it possible for the various establishments to play each other and a very healthy rivalry exists. At weekends teams from the camps are brought in and competition is very keen.

The football at the camps is a highly specialised game as the space available is limited and trees and roads and, in some cases, buildings come into the pitch. This no doubt adds to the skill of ball-control, but the results of dodging trees and cannoning off walls is most amusing to watch.

There are, I think, few serious problems facing the Prison Administration in Zanzibar. This is the only Service I have controlled in which the problem of over-crowding does not exist. Accommodation is adequate and there is still room to spare if numbers should increase. The question of after care and aid on discharge has not yet assumed any serious proportions. Work for the discharged prisoner is certainly more difficult to get now than it was a few years ago, but this is due to a general slight recession in the Protectorate and may change for the better.

One very significant thing struck me forcibly on my arrival here. No Prison Officer is armed. No rifles or guns are carried by Warders in charge of gangs working away from the prisons. I have always felt that the carrying of arms by Warders is something of an empty gesture as it does not in fact act as a deterrent to a determined escapee, and may be a very real danger to the public if improperly used. We have fire-arms, in the armoury, in case of emergency, but they do not come out. The general good order and discipline maintained by the staff without the inevitable rifle or Greener gun, to my mind destroys the argument that this cannot be done, and that the staff must carry arms. Of course, there are types of prisoners who must be guarded by armed Warders, but these are, I think, much fewer than is generally accepted.

It is difficult to compare the Zanzibar Service with those of other territories in which I have been. Where we think and work in tens, they do the same in hundreds and even thousands, in matters of staff, prison population and finance. In Zanzibar the Prison Commissioner (the title was changed from that of Super-intendent on the 1st January, 1957) is in close personal contact with every member of his staff and with a large number of prisoners, whereas in the larger territories he is a remote figure at headquarters who deals out the occasional rocket and constantly criticises and issues orders.

Coming direct from the large organisation of the Federal Prisons Headquarters in Salisbury, Southern Rhodesia, I found it difficult at first to revert to the detailed administration and day to day organisation of one security prison and the small minimum security camps. But it was a very pleasant change from the rush and bustle of new legislation, new staff conditions of service, and the thousand and one other things involved in the co-ordination of three separate Services into one.

Sitting in my office in the Central Prison, here in Zanzibar, looking out past the flag-staff with the scarlet flag of His Highness's Government, through the palm trees to the brilliant blue sea, soon made Salisbury seem a very long way off.

Map Reading

by BUNDI

Smoothe out the creases; in these names are found
The touch of sun warm day and star cool night,
The laughter on long marches and the sound
Of sleepy voices in the camp firelight.
Here still these contour lines recall the slow
Climb to the thunderous mountain where we came
To stand in breathless gratitude and see below
The sunrise strike the mist-grey lake with flame.
Here rivers ran together in the plain
Flashing their silver to our tented hill,
And all creation in the scent of rain
Rose from the dark, replenished earth. Here still
When day is new
Do crested cranes dance in the dew ?
Still does the lonely eagle's cry
Ring down the dawn-emblazoned sky ?

Here, where no forests were, trees grew at our command.
Our medicine here dealt witchcraft's first defeat
And here we built a school and from the land
Fear and corruption turned into retreat.
Here in the court, disputing cow or wife,
The elders taught us patience and bestowed
On us the timeless verities of life.
Here was the rich green valley where our road
Evoked new commerce from the unspent earth,
And here the market where we took our fill
Of gossip, when a minute's chat was worth
An hour among the office files. Here still
When evening cools
Do wildfowl talk in reedy pools ?
Still does the ibis slowly fly
Across the dusk-enchanted sky ?

P.R.O's and Cons.

by H. FRANKLIN

E VERYTHING new tends to be regarded with suspicion, especially, perhaps, when introduced into a long established Colonial Service. P.R.O's are new. As a result, one of the major difficulties in Public Relations work is to secure the full and willing co-operation of Administrative Officers and of officials in other departments. Yet without that co-operation Public Relations departments cannot fufil their proper function.

As " contacts " are to the newspaper reporter, so are Administrative and other departmental officers to the Information or Public Relations Department. These officers are, in the main, the real source of information material. It is for the technical department of Information, working under the general policy directive of its Government, to collect the right material, dress it up in the best clothes and send it out into the world along the right paths. Incidentally no newspaper editor would agree with that description of one part of an Information Officer's duties, and I should not blame him if the description applied anywhere but in comparatively undeveloped colonies. Unfortunately, however, in countries where there are practically no press representatives, no film companies, and no independent broadcasting corporations the Information Department, instead of merely leading the press and other organisations to the sources of information about the colony, has to shoulder the burden of actually producing and disseminating that information for the eyes and ears of the people both within and without its borders.

But this is a digression. How can the new P.R.O. get the necessary co-operation, without which he cannot do his job, from his colleagues in other branches of the Service?

An Information Officer who has served in his colony for a considerable time, preferably in the Administration (which automatically implies a good many transfers around the territory), starts off with the considerable advantage of knowing personally most of the people whose co-operation he needs. Personal contacts are half the battle and any I.O. or P.R.O. who does not start with this advantage should spend most of his first year touring the colony and making these personal contacts. That is by no means easy, but it is well worthwhile. Any P.R.O. whom I have ever met works at all hours (it is such an interesting job) and finds it very difficult to get away from the office and go out on tour. There is a staff conference every Monday, the Film Censorship Board every Wednesday and so on. And who would there be at Headquarters to arrange for the necessary broadcast feature, newsreel, picture story and press communiqué if the Secretariat should happily catch fire?

None of this matters. The P.R.O. who wants co-operation must go out and get it and leave the Secretariat to burn, which, metaphorically, it sometimes does when it finds him gone. But on tour, the P.R.O. will be making his invaluable personal contacts and is just as likely to get a good story anyway. I once knew a District Commissioner to be treed by a stray village cow which he had mistaken for a buffalo—but the story was never published.

Although personal contacts are half the battle, most of the P.R.O's dealings with his fellow officials must inevitably be in writing and, I believe, the less formal the writing, the better. I have very little faith in departmental circulars. There are too many of them and because of this too little notice is taken of them. When they *must* be issued, it is not a bad idea to issue them in such a form that the recipients can supply the replies required in a few words under headings typed on a tear-off slip at the bottom of the circular, which only needs folding and posting. This is useful, for example, in getting broadcast reception reports. But in cries for help of a kind which require more work on the part of officers of other departments, such as a plea for the supply of a weekly district news bulletin, more cunning methods can be employed. I write a personal letter every month to Provincial Commissioners, District Commissioners and certain Heads of Departments—the same letter to each, rolled off on the roneo. I try to make it amusing, to include some Headquarters gossip, as well as some straight news from Headquarters which is not for publication, but which officers " outside " would like to know. Within the sugar, however, lies the little pill asking for more news. It is not an infallible remedy, but it works better than any circular. Among the less tough members of the Administration the letter arouses a slight feeling of guilt, which can only be purged by the application of pen to paper in the compilation of a 'newsy' reply.

There is also the bribery and corruption technique. Every Information Department gets a good many illustrated magazines, newspapers, books and other attractive publications through the kind offices of the Information Department of the Colonial Office and the British Council. They are intended for distribution in the remote areas of the country, where they will do most good. I observe that intention by sending the best of them to those outstation District Commissioners who give me the most co-operation. It helps to encourage the others. The material, of course, is passed on to the local reading room or welfare centre so the Colonial Office need have no misgivings. If the P.R.O. adds his own magazines to the bundles, or better still his wife's, which are often of the kind that the Colonial Information Office would obviously not send out 'official free,' it is possible to create the illusion that this gesture is entirely his own, and still more sympathy is engendered.

It is the little things which so often count in seducing a District Officer away from his plans for a co-operative ghee factory for a few minutes to give the P.R.O. a hand. My photographic section has been known to repair a colleague's private camera if it entails no expense but only a little extra work. The condition precedent to such activity is always that the owner shall send us any usable pictures which he may later take. Similarly, when one of my broadcasting engineering staff is on tour servicing community receivers, he may do small private repairs for officials which cost the Government nothing and himself just a little time after sundown. There is obviously a limit to this sort of thing and I bar my staff from going so far as to take " stills " or movie shots of the Provincial Commissioner's new baby.

Yet, despite all these little dodges, there remain the hard hearted. Some officials still hold to the idea that any kind of publicity is in rather bad taste. Others think it more dangerous than dynamite. A few find it very difficult to remember that an Information Department exists at all. It is therefore necessary, whether the P.R.O. likes it or not, that he should talk and write about his own department a good deal, albeit modestly, so that the Service shall know what he is trying to do for it, for the Government and for the country. Putting one's country on the map of the world, helping officers in the field to put across ideas of development to their backward villagers—these and all the other tasks of the P.R.O. appeal a good deal to most officials when once they are properly explained. The media through which the P.R.O. works, broadcasting, films, photography and the rest, are fascinating to most people, provided they can see and hear something of them. They can usually hear, but have not always the opportunity of seeing.

Once having got publicity material from an officer, it is important to let him know what use is made of it—if he is unlikely to know that without being told.

If an illustrated article is obtained on his fish farming experiment which ultimately appears in the "Anglers' Weekly," it will give him quite a thrill to see the cuttings. Copies of the photographs can also legitimately be sent to him for display in the local club to the greater glory of the fish venture. Those who think publicity is dangerous must be reassured by letting them "vet" the copy before it goes out, whenever that is possible. This always breaks the P.R.O's heart and often does the copy no good, but it cannot be helped in the early stages of breaking down timidity. Those who think that all publicity is in bad taste must be left to the bitter end. By the time most of their colleagues have been helped in their work by the judicious efforts of the P.R.O. they may have changed their minds.

Finally the P.R.O. must always be careful to show officers in the field that he is fully aware that nothing he can do with film, radio and press is as effective as their own daily grind in developing the backward peoples under their care. He can only give help, quite useful help. But Administrative and Agricultural Officers who have been trying to get their tribesmen to adopt soil conservation methods for five years without much success will not be impressed with a P.R.O. who thinks he can get results through his magic media in five months.

It takes a good deal of effort, tact and persuasion to get co-operation from long established departments for the new-fangled work of Information. The P.R.O. just has to keep on trying like anyone else who wants to achieve anything worthwhile.

A Trade Unionist in the Colonial Service

by I. G. JONES

IT is said that the numeral seven has some significance of change in the ages of man, so, having now completed seven years in the Colonial Service in the Gold Coast, perhaps it is opportune that I should attempt to summarise some of my experiences and the task for which I was selected.

Coming as I did, from a mining union in South Wales, with its fast tempo of complex every-day problems, to West Africa was no small change and it will be appreciated that this caused me no little apprehension. Naturally I had read a little about the Colonial Empire but, I confess, not so much as one should; consequently my anxiety increased as each day brought me nearer to my task of assisting and educating the African worker in organising and working modern trade unions and negotiating machinery.

During my voyage to Africa my conversations with Europeans having government, industrial and commercial experience of the West Coast were endless. Such verbal exchanges had the effect of a barometer on my feelings, which alternated between optimism and despair. It appeared that there were three important things which I had to learn; first, whether the Colonial Government was really in earnest that the Trade Union Ordinance, which had been introduced in 1941, should become effective; second, what would be the reaction of the employers, who were possibly imbued with the ancient and forgotten prejudices of employers in Britain against trade unionism, and, last but not least in importance, what would be the attitude of the African workers, whose knowledge of real trade unionism could only be most elementary?

After a short period I learnt that many of my anxieties were groundless: I found the Government most benevolent and helpful in its attitude and almost too optimistic; it is essential to have straw before one can make bricks! The employers, very naturally, did not show much enthusiasm, but they were without exception prepared to be co-operative. Indeed, coming from South Wales with memories still very fresh of trade union struggles for recognition and even existence, I was agreeably surprised. The African worker's enthusiasm was high, but it was tempered by a slight suspicion of Government's motives, both in giving legal support to trade unions and in assisting in their organisation, even to the extent of recruiting a British trade unionist for the Labour Department. Possibly it seemed too good to be true, but there again it may just have been the apparently natural instinct of all of us to be suspicious of Government, not because it is a particular type of government, but just because it is one.

Problems quickly appeared: what organisations of workers should be assisted first? What should be their rules and constitutions? What parallel to the British form of trade union should the organisation take? Should it be on a craft basis, or should it be, as far as possible, framed to embrace all workers of a complete industry or undertaking? After long discussions with the officers of the comparatively newly-formed Labour Department, who, although they had no experience of trade unionism or industrial negotiation, were wise in their experience and knowledge of the people and the country, it was decided first to attempt to assist the existing union already created by the workers in the Government Railways.

The first meeting of the representatives of these workers gave some indication of the difficulties that would be encountered. It was not only the language; this could be overcome by interpretation and also many could speak and understand English, but there was little understanding of real trade unionism. The weather was extremely hot and the meeting seemed to be never ending. After six hours of constant explanation I told the meeting that they had better retire to have one more *palaver,* because I was exhausted. During the time they were absent I told my African clerk, who was in a somewhat similar state to myself, that, if they did not make up their minds, then I had had enough and I was going home. Eventually they returned and their principal speaker said that they had decided to form their union on the lines indicated and, with the usual engaging smile of the African, added—" We agreed with you after the first half-hour, but we liked to hear you talk." Never was I more flabbergasted, and I had to remember that in Africa patience is a virtue that must be practised above all others.

Endless difficulties have been met with, and many more would have arisen but for the reason that the rules and constitutions of all unions are practically identical and are based on modern British trade union administration and functional practices, thereby ensuring a uniform educational progress for all union members. Another great asset is the legal provision that only a *bona fide* worker in the craft or industry can become a member of the appropriate union. This prevents outside leadership of unions and necessitates the leadership coming from among the workers themselves. This safeguards the Trade Union Movement from being used for purposes far removed from the ideals of its founders.

Since the start of the Trade Union Movement in the Gold Coast there have been strikes, but it would be complete nonsense to say that, but for trade unions, there would have been none. Indeed it would be no exaggerated claim to say that, but for the Trade Union Movement and its acceptance by Government and the employers, there would have been many more. If there had been no recognised and accredited representatives of the workers during these times of rapid change, the improvisation of negotiating machinery would have been impossible and chaos in industry would have resulted.

As an example of the influence of the Trade Union Movement towards order and progress the mining strike of 1947 is a classic example. This strike lasted for five weeks and involved over 35,000 workers. It was finally settled by arbitration proceedings held by Mr. William Gorman, K.C., and, for the first time in the Gold Coast, a body of influential employers and the workers in a large industry presented their case in a manner that would be creditable in any form of society.

It is not my purpose to go into the rights and wrongs of the dispute but, as one who was wholly concerned with its avoidance and had intimate relations with both sides, I can say categorically that, if there had not been an existing trade union it would still have occurred and that, instead of the complete absence of incidents of violence during the whole course of the stoppage of work, there would have been disorder and racial ill-feeling on a large scale.

My personal experiences during this trouble were many, and the inevitable short-comings of a rapidly changing society in dealing with problems that have no precedents were vividly evident. The meeting of the Executive of the Mine Workers during which they declared a general strike is to me unforgettable.

Imagine a small room, very badly lit, filled with the representatives of the union, some dressed in European clothes and others in the artistically coloured cloth that enhances the natural dignity of the Gold Coast African. The meeting opened with a prayer, and the hymn which is sung at the beginning and end of all mine-workers' meetings. The President, a man of considerable character, bearing and personality, called on me to speak. I arose and through the Labour Inspector, who was my interpreter, I began. My purpose was to avoid the strike, sincerely believing as I did, that the owners were prepared to discuss once again with the Union wage scales and every means to avoid a stoppage of work. For two hours my voice and that of my African colleague and interpreter rose and fell with the intensity of argument.

The vote was taken, and our advice was not accepted. Both of us felt and appeared, in the increasing gloom of the room, utterly and completely disappointed and dreadfully tired.

The President rose and called the meeting to stand and they sang the hymn 'O God our help in Ages Past'. We rose with them and, looking at the faces around, which were now barely discernible, one felt to the full the tragedy and hopelessness of the misunderstanding between employer and employee that is found everywhere in the world. The same fundamental problem exists in Africa as elsewhere—how to achieve between employer and employee the realisation that both sides have one stake in common, namely the industry in which they are both engaged, and that if they kill that industry all will suffer equally; and furthermore that human reason can and should be capable of evolving a relationship that is to the mutual benefit of both sides.

Trade unionism is here in West Africa and it will stay. Its history will inevitably be that of mistakes and set-backs and also of progress. Its tasks, although lightened by the good-will of Government and employers, is no easy one. Illiteracy, the instability of migrant workers, the lack of industrial traditions, and the fast tempo of African social change are problems that seem insurmountable. But progress is being made and the Trade Union Movement will undoubtedly play its historical part in the march of African society towards a fuller life for all.

A Living Museum

by TOM HARRISSON, D.S.O.

MOST Colonies have a museum of one sort or another. But, for its size, Sarawak, with a population of about half a million, can justly be proud of its particular museum, at Kuching, the capital, thirty-six hours by sea from Singapore. It has the distinction of being the only museum in the great island of Borneo. North Borneo had a small embryo museum before the war; it was destroyed by enemy action. Brunei has nothing of the kind, though well represented in the Sarawak collections, and the larger territory of Dutch Borneo follows the general line of Netherlands East Indies policy, which is to concentrate collections in the great museum at Buitzenborg in Java.

The Sarawak Museum has a striking building in an extensive park. The upper storey is devoted to the colourful culture of a very varied population—Malay, Dayak, Kayan and Kenyah, Nomadic Punan; the extinct Sru stone carvers; pottery and beads; and the vivid tale of British influence since the first White Rajah, Sir James Brooke, a little over a century ago. Downstairs, in four main and four side galleries, are bright cases of mounted birds; mammals, including the giant orangutan, and the weird proboscis monkey; fish, snakes, a fine collection of butterflies and other insects; geological specimens, shells and so on. In a further building, down the hill, is housed the extensive series of spirit specimens. A third building holds reference collections and the library. As in all well-established museums, only a small proportion of the material is on display, and display to the public is only one function of the Museum. The success of this (the public) side of the Museum's work can perhaps be assessed by the fact that about 50,000 people enter it each year—equivalent to one-tenth of the population, a large part of which lives in areas remote from Kuching. On the reference (scientific and expert) side there are extensive collections, in frequent use for the benefit of students, other government departments, and museums and scientific bodies in other countries.

Like so many things in Sarawak, the first steps were made possible through the foresight of the second of the three White Rajahs, Charles Brooke. The Museum, as such, was first opened in 1878, and housed in the Kuching Clock Tower, which is nowadays considered no more than sufficient to house the office of the Development Secretary. As the collection rapidly increased it moved elsewhere; and then a special building was constructed and formally opened on the 4th August, 1891. This Museum building was copied from the architecture of a French Town Hall because the second Rajah had a great love of France. It has since been enlarged and modified. This year further extensions, in the form of a workshop, and the development of an adjacent building as a public reading room, are proposed.

The first Curator was Dr. G. D. Haviland, seconded from the job of Principal Medical Officer and after him came a series of men eminent in science, including R. W. Shelford.

The post of Curator is now combined with that of Government Ethnologist and, since I took up the work in June, 1947, I have spent the best part of a year in the interior, mainly among the Kelebits of the far uplands, previously the least known people in Borneo. As well as making a detailed anthropological study of these people, about 1,000 ethnological specimens were obtained, as well as some 900 birds and 150 mammals. Quite a bit of this material is probably new to science, though it is early to say yet. The first large collection of stone implements from Sarawak was made; it shows striking peculiarities. A good collection of beads is of special interest as showing close affinity with beads manufactured in the Eastern Mediterranean and the Near East, in some cases before the Christian era.

On the other hand pottery collected from this remote area is Chinese and Siamese, including several beautiful pieces, and some provisionally identified as of the T'ang Dynasty. Excavations in this area, where the Kelabits still have an active megalithic culture (making stone monuments and carvings) have also raised problems of wide interest.

The Sarawak Museum Journal, which is being revived after ten years, will carry preliminary reports on this expedition, as well as papers on Japanese occupation stamps, Celadon porcelain, Borneo reptiles, the affinities between the peoples of Burma and Borneo, orchids, vocabularies of little-known languages, and other topics which, we hope, will not only be of local interest, but have much wider implications.

Other jobs of the curator in this period have included the administration and regular inspection of the extensive turtle egg industry, centred on three islands off the coast; the preparation of rules in support of legislation controlling the edible birds' nest industry, and inspection of the fascinating birds' nest caves in various parts of the country; planning for a Colony-wide collection and exhibition of living arts and crafts; studies of the export trade in reptile skins, and the spread of the Giant African Snail (*Acathina fulica*); and duty as Deputy Superintendent of the first full Census of Sarawak, including personally conducting the count among the remoter upland peoples and the little-known Nomadic Punans of the northern jungles. These Punans, who make no permanent dwellings and live mainly by the blow-pipe and wild sago, provide a most interesting study subject, and I hope to spend some time among them at a later date.

It is the variety of the Curator's work—and I have only mentioned some aspects—which makes this, in my opinion, one of the most interesting jobs in the Colonial Service. I do not doubt that other Curators have duties at least as multifarious. Perhaps it is additionally attractive in Sarawak, which, although a land torn and tormented with mountain ranges and fierce rivers, is still remarkably free from political and racial divisions. Almost anywhere in this country the white man will be made more than welcome; the further inland he goes, the more this is so. In the crowded colourful life of the "long-houses" in which most of the inland tribes live, friendly contact with the people is easy, and study of them correspondingly so. But even among the more sophisticated coastal peoples— Melanaus, Malays and Chinese—there is a general atmosphere of friendliness, which is, alas, missing in so many other parts of the world.

Not that this Muesum job is all "gin and orchids." The Japanese occupation has left sad scars. The valuable plant collection is still in chaos; I hope to start reorganising it in 1949. It is laborious work to get the right specimen back with the right label, specially if you are dealing with something like a small green bead, which, although it may have no very obvious characteristic of its own, can nevertheless be of real importance from the scientific point of view. Shortly before the war a valuable collection of Malay manuscripts, mainly dealing with legends and the early history of the area, was obtained by Mr. Banks and Mr. McBryan. Unfortunately some of these have been lost during the war, and, though I have been able to replace some and obtain others not previously represented, the important project of obtaining and translating this material (which is in great danger of completely disappearing at the present time) has been seriously delayed.

Worst of all, much of the reference library of local books has vanished. It is a grave handicap to have to work with inadequate literature. Here perhaps, I may be so bold as to ask anyone who can send us such books to do so; we shall be grateful. Equally, we should be pleased to get in touch with other museums, collectors, or students; they only have to write to the Museum Curator, Kuching, Sarawak. We are particularly keen to exchange literature, ideas, suggestions, and specimens (at the moment especially beads and native designs) with other interested persons or institutions throughout the Colonial Empire and the British Commonwealth generally.

The Service on Ice

by JOHN LOXTON

THE International Geophysical Year has sent hundreds of scientists from many nations to the remote Antarctic wastes and hurtled space satellites through the defenceless skies of probably all the Colonial Office territories; it has also provided the occasion for no less than a dozen members of the Overseas Service to spend from two to seven weeks working together at altitudes between 14,000 and 16,000 ft.— probably a record in the Service for high-level team work!

The occasion was the I.G.Y. Expedition to Mt. Kenya in December, 1957, and January, 1958, the purpose of which was to study the structure and behaviour of the mountain's glaciers, together with associated phenomena such as weather and water run-off, during the period of the I.G.Y. when similar studies were being made in other parts of the world.

The expedition, which had the backing of the Royal Society, was organised and led by the Head of the Science Department of the Royal Technical College of East Africa, which institution also provided the Deputy Leader (who was responsible for logistics) and the Biologist. All the other members were either serving or past members of the Overseas Service: Medical Officer, Meteorologist, Hydrologist, Geologist, four Surveyors, Warden of the Mountain Royal National Park (a former member of the Survey Service), Photographer (from the Department of Information) and three Glaciologists.

At this point readers may remark that it is fairly obvious which Government departments the other specialists came from, but whatever branch of the Service harbours qualified glaciologists? Apart from the Falkland Islands Dependencies only three Colonial Office territories possess any glaciers at all and even these are too small and remote to warrant much attention from the respective Governments. As *Corona* will offer no prizes for the right answers, it may be revealed at once that they were a surveyor and a schoolmaster, and a former District Officer who flew in from the Rhodesian Copperbelt.

The R.A.F. provided radio communications and an air-drop of supplies, the King's African Rifles sent a mule transport detachment, while most of the provisions, non-technical equipment, air-photos, etc., were donated by local firms. An American institution which makes educational films sent along a cameraman.

Mt. Kenya is over 17,000 ft. high and the Equator crosses its slopes, which are clothed with forest (used for five years as a retreat by Mau Mau gangs) up to 11,000 ft., and with boggy moorland up to 14,000 ft. or more. Snow falls and lies in shady nooks down to 14,000 ft. or lower but melts on the summits on a sunny day. There are 13 glaciers, the largest of which is now only three quarters of a mile long. The area above 11,000 ft. is a Royal National Park, and no less than four districts of Kenya's Central Province converge at the summit—an arrangement which has not yet resulted in any administrative awkwardness, but neither has it provided a suitable venue for a District Commissioners' (summit) conference.

The expedition carried through its programme without any major hitches. The early days coincided with the local short rains which made the ascent of the mountain first a struggle with mud and then with deep snow and freezing winds.

On a later occasion, a commentator from the Forces Radio Station in Nairobi, trying to extricate his Land Rover from a sticky bit of the forest track, found a large elephant regarding him from close quarters. Unkind friends afterwards said he should have asked it to push, instead of firing in the air to frighten it away.

Three members ascended Batian, the highest peak on the mountain, a long climb of major difficulty, and were benighted during the descent. But they did not suffer the fate of the African whose body was found at 16,000 ft., apparently having died of exposure many years before. Had he been seeking the treasure which without doubt could be the only reason why so many of the *Wazungu* (Europeans) came to climb this inhospitable mountain ?

The scientific results of the expedition will be published elsewhere and will be correlated by the Royal Society with other I.G.Y. observations. Suffice to point out here that the size and movement of glaciers is an index of change of climate and particularly of rainfall—a subject of supreme importance in many Colonial territories. In East Africa glaciers and lakes alike are known to have been shrinking during the last half-century. Much of the effort which has gone into improving agriculture, stock-production, forestry, etc., may well be offset in the long run by advancing desiccation, so that every iota of knowledge gathered on this subject is more vital than is perhaps generally realised.

A Part-Time Job

by V. E. DAWSON

THERE were a few full time officials, such as the Supervisor of Federal Elections, with his headquarters staff, and the State (or Settlement) Elections Officers and their assistants. I write now as a District Administrative Officer, Executive Secretary of the District War Committee, Collector of Land Revenue, Deputy President of the Town Council (and Chairman of two committees), Chairman of the Liquor Licensing Board, Registrar of Marriages and Adoptions (there are, too, a few etceteras) who, like about fifty others, had to find time in the days and weeks preceding the first Federal Legislative Council Election in Malaya last year to undertake the duties of Returning Officer for a constituency of about 30,000 voters. As a Returning Officer, I shall not have anything to say about the registration of electors, except incidentally, or on the policies of the political parties.

The first impact came early in the year, when all prospective Returning Officers were 'frozen' in their appointments until after polling day. They were not to go on leave, be transferred, be sick, suffer accidents, or die. So far as I know, all of them except one saw the election through to the count.

In good time, the Supervisor of Federal Elections called a meeting of Returning Officers, produced a draft of explanatory notes dealing with the whole process of a general election and cleared several minds of doubts and apprehensions. Final explanatory notes, which were invaluable, were later issued to all Returning Officers and their assistants.

Our main theme was "this is the first Federal Legislative Council Election. Make sure that legal processes are observed, but bend over backwards in helping the candidates and their election agents on procedure; do everything possible to tell the people what an election means." This was done successfully although, as will be explained later, the contents of the ballot boxes, and the experiences of presiding officers, show that more electoral education is still necessary.

Soon the polling districts—thirty of them in my constituency—had been demarcated, the polling stations (mainly schools) had been chosen, and the presiding officers provisionally selected from among responsible government officers. As the district (divided into two constituencies) contains about a quarter of the population of the eight district State, we had to call upon nearly thirty senior officers from over a hundred miles away to preside at some of the sixty-four polling districts in the area.

The registered electorate per polling district ranged from 197 to over 2,000 In the small districts, two polling clerks were ample. In the larger ones, even four clerks per team, with a split register, were hard pressed to get through their voters in the 8 a.m. to 8 p.m. polling period. In the absence of polling cards, the register had to be searched, through addresses, to find the voter's name. There was no convenient street name and number for the address; in most cases it consisted merely of the name or the village and *mukim* and often there were several 'local' names for the village, which differed completely from the official name given in the register. Furthermore, as this was the first register prepared in Malaya for a 'General Election,' errors were inevitably found in the romanised spelling of Malay, Chinese and Indian names, and in the identity card numbers, any of which might require the voter to declare his identity on the forms prescribed for that purpose.

Everything possible was done to brief presiding officers, and their polling station staff—all told, for my constituency 140 people—before they went out on their own. About a week before polling day, they all attended a briefing conference, at which they also swore and signed their oaths of secrecy. They had already been sent individual copies of comprehensive 'Instructions to Presiding Officers' (or polling clerks). As busy departmental officers cannot be asked to waste minutes, let alone spend nights away from their bases unnecessarily, two way travelling and briefing were compressed into the hours between one rising of the sun and its setting; emergency curfews dictated movement, in some areas, for the rest of the twenty-four hours. This meant accepting something less than one hundred per cent certainty that polling staff would know exactly what to do when the big day overtook them. For example, the Malayan Film Unit made a most explanatory film on the conduct of a model polling station. We tried to black out the school hall, in which the briefing was held, and prayed for a dark, stormy day. But it was a brilliant day; everyone heard perfectly well, but sight was limited to a glimpse of a dark forearm or the ghostly movement of a black ballot box. Important detail was invisible. We hoped that the issue of copies of relevant legislation, the 'Instructions,' verbal explanation, demonstration, and answers to questions, would overcome this handicap, but we kept our fingers crossed. In the event, of six hundred spoiled ballot papers rejected at the count, only about a dozen were due to mistakes by election officials.

Fortunately, the preparation for polling day, and the count, progressed in well defined steps, although some of them were very close to each other in time, and it was important to ensure that five minutes' lack of care did not produce days, or weeks, of wrangles over some legal error or omission or commission. Representatives of the political parties (the names of the candidates were a closely guarded secret until the moment of nomination) were invited to a briefing on what had to be done. It was surprising how much there was to say, and how long it took to say it. Firstly, the nomination day timetable had to be emphasised. Nomination papers would be received between 10 a.m. and 12 noon—not a minute earlier or later; from 12 noon till 1.30 p.m. objections in writing would be received; from 1.30 p.m. to 4 p.m. decisions on objections would be given and symbols allocated, if necessary. Then followed various details which were noted, in single space typing, on one and a half sheets of foolscap paper, with six headings, 15 sub-headings and 14 sub-sub-headings. On nomination day, there were no hitches, and no objections. Watches and clocks had been synchronised with the telephone exchange and, at the appointed time, the two candidates' names, written in English, Jawi, Chinese and Tamil, were posted on a notice board together with the other documents required by law.

The period after nomination day was occupied, at first, with general preparation for polling day, and the following day of the count. There was no serious conflict between ordinary work—so far as work in Malaya nowadays can be described as ordinary—and electoral preparation. Polling day seemed a long way away. Publicity took most of the time. We received several thousand booklets, in the four languages, on 'Election Offences Law,' 'Don'ts for Voters,' and 'What Shall I do on Polling Day?' These were distributed through penghulus (headmen), local councils, estate managers (for their labour) and, of course, through the mobile field units of the information department. The campaign programmes of the political parties and the publicity programme of the information department were, by mutual consent, arranged so that clashes (with the possibility of sudden bad temper) were avoided. There was a steady flow, with sudden spates, of forms, notices, registers, and the rest, all told running into thousands.

Those eligible to vote by post—policemen, members of the armed forces, and a few others—had to receive their ballot papers in time to return them by 5 p.m. on polling day. This meant early posting, as many of them might be on jungle operations against Communist terrorists for a week or two at a stretch. The result was that about 85 per cent of the postal ballot papers despatched were returned for inclusion in the count. It is not necessary here to describe in detail the procedure for dealing with the issue of postal ballot papers and for receiving them on their return, it is all contained in the Legislative Council Elections (Postal Voting) Regulations, 1955. The most important point was that the candidates, or their agents, were encouraged to be present to check personally that every step taken was in accordance with the law, to affix their seals (if they wished) in addition to the official seal on ballot boxes and certain envelopes, and to give them absolute conviction that the election was conducted with honesty and secrecy.

On the eve of polling day, the polling stations were finally checked to ensure that polling booths, tables, chairs, lamps and other necessary furniture were properly arranged. At the same time, ballot boxes were filled with all the equipment and stationery necessary on polling day—registers, notices, rulers, pencils of various colours, perforators, forms, seals, sealing wax, string, and so on. These packed boxes were checked and accepted by the presiding officers, who then became responsible for them.

Some presiding officers had short, easy journeys to their polling stations. Others had longer journeys, culminating in a river trip or cycle ride, followed by Shanks' pony, no easy matter carrying a heavy and bulky ballot box. (In some areas, helicopters were used for the transport of ballot boxes and equipment.) As it was necessary for the polling station staff to be at their polling stations at least an hour before opening punctually at 8 a.m., some presiding officers set out on the afternoon of the day preceding polling day, sleeping for the night in a safe village or kampong near their station. Others began their outward journey from 4 a.m. on polling day.

On polling day, after having seen all the presiding officers on their way with their ballot boxes, I, as Returning Officer, settled to a twelve-hour sit at the end of a telephone, to act as a clearing house for complaints and to give any decisions or advice that might be wanted by the presiding officers, or the candidates and their agents. The four assistant Returning Officers toured specified polling stations for which they had been made responsible, ensuring that the staff there were on top of their problems. They also telephoned me every two hours to report progress, interesting or worrying developments, and to receive from me instructions on anything which needed urgent, personal attention. It was a gratifyingly quiet day, and I was able to get through as much, if not more, 'normal' inside work as on many 'normal' days.

About 8.30 p.m., I went to the school hall, which was to be the place of count at 10 a.m. on the following day, to receive from the presiding officers their sealed ballot boxes, the unused ballot papers, the returns which they were required to make and equipment which could be used again. This school hall (which was also the place of nomination) was outside my constituency, mainly because the constituency was bisected by a bridgeless river and a headquarters in any one half would have resulted in grave communication problems with the other half. The nearest ballot box had to be brought seven miles and the longest journey was 37 miles to the chosen focal point.

The first boxes arrived about 8.45 p.m. and several from other polling stations which were in the 'white' (from the emergency aspect) parts of the constituency arrived soon after. Most of the polling stations, though, were in areas from which boxes had to be fetched and convoyed by heavily armed escorts. The route and rendezvous timetable proved satisfactory, and the rumble of heavy police vehicles heralded from some distance away the arrival of the more outlying ballot boxes, until the last one arrived at nearly midnight.

The following day, the day of the count, the postal ballot box was opened at 9 a.m. and, after following the due procedure, the papers were included in the count which began at 10 a.m. At long rows of tables sat the counting clerks and opposite them sat the counting agents of the political parties. All the ballot papers which the clerk himself considered to be doubtful, or on which an agent raised an objection, were brought to me for decision. The two candidates were, by invitation, seated at my side with the knowledge that their views on the validity of any ballot paper would be welcomed. Provided that there was no legal reason for rejection, I decided to accept every ballot paper which clearly showed the voter's intention, even though not marked with a perfect cross! In following this decision, I never had to overrule strong objection from either of the candidates.

The presiding officers, in their comments the previous night, had told of their fears that there would be a large percentage of spoiled ballot papers. In spite of the Government's and the political parties' efforts to educate the public on how to vote, they had seen many people with every appearance of bewilderment in the polling booths. As the day wore on, they found an increasing number of X's, with a fair sprinkling of O's, on the walls of the booths, on the notices affixed for information inside the booths, and even on some fastened to the walls of the polling station. Presumably the people making these hieroglyphics were either practising making their mark, or believed that provided a mark was put somewhere near the voting place, electoral duty was done.

In the ballot boxes, when we opened them for the count, we found a birth certificate, several identity cards, many handbills issued by the political parties and, of course, the number of ballot papers found in boxes did not agree with the number recorded as issued in the return submitted by the presiding officer. In spite of everything, it was found when the result was announced at 1.30 p.m. that less than three per cent of the ballot papers had been rejected, which was satisfactory in a poll of over 83 per cent.

All the correspondence in connection with elections was brought into one or other of the following files:—legislation, nomination, staff, transport, finance, postal voting, publicity, polling, count. When the result had been declared, these files, stacked, were a foot high. Not bad, for two part time months!

There were, of course, some loose ends to be cleared up later such as returning the candidates' deposits, dealing with the travelling and subsistence claims of the staff who had taken part, and paying their honoraria. But, after the day of the count, our minds were turned to new affairs—the celebration of the diamond jubilee of His Highness the Sultan of Johore, the amnesty offered to the Communists (an important feature of the successful party's election campaign); charities week; measures to meet the likelihood of floods and, of course, normal work.

Teaching the Tanganyikan Agriculturist

by D. R. BREWIN

A NEW Agricultural College, a new Agricultural School for Africans, nine new Farm Institutes, a Fisheries Training Centre, a programme for the training of Engineers in the Cotton Ginning Industry, the expansion of existing staff training facilities and an increased programme of staff in-training courses in Tanganyika and overseas—such is the size of the agricultural education programme now being tackled by the Agricultural Department in Tanganyika, as part of the Government's policy to prepare Africans to undertake increased responsibilities.

Tanganyika, which relies largely on agriculture and is on the verge of independence, has a long way to go in agricultural development if it is to expand its economy and keep up with the increasing demands of the people for schools, hospitals, roads and other social services. Comprehensive schemes for the expansion of existing coffee, cotton and other cash crops are being supplementd by entirely new schemes for the cultivation of crops such as tea, cocoa, pyrethrum, Turkish tobacco and peas for sale overseas as seed-crops which have not been grown previously by African peasant farmers. Irrigation schemes are planned to utilise the vast water resources of the country, and co-operative farming settlement schemes are being actively encouraged.

Each new scheme and new crop creates a demand for advisory staff and in particular for more highly trained advisory staff to show peasant farmers the correct way to undertake these new tasks. The size of the problem is indicated by the fact that there is at present only one extension worker to every 8,000 farmers in Tanganyika and this extension worker has probably had only eight years of basic education and two years of agricultural training.

As Tanganyika approaches independence, there is an urgent need for Africanisation of senior posts, not only in the Civil Service, but also in the plantation industries and other outside agricultural enterprises.

In the Three-Year Development Plan recently drawn up by the Agricultural Department, top priority was given therefore to staff training. There are three main categories of staff—Agricultural Officers, who are University graduates; Field Officers, who normally hold diploma qualifications; and Field Assistants and Agricultural Instructors, who receive two years' agricultural training after completion of between eight and twelve years of basic education.

The training of Agricultural Officers is already under way at the University College of East Africa at Makerere in Uganda. Unfortunately the present output of agricultural graduates is only about five per year and it is hoped that this number will be increased in the near future.

The training of Agricultural Officers presents little problem but, on the other hand, there are no facilities at all available in Tanganyika for the training of Field Officers. The Field Officer is the key man on the practical side of extension work in Tanganyika. He normally lives on a small administrative station and spends more than half his working month on safari, supervising perhaps twenty Field Assistants and Agricultural Instructors, who are themselves in day-to-day contact with the peasant farmers. As an interim measure, strenuous efforts are being made to place local students in agricultural colleges in the United Kingdom, Australia, New

Zealand, Holland, Kenya and other countries, but it is proving very difficult to obtain enough places at such institutions.

In view of the importance of training this category of staff, plans have been prepared for the construction of an Agricultural College in Tanganyika which it is hoped will be completed and ready to accept its first intake in 1963. It is planned that this College will be associated with the proposed University College of East Africa and in particular with the proposed University College of Tanganyika. It will be independent, however, and manage its own affairs under a Governing Council. The aim is for the diploma of this College to be equivalent to that of the Gwebi College in Rhodesia and the Egerton College in Kenya. Staff of the highest possible ability and calibre will be appointed. The syllabus and practical work will be drawn up after careful consultation with the East African University Authorities who will be asked to sponsor the examinations and awards and advise on the appointment of staff and external examiners. A big stride forward is the contribution of £100,000 which the Rockefeller Foundation in New York has agreed to make towards the £300,000 capital and £50,000 recurrent expenditure which it is estimated will be required.

The third level of staff training concerns Field Assistants (permanent and pensionable staff) and Agricultural Instructors (Subordinate Service). There are in Tanganyika at present 785 Field Assistants and 1,172 Agricultural Instructors. It is planned that the Instructor cadre will be replaced by Field Assistants and the main emphasis is being given to Field Assistant training. There are two training centres in Tanganyika which concern themselves with the training of these cadres of staff. At the Agricultural Training Centre, Ukiriguru, in the cotton-rich Lake Province, some 50 students are trained each year in the basic principles of practical and theoretical agriculture, and at the Natural Resources School, Tengeru, not far from the famous Mount Kilimanjaro, some 80 Field Assistants are trained each year. But in order to cope with the increasing tempo of agricultural development, this output of approximately 130 students per year will be doubled as soon as possible and plans have now been drawn up for expansion of facilities and raising of standards at both institutions. Until comparatively recently, students accepted for training at Ukiriguru or Tengeru had only eight years of basic education but now, with the increasing output from secondary schools, it is possible to recruit School Certificate holders.

At the same time, in-training courses are being arranged for all categories of staff of the Agricultural Department. It is only necessary to mention a few. A new hybrid sisal plant, which shows promise of revolutionising the sisal industry in Tanganyika, formed the subject of a course held recently at the Sisal Research Station. Animal husbandry, which becomes more important as the idea of mixed farming becomes more widespread, has been the subject of a number of courses arranged at various centres. At the Coffee Research Station on the slopes of Mount Kilimanjaro frequent courses are provided on aspects of coffee cultivation, with special emphasis on methods of pruning. Other newly created centres are concerned with the training of oxen and donkeys for draught and with the training of staff to handle them.

Tanganyika also possesses a training centre specifically for Land and Farm Planning. It is believed that it is the only one of its kind in English-speaking Africa and a continuous series of courses are conducted for staff of both the Agricultural and Forest Departments at this centre.

The courses mentioned so far are being run within Tanganyika. A recent development, however, is the receipt of aid from a number of countries overseas and already 19 students have been selected for courses of approximately six months duration in the United States and Israel, to study various aspects of agricultural extension and co-operative farming.

Hitherto, all our efforts have been centred on the training of Government and Commodity Board staff, but now the time has come for consideration to be given to the training of the farmers themselves. Plans have been worked out recently for the construction of a Farm Institute in every Province of the territory. Groups of farmers will be encouraged to attend with their wives, accompanied by the local agricultural extension worker. The courses will be of ten days to three weeks duration, and the type of course to be given will vary considerably and will depend on the needs of the area from which the farmers come. The simpler aspects of animal husbandry, pest and disease control in animals and plants, the management of grassland, the use of artificial fertilisers, cultivation of new crops, and the use of new types of ox-drawn implements, are examples of the kind of courses which will be given. The Institutes will be on a small scale in the first instance and numbers on each course will not exceed 30. A capital expenditure of £25,000 will be required for each Institute in its early stages and recurrent expenditure is estimated at £7,500 per annum. Application has been made to the International Co-operation Administration of the United States for aid towards the cost of these Farm Institutes and it is hoped that two or three Institutes will be able to accept their first students some time in 1962. The training of staff for the Institutes is already under way at Moray House College of Education in Scotland and in the United States.

The Farm Institutes will cater for peasant farmers. Sisal, however, is Tanganyika's main crop and it is grown on large estates. Here, too, plans are being made for the training of managerial and engineering staff. A bequest of over £250,000 has been made to the Tanganyika Government by the late Mr. Christos Galanos, a well known sisal plantation owner. Trustees have been appointed to administer these funds and plans are being drawn up for the establishment of an agricultural school.

The second most important crop in Tanganyika is cotton, and there are 35 ginneries in the territory engaged in processing this crop. In the past, the managerial and engineering work in these ginneries have been handled largely by Asian staff but two new trends in the industry have created a need for more trained staff. The first is the establishment of co-operatively owned African ginneries, of which six have been built so far; the second trend is the installation in these ginneries of a new type of automatic American machinery and the general introduction in all ginneries of much more electrically-operated equipment. The Agricultural Department is offering advice to the industry on the development of a training programme, to be run in conjunction with the Dar-es-Salaam Technical Institute and the two Tanganyika Trade Schools, for the training of ginnery staff.

The Agricultural Department does not only deal with crop and animal husbandry; fisheries—both inland and marine—are the responsibility of the Department. Plans have recently been drawn up for the establishment of a small fisheries training centre on the shores of Lake Victoria. Only about ten students will be trained at a time, but they will receive a thoroughly practical and comprehensive two-year course on all aspects of their work, from the use of outboard motors in African canoes to the transport of fingerlings with which to stock inland dams.

An Experiment in Administration

by A. H. M. KIRK-GREENE

A FEW months ago there opened, at Northern Nigeria's Institute of Administration, a course that is believed to be unique in Africa: it is the Administrative Service Training Course, which caters for 16 potential Assistant District Officers. All of them are Northern Nigerians.

What is the background to this experiment? With the succession of Constitutional Conferences and the steady march towards self-government, it became inevitable that—as the White Paper of May, 1956, on the Reorganization of the Overseas Civil Service recognised—it would no longer be possible to offer the hope of a full-spanned career in Nigeria to candidates nominated by the Secretary of State for the Administrative branch of the Overseas Service. It was therefore doubly imperative that an indigenous Civil Service should be built up. The peculiar structure of local government in the Northern Region had already developed a competent, responsible body of Native Administration civil servants, while the accelerated output from higher educational institutions had, during the last few years, begun to find its way into the professional and technical departments of the Government; yet, apart from a lilliputian handful of Assistant Secretaries, there was in 1955 not one Northerner in the Administrative Service.

The Executive Council, the policy-making body of the Region's Government, was acutely aware of this hiatus. A dozen local direct appointments were made to the Administrative Service in 1956/57; in the main, these have proved an outstanding success. But more than this was needed, for, platitudes apart, an efficient impartial, enthusiastic Administration is a *sine qua non* of any technical development: "If the administration collapses, chaos will ensue and there will be little scope for departmental officers", commented a recent Commissioner invited by the Government of the Northern Region to advise on the future development of local government units. The staff position was further underlined by the House of Assembly's approval in principle, last March, of the Hudson Report, whose implementation of the Provincial Authority system might well demand an increase in the cadre of Administrative Officers, besides catering for the replacement of the normal wastage brought about by expatriate retirement or transfer, and the expansion already called for by the staffing of Ministerial offices at the Assistant and Permanent Secretary levels. Finally, the corollary of such a demand: the supply. "Africans of the normal university graduate academic qualification", wrote Mr. R. S. Hudson, in his report to the Northern Regional Government in 1957, "are not yet available in the Region in anything like the required numbers. Therefore I suggest that there is a strong case for selecting the best young men . . . for training as Administrative Officers. . . . This recruitment should be given priority by the Regional Government. . . . I also suggest that concentrated local training courses should be provided for these recruits as well as short courses in the United Kingdom."

The Northern Regional Government acted swiftly. In June they announced their plans to accelerate the introduction of Northern Nigerians into the vital ranks of Assistant District Officers. The Public Service Commission called for applications for admission to a training course designed to lead to appointment as Administrative Officers. While stressing that the normal academic requirement for such an appointment was a university degree, they declared that, as a temporary measure for this first course, consideration would be given to Northern candidates who had supplemented a good secondary education with an honourable period of subsequent employment and who possessed evident qualities of ability, energy, responsibility and adaptability. The maximum age was 35, which upper limit allowed Native Administration staff of several years' service to apply for consideration.

The enthusiastic response to this advertisement in the Gazette dissipated the qualms of any pessimist who might once have muttered his doubts about the reaction to such a step. Over 400 replies were received for the 16 places available. A few applications could, of course, be committed to the waste-paper basket without further ado: a scribe who had already failed his clerical confirmation test three times would be unlikely to cope with the complex circulars that are apparently inseparable from life as a myrmidon of the Ministry of Finance; an applicant who showed barely a glimmer of literacy in completing his form for admission would be unlikely to hold his own in a Division where the Native Authority Councillors are largely ex-teachers, even ex-Ministers. Others, though *prima facie* eligible, could perhaps wait a year without losing anything: the secondary schoolboys resplendent with distinguished certificates, were still on the young side, and postponement of their consideration for a twelvemonth would allow this first Training Course to be devoted to those who, a little older in experience as well as years, might find a year's deferment tantamount to a blocked career.

So it was that our first Administrative Service Training Course opened with 16 students, all armed with several years' previous administrative experience in either Government or Native Administration service, and returning an average age of 29 plus. Let us briefly analyse their background.

Educationally, they run the gamut from University College, Ibadan, down to Middle IV. This last certificate, though below the secondary education called for, has been supplemented by several years of administrative work carried out in the English language, and by success in either the Clerical Training Course or the Native Treasury Diploma Course (or both!) held at the Institute of Administration. Half the students have travelled abroad: two visited England as private secretaries, to an Emir and to a Minister respectively, one worked in the London office of the Commissioner for Northern Nigeria and four completed study courses at various colleges in the United Kingdom. Another student has undertaken the holy pilgrimage to Mecca. Their previous occupations include Bursar and lecturers at the Institute of Administration, headmaster of a Provincial School, Native Treasurer, Chief Scribe, Development Secretary to a large emirate, Supervisor of Agriculture, Provincial Accountant, Adult Education Officer, Information Officer, etc. Of the parental background, the fathers of over 70 per cent of the students were either farmers or Native Administration employees, while others were a tailor, a Government pensioner, an *imam* or Muhammedan priest, and a United Africa Company factor. All are married, some heavily so, but nobody could suggest that such an arrangement in any way impedes study: the experience of the universities in the immediate post-war years has been spared us.

So to the present course itself. During their nine months at the Institute of Administration, lectures are given on Law, Public Finance and Local Government as the principal subjects, with further instruction in the Constitutional and Economic History of Nigeria, Comparative Religion, Political Theory and Current Affairs. Outside lecturers give talks on the functions of their own Ministries. Emphasis has been placed on attaining a high standard of English (written, in particular: the spoken English of the Northerner is a proud by-word among pedagogues) so that those students who subsequently attend any further training in the United Kingdom will be able to derive the maximum benefit therefrom. For the same reason, much care is devoted to the social education of the students, many of whom will, one hopes, soon be mixing in dizzy circles at home and abroad. Another interesting feature of the course is the university tutorial system of instruction, which is proving of considerable value.

The practical side of an Administrative Officer's training is not overlooked. Field engineering, map reading, elementary survey work, vehicle maintenance and First Aid are all included. There is a five-week attachment to Divisions, where any starry eyes will have a chance to be slightly glazed over by the hard reality of life in the bush. The Course aims to finish with a fortnight at the famous Man O'War Bay, which seeks to assess a man's determination, endurance and qualities of leadership in a course modelled on the Outward Bound principles.

Those who successfully pass the Administrative Service Training Course will be eligible for immediate appointment to the long grade of the Administrative Service, though they may then, or at some later date, be sent to the United Kingdom for an advanced course of training. Naturally, like any pilot scheme, this experiment has to prove itself. It is too early for us, still in the first term, to estimate its success; but it is already clear that morale is high and that all the students are aware both of their heavy responsibilities ahead and of the value of the careful training they are now being given.

And then? The Administrative Service Training Course is the beginning, not the end. "There is no short cut", noted the Commissioner quoted above. "The most intense efforts will have to be made to recruit the cream of the young men and to train them. . . . They must gain region-wide experience, loyalty, integrity and versatility through years of field work in different provinces, as well as through experience in provincial and regional secretariats."

The future is unknown but we believe that Northern Nigeria's experiment in administration has got off to a promising start and that those whom it launches will, given a fair wind, soon be able to sail as smoothly as the former ships of their line.

Beachcombing

by J. DARRELL BATES

ADMINISTRATIVE OFFICERS in the Colonial Service seconded to the Colonial Office are commonly known as Beachcombers. Why this is so I don't know. Beachcombing conjures up visions of retired civil servants sitting outside gimcrack bungalows on a Tropic Shore in well-worn tennis shoes, waiting for last month's Blackwoods. It describes a picturesque way of doing nothing in particular abroad on a small income. It is idleness in exile. None of this, however, really seems to explain why we Beachcombers are called Beach-combers. So, having no dictionary at hand, I asked my wife what she understood by the word. "Cheerful old men picking up anything they can find as they wander in strange places, and spending the proceeds on gin," was the answer. Asked if this really applies to D.C.s on loan to the Colonial Office, she said: "It doesn't. They are not old." Perhaps we had better leave it at that.

First of all, how does one become a Beachcomber? The only answer I can think of is Malvolio's. "Some are born Beachcombers. Some achieve beach-combing, and some have beachcombing thrust upon them." There doesn't seem to be any one answer. Some are no doubt carefully chosen on merit for this honour—but most of us, I think, get to the Colonial Office more by accident than by design. One thing's clear, though: you don't become a Beachcomber by going to the Colonial Office and asking to be taken on. If you do you will properly be told that the decision lies in your colony. Beachcombers are drawn from all parts of the Colonial Empire. They come generally when they are about thirty, and stay for two or three years. At present there are about twenty of them in the Office.

The first six months are usually depressing. There is United Kingdom income tax to pay and the 8.15 to catch every morning. One has to wear a tie, and pay for firewood. In the office one must get to understand strange formalities of method and phraseology, as bewildering, and sometimes as archaic as the sacrosanct peculiarities of school or university. Not only the procedure but the people are, for the most part, new to one, and one has to cope, perhaps for the first time, with horrors like the disconcerting aliveness of a stenographer and the disconcerting deadness of a dictaphone. If in the first six months you have discovered how to get your drafts typed and your telegrams despatched; if you can extract both the right file and a morning cup of tea from the registry staff, and know half the office staff by sight, by location and by illegibility of signature, you won't have done too badly.

The Colonial Office is divided into Geographical Departments, which are concerned with groups of territories, and Subject Departments which deal as experts with particular things like supplies, finance and communications. Beach-combers are, of course, distributed to Departments as vacancies exist: but often there is a choice of vacancies at the outset, and opportunities of transferring from one Department to another while one is at the Colonial Office. This being so, it is helpful to know beforehand enough about the organisation of the office, to know which Department to choose, or to set as one's goal. My own view is that every Beachcomber should at some stage go to a Geographical Department—where he can, I think, best see the Colonial Office end of his own work as an Administra-tive Officer, and study, so to speak, the reverse of his own particular medal.

This leads me on to make two other points. Generally speaking the best way in which an Administrative Officer can hope to make any contribution of his own to the Colonial Office is to bring to bear on his work and on the permanent staff of the office the realities of his own experience and responsibilities in the field as a District Officer. It is less often that experience in a Colonial Secretariat is of the same value to the Colonial Office, whose own staff are so obviously much more competent and experienced in this type of work. For this reason I feel that, as a general rule, Administrative Officers should be sent as Beachcombers when, and only when they have actually been in charge of a District. Secondly, it is clearly desirable that territories should be encouraged to send to the Colonial Office the people they think best able both to benefit from this experience themselves, and to make some contribution of their own to the Colonial Office. It is unreasonable to expect them to do so, however, if, as sometimes happens, the Beachcomber gets posted to another job or another colony when he has finished at the Colonial Office. Colonies may well feel that a man sent to the Colonial Office is a man lost, and consequently tend to send the people they are quite prepared to lose rather than those they want to keep.

I personally enjoyed my time at the Colonial Office immensely, and came away with great respect and admiration for the work of the office and for the people in it. This I think is the impression made on most Beachcombers. There is, however, a danger in excessive admiration of this kind. Administrative Officers should come to the Colonial Office not only keen to learn, but keen also to inject—if they can—something of what they regard as the hard realities and practical difficulties of colonial administration. Too often this zeal is quickly exhausted and the Beachcomber assimilated by the office until, after a time, he is almost indistinguishable from the genuine article. Instead of converting his chosen flock the missionary from the bush is converted by the heathen of the city. I think myself that Beachcombers should continuously resist this tendency and try to retain their distinctive status as long as they can. To succeed in this it should not be necessary to exude all the time the obvious aroma of the bush or the rugged atmosphere of I've-quelled-a-riot and remember-the-lion-I-shot-in '37, but better this than the furled umbrella and the black hat.

A word about the functions of the Colonial Office as they appeared to an outsider. They seem to fall roughly into two parts, which can be summarized as positive and negative functions. The positive functions of advice, of direction and of co-ordination are, I think, well enough understood and appreciated in the Service. But it was oddly enough the negative functions which seemed to me to be the more important of the two. I would define them firstly, as ensuring that nothing is done in the Colonial Empire which cannot, if necessary, be justified in an Answer to a Parliamentary Question; and secondly, as seeing that nothing is done which is contrary to the general policy of His Majesty's Government. The constitutional importance of collective Cabinet responsibility dictates the necessity for the latter, and the absence of reasoned and detached criticism in many colonies emphasises the need for the first. These two functions alone, to my mind, entirely justify the existence of the Colonial Office, and explain a large part of the otherwise inexplicable attitudes sometimes taken by the Colonial Office to what goes on or is proposed in the colonies. If every member of the Colonial Service had these negative functions of the Colonial Office clearly in mind, a host of misunderstandings, of irritations and of correspondence would, I am sure, disappear.

It is not, I think, generally known that not only are there Administrative Officers serving as Beachcombers in the Colonial Office, but that there are also members of the permanent Colonial Office staff serving in District Offices and Secretariats. As far as I know no corresponding term of abuse has yet been invented for them. Since 1939 this excellent practice has, owing no doubt to shortages of staff, tended to fall into abeyance, but it is, I believe, now being revived. Certainly there are many of the Colonial Office staff who are desperately keen to serve for two or three years in a colony.

When we were in the field we all get irritated with our Headquarters ; and when we are at H.Q. we all get equally irritated with the field staffs. To serve at both ends is perhaps the only cure for this irritation, which is so often unreasonable on both sides and never does anybody any good at all.

Marchant on Malaita

by D. C. C. TRENCH, M.C.

(William Marchant, C.M.G., O.B.E., joined the Kenya Administration in 1919 after service in the first World War, in which he was wounded. From 1935–37 he was a Deputy Provisional Commissioner in Zanzibar, occupying a similar post in Tanganyika from 1937–39, when he became Resident Commissioner in the British Solomon Islands. What he did there on the outbreak of the second World War is told in this and the two following numbers of *Corona*. The story is named after Marchant who was the senior Colonial Service officer and made the first important decision not to leave his post as the Japanese advance rolled nearer, but it remembers no less those others who shared his hazardous enterprise. The writer of this story himself saw stirring times in this area.

Marchant's Colonial service ended in 1947 when he retired from the post of Chief Native Commissioner, Kenya. He died in February, 1953.)

ON a double page towards the back of your atlas you will find a map entitled "Oceania," which covers nearly half a world of water: no doubt you have sometimes glanced at it idly before turning the leaf to study some other map—which also probably wasn't the one you were really looking for, either. Turn to that double-paged map now and look more closely at the British Solomon Islands Protectorate, which you will find lying just east and south of the easterly tail of New Guinea.

In a good atlas, a few names will be shown: perhaps Tulagi, the pre-war capital in the centre of the group, will be marked; also the island groups of Savo, New Georgia, Florida, Malaita and one whose name may be more familiar— Guadalcanal. At the north-western end of the double chain of islands you will find Bougainville, which is geographically a part of the Solomons but politically a part of Australian New Guinea. Few in Great Britain realise the fierceness of the naval battles that were fought in this general area or know that at the bottom of the 29-mile channel between Guadalcanal and Florida lie more ships of war than in any comparable strait in the world, excepting only the English Channel.

The little smudgy dots your atlas shows are not really small; it is just the scale that makes them seem so. Guadalcanal, for example, is 90 miles long by some 30 miles broad and has a mountainous spine peaking at 8,000 ft. The other major islands are of comparable size and are almost equally mountainous: but whereas the rest rear themselves straight up out of the mangroves or coral sand at the sea's edge, Guadalcanal has along its north-east shore an extensive plain covered with coarse, thigh-high grass and bearing patches only of the coconuts or rain forest typical of the group as a whole. The wartime importance of Guadalcanal lay in this plain, for here alone for many hundreds of miles in any direction was there a really good site for airfields. True, they were built elsewhere before the end of the campaign, but Guadalcanal none the less remained the obvious place to build them and in this lay its military attraction.

After the 1914–18 war a natural harbour near Tulagi was briefly considered as a possible Pacific base for the Royal Navy. Although this idea came to nothing, pre-1939 appreciations did give warning that major naval battles could be expected in the vicinity if Singapore ever fell. These appreciations, however, gave no hint of possible warfare by land and in consequence the Resident Commissioner, W. S. Marchant, had no military forces at his disposal at the outbreak of the Second World War, except the small Armed Constabulary. In those days a Japanese entry into the war was considered imminent, and so to this force was added a hastily organised platoon of Europeans and a few Chinese, sonorously entitled the British Solomon Islands Protectorate Defence Force. The Defence Force's beginnings were unassuming. Rifles and three ancient Lewis guns were its only arms and it was at first uniformed in classic South American revolutionary style—khaki trousers and shirt with a red arm-band, topped off with a red-banded straw hat of the type affected by horses. This curious get-up was practical enough and had the merit of being instantly (and cheaply) purchasable in the Chinese stores of Tulagi.

The 'phoney-war' days of 1939–41 were also more profitably used to build up an organisation which was later to play a part out of all proportion to its size—the so-called Coast Watch organization. Naval responsibility for the Solomons area was vested in the Australian Naval Board, and the Resident Commissioner was an Admiralty Reporting Officer, charged with the task of reporting all shipping movements in the area. To assist in these duties, the Board lent a number of teleradio sets to the Protectorate Government, who also purchased a few more. These sets were of a type manufactured by Amalgamated Wireless (Australasia) Ltd. for use in the outback of Australia. They were powered by two 6-volt car batteries charged from a small petrol driven generator, were extremely simple to operate, portable, and so well constructed that they gave yeoman service even under the most gruelling conditions. Working on a wavelength of about 40 metres, they gave good voice communications in daylight at distances even up to 400 miles; but on this frequency no contact could ever be maintained after dark. The sets were distributed at suitable District Headquarters, mission stations and plantations; the reporting of incidents to stations at Tulagi and Port Moresby was practised, and by the latter part of 1941 the Coast Watch radio net was everywhere working smoothly.

War with Japan and the subsequent fall of Singapore, with the realisation that now nothing barred the southward Japanese advance, was a severe shock. By February, 1942, it was already obvious that the Protectorate was gravely threatened, and an evacuation was arranged. The Resident Commissioner himself was given discretion to leave, but he elected to stay and with him stayed the Administrative Officers in the group at the time, some planters and business men and a number of missionaries including the Roman Catholic and Anglican Bishops. As Tulagi was too small an island to allow any chances of evading capture, Marchant with a small staff established himself in the hills behind District Headquarters, Malaita. There was a pause, while the news of the advancing Japanese grew steadily worse.

Meanwhile the American High Command had acted with speed and resolution. The hastily formed "Americal" Division secured the French island of New Caledonia. Other forces garrisoned Tongatabu, the island capital of the Queen of Tonga, and the Anglo-French New Hebrides. In addition to these forces which were holding forces only, protecting the lifeline between America and Australia, a naval striking force, with aircraft carriers, was collected and the 1st Marine Division was assembled on transports ready for an assault wherever required.

While the Americans collected in the south, the Japanese made themselves felt in the Solomons by bombing Tulagi. Fortunately they concentrated their early efforts on the antiquated government radio station, leaving alone a more powerful Royal Australian Air Force station recently established nearby. These attacks intensified during March and April, culminating on the 1st May, 1942, in an attack on the by now discovered R.A.A.F. base : this attack did so much damage that the base was abandoned and the staff withdrawn to the New Hebrides by schooner.

The Coast Watchers were by this time all at their operational posts. In the extreme south-east, Mrs. Boye, wife of the manager of the Vanikoro Kauri Timber Company at Vanikoro, relayed messages when radio conditions were bad between the Coast Watchers to the north-west and a new control station in the New Hebrides. On San Cristobal, the most south-easterly of the main islands, was Michael Forster, the District Officer, gravely encumbered by numbers of Chinese refugees placed in his care. With Marchant on Malaita were the District Officer, C. N. F. Bengough, T. W. Sexton, the Government Wireless Officer, and H. W. Bullen of the Melanesian Mission, who acted as a Cypher Officer. Three Coast Watch stations were established on Guadalcanal. The District Officer, Martin Clemens, was in the south-east; in the centre were K. D. Hay and A. M. Andressen, planters of great experience, accompanied by Lieutenant Commander D. S. Macfarlan, R.A.N.V.R., the Naval Intelligence Officer; while at the north-western end was F. A. Rhoades, another planter of great experience. Lafe Schroeder, a trader, was on Savo Island; and Geoffrey Kuper, an Assistant Medical Practitioner, went to Tunnibulli at the south-eastern end of Ysabel Island. The station furthest to the north-west in the Solomons proper, and therefore the most exposed, was operated by D. G. Kennedy, another District Officer, who eventually stationed himself, after a number of moves, at Segi at the southern end of the New Georgia group. Even further north-west, however, were W. J. Reid and P. E. Mason who were established at the two extreme ends of the Australian island of Bougainville.

Lieutenant Commander Macfarlan's position at Guadalcanal needs comment. He was the only trained intelligence officer available, and Marchant thought Macfarlan should be with him to help collect, sift and pass on reports from the other Coast Watchers. Macfarlan was, however, ordered by his Service superiors to go to Guadalcanal to be as near as possible to the probable centre of greatest enemy activity but where, being a stranger to the Solomons, he was reliant on Hay and Andressen; Marchant's desire to have the Intelligence Officer near him, where he considered he could be most useful, was reasonable but unfortunately it was construed in some quarters, both at the time and afterwards, as an improper attempt at control by the civil authority. The consequences of this misunderstanding were an additional source of worry to Marchant which he should not have had to suffer.

Towards the end of March, 1942, Kennedy, anxious about events in the extreme north-western end of the group, sent Wheatley, another Assistant Medical Practitioner, up by schooner to reconnoitre. Unfortunately Wheatley's arrival there coincided with the first Japanese move into the group and he was not heard of again. There was no further troop movement southwards until the 2nd May, the day after the last heavy bombing of Tulagi, when Kennedy reported a considerable fleet in the waters south of Ysabel. Three days later this force appeared off Tulagi but the U.S. Navy, warned by Kennedy's reports, was ready for them. The occupying force was heavily and successfully attacked by U.S. carrier-borne aircraft while in Tulagi harbour and the adjacent waters, the battle straggling off to the westward in succeeding days to become known as the Battle of the Coral Sea. It was therefore in Tulagi harbour that the southward Japanese advance was first met and seriously checked; and here the Coast Watchers drew their first blood.

Schroeder on Savo had a ring-side seat at this opening battle and was able to report the sinking of nine enemy ships during the action. Nevertheless the Japanese were checked only and next day occupied Tulagi in some force. This done, they reconnoitred further afield and parties started to investigate the grassy plains of Guadalcanal. The Guadalcanal Coast Watchers carefully watched and reported these movements. Clemens turned his police and a few volunteers he had with him into a Defence Force detachment and these men kept in touch with the Japanese by offering their services as carriers, on one occasion insuring themselves by carrying the party's heavy machine gun! More than once the Japanese were led into the bush by volunteer 'guides' and lost. The other Coast Watchers similarly sent trusted men to mingle with the Japanese and report, all these reports being received and passed on south by Marchant on Malaita. Aircraft movements were also reported, to give the Allied Command some idea of Japanese search patterns. There were many similar exploits, but the Coast Watchers were, nevertheless, in a most exposed and dangerous position with no possibility of relief so far as they knew and in constant danger of being harried by Japanese patrols. Schroeder had to move over to Guadalcanal to join Rhoades and it was at this time that Kennedy and Kuper moved to their final positions.

The Japanese finally selected a part of Guadalcanal, near Lunga, and in late June, 1942, started to make an airfield. This base was not far from the mountain eyrie where Hay, Andressen and Macfarlan were perched and they and the other Guadalcanal Coast Watchers continued to keep in touch with Japanese activities by sending their men to mingle with the labourers pressed into working on the airfield. In this way continual reports on the progress of the base and the extent of Japanese consolidation winged southward by radio from the Coast Watchers through Marchant's station on Malaita to the Allied Command.

(c) From the Woman's Viewpoint

One of the most revealing and rewarding dimensions of the post-colonial study of Colonial Service work and life has been the exploitation of the experience of that life (conventionally very much a male one) by women. For all the post-1970s phenomenon by way of memoirs and novels, from wives of Colonial Service officers as well as from woman officers, the pages of *Corona* throughout the 1950s reveal an interest in and encouragement of writing about women's experiences and views, whether as wife or career official, far ahead of the time.

In this Section, besides the accounts of different kinds of Colonial Service employment, there is a selection of contributions to the debate about children in the Colonial Service life which preoccupied the editor and *Corona* readers in the journal's early years. The historic "War Song of the Amazons" was composed by two women who were working in the Colonial Office in 1944, where A.M. Grier (N. Borneo) was in charge of the new project of recruiting Women Administrative Officers for service in the colonial territories. "One of the two, it is fair to say", the editor commented in 1953, "became herself an 'Amazon'".

Queen Elizabeth's Colonial Nursing Service

by FLORENCE UDELL, M.B.E.

IT was in 1896 that the first trained nurses were officially sent from the United Kingdom to the colonies. Before that time skilled nursing care was unknown in isolated places within the Colonial Empire and, though there were Medical Officers, their work for the sick was handicapped by the lack of trained nurses.

The idea originated in Mauritius and began with the formation of a voluntary society to provide trained private nurses for the care of British officals and settlers and their wives and children. "The Colonial Nursing Association," now "The Overseas Nursing Association," was formed in London to recruit suitable nurses, and local branches of the Association were set up in some of the colonies, who were the employing committees. The first two members of the nursing profession appointed by that body left for Mauritius in the spring of 1896.

Later in the same year the then Secretary of State, Joseph Chamberlain, who had shown great interest in the scheme, sent a circular despatch to Governors of all colonies drawing their attention to the work which had been started, and recommending its development. The interest and approval which this suggestion received is shown by the fact that the first two government-employed nurses sailed for the Gold Coast in January, 1897.

In this way was started the first work of professional women in the Colonial Service from which has grown the present Colonial Nursing Service, the only Unified Service of which membership has, up to the present time, been exclusively for women.

At first Colonial Governments employed these trained nurses to care for European officials and their families, the care of the colonial peoples being undertaken by the Missionary Societies. It was soon realised, however, that the provision of trained nursing care for the colonial population was also a government responsibility, and the service expanded rapidly. Three appointments were made in 1897, the figure increased to over one hundred in 1925, and in the last two years an average of two hundred and thirty new appointments per annum have been made.

The Unified Colonial Nursing Service was formed in 1940 and, in April 1948, a signal mark of Royal recognition was conferred upon it when Her Majesty the Queen consented to allow her name to be included in its title, and the " Queen Elizabeth's Colonial Nursing Service " came into being. Already professional circles speak familiarly of Q.E.C.N.S., and the " Q.E's " are taking their place with the other nursing services similarly recognised in the affectionate regard of their professional colleagues.

Many thrilling stories could be told of the pioneer work carried out by members of the Service in many parts of the world and of the difficulties and even dangers which they encountered. But these experiences can best be recounted by those who have had them and cannot, in any case, be included in a short account of the history of the Service such as this.

The records of the Service show that these British trained nurses have carried the fine traditions of the profession into their work overseas. Yet it is obvious that tradition alone has not been sufficient. Ingenuity and the ability to adapt both herself and her professional work to varying conditions have played a large part in the help which each Nursing Sister has given to the development of colonial nursing. The success which has already been achieved shows how much those qualities and a sense of responsibility and leadership have been, and still are, possessed by members of the Service.

The Service has not escaped the dangers and horrors of war and, between 1939 and 1945, fifty-two members lost their lives, most of them serving in Malaya, who were killed, presumed lost at sea, or died in internment in the Far East. Many members have been honoured by the King for their services, and the long Honours list includes several who were specially recommended for service rendered during the war.

The Service has always had an exceptionally high marriage rate. In professional circles this is regarded as " wastage," and it certainly causes serious problems for those who are responsible for maintaining a nursing service in an individual colony, or for recruitment at home to fill the resulting vacancies! But a trained nurse married to an official in a colony is always a useful member of the community and, during the war years, when new recruitment was almost impossible, married ex-sisters returned to professional work in all parts of the Colonial Empire and, by doing so, often prevented the very serious situation which an acute shortage of trained nursing staff always creates.

The present establishment of the Service is over eight hundred. Its high reputation, in spite of the difficulties members may have to face, is shown by the fact that it is almost the only nursing service in the world at the present time which is not faced with a serious shortage of recruits. In fact, for some of the most popular and best known colonies there is a waiting list of candidates. The membership of the Service already includes several nurses born and educated in the colonies, who have come to the United Kingdom for training and have qualified here. Nurses' training schools already exist in some colonies and others are being built or planned. As soon as these schools turn out nurses with qualifications equivalent to those obtainable in the United Kingdom, reciprocal recognition can be applied for by the Government concerned and, thereafter, locally trained and fully qualified nurses will be eligible for appointment to the Service. The result should be that the Service will rapidly expand and will, in years to come, include a great many members recruited from and serving in their own countries.

The white overall and cap of the Nursing Sister is a familiar sight throughout the colonies. Soon it is hoped to have a recognised uniform and badge of which members of the Service can be proud.

Nursing Sister

by MARY GRIFFIN

WHEN I was first asked to write an article on the Queen Elizabeth's Colonial Nursing Service, now the Queen Elizabeth's Overseas Nursing Service, I was full of trepidation, as I felt quite unable to do justice to this great, if little known, Service. Then I thought that if I put down some account of my own life in it, it might help to give some realisation of the great work this Service has done and is still doing in many overseas territories: a work which first consisted purely of nursing care for Europeans and then for local peoples, and has since gradually widened until the present day, when the Matrons and Sisters of the Queen Elizabeth's Overseas Nursing Service are training local girls to the English State Registered standard, in order that they may take over entirely their own Services.

I entered the Service first just before World War II in one of the most delightful overseas territories of the Commonwealth—Gibraltar. To begin work in the Service in Gibraltar's lovely climate, amid its sub-tropical flowers and trees, is to be prepared gently and gradually for the more rigorous work of some of the larger territories.

There are three Government hospitals on the Rock: the general hospital, near Moorish Castle, a mental hospital and a T.B. hospital. The latter was finished just about the beginning of World War II and was not used as a hospital until the war finished, so that I did not know it as a working unit. It was built as a memorial to King George V, and, as there is a great deal of T.B. on the Rock, serves a very useful purpose.

The work in the general hospital, which consisted of 120 beds before the war but was built up to 300 during it, is most interesting. Naturally, as the hospital serves a port, a good proportion of the patients are merchant seamen from every quarter of the globe. The language problem presents considerable difficulties at times and, although in my time the local and English staff between them used to muster up a mixture of Spanish, Italian, German, French and English, the occasional Lithuanian or Chinaman who used to appear without a smattering of any of these caused exasperation or amusement, according to the success of the sign language employed.

I was the Theatre Sister in Gibraltar for three years of the war, and I would not have had any other job in the world. I could look out of the window while sterilizing or cleaning and I shall always remember the Sunday in November, 1942, when I came on duty at 8 a.m., while the wireless was giving out the news of the North African landings, and I was watching the fighter planes coming back from protecting the landings, from the theatre window.

The nursing here before and during the war was carried out by Nursing Sisters of the Overseas Service assisted by local orderlies, but at the time I left in 1944 some organised training for local girls was being planned and has since been carried out.

And so to Cyprus in 1945. I arrived in that lovely island one week after V.E. Day, and, from a work point of view, it was rather a wider field than Gibraltar. There is a modern 300-bedded hospital in Nicosia, the capital, a very fine T.B. hospital in the western mountains, as well as a leper colony and mental hospital, and there are small hospitals in each of the five main towns. By the time I arrived an attempt was being made to start a health service, and during the four and a half years I was in Cyprus the one English Health Visitor had made very commendable strides in training some of the local nurses in public health work which, of course, was invaluable in an island whose population consists mainly of small farmers, often in remote country districts. Unfortunately, in Cyprus the value of the injection is rated very highly, and for this reason treatment was considered poor by some of the country-folk if they had no injections during their stay in hospital. I have heard it said that in some country districts the inhabitants used to boast of the amount they had to pay for an injection, those who were able to say they had paid £1 for one gaining considerable status over those who had paid a paltry 10/- only! However, for all that, the hospitals remained full and there was always plenty of work in them.

The education of the local girls, however, up to the end of the war had not reached a very high standard, only a comparatively few having reached School Certificate standard and, of these, those who were interested in nursing had been sent abroad for training. Local training, at the level of the assistant nurse grade, was started in 1947 and has gradually increased until now it has almost reached the registered nurse level. The training is still being carried out by the Matrons and Sisters of the Overseas Service, side by side with the trained local staff, the Matron of the general hospital at Nicosia being the first Cypriot nurse to be trained in England.

At the end of 1949 I was transferred to Kenya to begin probably the most interesting period of my career. I was extremely lucky to begin work there under a most able and vigorous Director of Medical Services, Dr. T. Farnsworth Anderson. The scope in Kenya was very wide. There are 52 hospitals in the country, verging from the lovely modern 660-bedded African hospital in Nairobi (the King George the Sixth Hospital), to the 12- and 20-bedded hospitals in the desert of the Northern Frontier Province. When I first went to Kenya, there was the same problem of lack of education for the girls, but by the end of 1950 their education was being stepped up, and so it was decided to start two proper training schools at assistant nurse level, and a further one for registered nurse training in Nairobi. A Nursing and Midwives Council was formed at the same time and from these small beginnings now have arisen training schools for assistant nurses at all the main district hospitals, and the registered nurse training in Nairobi was recognised at the beginning of this year by the General Nursing Council for England and Wales. All the training is done by the Matrons, Sister Tutors and Nursing Sisters of the Queen Elizabeth's Overseas Service, often under considerable difficulties in the districts. In the more backward districts, where the educational standard is not so high, and where the majority of the trainees are boys, it takes time and patience to get the theoretical knowledge absorbed by the students, who sometimes produce unusual answers. A nursing sister in Kilifi, 40 miles north of Mombasa, once asked the students, in an anatomy and physiology paper, to describe the occiptal bone, and one of the answers came back: "My occiptal bone is the part of my head which, if I were travelling in the 'bus to Mombasa, would be looking back towards Kilifi."

The Public Health Services in Kenya are being very widely developed and it is certainly a fascinating country in which to do health work, as indeed is the whole of Africa. The Africans are so likeable and so teachable if patience is spent on them, that one comes to feel it is indeed a worthwhile job to educate them, not only in the basic care of healthy children and clean homes, but also to combat bilharzia, onchocichiarsis, trypanosomiasis, malaria, leprosy, trachoma, and the various other diseases prevalent in the area.

In 1950 in East Africa a series of yearly Matrons-in-Chief conferences was begun. These embraced all the East African territories—Kenya, Uganda, Tanganyika, Northern Rhodesia, Nyasaland, Zanzibar and, from time to time, British Somaliland. Each year the meetings are held in different territories and common problems are discussed and action taken on them when necessary. It was out of these conferences that the present Queen Elizabeth's Overseas Nursing Service uniform was born, a uniform which is possibly not widely known, but certainly surpasses any other uniform I know in its smartness and colours—white and the Overseas Service blue. Quite apart from anything else, the visits to different territories give the Matrons-in-Chief a very good insight into other territories' problems, and a few ideas on how to solve their own, and, although these conferences now take place every two years, their usefulness remains.

From Kenya I went to Singapore in 1955—an entirely different field of work, but also most interesting. I found a nursing service here already built up, but, with the highest birth rate in the world, an increasing pressure being brought to bear to develop, as fast as possible, the existing nursing midwifery and public health services, and to cope with the great problem of T.B. Unlike Kenya, where the midwifery hospitals are run by the city councils in the big towns, the Singapore Government is responsible for the extremely busy obstetric and gynaecological hospital (the Kendang Kerban Hospital) where, at rush periods, around 90 babies are born a day. Every member of this staff does an amazing job of work.

The extremely busy 1,200-bedded general hospital is a heterogeneous mass of buildings which have, like little Abner, simply "growed up", unlike the well-planned economical African hospital in Nairobi. The outpatient department of the general hospital at 9 a.m. in the morning has to be seen to be believed, and one wonders how the staff ever cope with the thronging, jostling crowd of men, women and children of various races, which include Chinese, Eurasians, Indians, Singalese and Malays, many speaking completely different tongues and dialects.

In the nursing school there are around 500 students being trained at a time, and a further 150 assistant nurses at the well-run 800-bedded T.B. hospital which, with the 2,000-bedded mental hospital and the 150 children's orthopaedic hospital, completes the Government curative services in Singapore. They are augmented by a good rural health and maternity service in the rural areas, which comprise the main part of the island, outside the crowded five square miles of Chinatown and the city.

All these services have been built up on the nursing side by the Queen Elizabeth's Overseas Nursing Service Matrons and Sisters, who have trained the local nurses to the standard which, in 1952, was recognised by the General Nursing Council for England and Wales. Now, with Malayanisation, the nursing sisters of the Service are rapidly departing, and in two to three years' time the last member of the Service will probably have gone, leaving the local nurses to carry on their traditions.

I have not mentioned the Service in many of the other territories, in West Africa, the West Indies, the Pacific Islands, Hong Kong, St. Helena, Borneo, etc., but from all I have learned of them the smaller territories have similar problems to Cyprus and Gibraltar, the larger ones to those of East Africa, Singapore and Malaya. I know the nursing problems of Hong Kong are very similar to those of Singapore, and those of Kenya to Malaya. In every territory, the standard of training of the local nurses has depended, and still depends, on the standard of education in each territory, and on the number of girls with the School Certificate who complete their education.

In all the larger territories there is the problem of giving adequate nursing and health services to the people in the outlying districts far from the main centres, whether they be in bush, desert, jungle or swamp country. Invariably, the local girls have to be sent to the nearest big town for training and, once having seen the bright lights of the cities, they seldom wish to return to the quiet of their own countryside. But in all the territories in which I have worked, and the others I have visited, there has always been the most wonderful enthusiasm for their training from the local students. It is indeed heartening and inspiring to feel the confidence and affection which the majority of local girls have for their Overseas Nursing Service teachers, and one is constantly being touched by the many small acts of kindness and gratitude which one receives from time to time from both nurses and patients.

There are, naturally, difficulties in working in the Service. Students to whom the tradition of learning is so new take much more time and patience to teach than their European counterparts. Patients have customs and tabus that one has to learn to respect if one is to gain their full confidence. Often the Matrons and Sisters are working in temperatures and humidity unknown in Britain; sometimes dust or insects are causes of discomfort. There is, especially now, when local Governments are gaining experience, a good deal of red tape and misunderstanding from time to time, which add to difficulties but, in spite of this, life in the Service is infinitely worth while—the feeling that one is taking a real part in the building-up of a nursing service, thereby helping in the building-up of a country; and being able to contribute something to the happiness and well-being of its people, especially its women and children, is a very thrilling thing, and, although some territories have now passed out of the orbit of the Queen Elizabeth's Overseas Nursing Service, there are others left, especially in Africa, where much remains to be done, and where a Sister in the Service can still find a busy, happy and amusing life.

Let us pay tribute to those in the past who have helped in the building up of nursing overseas, and have even given their lives in the Service, and wish happiness and success to those who continue the good work.

Domestic Science in the Bush

by JANE BELL, M.B.E.

BESIDE a tarmac road, a few miles from Kampala, among the untidy elephant grass and ragged banana leaves, stands a new neatly-lettered signboard: "Busega Domestic Science School for Women and Girls", it announces confidently to the passers-by. A hundred yards up a rutted earth road a second board points the way into a small compound, shaded by tall trees. There are two dwelling houses in the compound, a few yards distant from each other. They are built of plastered brick, with corrugated roofs and shuttered windows barred against burglary, and each has concrete floors and verandah. The only real difference is in size and age.

The nearer one, smaller and shabbier, houses the domestic science school, and here in two small rooms about a dozen teenage girls gather every day in search of education.

Private schools in Uganda are not unusual; they are recognised by the Government, provided they comply with a few minimum requirements; they are given help and advice and, in certain circumstances, financial assistance. This one, however, as far as I can discover, is unique: it is the only private domestic science school in the country.

Girls who have completed six years in primary schools have only a few opportunities open to them; the best go to Junior Secondary Schools, others enter teacher training colleges; a new and admirable development in various parts of the country is the establishment of Homecraft Centres usually under Mission auspices, where girls can go for two or three years to study family life in a way somewhat similar to that which the Americans call Home Economics. The Buganda Government, in many ways the most advanced of the Provincial Administrations, has lagged behind in this and has not yet provided Homecraft Centres. So Mrs. Kiwanuka has taken the initiative and boldly put out her sign and taken in the girls.

The main classroom is small and cramped, with awkwardly bulky but solidly built benches and desks. An unexpected luxury is two blackboards. In an even smaller back room two sewing machines, two stools, a narrow table and bench provide the needlework equipment. Outside the back door, in the thin line of shade of the roof overhang, on reed tables made by the girls, cookery classes are held. The food is cooked in a makeshift oven. A heavy metal pot is placed over a charcoal burner; a layer of sand covers the bottom and the cake tins are perched on flat stones within. A thin layer of live coals is strewn on the lid. The products are remarkably good.

But no one will go to a school of any sort unless English is one of the subjects in the curriculum. Mrs. Kiwanuka's English is wildly inaccurate and erratic, so she arrived one evening to ask for help. We arranged that the week's English should be concentrated on Tuesday mornings—educationally indefensible, but with difficulties of transport and other commitments, the only way.

One may well ask what point there is in spending time on the teaching of English, since it is unlikely that the girls will ever become sufficiently proficient to use it either to increase their general knowledge or for enjoyment. But it can be very useful in two ways for girls like these. They need to know enough to be able to follow printed instructions in books on domestic subjects: to use a recipe, to act on instructions about laundry, to make cushions, curtain covers etc., to use paper patterns and to understand simple books on child care.

It has also immense psychological value if they can speak enough English to be able to make contact on the simple level of domestic interests with English women whom they may meet.

Our English lessons, consequently, have a highly unorthodox flavour. Writing is slow and laborious and the results out of all relation to the toil. So we concentrate on conversation and the interpretation of the printed word into action. They learn, in fact, through doing. There is nothing original about this: it is largely infant method adapted to a different level. Accurate weighing and measuring were used to make personal record cards for the class members. Comparative weights were introduced into a conversation built round a visit to the weekly children's clinic. Relative sizes were learned in connection with the plates, knives, spoons and forks used in setting a table for a meal.

Sets of cards with typed instructions for various simple activities ensure that each girl is using her knowledge of English, and it also economises in space and equipment, because each one does something different. At first, they were extremely bewildered at receiving written instructions and found it difficult to believe that it was not sufficient to understand the words, but must also, on their own initiative, act upon them. Once they had grasped that, it assumed a sort of treasure hunt atmosphere, with a growing sense of satisfaction in success.

Conversations are an important part of the work and take the form of little playlets, which are built up on some topic which has been the subject of vocabulary and sentence structure study: a visit to the hospital, to the dressmaker, a quarrel over a piece of lost property, a family gathering with its exchange of news. The girls soon show a delightful sense of character and are beginning to hear the stress and inflection of English speech. The old jerky word by word reading aloud from a book has been eliminated from the timetable for the time being.

Their stay in the school varies with circumstances. One girl had in fact gained a place in a Junior Secondary School but could not produce the money for the fees and other charges. She put in time with us, until by persistence, she had successfully settled her financial problem and departed to higher spheres. Another got married. Another took a job as assistant to a bush dressmaker. An older woman will sometimes come in to brush up her English before going back into the job which she had left in order to marry and bring up a family. And with truly delightful humility and common sense, the teachers join their pupils and take part cheerfully and energetically in the lessons. Their presence is accepted without any apparent feeling of incongruity.

It seems quite likely that some of the work that we do fails to achieve its full purpose because circumstances are against us. We go out to classes and clubs, teach and disappear. Our students can have little or no real understanding of why we suddenly appear, business-like, energetic and compulsive. Neither have they any possible means of visualising us against our own home background. We appear, perhaps, a little inhuman and that makes it difficult to reach a stage of easy friendliness where confidence and the sharing of laughter and distress are possible. African women, like most others, feel most at ease in the framework of family and home and respond to strangers most easily in these familiar conditions.

With this in mind, I invited the schoolgirls and their headmistress to my house to tea. Each one shook hands with me as she entered the house and then they settled silently into a wide circle in the sitting-room. All were congealed in shyness. In a recent lesson they had studied with me European furniture and its uses. I reminded them and drew their attention to some of the things I had described. Their shyness melted in a flash and soon they were touching, naming and examining the things they had only seen in pictures. The party soon loosened up, chairs were abandoned as they moved around, heads together, handling cigarette boxes and ornaments, fingering curtains and looking at pictures. "It's so clean!", they said.

The ice broken, they all helped to pour out, carry trays of teacups, hand cakes and sandwiches. After tea, they wandered all over the house, opening cupboards and drawers, at my suggestion.

"How do you use the bath ?"

"Who sleeps here ?"

"What is this room for ?"

"O-o-oh! You have *too* many dresses!", looking into my wardrobe. Gentle hands drew out an evening dress—"What is this one for ? When do you wear it ?"

They went into the kitchen and pantry and talked at length with the cook, pressing him on technical points connected with the cooker and filter. He is of an elder generation and spoke with fatherly kindliness.

Two young men, playing for a visiting football team from England, came in. The girls retreated into demure downcast-eyed groups. But the guests were not in the least disturbed—introductions were performed and every hand shaken. The girls were amazed at the courteous good manners and I saw quick glances flicking between them under dropped eyelashes. But they managed a quiet "Good afternoon", and even gained sufficient courage to ask, "Do you like our country ?", "How long are you staying ?".

I was conscious of the effects of this visit in the ensuing weeks. There seemed to grow between us an ease which had been lacking before which showed itself in greater spontaneity of behaviour and a noticeable increase in the number of questions asked in class.

Just before I left, they organised a tea-party to which they invited several guests of both races and were deft and thoughtful hostesses to us.

It may well be that the by-products of the lessons will prove to be of more lasting value than the lessons themselves.

I was a Homecraft Officer

by BRIDGET WAINWRIGHT

WE had been in Kisumu, on Lake Victoria, just four days. I was resting wearily on a packing case and contemplating the curtains—all too short for the new lot of windows—wondering which corner would be best for the wireless, and generally rather in despair of ever getting the house in order. My day-dreams were interrupted by the arrival of no less a person than the Commissioner for Community Development who had come to ask if I would join forces with another girl and start clubs for African women in the country around Kisumu. Now that the children were at school I had been playing with the idea of finding a job of some sort and this one sounded interesting—so I became a Homecraft Officer.

This land where I was to work lay on the north-east shores of Lake Victoria (which incidentally is a long way from the "Mau Mau" country), and the part we covered was within a fifty-mile radius of Kisumu itself. In Kenya the climate is determined almost entirely by the height above sea-level—anything over 5,000 feet being temperate and pleasant. But most of this land is around 4,000 feet and is therefore decidedly hot at times and, for most of the year, dry and dusty too. Part is rocky and covered with tsetse-fly infested bush, other areas are completely flat plains, and a small part is above 5,000 feet with a high rainfall and fertile soil. The people who live in this land are the Jaluo, a Nilo-Hamitic tribe. They are tall, well-built people and, being great fish-eaters, have plenty of protein in their diet, unlike many other African tribes. They are notable for their large protruding upper teeth, and they are, on the whole, sensible, happy and most likeable people.

When I first became a Homecraft Officer in 1951, the club movement for African women in Kenya was in its infancy and we had not much to go on. But the aim of the movement was to go out to the women living in the outlying parts of the district (which reached to the borders of Uganda over 100 miles from Kisumu itself) and, by starting clubs, to try to help the women to learn cooking (using local materials as much as possible) child-care and hygiene, and also to learn to sew with the stress on mending and dressmaking rather than embroidery, and in fact generally to improve their living conditions. We decided to model the clubs more or less on the lines of the Women's Institutes in England, with a small subscription, but where possible meeting more often than once a month.

We started off by discussing the idea with members of the African District Council and various Chiefs and Elders—all of whom said it sounded a wonderful idea and just what the women needed. So then we took the plunge and started clubs in several different places at once. The response was varied, but on the whole we found the women very eager to come and see what it was all about, and they became quite excited when they heard that they could learn to make their own clothes. In fact sewing, in a sense, was the biggest obstacle we had to overcome, as the women were not really very interested in anything else!

When the European first penetrated to this land of the Jaluo at the turn of the century, they found the women completely naked. But they have long since decided that they prefer to wear clothes and they are now more "dress-conscious" than any other tribe in Kenya. Every woman wears a bright cotton frock and head-scarf, and under the dress she wears a calico petticoat and a sort of short skirt under that, and sometimes knickers as well. At one meeting a girl asked if she could make an "apron-ya-titty" which after a good deal of puzzling we found to be a brassiere! The idea of being able to make all these clothes themselves and so save a bit of money appealed enormously, but the majority just could not see the point of learning to look after their children better, of keeping the back garden clean, or giving the children a mixed diet. They were apparently perfectly happy with the way of life they had always known, and in a way one couldn't help sympathising. The only exceptions were the girls who had been to the good mission schools in the district, and they were only too keen to be sent, at government expense, to the Jeanes School, near Nairobi, to do a year's homecraft training course. Only the most intelligent ones, and those with powers of leadership and personality, were sent there. On completion of the course they were supposed to return and help to run the clubs nearest their homes. In fact, it is on these girls that the whole future of the movement will depend, because as the clubs increase in number, each one can be visited less often by the Homecraft Officer. The men are very keen that their wives should learn more varied methods of cooking, and to feed their children properly, and they are pushing the women to take an interest in other "homecrafts" besides sewing.

The clubs met never less than once a month, and as often as twice a week if there was a Jeanes School trained woman in the neighbourhood. Most of them met under a tree and often a meeting has ended in chaos in a sudden storm.

The subscription was 2s. a year, paid into a Post Office Savings account, and used to buy thread, saucepans, cooking materials, etc. Material for clothes members had to buy separately, and half of it had to be paid before the garment was started (receipts were given for every bit of money paid) to stop our being landed with a lot of half-finished and unpaid-for garments, which happened before we got wise to it. Nothing could be taken away and sewn at home, the most astonishing things happening to garments when there was no supervision. Some of the old ladies who came to the meetings could hardly hold a needle, much less thread it—but they were so keen to learn. One usually had to start by teaching them to sew towards themselves and not away.

The Agricultural, Marketing and Medical Departments were very co-operative about sending African Instructors and Dressers to talk to the women. One day we arrived at a meeting to find that the Dresser at the local dispensary was ill and could not give his regular talk on hygiene. However, at the end of the meeting he turned up together with the cause of his illness—a large tape-worm, in a glass bottle which illustrated his talk! The women were most intrigued and I am sure the lecture was much more effective than it would have been without the exhibit.

We had many adventures on the road. Once we hit a stone and punctured the petrol tank, but we managed to fill the hole with a piece of chewing-gum bought at a tiny Indian trading store, and then to do a further fifty miles home. We got quite expert at driving through lakes where the road was meant to be, and once skirted a hail storm in which the hail stones were almost as big as tennis balls—we got out and drew the outline of one on a piece of paper as we knew no one would believe us otherwise. On another occasion my car broke down and I was given a lift into Kisumu by an Indian who was driving the car himself. When we reached the outskirts of the town he changed places with an African who had been sitting in the back. Upon asking the reason for this I was told "Me bad driver, Police no give any licence"!! I didn't let on that I was the D.C.'s wife!

My husband was transferred again after eighteen months, and so I gave up being a Homecraft Officer, but I had got to know the Jaluo women fairly well and to like and respect them. They are nearly all extremely honest, sensible and quite remarkably clean. They laugh easily and ask for very little in life beyond a simple house and some land on which to grow their food. Their chief weakness, like that of so many of us, is clothes. Of any pocket money they get from the sale of fish, surplus crops or cotton, a large part goes straight into a gay new dress and a new set of undies. But they must move with the times or be left behind by others, and that is what the women's club movement, organised from the Jeanes School, is trying to help them to do.

The only trouble about this work in our little corner of Kenya was that I found it so absorbing I never got our own house really straight!

War Song of the Amazons

Chorus : Oh I'm a Sergeant-major in "Grier's Amazons."
We'll show the British Empire what we are
Rosita Forbes is nowhere
When the Amazons first go there,
Be it Aden or Mombasa or Accra.

I want to go where men are men and life is blood-red raw.
I'll bear the White Man's burden as it ne'er was borne before.
I'll shed my solar topee, get leather-skinned and tough ;
Become the Governor's pin-up girl, the D.C.'s bit of fluff.
Chorus

We'll just ignore tarantulas and spurn the tsetse fly,
We'll stamp on snakes and pot at crocs—smite scorpions hip and thigh ;
We'll ostracise anopheles, cock snooks at all white ants ;
We'll justify the Empire's call, we'll show who wears the pants !
Chorus

I'll outride Rider Haggard, turn over Gertrude Page.
I'll go where clothes are never seen and scalps are all the rage.
Where white man's foot has never trod I'll leave my dainty prints
And lecture to the cannibals on meatless cooking hints.
Chorus

I'll hunt the fierce bilharzia, I'll shoot at Chota pegs.
I'll sleep out on my *ju ju*—quaff sampan to the dregs.
I'll dance a merry baobab and houri with the best
At the Governor's formal soirée I'll put on my lace safari
And ensnare like Mata Hari, 'neath the scented rinderpest.
Chorus

Mrs. D. P. W. in British Honduras

by PEGGY PEACOCK

AT 10 p.m. the telephone rings: Mrs. W's sink is stopped up—could a plumber be sent at once ? At 3 a.m. it rings again—a main bridge across a road has been swept away by a flood. Things like this have a habit of happening at night in British Honduras, and people expect the Director of Public Works to deal with them at once—even Mrs. S. who finds she hasn't a drop of water left in her vat. As the Director's wife I, too, am on the receiving end of the telephone.

But this is a very pleasant life (apart from separation from children), and I like Belize very much—its people are friendly and very kind, and though the climate is hot and sticky from May to October the other months are most pleasant, temperatures varying from 60° to 80°. During our previous tour in Belize we had our youngest boy with us and he went to the kindergarten of Wesley College. School fees were one dollar a week (five shillings) and he went by taxi which cost us ten shillings a week (I think the fees have since increased). He now goes to boarding school in England and it costs approximately thirty shillings a day.

I live in a Government furnished quarter within ten minutes walk of the shops. There are a few good stores where most ordinary things can be obtained, but no ready made clothes; however, there are lots of material and good tailors and dressmakers.

My house—"Peacock Lodge"—is of local pine, on stilts, eight feet in the air. Most of the houses in Belize are off the ground, as this was once swamp land—rumour says that it was filled in with mahogany chippings and empty rum bottles—but they are also built this way to get the breeze. My house has a verandah, where we spend most of our spare time, a large sitting-dining room, two bedrooms, bathroom and lavatory, and kitchen—all very compact. The floors are of polished pine, and the furniture is local mahogany, beautiful and very different from the furniture issued in Somaliland, our previous posting. Under the house is a maid's quarter, a large space for washing and drying the clothes when wet and a garage—all with concrete floors. I cook on a Florence paraffin three burner stove, but shall shortly change over to Butane gas (calor gas) which most houses now have. They are dearer but cleaner and cooler to use. Our 'frig' is on hire from the Electricity Department.

I am very proud of my house. It looks like home, with all our personal things about, copper, silver and brass—we even have a copper warming pan engraved with a peacock hanging on the wall, and this is of great interest to Americans who visit us.

We have a small garden round the house, and a hibiscus hedge which has bloomed continually ever since I arrived. Things grow very quickly here. I planted a bougainvillea cutting and within eighteen months it had climbed over the verandah roof. We have several local rose trees in drums, and some chrysanthemums which bloom in November. The garden is mostly lawn, and also has a banana and mango tree, frangipani, oleander and a few other shrubs. This is a great joy to me and I always have flowers in the house. Roses bloom all the year round, and I have a few white and purple mountain orchids in hanging baskets. The plants and cuttings are planted in drums to keep away the land crabs which are a perfect pest, and eat away the roots if they get at them.

We live about fifty yards from the sea and near the Customs. It is very pleasant to sit on the sea wall in the cool of the evening and watch the moon come up over the horizon. Sailing and fishing here are excellent. We have an eighteen foot boat, and have had many good sails in her. We trail a fishing line and can catch anything from a two to a 20 lb. fish.

Our water supply is rain water from the roof; this runs into a huge vat, where it is stored for our use only. Each house has its own vat. Some houses now have piped water but I prefer the soft. It is always boiled before use—I hope!

Domestically this is an easy life, though one quickly becomes so involved with different things that it can be hectic. I am fortunate in having a very good maid, and my husband's driver works for me in the evening; he looks after the garden and does my shopping at the market, for which I give him ten per cent commission. The maid is exceptionally good at washing and ironing and it is a wonderful thought to know that it will be done twice a week—or more if necessary—and be ready the same day. All the washing is done in cold water but is left out to burn (bleach) if extra dirty. Also local starch is used, made from cassava and mixed with a piece of candle; the result is excellent.

Morning coffee parties are popular here, but I am a little wary of them—the conversation, if only Government wives are present, invariably turns to the P.W.D.! We become then "The Public Won't", "The Public Waste" or "The Public Wait" Department and when all the chat is about who wants what and who has got what, I can only repeat that Mrs. D. P. W. is usually the last to get anything! And, of course, there are the stories, apocryphal or otherwise. A favourite one is about the lady V.I.P. staying for one night at an important house where the plumbing in the guest quarters was not quite finished. She had a fine hot bath on the night before she left, but her aeroplane was delayed and she came back again—no hot bath this time: the P.W.D. had withdrawn the plumber who, on the previous night, had been making the necessary connections on the other side of the bathroom wall.

When my husband goes into the out-districts I accompany him and we stay in Government rest houses. We stop many times on the way to inspect road gangs and bridges, hospitals, health centres and police stations. The favourite trip of mine is to Stann Creek, about ninety miles south of Belize. We go through fifteen miles of orange groves in the valley. Citrus fruits are exported, and we have paid an interesting visit to the canning factory, seeing some grapefruits being washed and squashed for juice, then others washed, peeled, quartered and tinned. Even the oil is extracted from the skin and exported. The speed of the workers is terrific and they receive piece time rates of pay plus a bonus. The grapefruit season starts in August and oranges in December.

Another interesting trip is to Corozal about ninety miles north of Belize and on the borders of Mexico. Corozal was almost flattened by the 1955 hurricane 'Janet' but now a new town has been built, with a new rest house quite as good as some hotels I have stayed in. When we visit Corozal we sometimes take a trip to Chetemal across the border into Mexico—our driver doesn't altogether approve of this as he has to drive on the right and he doesn't like to see the police all carrying revolvers. We spent our local leave last tour in Merida in Yucatan, Mexico. It was very pleasant —and how popular the British are there!

We live almost next door to the Colonial Development Corporation's super hotel, "Fort George" and Americans come here in the winter for some sunshine—we often meet them on our evening walk along the sea front, and bring them back home for a drink. One of our guests looked doubtfully at the egg-lettuce sandwiches I offered him and asked if the lettuce was clean and good to eat: I told him it was imported from America and had cost 3s. 6d. a pound. I showed him some 'Obeah' candles, that were stuck all over with pins, and he wouldn't hold them in case they were poison. These two candles were found in the sea by my son when he was fishing.

They were green piano candles, tied head to tail together with lots of black cotton. Spanish writing was on each and they were stuck all over with pins. My maid said they would bring bad luck to the house and we must throw them back into the sea, but we still have them. They probably represent a couple, and some mumbo-jumbo had been said over them before they were thrown into the sea. Maids who want to finish their work sometimes practice a bit of 'obeah' if you have visitors who won't leave: they stand a broom behind the door and stick a fork into it—and off goes the visitor. Try it yourself sometime if your drinks are getting low!

If 'obeah' is still important here, so are funerals, particularly of Lodge members. Then you have all the Lodge Brothers and Sisters dressed in mortar-boards, sashes and aprons and all walk behind the one horse-drawn hearse that has four black plumes at each corner. A recent funeral was of an old woman said to be 126 years of age—she had remembered being brought into Belize at the age of five to attend the celebrations of Queen Victoria's coronation!

The boledo lottery is a big thing here. Five cents a chance, any number from o to 99, and if it turns up you win three and a half dollars. Winning numbers of boledo are given out each evening by the local radio station. My husband and I often make a guess at it and only once have we been right. The local people connect numbers with most things—for example, if a car has an accident they play the last two numbers of its registration on boledo. Recently a child was killed accidentally, and its coffin was put under a mango tree full of fruit, prior to the funeral. The next day a large mango had the child's face quite clearly marked on it, and people said that meant number nine. That evening nine was heavily staked on boledo and it turned up.

Our friends and relations at home think we lead a very easy life. No housework, lots of sunshine, cheap alcohol and cigarettes, many parties, plenty of bridge, etc., but life can be exhausting. You help to run a coffee shop, all of whose profit goes to the Red Cross rehabilitation centre for T.B. If you happen to be a nurse, there are lectures to give to Red Cross and hospital staff; there are the hospital library, the girl guides, and the Y.W.C.A. I have helped with the Red Cross Bazaar and the church bazaar; put on concerts, formed a drama group, taught Scottish dancing; catalogued the medical library, put hospital records in order and last but by no means least helped to entertain the Royal Navy when they visit us twice a year. No, time does not hang heavy on the hands of a D.P.W's wife in British Honduras.

Mrs. O. S. in Malaya

by V. E. DAWSON

OUR wives are not unsung. *Corona* contains many pieces by, and about, them in different lands. *Dearest Priscilla** was devoted to them in its delightful entirety. *A Pattern of Islands*† gave glimpses of the author's wife. What follows is an attempt to give a composite picture of Mrs. O. S. in Malaya—O. S., I hasten to say, stands for Oversea Service and has no physical implication!

The majority of Oversea Service wives now in Malaya are post-war arrivals. Each of them had to become acclimatised rapidly to the new status of being wife of a husband immersed in the stimulating, but exacting post-war work of reconstruction and rehabilitation which jostled for priority with economic, political and social progress; a new climate; new domestic arrangements; a new language; new—and idealistic—people, and probably, a new family of her own. All in all, Mrs. O. S. may have had an occasional twinge of doubt, during the first year or two, whether she enjoyed the life of being her husband's wife.

But remarkably soon, or so it seemed, the new family was at school in Britain and the new husband, still immersed, had been transformed into a vintage model. Well before this happened, Mrs. O. S. had discovered new interests and would not, even if she could, exchange her way of life for any other.

Wherever she happens to be, it is not long before she meets the women of the country—at meetings, in their houses, or they in hers. At first, this is a strain owing to the language barrier but after she has taken lessons, practised conversation, and gained confidence, the friendly smiles of before can be backed up by fluent speech.

There was a time, not long ago, when it was almost inevitable that Mrs. O. S. would have had to take the lead in persuading a few 'advanced' women to look beyond their domestic walls and to do something for the good of the community. Now she can join or visit, in a comparatively small rural area of a few hundred square miles, many well organised women's institutes, with hundreds of members who meet regularly to learn and teach cooking, dressmaking, hygiene, child welfare —in fact, practical domestic science. The women's will, and ability, have probably always been latent, and with unobtrusive encouragement are now being displayed. Mrs. O. S. can still teach but perhaps her most important rôle now is to show, by association and example, how this community consciousness can be expanded.

Adversity always evokes sympathy, but some people now doubt whether it is their personal concern, pointing to official social services as one of the causes of taxation. The Social Welfare Department, with the best will in the world, has neither the organisation nor the resources to be all embracing. In the few urban areas, and comparatively large rural areas, there is almost limitless scope for what is sometimes cynically described as "do-gooding" but is better defined as "the giving and spending of time and money to and for distressed people." Here Mrs. O. S. (and other public spirited men and women) is well in the picture in raising money to fight tuberculosis and to alleviate the hardship it causes; to give, or lend, small business capital to the handicapped so that they can, within their limitations, be independent; to provide homes for the young who may need them, and the old who have no other refuge. It is almost certain that, every year, she will assist as

* By Emily G. Bradley. (Max Parrish, 12s. 6d.)
† By Sir Arthur Grimble. (John Murray, 18s.)

organiser, secretary, or maid-of-all-work in the distribution and sale of Remembrance Day poppies.

Raising money calls for hard work in arranging dances; badminton, football and basketball matches; fashion or beauty parades; film shows; sale of flags; collection of donations either in cash or in kind; a fun fair or 20 or 30 stalls manned entirely by volunteers. Then, when the event is over, and the accounts have been prepared, Mrs. O. S. will be concerned in 'follow-up' action—the expression of appreciation to all those who have given large or small voluntary effort (with an eye to a generous response next time, of course).

There are also the hospitals. The record of the Malayan Medical Service over the past ten years has been impressive but, as elsewhere, provision of new buildings and recruitment of staff have not kept pace with demand. Mrs. O. S. can, with the blessing of the hospital staff, bring comfort and interest to patients by collecting flowers and shrubs from many private gardens for the hospital grounds, by occupational therapy such as knitting, making domestic knick-knacks, painting and drawing, tapestry work, and many other interesting and useful pastimes for all ages.

There are other calls on Mrs. O. S's time. A baby show, for instance; a family planning association—a delicate subject, but one which is receiving increasing attention in Asia; school, sporting, and youth occasions at which she is frequently offered the courtesy of giving away the prizes, and of course her own social occasions; Mrs. O. S. must often be hostess for cocktails or dinners to transient VIPs, and friends and colleagues of her husband's. The remarkable thing is that, as a rule, she enjoys the stimulation of these human contacts in spite of the cost in energy and money.

Even now, her voluntary work may not be finished. Her husband keeps his official shorthand/typing resources fully employed, yet still has enough left over for Mrs. O. S's shorthand book, stenotyping machine, or portable typewriter, in the evenings. Bedtime arrives either when physical fatigue brings to an end her attempt to work, or when she falls asleep doing it. A labour of love indeed, with no working to rule!

So Mrs. O. S. in Malaya is far from being a languorous, sherry and gin drinking, mahjong and bridge-playing drone. She sees a great deal of life, both good and bad, and leaves what she meets the better for the encounter. It need hardly be said that she has a profound influence on her husband's performance and on his career, and that as long as the Oversea Service endures, with its need of the personal qualities of tolerance, humanity and sympathy, she will continue to be a power of good behind the scenes, as she always has been.

I Married an Auditor

by WINIFRED BARTON

IN the words of a learned judge—so I'm told—"An auditor is a watchdog ; not a bloodhound." In the Colonial Service the watchdog wears a green collar and the pages of tiresome looking account books in Government offices are bespattered with the green imprints of his persistent pawing. Those aspiring to be auditors are probably best advised to remain unmarried, for these strange creatures appear to develop a singleness of mind which, at times, fiercely excludes family ties. And yet, contrary to some opinion, as a species they appear to be generally human in their attitudes and values. Like most males, I suppose, with the right kind of treatment they can be persuaded to put away their toys.

One would imagine that a bride entering upon an enterprise as lifemate of an auditor might reasonably anticipate a life freed from all forms of housekeeping accounts. Imagine my chagrin when I found that my husband handed this troublesome job to me in its entirety ! My worries began early as I soon discovered that our Bank Manager does not share my husband's confidence in my accounting, and when I am unable to convince him that his accounting shows a jaundiced picture of our money matters the Auditor must be called in. Then, alas, his examination is most searching. The arrangement I adopt for my accounts makes his hair stand on end. Grimly whittling away at a green pencil he asks for "vouchers"—whatever they may be—and starts adding and ticking away at a furious pace. Yet why he should quietly put a tick against such items as "Evening Dress £8" or "Dinner Party £3," but ask for a long explanation as to why one side adds up to 14/9d. more than the other I can never quite understand. An even more heinous crime, apparently, is forgetting to fill in the stubs of my cheque book. This is always followed by a "Reconciliation statement" before accounts (and marital relations) are put on a "sound basis." And, although after a few weeks the whole process has to be repeated—with slight variations—he still insists that I should keep the accounts.

Auditors, it seems, must subscribe to all sorts of dull periodicals full of statistics, accounts, graphs and long columns of figures. Our infrequent mails in Seychelles bring large bundles of the *Economist*, the *Accountant*, financial pamphlets of all kinds and Auditors' Reports from many other Colonies, ranging from remote and historic St. Helena to metropolitan Hong Kong. These unromantic papers become untidily distributed throughout every room in the house ; even the bathroom is not exempt. From time to time, when a spring-cleaning urge takes possession of me, some of the copies become caught up—not always inadvertently—in the general process, and are effectually disposed of. Some time later the Auditor will invariably demand a copy of an *Accountant* that has gone to this unhappy end. The explanation offered is never accepted as satisfactory, but the fact seldom appears to have any serious consequence.

There is apparently an unwritten understanding among the "financial fathers" of all Colonies that the Auditor should, in no circumstances, be allowed a personal secretary, so that wherever we go I am obliged to accept appointment as his temporary-acting-unpaid-overworked-private secretary, or, as I put it, "stooging for a stooge." This job could be largely a labour of love were it not for the jade-green monster Annual Report that rears its hideous head with relentless certainty every year. It might still be bearable did the brute confine its devastating influence to the office. But, alas, during the seemingly interminable weeks that the preparation of each Annual Report demands, the influence of the beast is only too apparent at home. Social engagements of all kinds must be brought to a standstill ; the household must tread softly, the children must be put early to bed and, amidst a pile of files, statements, returns, and quite incomprehensible papers, the Auditor scratches grimly away at one draft after another. Each morning—for the Auditor cannot compose a report to the accompaniment of a typewriter—a little pile of paper denotes the previous evening's illegible scribbling and awaits my transcription. But one day he will announce himself satisfied and it remains only to tie up the Report with green ribbon and implant the auditorial seal. On the evening of this day it is always safe to throw a party.

The official blurb has it that an Auditor may expect to be stationed in four or five different Colonies—assuming he survives a normal career. For those, like myself, who find a lasting happiness in going to new places, this adds seasoning to the pie that Auditors' wives may expect to eat. There is a pleasurable excitement in poring over a map and wondering to which tiny red patch we will go next ; in guessing when the move will come ; in deciding where one would like it to be ; in knowing that there is another new place in store. Not that one is restless to move. Now, almost at the end of our present tour, I still look back with happiness to the days in our previous Colony—and it will not be different when we transfer again. And even when the Auditor is safely installed in the Colony of his appointment, the wife with a wanderlust need not fret. In the larger Colonies there are inevitable transfers between stations adorned with Branch Audit offices, and in all Colonies, tours of inspection that vary from West Indian island cruises to foot-slogging in Darkest Africa. And let not my brown-kneed sisters in the rough-riding Administrative Service sniff ! The wife of an Auditor who recently toured the Falklands Islands Dependencies proudly affirms that she was present when her husband put a green tick on the South Pole.

So I dare to remember the pleasurable day when I first accompanied the Auditor on a day in the country away from the clangours and humidity that enervated his Hong Kong Office. Across the feverish roadstead, where all the commerce of the East seems to ply in innumerable craft, varying from sampan to ocean liner, we came to Kowloon and at last found quiet in the New Territories, with its variegated paddy fields where women and children were up to their knees in mud tending the rice shoots. There, while the Auditor counted the stamps in wayside Post Offices and pried into complacent Police stations, I could idle in the green shade of a weeping willow tree or on the deserted beaches. We made a picnic lunch while curious Chinese in broad coolie hats and pigtails turned to stare. Here in the Seychelles we cross from Mahé to sleepy Praslin on a luxury motor yacht that Government allows us to call our own for a few days. The Auditor's mood is abstracted as he buries himself in a variety of odd-shaped buildings which find it a fearful struggle to muster dignity as Government offices. But I have brought our children, and they have brought their little friends, and in excited company we visit General Gordon's "Garden of Eden" in the famous Coco-de-Mer valley, where giant trees tower to heights of a hundred feet and the rare black parrot makes this seeming primeval forest his home. Next day we set course south for La Digue where the Rest House proves too small to accommodate my brood of children, and we are provided with an excuse to make our beds on the beach and sleep under a bright canopy of stars. But the romance of a tropic night is a brittle thing and ours is tempered by the necessity for building little fires under the *takamaka* trees to smoke away the merciless myriads of sandflies and mosquitoes. North again to Curieuse where we visit the patients in the Leper Settlement and, in the revelation, find grace from their cheerfulness and busyness in affliction. Here the sea is crystal clear and alive with exotic fish— rainbow coloured, dappled, striped and iridescent. Huge turtles swim to the surface only to think better of it and plunge again into the depths. Next day the inspection is complete and the Auditor can relax as we race before a spanking breeze over tropic blue waters to return to Mahé. The line which the crew has patiently trolled over the stern for four days suddenly comes alive and amidst childish shouts a gleaming "Job" is hauled on board, only to be followed almost

Wife on Safari

by SUSAN HUDDLE

PERHAPS I have not chosen the most auspicious moment to begin this article, for one of the main social events of the present safari is now taking place, and I sit in the resthouse surrounded by the wives, elder daughters and babies of the local chief. The babies are alternately crying and sucking, while the women are keeping up a noisy high-pitched commentary on my appearance, safari equipment, the way I write, the fact that I can write and, most extraordinary of all, the peculiarity of my sitting in a chair with a table before me as though, they declare, I were about to drink tea with an important guest. When their state visit is almost over I shall speak to them in their own language, and thereby produce amazed giggling and delight, but at the moment I find it most amusing just to listen in.

I don't think that a Government official's safari differs much throughout East Africa, but this is what it is like in Lango, in the Northern Province of Uganda, and in our own particular case. John is in the Administration, and we are likely to be out for anything between ten and 20 days at a stretch, moving camp every second or third day.

First, we pack. There seems to be an unwritten rule of Fate which requires that nobody shall ever go on safari without forgetting at least one essential piece of equipment. In fact, a common question among the safari wives on our station is: "And what did *you* forget this time?" It might be the shaving mirror, the pricking needle for the primus, the filter, bath towels, the insect spray, spare mantles for the pressure lamp—the absence of any one of these things can, it is obvious, be very awkward. But by far the worst sin I can commit is to come without full radio equipment. "Good heavens, girl, d'you realize that some international crisis might blow up during the next five days, and we shall be none the wiser?" What John subconsciously feels, in common with many other men, I am sure, is that so long as he is kept in touch, no crisis will arise, but once loosen his grip on the threads of international affairs for a moment and something is bound to go wrong.

I have an aunt who lives in a beautiful flat in London. Everything in it is spotless, the kitchen gleams with chrome and tiles, mint and parsley grow in pots on the sill, all the food comes hygienically wrapped from Harrods—in fact the whole place would be a hygiene-maniac's dream. My aunt, far from being a maniac, is an extremely nice and sensible person, but time after time on safari I find myself speculating: "What would Aunt D. think of this?" I find it amusing to imagine her with us, bearing shock after shock with horrified but resigned acceptance.

When everything is packed into the car and its little box trailer, we set off for the first resthouse. It is made of rough wooden poles and thatch, and the low walls and floors are plastered with a mixture of mud and cattle dung. (Aunt D. sustains her first major shock!) On all sides there are numerous open doorways and windows, and it is no easy matter to select a relatively private site for the camp bath. The 'little house' is some distance away, a minute hole in the ground, often surrounded by a sort of Hampton Court maze of rush screening. The view is not spectacular, the usual horizon being tall grass and shrubs a few hundred yards away.

As soon as the stuff is unloaded, John goes off to read court books, hold meetings and inspect prisons, while I settle down to getting the camp in order.

In this I am probably more hindered than helped by our 'boy', and I have a busy time re-erecting the tables and chairs he has set up, rescuing the dog's meat from its tempting position on the floor, and removing sooty pots and pans from the bedding roll. When order is restored the 'boy' retires to his smoky black den behind the resthouse, there to cook the milk which has been delivered by the locals in unsavoury looking teapots, dirty beer bottles or calabashes, with about a teaspoonful of mud in the bottom of every pint. (Poor Aunt D.!)

Safari food in our particularly hot district is rather difficult. After the first day or two of trying frantically to eat all the fresh food we've brought before it goes bad, we resign ourselves thereafter to alternate meals of tinned food and stew or curry made with local chickens. Surprisingly enough, these tough athletic fowls can be coaxed into quite a reasonable state of tenderness if pressure-cooked for a few hours.

Safari seems to have had a surprisingly good effect on many of the women on our station. The most unenterprising of them may suddenly be inspired to experiment with different arrangements of tins, stoves, red-hot embers and so forth to evolve an efficient baking oven. Some take up hobbies for which they would never otherwise have found the time or impetus to begin. I myself have been induced to take up painting, puppet-making and photography, and still have time to catch up on months of neglected reading and letter-writing.

At any time of the day I must be prepared to receive the local ladies. They are invariably cheerful, friendly women who come right in and sit down, sidesaddle, upon the floor. Sometimes they make a close inspection of our possessions, and demand to be shown the uses of various articles, so that the visit may develop into an impromptu cooking or sewing lesson, absorbed with much interest, but seldom, I suspect, with any intention on their part of applying my astounding revelations to their own homes. Sometimes they treat me as an enormous joke, asking me why I can't talk Lango well enough for their liking, or why I don't join them in the morning expedition to get their husbands' bathwater from the borehole.

I have other visitors, of a much less welcome kind. I am one of those unfortunates who seem to attract every insect for miles around. Everything that bites, stings or merely buzzes, finds its way unerringly to me. I shouldn't be surprised if my magnetism isn't enough to divert the path of whole safaris of ants. As for spiders, I've never yet set eyes on one that wasn't crawling menacingly in my direction, a poisonous gleam of anticipation in its eyes. Bats also are a nuisance, bickering at one another in the rafters overhead .I once produced a catapult to deal with the little horrors, but gave up when the floor was strewn with the stones of my ammunition, and the bats were still there, hardly having bothered to move their positions.

Quite often I go with John on his various expeditions in the afternoon or evening. We may attend a village council meeting, and this often means a bicycle ride for several miles along narrow twisting paths. The whole party from the county chief downwards is supplied with borrowed bicycles. I used to wear slacks on these occasions, but this produced so much loud and controversial speculation as to whether I was a man or a woman that I gave them up. Lango is marvellously flat, so almost the only time one has to get off and walk is when there is a swamp to be negotiated. Wading is then the order of the day, and sometimes a few naked bathers are enlisted to give a hand with carrying over the bikes. A couple of these once kindly offered to carry me as well, but I managed, politely I hope, to decline the offer.

On every safari there is the chance to do something slightly different. We may be near the Nile, where a Tsetse Control Officer has his camp, and go for a trip in his little outboard motor boat, chugging along between floating islands of papyrus in search of hippo, and feeling like the stars of *The African Queen*. One morning we were called out to see an elephant one of the chiefs had shot when it wandered into a populated area. Much to my dismay John climbed onto the carcass to make a speech to the crowd, all of whom were brandishing knives and impatiently eyeing their choices of steaks. Luckily they held off until he was finished, but it was a near thing.

Sometimes we are asked to a meal at a nearby Roman Catholic mission. Excellent fare is provided, but we have learnt to be wary of drinking their water, for they are often such tough old-timers that they are not over-fussy about boiling and filtering it. Members of the small Asian communities scattered around the district are equally hospitable, but woe betide me if we have to partake of their curries. I cough and choke and tears pour from my eyes, while my kindly hosts set up a refrain: "Not hot, Memsahib, not hot, not hot!"

But the nicest visits we pay are those made on an evening stroll to the homestead of some nearby farmer. The inhabitants appear not at all surprised at our sudden appearance in their midst, despite the fact that some of them may seldom have seen a European before. The women sitting in the shade of their huts beam and send up a chorus of greetings, the young girls pounding grain between stones stop work and look bashful, and old Grandma, a delighted grin on her wrinkled face, grasps my arm with her skinny claw, gabbling her welcome. The head of the family appears and introduces his sons and brothers, and proudly points out his own wives and children. Then, if we wish it, we are taken to see his crops and permitted to peep into his little thatched grainstores. John enters into a discussion on the state of the crops, the health of local cattle, and all the various topics which lie closest to the hearts of these people. Someone points proudly to a small hut set behind the others. "There is our 'bye-law'!" The recent enforcement of a health bye-law has resulted in this, the first latrine thay have ever possessed, and thus it will be for ever known as a 'bye-law'.

We are soon invited to partake of a pot of 'pombe' (the local beer, made from grain). A grimy-looking earthenware jar is produced, holding a scummy liquid with what looks like coffee-grounds floating in it. Thin hollow sticks with metal filters at the tip are offered. John has a sip and declares the taste to be "interesting". I however, suddenly remembering Aunt D., decline the honour and we take our leave, escorted right down the path by Grandma. One last look back and the family is settling down comfortably round the jar, sucking gently at their reed-like filters, and laughing at the joke of the Assistant District Commissioner's wife having declined their wonderful brew.

Barriers and Bridges

by ROSEMARY SMITH

THE YEAR is 1957. The scene is the District Commissioner's sitting room, where a multi-racial sundowner is being held. In parts of the room small groups of men, Africans, Indians and Europeans, are talking happily together. No thought of racial differences occurs to them, for they are used to meeting one another every day at work.

But the rest of the room presents a different picture. Conversation is animated enough, but there is no attempt among the women to mix with different races. In one corner there is a huddle of four or five Indian women, beautifully dressed, gossiping in their own language. The African women, too, are shy, and flock together in another part of the room. The European women, sitting apart and looking rather superior, are discussing their own affairs.

The D.C. catches his wife's eye. She sighs, says something to her friends which makes them laugh, and advances on the nearest group of African women with a look of determined resignation. Her victims brace themselves at her approach; they can almost see her thinking. "What on earth can I talk about to these people?"

Today this is no longer an entirely true picture of a "mixed" sundowner. Tanganyika's independence has placed the different races on an equal footing, and the African women whose husbands have been given positions of responsibility are eager to learn more about the European way of life. I must add, however, that I am expressing only my own opinions, formed in my four and a half years as a District Officer's wife in Tanganyika. The relationship between women of different races is a wide subject, and the views of someone like a Social Development Officer are probably quite different to mine.

On the whole I have found Indian women more difficult to talk to than many Africans. The younger and probably better-educated ones take more interest than their elders in the usual feminine gossip about clothes, children and food, and some of them are interested in European ways. I remember meeting the young and most attractive wife of a Prisons Officer who gave an amusing account of her struggles to cook the European food her husband preferred. There are, too, many highly educated Indian women—doctors, welfare workers, teachers—with whom I feel as much at ease as with a European woman of my own background and with whom there are as few reservations. But I have found that, with most of the Indian women I have met, conversation ceases abruptly once it leaves the safe confines of domestic affairs. Outside those we have as little in common as a suburban housewife and a farmer's wife from the muddy depths of the country.

Then there is the additional difficulty of language. Many Indian women speak no English and little Swahili, and the resources of sign-language are soon exhausted.

The African women one meets at sundowners are generally the wives of Government officers, from clerks to D.Cs. Language is still the main problem, for although most of these better-educated Africans have at least a smattering of English and understand it quite well, they are shy of speaking it. Few

European women take the trouble to learn more Swahili than they need to instruct any domestic staff they may have; consequently their range of conversation with an African woman who knows little or no English is strictly limited. I think this is a real cause of resentment, especially with more intelligent African women. Lack of a common language widens the breach already caused by the differences in African and European ways of life, income and skin colour.

Europeans who do speak reasonably good Swahili are at a great advantage in getting to know Africans, for the more intelligent Africans appreciate the effort made to learn it. An African friend of mine once told me she thought it unfair that I should expect her to speak good English while I, after four years in Tanganyika, spoke only moderate Swahili; after all, Swahili is a far easier language. Europeans sometimes complain that well-educated African men so often have wives who can't speak English. They don't seem to blame themselves for not learning better Swahili.

However, it seems that even an excellent knowledge of the language does not ensure understanding between European and African. The same African friend told me that she finds many European women quite unsympathetic. However good their Swahili may be, she feels that they are always looking down on the Africans with whom they come into contact and laughing at them for their lack of *savoir-faire*; while others, who may know only a little Swahili, have a genuine sympathy with Africans and are eager to learn how they think and how they live.

Many African women are undoubtedly too self-conscious and afraid of criticism when with Europeans. This is partly why so many take little or no part in general conversation, even with people they know well. The problem is how to make them feel that others are ready to listen to what they say without sneering or laughing at them; this is aggravated by the fact that even now African husbands still believe the woman's place is in the kitchen with the children and do not allow their wives to hold or express opinions on subjects like politics. Until this attitude changes, most African women are going to be at a loss when conversation turns to more serious topics. Quite understandably, they are afraid of appearing stupid and ill-informed.

This problem is made even more difficult by their upbringing. Another African friend told me that if a European came into the school where she was a pupil, she and her companions were so full of awe that they would have been tongue-tied if asked to talk to the visitor. This attitude, I am sure, is changing fast, and the schoolchildren of today are no more in awe of a European than of one another. But the slightly older women find it difficult to shake off their childhood conditioning, and it is almost always the European woman who has to take the initiative in conversation.

At a sundowner it takes quite a brave woman to break into a group composed entirely of another race, but it must be done, and done with tact and sympathy; otherwise the barriers will remain up indefinitely and the Africans will continue to think of the European women as aloof and superior.

What happens if you detach yourself from your European companions and approach a group of African women? You are greeted politely, probably with some giggling, and it is left to you to find a topic of conversation once the ritual greetings are over. Usually you choose children, clothes or cooking, according to what you already know of your new companions. Sometimes the conversation becomes quite interesting; but only too often it degenerates into questions from you, met with monosyllabic answers. Large parties present conditions which are far from ideal for getting to know one another. Small informal gatherings—perhaps a morning coffee party, but preferably a group which has met to do something together like cooking or sewing—are far more rewarding. In the more intimate and relaxed atmosphere you can forget most of the barriers which divide the women of different races at a larger party, and begin to learn about and appreciate other points of view.

These days even a normally shy African woman will sometimes take the initiative. I should never have become friendly with the two Africans I know best if they had not first come to me for advice and help with cooking,* etiquette and clothes. The only trouble is that they expect me to be an infallible guide. "*You* know about these things," they say. "You must tell us what is the right thing to do." And so often I have to disappoint them.

But even when one has made friends, there are still bound to be reservations, caused mainly by the differences in background. They will never talk as freely as European women will about their personal affairs; for instance, how they met their husbands. They have far more dignity in many ways than we have. In some respects I think they almost despise the freedom of speech and action which a European woman enjoys, while at the same time envying it

So far I have written only of the better-educated African women I have met, mainly because I have met few others socially. The barriers are made higher by the fact that many uneducated Africans are afraid of speaking to a European woman and relapse into embarrassed giggles as one approaches. One usually meets them at sewing circles or child welfare classes run by such organisations as the Women's Service League. I have had no experience of these, but a friend of mine who started a sewing class said she felt the women resented her presence. The afternoon was a social outing for them and the instruction an unwelcome interruption to their gossip with their friends. Of course, many African women are pleased to be taught how to make clothes for the children and how to improve their health, but I think that many of them regard us Europeans as interfering busybodies—in some cases probably quite rightly. It is difficult to avoid the air of the lady of the manor: patronising and proudly conscious that one is doing "good works". The benefits are better appreciated these days if the teaching and advice come from a fellow African.

In my somewhat limited experience, then, the chief barriers to an easy relationship between the women of different races seem to be, first, the lack of a true common language; though where sympathy is lacking, even good Swahili is not a passport to friendship with an African woman. Secondly, the shyness and lack of self-confidence of many Africans and Indians, aggravated by the perhaps unconsciously patronising attitude of some European women, prevent them from taking a full part in social life. This

* *Rosemary Smith wrote about this in* Cookery for Independence, *Corona, March,* 1962 . . . *Ed.*

is sure to change in the future as they gain poise from experience.   There
certainly seems to be no animosity, apart from the occasional resentment of
African towards interfering European, and happy relationships can be
achieved, given genuine good will, patience and a sense of humour.

Sleeping Water

by "CORIN"

I gaze into the sky-reflecting lake
And watch the picture cloud-battalions make,
As floating in the mottled depths and cool
They pass serene across the sleeping pool.
The hills' inverted pinnacles extend
In brown fantastic shadows that descend
Towards the deepest depth of sombre sky
Where birds and little fishes seem to fly,
Or do they swim ? For this quaint looking-glass
Bordered by daffodils and daisied grass
Creates a fairyland of chastened hues
Exquisite in the mingling of its views,
Bewildering to the unaccustomed eye
As honey-bee and blue-winged dragonfly
That skim the lake and drone among the flowers
In endless lullaby for sultry hours.
And yet this mirrored and unruffled world
Can be destroyed if but a stone be hurled
Into the liquid depths of fragile calm
That hold its picture in aquatic charm.

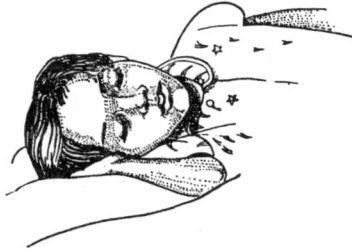

Unwanted Priscillas ?

by MARGARET DERRICK

I AM myself a Priscilla* and, therefore, presumably biased in the question of whether or not wives are an asset to colonial servants or to the colony in which they serve. Indeed, until a short time ago, I was not merely biased about the question ; I simply never considered the answer to be in doubt. Which only goes to show, I'm afraid, how ignorant I was. Recently I have thought more about the whole matter, and realise that the arguments are strong on both sides ; the anti-wife contingent has doughty forces—indeed it has almost persuaded a wife to its side. But not quite.

Before the 1939 war, cadets in the Colonial Administrative Service had to be unmarried or at least unaccompanied for their first tour. This was for a period of as much as four or five years in some colonies, and in others, where tours were shorter, strong discouragement was offered to early marriage, or even to marriage at all. Wives' passages were not paid, accommodation was not guaranteed, few medical and certainly no maternity facilities were offered. We were warned off. The war broke into these regulations, which have not, so far, been entirely re-established. Nevertheless, they were not wholly the work of prejudice and many of the arguments against wives before the war are valid today. What are these arguments ?

"Strong discouragement to marriage"   M.D.

The two main propositions put forward are that the physical conditions of the colonies are not suitable for women, and that a wife prevents a man giving his whole time to his work. Let me elaborate. Twenty years ago, and still today in many parts of the Colonial Empire conditions of living and of travel are difficult ; climates are trying, tropical diseases are numerous, and all the medical and nutritional benefits of more civilized countries are scarce and difficult to come by. It is enough for the Government to be responsible for the health, housing and transport of an officer without the addition of a wife and perhaps children.

The second argument is valid too. The bachelor or grass-widower will happily spend an evening with the indigenous people—at their club, in a game of football, in his house or in their houses. His free time will often be at their disposal. Again, he can be sent on tour or to enquire into some trouble at short notice without having to consider the well-being of a wife and family. He can concentrate his mind and energy on his job, and get to know the country, the people, the language, without the back-lag and counter-attraction of his own personal life.

Contingent on these two main arguments are several others, the anxiety caused to a man over his wife and family, when he leaves them for some time, if they are ill, or unhappy, or if he himself is in danger ; then there is the liability of the Government to help in cases of illness and to provide security and accommodation. In some colonies these difficulties are less, in others still considerable. In some countries, particularly in Muslim areas, wives are not even acceptable to the local people, and modesty of dress and behaviour is absolutely essential.

These arguments, surely, are just, and to them are added a few more which, we hope, are unjust ; that wives are possessive and clinging, doubly hampering

*The name is taken, with permission, from "Dearest Priscilla : Letters to the wife of a Colonial Civil Servant" by Emily G. Bradley (Mrs. Kenneth Bradley), published by Max Parrish, 12s. 6d.

their poor husbands ; or that they quarrel among themselves, and their husbands have to be posted elsewhere before the district can function in peace ; or that they are flirtatious, causing heart-burning amongst the other officers, married and unmarried, and generally disrupting the peace of the station.　Oh, Priscilla, I hope this is not true ; but even if untrue, the charges against us are many, and we are put much on our metal to justify ourselves.

Nevertheless, I am sanguine of a final judgment in our favour.　Without doubt a Governor is better equipped for his duties if he has a wife.　At what stage, then, does he acquire her ?　From the moment a man gets a headquarters job, be it as a senior District Commissioner, a Provincial Commissioner, or in a Secretariat, his work involves him in a great deal of entertaining.　The higher he rises, the more he requires the social graces of a wife.　Even the dullest, most uninspiring wife can take the other end of the table at dinner, lead out the ladies, or be present in flowered hat and gloves at the many official ceremonies.　At minimum she is an asset; at maximum she can do untold good to her husband's cause and relieve him of a great burden of social responsibility.

"*A Governor is better equipped*"

That is for the headquarters wife.　What about the more modest violets in the wilds ?　Here, quite frankly, I think our main function is to keep our husbands sane.　Do we not all know that glint in the eye, that roving look bespeaking lack of concentration, those odd habits, perhaps those unbreakable silences of the bachelor who has lived alone in an out-station for some time ? Even the elderly bachelor whose life has coursed out a settled way exhibits strange traits—excessive personal vanity, unbreakable routines, self-centredness, or the restless energy demanding continual activity with no breaks into which could rush that engulfing sea of loneliness.　I do not exaggerate ; rarely is a bachelor a balanced happy man.

Moreover, the coloured races consider bachelordom to be unnatural, and this cannot fail to add to the distance between white and black, let alone to give rise to scurrilous gossip and rumours.

A wife, be she never so ordinary, will make a home in which the habits and way of life natural to an Englishman will be found, and in which conversation need not be entirely "shop" (I only say "need not" ; I make no promises !).

She can also take an active part in her husband's work.　This sounds like a recruiting slogan, but is nevertheless true.　Everywhere the indigenous woman lags behind her menfolk, and the white woman can help in varying ways, from simple entertaining to visiting, medical assistance, teaching of crafts and encouragement of better standards of cleanliness and feeding.　Much can be learned in this way that would pass unseen by the officer, especially in such Mohammedan countries as still enforce the keeping of purdah upon their women.　In her own way, also, the European wife is the unconscious representative of all she is trying to teach—a responsibility that can be turned to good advantage.

What an angelic band of admirable, perfect characters we have got to be, it seems, to justify ourselves !　We must have the arts of housekeeping at our finger-tips, the graces of a hostess in our blood, the devotion of a social worker in our hearts.　Do not be too alarmed, Priscilla ; I doubt if those admirable Colonial Service officers, our husbands, themselves attain to such perfection.　If they weigh our merits, perhaps they may overlook our offences.　And surely, our final justification lies in the fact that, with one exception that I know of, all the consistent critics of wives in the Colonies are themselves bachelors ? Perhaps it is only that our husbands are very faithful, and now conceal their real views. But one fact seems clear, however the issue is judged, that, like atomic energy or the man who came to dinner, Priscillas, wanted or unwanted, are here to stay.

Nocturne

by RUTH BULMAN

The gothic domes of bamboo spread
Their soaring splendour overhead.
The warm winds of the darkness shake
Their starry petals o'er the lake.

A purple frieze against the sky,
Nyanza's hunch-backed islands lie.
Her many-jewelled fingers spread,
Poking and prying by the dead
Sea-flowers of some ageless cave.
And there the quiet waters lave
Pale bones, gigantic shapes that keep
Eternal attitudes of sleep.
Nyanza draws a breath once more,
Sends her soft laughter to the shore.
Her rocking wavelets toss and break
To where insolent palm-trees shake
Their cool leaves at the tranquil moon,
For well know they that very soon
This flimsy rapture will be crushed,
The withering stars, night's blue stole pushed
Softly down the precipice of dawn
And all that trembling magic gone.
Or sooner still, some lusty storm
With loins unleashed might hotly come,
Raping and raddled with desires—
All's over, gone those fairy fires
That put the quivering stars to light
And made the lake one flame of white.

Now with reverent whispers filled
(At daybreak when the moon is spilled
Into the milling broth of day)
How dreamingly the voices say
From green and honey-coloured choir,
Soft Aves to the morning air.

Wives in Perspective

(From an article in The Cambridge Review *by Kenneth Shadbolt, a District Officer in Tanganyika.)*

". . . Things, and what people think about them, alter quickly in Africa today—each annual intake of Cadets, for example, holds opinions, usually progressively liberal ones, always a degree different from those of the intake of the previous year. What has altered more quickly than most attitudes is that towards the married District Officer. The archetypal boy scout-subaltern type, for whom the job's greatest appeal lay in its being largely conducted out of doors, has given way, if grudgingly, to a perhaps softer yet perhaps more civilized officer. A wife who was supposed to hinder a young officer's movements on transfer or safari and to prevent him making proper or improper contact with the people in his district has on the contrary shown herself able to make just that sort of contribution needed in present-day conditions to make him a better officer, off duty and on, than he was before. He is more likely to retain his sense of proportion and balance if he works with a background of home and family close behind him, and repetition does not dull the truth of the saying that a happy officer is an efficient one.

The presence of a wife and family reflects, too, an aspect of the work which has come more to the fore in recent years. An officer-to-other-ranks relationship, superficial, coldly just, dignified, satisfying in its formality, sufficed for as long as the other ranks were content to remain other ranks. But the new wind informing African life today is altering all that; the canon law of Lugard is being challenged by the secular and popular renaissance of its own making. Government can no longer find it enough to deal with some of the people some of the time but has to countenance a whole society on the move. An integrated clamour must have an integrated response. Government Officers in the field are not yet organization men but certainly they are nowadays working more as a team than as individuals; so, too, the individual officer must have the fully rounded, integrated sympathy of outlook which bachelorhood often finds difficult to produce. The sort of wife, enjoying a range of positive, creative social contacts at all levels, who can evoke the local greeting "Mama" in place of the older term "Memsahib" with its undertones of British Raj has won half her husband's battles already. I confess unashamedly to using my wife's friends in the village as an entrée in the society we are living amongst.

There is thus seldom any division between home, office and neighbourhood, and I feel glad I have never experienced the division of interests which commuting makes so inevitable in England. I think this greater unity is thoroughly wholesome and psychologically a good thing; and for us it is the only way by which transfers between stations can be made as little disruptive as they are. There is a drill and a routine which cushions you against any amount of outside change in the work, the tribe, the countryside or the climate. Soon one hopes one's magic will begin to work in the new context, the feelers will be out, contacts made and we shall be working, thinking, talking shop again, wedded to yet another African community until the time for leave or transfer comes round again . . . "

Educating Our Children

by HELEN GRIFFITHS

IN the November number of *Corona* there was an interesting article stating the case against the education of English children in East Africa, and the author argued that it would be better for the children themselves and for the future of East Africa if these children could have their schooling in England. The problem is no new one. It was after the Norman invasion that Norman lords were anxiously sending their children to be brought up in Normandy, lest their accents should suffer in barbarous Britain. But the topic is certainly a thorny one, and one that today is constantly discussed by parents in East Africa. I should like, however, to show the other side of the picture, and show that children need not in fact suffer by spending their schooldays in East Africa.

It was stated that a child brought up in East Africa lacked the opportunity for helping others and that, by being waited on by servants, he missed the training that his English cousin gets in helping in the home. But surely the important aspect for the child is the fostering of a general willingness and desire to be helpful ? It does not matter that there is no need in an East African home for dishes to be washed. It is equally good training when small boys voluntarily make their beds to help the servant, or cook the Sunday supper for the pleasure of learning to crack eggs. And these things do happen in many homes. On the other hand, I have noticed how mothers in England try to save their children as far as possible from irksome chores, remembering their own carefree childhood. Boy Scouts and Girl Guides in East Africa, like those elsewhere, are enthusiastic about learning to do things for themselves with never a thought as to whether the task is menial.

Another point mentioned was the fact that only a second-hand knowledge of English culture could be obtained. It cannot be denied that much is missed in this way, but it is the years immediately following school that are really important for adjusting the perspective—and it will need to be adjusted. And it is at this age that the fullest benefit is obtained from theatres and concerts and general background, when powers of appreciation and critical faculties are developing. The child going to school in East Africa and then going to England for two or three years of professional training will quickly absorb that culture which he has been hearing about at second-hand. In East African schools the teachers are all themselves from England, which is not the case in any of the Dominions ; so the pictures they give of English culture should be true ones. The child introduced in school years to good music and the romance of history will not take long to appreciate music at first hand or old historic castles when he sees them. Even the poetry he has learnt of the English spring will suddenly spring vividly to life when he later walks in English lanes in May time. This I know from my own experience.

But what of his East African background ? How fortunate the boy in this austere and urban era, with Africa for his playground, with all the wealth of its wild life to be explored—not looked at through bars in a zoo. What if the standard of competitive sport is not so high in this country, when all the joys and excitements of *safari* are his ? Here, if anywhere, self-reliance and manliness are at a premium and attained at an early age.

The problem of girls was mentioned and the precociousness which results from too early an introduction to adult society. This surely is dependent on the discretion of the parents. I, too, had heard many years ago the legend of East African teen-agers, and an alarming picture grew in my mind of ultra-sophisticated teen-agers ordering repeated gins at sundowner parties. I can only say that I myself have yet to meet the damsel.

Parents who discuss this problem of the education of children in a different country, with the long separations that that involves, generally agree on one matter—that the parents suffer more from these partings than do the children. For the children it is often only the exchange of one home for another with a kind aunt or guardian instead of a kind parent. For the parents it means much more—a childless home, and the forgoing of that liberal, if occasionally painful education which growing, lively children so fully give us. And for those of us for whom an English education is an almost impossible financial strain, is it not better both from the point of view of our family relationships and even of our social relations as members of the European community of this country, that we should let our children spend their schooldays in East Africa ? This must always be a matter of opinion ; I have simply tried to show some of the factors which influence those of us who decide that our children gain as much as they lose by going to school in East Africa.

In a Tropical Forest

by RAYMOND TONG

Deep in this forest's primeval innocence,
where Time is lost in green philosophy
that knows no change, the past, like the future, seems
to wear a mask of kindly reticence,
while the present hears no more of history
than it can learn from silence and from dreams.

Beneath the grandeur of these giant trees,
by this impenetrable wall of green,
humanity contracts to its true stature,
and we forget our world that's ill-at-ease,
our world of maybe or of might-have-been,
dwarfed by the immense frugality of Nature.

Don't Send Them Home

by ELIZABETH JUNE KNOWLES

CECILY EVANS, in writing about "The Problem of Our Children," describes her own comfortable English childhood. "There were four of us children, but every holidays there was an influx of cousins whose parents were in India. They fitted into the household as part of the family, we all sorted ourselves out, and no one was lonely or left in the cold or made to feel an interloper. These cousins saw their parents about every four or five years, and although we were slightly sorry for them, I doubt if they felt particularly sorry for themselves."

Surely the main obstacle in sending children home is to have them live through their most impressionable years with everyone slightly sorry for them, and perhaps only those of us born of colonial parents who have ourselves experienced the undiluted gloom of years of pity can appreciate the effect it has on a child. Thanks to the interruption of my schooling by the outbreak of war, I had only three years at school at home on my own; both my sisters had considerably longer periods, and inevitably we were in touch with many other colonial children. Most of us are determined never to inflict on our children what we ourselves went through.

Of course, there are today mercifully few young Kiplings—in his autobiography Kipling describes how his mother, back from India after six years, came up to say good-night to him. He was eleven years old, and automatically he put up his arms to ward off the blow he expected from those who came to bid him good-night. During the same six years he had almost lost his eyesight through neglect and misunderstanding on the parts of his guardian. But even today, suffering, physical or psychological, can be very real. The physical risk is I think less great but none the less important. In my own case a crank matron believed warm clothing in winter to be unnecessary, and put all mine away. The subsequent strain of cold and illness on a heart unaccustomed to cold and perhaps already tired from Kenya altitudes, had me on my back for six months and away from that school for ever. The specialist told my mother that another six months would have put me on my back for life. The merciless bullying endured by another member of the family destroyed all her confidence in herself, her family, and even in others. She was never again a member of the family in the same way the rest of us were, and is only now—in her own home—recovering some of her self-confidence. The worry and suffering caused to ourselves and our families has not been compensated by the English education. I do not regret the education, but I think that as a family we paid for it too dearly. The public school system depends on the survival of the fittest, but those of us who cannot be certain that our children are both physically and mentally amongst the fittest much assume a more personal responsibility for those children than schooling them thousands of miles away.

Apart from the schools, there are the holidays, and any colonial child will tell you these can be far worse than the worst school in term-time. However plentiful and kindly relatives may be, they can never give you the sense of security and of belonging that you obtain in your own home. You do not, unless you are very fortunate, come back to the same room every holidays, you cannot leave your treasures at home, you must leave your trunks at school, you cannot ask your friends to stay, you must always be on your best behaviour. And then comes the dreadful holidays when the family you usually go to cannot have you, usually owing to illness or other unforeseeable calamity. There follow the hurried cables to Africa, and back from Africa to other relations, the refusals and finally the slightly grudging offer of a temporary home. "Of course, we can have her, but I am afraid that she will have to amuse herself." More than ever, you are once again on your best behaviour for a long and dreary holiday.

And through all this, the child becomes acutely conscious of the English attitude to colonials, and of colonial inferiority. "This is my little niece, her parents are in Kenya," says the gossipy aunt over the dull tea-table, and looks are exchanged, the 'are you married or do you live in Kenya' looks which you learn later to laugh off, but which cut to the quick in the early teens. And always she overhears such gems as :
"What a pity she should be tone-deaf."
"Yes, but after all she is a colonial."
Whereas the "It's very good she should captain the tennis VI," is invariably greeted by : "Yes, certainly England is doing her all the good in the world." So the colonial child learns that all her failings are because she is a colonial, and her abilities—if any—are due to her English blood and the splendid opportunity she has to enjoy the English Way of Life. So strongly was this feeling inculcated into me that until I was twenty-five or so, I could not bear to admit to strangers in England that I had ever lived in a colony.

But although these memories have survived in my mind despite the grimness of an active war, and are still bitter to me fifteen years later, I cannot but agree with Cecily Evans' reasons for sending a child home. There is nothing that can ever replace the English traditions and background. The question is, which is most important to each individual child, the English background or the security of its own home ? It can only be decided separately for each child. Undoubtedly, some few children, especially those exceptionally gifted and independent, will do better with an all-English schooling ; whereas some few nervous and backward children will do better never separated from their own homes. But I think that the vast majority of those who have been sent to England in the past have been sent to England too young. I think that until the middle teens the home background and security and sense of belonging is far more important that anything else in the world ; and that a child should not leave home until it has been recognised in that home as a person and not merely a child. Too often parents bring children, especially girls, back to the colony at the age of eighteen after six or more years of expensive English education. The child is welcomed with the same treatment that it received at the age of eleven or twelve, finds it impossible to accept parental advice or companionship, finds it difficult even to live at home. How often do you hear these parents complain, after long separations, "We have lost our child."

If the child is not sent home until fifteen or sixteen, this loss of contact is much less likely to occur. Also, the child is now old enough to do for itself those things it would rather not depend on relatives for. At sixteen you are old enough to manage your own dress and travelling allowance (oh, those dreary shopping expeditions with un-understanding aunts !) ; to make your own holiday arrangements in case of emergency, and generally to look after yourself. You are not too old to absorb all that is best in the English way of life, or to develop academic, artistic, or sporting abilities ; neither are you so young as to suffer agonies from insecurity and unwantedness, real or imaginary. You are old enough to acknowledge colonial characteristics in yourselves and your parents, and to be proud of them. Most schools can and do absorb children from overseas after the school certificate stage into the lower sixth forms, and in this way the child gains most of the advantages of English schooling and risks fewer of the disadvantages of being away from home. There is the additional advantage, that if there are only two, rather than six, years of schooling to be met parents are more likely to be able to afford further training, university fees and suchlike. And personally, I got far more value from three years at a university than from six at English schools.

Given then that every child should spend some part of its educational years in England, and that some children do better to spend all their educational years there, I cannot see the advantage of the hostel system as recommended by Cecily

Evans. It is too reminiscent of the usual English welcome: "Now let me see, you come from Kenya—I know a delightful South African you simply must meet," and all the while you want to scream that Kenya is full of delightful South Africans, and in England you really want to meet the English people at home. Sending a child to live in a colonial hostel defeats the point of sending a child home. It does not give the child English home life, it does not give the child English school life, and institutional life is only tolerable when you can get away from it at definite intervals. The colonial child would have no such intervals. Since the end of the war it has been surprisingly easy to find foster-parents for every type of child in unfortunate circumstances. According to the popular press, the number of homes still outnumbers the number of children available. Surely some scheme of foster-parents to take charge while the parents are away would be far more satisfactory? It would cost the parents no more, the Colonial Office less, and the 'retired colonial servants' who would have been employed to run the hostels would be able to provide the close supervision and individual contact needed in any such scheme. The children would still be able to go to day or boarding school as their own parents chose, and in the holidays brothers and sisters would have the security of always re-uniting in the same household. The Colonial Office might use the money which would otherwise have been spent on the hostels in assisting parents with school fees—it might even follow the excellent Foreign Office practice which allows parents £100 a year for every child at boarding school in England.

Thus while agreeing with Cecily Evans that nothing can take the place of an English background, I think she over-estimates its importance in comparison with the importance, to a child, of its own happy home and family ties. I think she entirely under-estimates the suffering experienced by children who have been sent to England, who are only too aware of the sacrifice their parents have made for them and who would never admit to unhappiness. And even when parents have decided to risk this suffering for their child, and the possibility of broken family ties in later years, by sending the child to England, I think that to send it to a hostel for colonial children would defeat the purpose of sending it to England, and that English home life is the only thing that can ever compensate the child for the dreaded separation from its own home.

Have Them Out For The Holidays

by BLANCHE PETTY

SEND the children to England or keep them with us in the Tropics ? This problem is one that very few "Coaster" parents had the chance even of contemplating during my years in West Africa. There was no choice. Nevertheless, it was with much interest and sympathy that I read the views of Cecily Evans, Elizabeth Jane Knowles and Helen Griffiths, who have had first-hand experience of this difficulty in East Africa.

A variation of the problem of splitting up the family circle does, of course, obtain in the West African colonies. My experience of colonial life has been confined to the Gold Coast. Naturally, there has been a very considerable change in conditions and viewpoints since my early days there. Eighteen years ago, when my daughter was a baby, it was regarded as out of the question—quite wicked, in fact—to think of taking one's child to West Africa. The authorities actively discouraged such a course and the idea of one's baby being born on the Coast was looked upon as criminal folly. Certainly no provision was made for such a contingency.

There were, of course, the valiant few (there always will be, thank goodness) who accepted the risks and ran the gauntlet of public disapproval. But the children of these pioneers were sadly pitied and, as for the parents, woe betide them if anything went wrong ! At once the blame was laid on their cruel selfishness and their inhumanity in exposing a child to the perils of the "terrible climate." The fact that even in their own countries white children fell sick and sometimes died was completely ignored.

Having a baby was a very costly business indeed. One was advised—nay, urged—to get away from the Colony long before the baby was due and this often involved long separation from one's husband and the consequent expense of running two homes. Doctor's fees and nursing home charges were high and when, eventually, we returned to the Coast we had usually, of necessity, made some very expensive arrangement for the care of the infant left behind. If, alternatively, one stayed on in England, poor father had a very thin time. Not only was he cut off from his wife and family but the severe strain on his financial resources caused hardship and in many cases he was forced to drop out of the social life of his friends.

However, we have made good progress and nowadays there is a much pleasanter picture. In the Gold Coast, particularly in the bigger seaside towns, there are many healthy European babies and young children living a life of absolute bliss. So many things that contribute to a happy childhood are at hand : warmth, sunny sandy beaches, skilled medical care and a home running smoothly and at so leisurely a pace that even mother has time to enjoy life. But with the passing of kindergarten days this halcyon existence comes to an end and one must face up to *the* problem—education. What is to be done ?

Finding the right school and the wherewithal to pay the bills gives us many a headache. Mrs. Knowles paints a terrifying picture of the almost irreparable physical and psychological damage done at schools she and other members of her family were sent to in England. I venture to suggest that treatment such as she mentions is extremely rarely met with these days and that it may, like those delightful homes of half-a-century ago referred to by Cecily Evans, be regarded as among the things of the past. I think that present-day life is not void of virtue and that by careful choice there is every hope of finding a school approaching closely to our ideal. This has certainly been my own experience.

School fees, alas, are high and soar ever higher. All kinds of economies have to be practised in the endless struggle to make ends meet. Among the more material advantages afforded to present-day parents is the opportunity to save during that enviable period when their young children are with them on the Coast.   A start can be made towards the provision of school fees through education policies and so on.   Unlike the old-timers, parents now do not have to worry, at this early stage, about how to keep two homes going.

I have found that by far the greatest worry and the biggest heartaches arise with the approach of the holidays, in particular, the long summer holiday.   And I have heard many others say, "We could manage quite well but for the summer holiday."   It is here that I think that local Governments, backed by an understanding Colonial Office, should do something to ameliorate matters.   It is

possible nowadays for schoolchildren at home to be with their parents abroad within twenty-four hours but very few officers can afford the cost of the air-passages.   What a great difference there would be if an officer's conditions of service included the provision of air-passages for schoolchildren in Britain, once in each tour of duty.   The resulting lessening of financial worry would lead (among other things) to higher efficiency all round and, incidentally, I feel sure that such a concession would quickly bring about a marked improvement in recruiting for the Service.

Towards the end of his service in the Gold Coast my husband received a small legacy which enabled us to carry out a long-cherished plan.   We were able to arrange for our daughter to come out by air and spend the whole of her summer holiday with us.   At the age of sixteen she saw for the first time the place that had long been our home.   Strangely enough, there were a good many things in Africa that I, too, saw for the first time, or saw more clearly, because she was with us.   The visit was a tremendous success and I felt that subsequent ones would have been even better.

In my opinion a scheme for assisting overseas officers in the uphill battle to give their children a proper education and at the same time to make possible at least one long spell of family life each year, is urgently needed.   Although it is difficult for me to make constructive suggestions regarding the financing of such a scheme, it is only too easy to produce cogent arguments demonstrating its need.   Here is one of the many.   It is most undesirable that a child should know its father only when he is on leave.   The impression many children receive is of a perpetual holiday-maker, maybe over-indulgent and liverish by turns. This would not happen if there were opportunities to see father under normal everyday conditions; to see him dignified by his labour and to appreciate him as head of his own household.

On The Move

by ELIZABETH KNOWLES

WE have found an infallible way of obtaining a posting. Indeed it has brought us postings when we would rather not have them. For I have only to make a large batch of marmalade (jam and chutney are almost as good), and sure enough, while the beastly stuff is cooling in its paper-topped jars, the telegram arrives. In three years of married life we have lived in five different houses in three totally different climates. My 1954 resolution—no more marmalade!

The first occasion, like all first occasions, remains unforgettable. Himself was out on a foot safari, expected back on the 1st June. On the morning of the 31st May I was stirring my marmalade, when the telegram arrived. "Move in May to Malindi." I looked up Malindi on a map. It was just under one thousand miles away. At ten o'clock that night himself walked into the house, to find it in a chaos of packing. Masculine displeasure showed itself. "And where do you think you are going?" he enquired.

"We are leaving for Malindi, tomorrow!"

We eventually left on the 6th June, and for all that week we lived in chaos. Since then, I have much improved my packing routine. I say "I" advisedly, for himself can produce an active malarial slide whenever he sees packing cases.

Although we move well within the statutory two tons, it is amazing what a lot of packing two tons can take. During service in the more remote districts we found we were often paying 2½ per cent of salary, or £20 a year, for furniture with a total value at the most generous estimate of £30 a year. So we soon acquired our own furniture. In different conditions different equipment is needed, paraffin lamps *and* electric lamps; paraffin, electric, *and* charcoal irons; desert, mosquito, and gum boots; the list seems endless.

The following seven-day routine of packing allows for a family moving complete with all furniture and livestock, (cats, dogs, chickens, ducks). The packing is based on a household of two servants, one to help me and the other to continue the ordinary routine of the household. I pack everything myself, working seven to eight hours a day for six days (allow an extra day for those with children). Where for reasons of climate, health, or other responsibilities it is not possible to devote so long to packing, then the whole operation must, of course, be spread over a longer period.

In view of unexpected moves, we try to keep the following two rules all the time. The first is to be ruthless regarding junk, to keep writing tables, workboxes, pantry cupboards, as free as possible from unessentials. The second is to decide, whenever anything new is bought, what sort of packing is required and to provide that packing at once. This often saves money as well as time, for example when we moved into an electric light area, the shop where I bought all my lampshades gave me a box into which they fit, one inside the other. In case of second-hand furniture, a carpenter will knock up crates for a few shillings, and I make the hessian covers where necessary.

The first day of packing is spent on all the safari boxes as if the whole family were going out on safari. The cook's box takes all the safari saucepans, and leaves space for provisions. The "housemaid's" box takes the crockery and cutlery, with empty screw-top jars for butter, sugar, jam, etc., and space for sauces. Another box takes paraffin lamps, an iron, wash-basin, and shoe-cleaning materials. The pressure lamp has its own box. There is a bedding roll for each member of the family, complete with blankets and mosquito nets to provide for expected climatic changes. And then of course there are clothes for all contingencies on the journey.

In a household well trained to safari, this whole routine takes but an hour or two. In one not so accustomed, it will probably take the best part of a day. In any case it is as well to check at this stage that all safari boxes, together with servants and livestock, will in fact go in the car.

The second day, our mattresses go into their crates, the beds are dismantled and the bits tied together; from now on we sleep in our camp beds. Then the servant assisting me washes all the sheets, blankets, etc., while I concentrate on my personal possessions. This includes clothes and dressing table oddments, three boxes in two hours; typewriter and contents of desk, one hour; sewing machine and work-box, one hour; gramophone, records, and piano accordion, one hour; golf clubs, tennis rackets, fishing rods, etc., one hour. This is a long day and often spreads over into the third day.

The third day is only at the most a five- or six-hour day. Five hundred books go into five large crates at the rate of one crate an hour. One servant assists, and sews up the book cases in their hessian covers as they are emptied.

Thus until the fourth day, the household is running on almost normal routine, up to entertaining standards. From the fourth day on entertaining becomes impracticable. All pictures, photos, lamps and shades, ornaments, trays, occasional tables, book-ends, clocks, cigarette cases, and other paraphernalia are packed. Carpets are brushed, sprinkled with a D.D.T. compound, and sewn into a canvas cover. Linen and blankets not in use are repacked in the chests in which they normally live. A long and tiring day—for us seven boxes and the roll of rugs.

On the fifth day all the pantry and kitchen equipment is dealt with. The china goes into two tea chests, glass into two small wooden boxes, kitchen utensils into one very large crate and one small one, silver into one box, half used provisions and drinks not required on the journey into another box. As the shelves are cleared, the servants unpack the safari boxes on the first day, transferring butter, sugar, and other provisions into the screw-top jars.

For those with children, it is a good idea to have one clear day on which to pack the children's possessions, clothes, toys, and furniture. The nearer the end this day can be, the longer the children can be left undisturbed. The sixth day is perhaps the latest date to which this task can be left.

The seventh day is the last, and quite the worst. It is essential to have the services of either one's husband or a trained carpenter, preferably both, and both servants are called in to help. This is the day to accept invitations to meals from kind neighbours, otherwise the family picnics amongst the cases. I start the day going round the house fitting hessian covers to everything which needs them. Meanwhile the carpenter is crating all cases, roping all boxes, already filled. The refrigerator has been switched off (or lamp removed) the night before. The carpenter follows me, crating the dining room furniture on top of its hessian. Extra assistance is called in to push the piano and refrigerator, both of them pinned into hessian night-dresses, into their crates. The rest of the furniture is sewn into hessian and travels uncrated. Crates for the livestock are checked on. Then curtains come down, their hems are pulled out to let them down to their full eight-foot length, they are folded into a suitcase and left at the laundry nearest to our new station, to be sent on when clean. The old hem-line is laundered out, all I have to do is to adjust them for the new windows and put them up. For an early start, the luggage is loaded onto the lorry overnight.

The household is now living on full safari kit, as in a rest house or in camp. Departure in the morning is but slightly worse than breaking camp. Wash-basin and kettle as always go in last, come out first—and when moving so do brushes and brooms and the tool box.

The advantage of this routine is that it is so easily adjusted to all the well-known variations. The family can continue to live off safari kit while their heavy luggage goes on by rail. When handing over to a large family, the outgoers can complete the whole routine except for the routine of the fifth day, leaving out also beds and dining room furniture as necessary. All completed packing cases can be removed to a shed or garage, the outgoing family can themselves retire to the guest house, thus giving the newcomers all possible room in which to unpack. After a few days, the outgoers pack all china, glass, kitchen equipment, etc., while on the same day the newcomers unpack theirs and take over the catering for the entire household.

Again, if on taking over a new station one is expected to live in the guest house during take-over, then the fact that one is completely self-contained enables the outgoers to pack their kit with the minimum of trouble. Even prior to going on long leave this method works admirably, the heavy luggage can go on in advance to store, the safari kit following as the family leaves for the airport. What, one wonders, is it like to live 365 days a year in the same house, to make marmalade unperturbed by that moving feeling?

Safari

by RUTH BULMAN

When we rode on in the heat of the day
It seemed we struggled in a blood-red basin,
Slithering along the same repeated landscape
　　　As in a childish nightmare.
Open to the sky we were and vulnerable,
Our world a decaying globe of fruit
Blistering in the passionate heat of the sun,
Oh! He smote with the utmost power of his heart!
Beating, beating on the rotting fruit of us.

Came an occasional stench of swamp—
Papyrus stretching to the long horizon
Under sky bunched with savage cumulus.
From hot red sand we ran into the storm,
Where sullen clouds had mutinied at last.
When the rain stopped the sun came out
For a while, and rainbowed veils of steam
　　　Encircled us.
Trees gave thankful chatter with their arms
And the scent of mimosa smote us as we slowed
To meet the lovely pain of sunset.

In an amber light the forests glimmered palely,
Cactus fangs were muted in the mist.
Suddenly, loudly, a wood-pigeon
Sang a sentimental song, cut off mid-note
　　　As night swung sharply in
Engulfing us in throbbing blue,
The very puddles on the road thrilled with the mad
　　　Electric blue of it.
And we went winging, winging, winging
Through a star-hung night of Africa.

An Introduction to Minuteship
(*Reprinted from the "Sarawak Gazette"*)

IT is with diffidence that these few notes on minuteship, which may be defined as the delicate art of replying to minutes *without actually answering them*, are submitted, and the author is sensible of the debt that he owes to Professor Potter, the leading authority on Gamesmanship and Lifemanship. That some introduction, however short, is necessary to any apprentice to the Secretariat has become almost painfully obvious to any diligent student of Secretariat files ; and it is, therefore, in the hope that the following notes of basic principles will be of assistance to the tyro, and that they may not only persuade him to develop this particular art as fully as lies within his powers but even encourage him to extend the operation of its principles, that these notes are offered.

Those familiar with the fundamental principle of Gamesmanship will be aware of the fact that "if you're not one up (Bitzleisch) you're one down (Rotzleisch)," and that (respectfully to quote the critic of the Times Literary Supplement) "the whole art . . . lies in putting oneself in a position of perpetual one-upness, of projecting, as it were, a fifth-column microbe from one's own mind into that of the other person—the eternal opponent, whoever he may be—thus causing him to *'feel that something has gone wrong, however slightly'*."

Adopting this well-tried principle, therefore, we may observe that the true exponent of the art of minuteship must treat every other member of the Secretariat as an antagonist, if not an enemy ; it must be his aim to persuade his opponent, whom we may for practical purposes define as the writer of the preceding minute on the file, that he has, in some way or another, blundered grievously. It is in securing this end by such means that your opponent is incapable, unless he is himself an expert minuteman, of adequate reply, that your skill in the art of minuteship must be measured ; and your minute will thus remain on the file, for all to see, as a first-class illustration of the finest art known to the CSO.

A basic principle, depending of course on the nature of the file under minute, may be laid down as follows : Scrutinize the file carefully, then meditate upon the particular department to which it might have been despatched, *other than your own*. If you can thereby pass on the file to some other person, without replying to it yourself other than by, say, the polite comment "I think X should be given an opportunity of expressing his views on this matter," then you may indeed congratulate yourself on an artistic use of the first principles of minuteship.[1] Use of this ploy may keep a file away from your office for a matter of months ; and, of course, there is always the possibility that the file may in the meantime be lost.

A second principle is that of catching your opponent out in law, General Orders or Colonial Regulations. It is appreciated that this may require some little research, but no minuteman worth his salt will consider such time wasted. For example, the chances are that your opponent is unaware of the latest amendment to the Ordinance ; in fact, he may even be unaware of the existence of any piece of legislation affecting the subject under review. If this is so, you can demolish him in a line ; if not, cast doubts upon his interpretation of the law, then lie low. This technique is remarkably effective in dealing with pensions legislation, and, generally, the minuteman apprentice will find back numbers of the *Sarawak Tribune* containing Circuit Court judgments of remarkable assistance in his evolution of this particular technique.

Certain minutes may, by their very length and complexity, tend to overpower the inexpert minuteman at first sight. The true minuteman will, however, be aware that by his very prolixity his opponent has delivered himself into his hands.

[1]The author is aware of one expert minuteman who adopted this procedure and referred a file to the Fisheries Department, which had (by the time the file passed through the Secretariat) *ceased to exist* : this is minuteship *par excellence*.

With the skill born of years of study at the art, he will politely minute back, "Noted. Thank you." This particular ploy will dishearten an opponent, and shake his morale : he will feel, somehow, that *something has gone wrong*. It should be emphasised that of course this should only be employed with certain minutes, in which the personality of the writer has made him unaware of his own failings ; nevertheless, the technique may be used most effectively in certain debatable classes of minute, such as those dealing primarily with finance.

Arising out of the preceding paragraph, is the alternative ploy in playing with your opponent's grammar. This, admittedly, is only a secondary exercise in the art of minuteship, but may be rendered remarkably effective by an ironic use of double negatives in relation to assertions of your exponent, or, better still by an even more prolix reply. This takes all the skill of an expert minuteman, but he will assuredly find Fowler's *English Usage* an admirable companion at his elbow ; and to throw into a minute some such observation as "Fowler says . . . ," or to quote from Fowler some sentence such as, "it will save repetition to state shortly here what is explained more fully under which with and or but, that a defining clause, whether that is used in both or which in both, or that in one and which in the other, ought to be coupled by and or but as if they were parallel things," will not only throw an opponent into confusion, but may even succeed in keeping the file away from the office for a further six months.

The earnest minuteman will naturally collect his own dictionary of useful phrases, reference to which will save him considerable time. To assert that "I am doubtful of the practicability of . . ." or "Admirable as the above minute is, I cannot help feeling that . . ." are both useful in their context, as causing your opponent to think again, and thereby to render himself uncertain of his facts ; and, if he is foolish enough to number the paragraphs of his minute, the expert minuteman should not miss the opportunity to observe, *simpliciter*, "I agree with the proviso to your para. 2" : thereby causing his opponent to speculate uncertainly on the minuteman's opinion of the other matter of his minute.

As stated above, these are merely a few elementary principles offered for the guidance of the minuteman apprentice, and will be of little interest to the experienced minuteman of the Secretariat. In making it clear to the minuteman apprentice that minuteship is indeed an art, it should be added that conversation concerning your minutes, or indeed those to which you seek a minuteman's reply, is anathema to the expert minuteman. Implying that he has far too much work in hand to tackle the file that he has been wrestling with for the past three weeks, the expert minuteman will reply, when asked his oral opinion of the question put to him in the file, "What file ?" This example of the "off-balance" technique will make his inexpert opponent wonder whether in fact such a file exists, or has indeed ever existed, and he will attempt to trace it through the Secretariat file indices ; this particular ploy is guaranteed to keep an opponent out of your office until after the next Council Negri.

The following list of approved minuteman words and phrases, all of which have been adopted by expert minutemen, is appended for the guidance of the minuteman apprentice :—

I do not know where this file has been—I have not seen it till today.
I should have thought that . . .
Do hypothecated reserves cover this ?
It is now too late for . . .
(2) in this file seems to have been lost sight of . . .
On further consideration, it would be more expedient that . . .
Nebulous.
This is somewhat mysterious . . .
I must enter a caveat . . .
We must discuss this, *later*.   "DRYAD"

Hobbies for the Out-Stations

by R. J. A. W. LEVER

THE average young man taking up his first appointment in the Colonial Service may not be much concerned with a hobby before arrival. However, a little time spent in considering the matter pays good dividends and although the choice is obviously a personal one, suggestions may not come amiss from one who for over twenty years has seen many unorthodox choices prove successful.

The newcomer is likely to be posted in due course to a fairly remote area where other Europeans will probably be few and possibly well scattered, and it is under such conditions that the choice of a hobby assumes much importance.

For those fortunate enough to be posted to island dependencies in the Western Pacific, West Indies, Zanzibar or in the Indian Ocean, tortoiseshell work offers an unstereotyped hobby, especially if fretwork was ever indulged in as a boy. A wide range of acceptable presents such as buckles, buttons, monograms, combs (rather tricky) and paper knives can be turned out at only a minute fraction of their present-day prices in the shops. In some Pacific islands during the war it was virtually impossible to satisfy the demand for objects of tortoiseshell (actually, of course, made from turtleshell) and cat's eyes, which are formed from the hard bun-shaped structure covering the opening of certain whelk-like sea shells.

From cat's eyes to cat's cradles is an easy transition and in the Pacific string figures are made by women and children. Their study offers a hobby particularly suitable for women and the wife of a former District Officer took it up to such purpose that a learned anthropological journal published an article by her on cat's cradles of the Central Pacific. Here the hobby extended to writing about it.

Many subjects concerning the position of women in primitive tribes lend themselves particularly to investigation either by wives of officials or by the increasing band of young women in today's Colonial Service. A book which one might think would have but a limited appeal, Margaret Mead's *Coming of Age in Samoa*, has been published in the Pelican series and indicates the way in which much valuable information can be secured. Not even the most tactful male officer could reasonably be expected to find answers to some of the questions given in the appendix to this book.

Sketching is usually considered a hobby only for those of proved artistic sense, but the least artistic can get great satisfaction in the execution of panorama drawings and simple landscape sketches. Subalterns are, or at any rate were, assured that for the accomplishments of "The Manual of Map-reading, Photo-reading and Field Sketching," "no artistic sense is required but practice is essential"—so why not the Colonial Service officers ? Here is a useful hobby to take up whether or not one holds a service protractor 11 inches from the eye by means of a length of string between the teeth. I, indeed, admit to failure in making a rough panorama of a favourite insect-hunting spot on one of the Solomon islands—most unfortunately, as a few years later this site became temporarily famous as Edson's or Bloody Ridge near Henderson Field, Guadalcanal. Post-war accounts have revealed an acute dearth of sketches and photos of this area in mid-1942, and a few rough but reasonably accurate panoramas available to staff officers of the 1st U.S. Marine Corps would have been of great value had it but been possible to contact them before the landing in August.

For portrait sketching on the other hand, the beginner really does require some kind of coaching as completely untutored efforts are often most disappointing. But it is an excellent hobby for those who can do it and opportunities for portraiture often occur on tour, when porters, hunters and camp followers readily provide good subjects which are often lacking at headquarters. Even there, however, orderlies, house servants or estate labourers can generally be persuaded to pose for a small sum.

One of the most popular hobbies is photography which in its more straightforward aspects leaves little room for comment. But often the very act of residence in a place for some time has the effect of dulling one's sense of what is photographically attractive so that there is a tendency to ignore interesting subjects which strike the eye of a visitor. The continual search for more and arresting photographic angles on familiar things is, in itself, a pleasant hobby.

Nowadays with refrigerators even in remote stations, it is easier to obtain water at the right temperature for developing and printing, so the photographic hobby can be complete. Enlarging is not impossible even without mains electricity— there was a District Commissioner who enjoyed himself a lot enlarging through his own camera with a car battery and torch bulb mounted in a tube cut from a petrol tin.

Readers may recall the War Office asking in 1943 for photographs taken on Continental beaches; they were wanted in connection with D-day planning. Out of the thousands of photographs submitted of happy pre-war holidays there came at last a hackneyed snap of a family bathing group in line, standing on a shelving, sandy shore. What this snap revealed, however, was the depth of water at a particular beach in Normandy. So in the Colonies in peace time, information is waiting to be recorded for future use. A series of my photographs when shown months later to an American G2 (Intelligence Officer) raised the comment that had they been able to reach the right hands at the right time they would have saved some casualties as the photos revealed then unknown topographical details of what was called "Beach Blue" and a rocky ravine on Tulagi in the Solomons; in the latter spot there was heavy, organised resistance.

So it is with projects such as the construction of dams, bridges or roads, where photographs before the work begins can point the way for bulldozers and earth-moving machinery; how often one hears regret expressed that there is no photographic record of the early appearance of some large estate before buildings and crops transformed the jungle. In photography, "spotting the winner," in choosing what seemingly commonplace picture may later become valuable, is an additional skill which should accompany this particular hobby.

Turning now to natural history, there is a wealth of material from which to choose, even when the over-popular butterfly collecting is excluded. No matter where the would-be naturalist is stationed he can always count on willing assistance from the authorities of the British Museum (Natural History) once it is clear that he takes trouble in collecting and forwarding his specimens. The *bona fide* collector may even be provided with a certain amount of apparatus for the preparation of good specimens for the National collection (though it is unlikely that they will be shown in the exhibition galleries which represent only a small fraction of the collections at South Kensington).

One essential item for most natural history work is alcohol for the preservation of fresh specimens. A frank statement to the local Customs of the proposed use of the fluid will usually resolve any difficulties especially as the particular kind used is not drinkable by anyone but a dipsomaniac. Conversely, I know of one enthusiastic collector who sacrificed more than a wineglassful of Scotch whisky in order to preserve from putrefaction a rare jungle frog on its long journey to a specialist in Cromwell Road.

The interest and satisfaction to be obtained by the keen amateur botanist living in out of the way parts of tropical Africa has already been described in *Corona* for July, 1952, where hints on what and how to collect and press plants for dispatch to Kew Gardens are given. Before sailing on one's first appointment, or when home on leave, a visit (by appointment, please) to an official at South Kensington or Kew Gardens will often put one on the road to secure scarce or even undescribed specimens of plants or animals.

The following example will show how an enthusiast with absolutely no specialised knowledge of natural history was nonetheless able to make a worthwhile contribution to science. A retired business man took up the study of mosquitoes in the particular colony where he was living, a sympathetic Director of Medical Services arranging for him to be attached to the Public Health Department where he trained a body of mosquito-searchers. So well were they trained and so keen did they become that it was not long before they discovered two new species of mosquitoes in crab-holes and in a quiet weedy part of a river. This keen amateur then prepared an illustrated manual to supplement previous knowledge of mosquitoes in the area which had been fairly well studied pre-war.

Languages may not appear to be a subject for a hobby but for anyone born with the gift of tongues they are most valuable. I know of one young District Officer who, soon after passing the compulsory language test, wrote a first-class Melanesian grammar which still helps successive batches of cadets.

While neither wives of serving officers nor women government servants can all hope to write so much concentrated wisdom as appears in Mrs. Bradley's delightful "Dearest Priscilla," writing remains a first-class hobby for them, as well as for men. A Governor's wife has written about the West Indies, a former District Officer's wife on the Central Pacific and a Customs Officer's wife on Malaya.

Sir Arthur Grimble's "A Pattern of Islands" shows outstandingly what can be done in writing up the day-to-day activities of one's earlier service.

Without doubt the largest scale job of curio-production occurred during the Pacific war where on some islands the Sea Bees (Naval Construction Battalions) turned out on their lathes hundreds of clubs made from green timber. These objects were sold to unsuspecting G.I's as genuine Solomon Island war clubs ! Those readers of *Corona* who during the last year or so have been to see the musical play "South Pacific" will be familiar with the mass-produced dance skirts made for sale to the natives for resale to the troops who sent them "States side" as valuable curios.

One must avoid riding one's hobby horse too hard : some people, indeed, may find their work all the hobby they need, but where something else is required time spent in choosing and pursuing a hobby that will give a lasting interest is well worth while and one may in the process be able to add some concrete contribution to the knowledge of some little-known Dependency.

(To the reader who may say "What, no birds ?" we are glad to reply that a well-known ornithologist has promised to write for *Corona* on possibilities offered by bird study in the tropics.—*Ed.*)

Good and Faithful Servant

by ANTHONY KIRK-GREENE

ALL GOOD things come to an end—the Colonial Service, *Corona*, the days of the District Officer—and to mark this acknowledged end of an epoch, I should like to offer a slight tribute to those whom I believe most of my Overseas Service colleagues, past and present, would wish to thank: our personal staff, from khidmutgar to chokra, from steward to mpishi, from dhobi to doki-boy, from toto and night-watchman to chaprassi and gardener. In short, our 'boys.'

If I name any names, let these be symbolic, let the part represent the whole: my Abdullahi Mahmud and Sunday Okeke are Smith's Joseph Karuga or Brown's Ram Lal. For all we cursed their covetousness, damned their deafness and muttered at their miserable memories, we retain a warm spot in our hearts for our personal staff; and the colder the British climate, the warmer that memory.

Isa came to me in my second month in Northern Nigeria and he is now in his twelfth year. In a tribute like this, the best method of presentation is perhaps that of the traditional cinema flashback. Isa serving at table with quiet competency and darting glances of thunderous ire at the nervous second steward whose Islamic upbringing forbids him to believe that any woman can possibly be served before any man; Isa's alarum-like punctuality as he brings in the morning tea at 6.15; Isa proving to a friend that his master had a pretty fair temper, by solemnly informing me that he had "forgotten" to heat the bath-water, his subterfuge then given away by the hoots of mirth as I stepped furiously and then howlingly into a furnace-hot bath; Isa insisting in a photograph that if the cook was to display his insignia of office (one frying-pan and one-egg-beater, better known as beater-egg) he too must show his badges of rank (declared to be one bottle-opener and two tea-towels); Isa, still refusing to believe that on leave I ever would (or probably ever could) do the washing-up; and Isa obviously putting on more vicarious dog about my gradual promotions through the years than I ever dared to do.

Next, Audu the cook. How often have we, cursing in our temporary wrath engendered by a too liberal *caramel brûlé* or the ineluctable stand-by of chicken *sitew*, been convinced that African cooks are the lost and damned ones of Adam's tribe? Who but a subnormal dunderhead could, in the middle of bush and miles away from the shops, calmly announce without rhyme, reason or even excuse: "There is *no* dinner tonight"? Who but a magician (or an African cook) could persuade you that two pounds of sugar *never* last more than three days?

Audu came to me first as a "small boy," as we call them on the Coast, and on a number of bush safaris proved himself exceptionally resourceful on all sorts of matters outside his 'profession', such as dealing with car punctures, recalcitrant Post Office clerks, and elusive wildfowl. Extending his intelligence to initiative, Audu fixed himself a kitchen course with a brother-officer's wife when I was away for a sabbatical year, so that on my return I found myself confronted by a self-taught, self-advertised and self-confident cook.

Audu really rose to fame and favour on Christmas Eve three years ago. The Resident had thrown a big traditional party and I remember wishing my cook could show as much culinary imagination. As the guests left, they congratulated the Resident on his chef. "Not mine," he replied, "it's Kirk-Greene's Audu." I was not as gruntled as I should have been at hearing this unexpected compliment, and next morning I sent for Audu. Isa marched in the prisoner in his best orderly-room style and the following interview took place:

K-G (*disbelieving*): "Did you make that *bombe glacée* at the Residency last night?"

Audu (*hurt*): "Of course I did, may your life be prolonged!"

K-G (*puzzled*): "Why have you never made it for my dinner parties?"

Audu (*triumphant*): "You never asked me, may your life be prolonged!"

K-G (*groping*): "I never knew you could."

Audu (*hurt*): ?

K-G (*challenging*): "In fact, I still don't believe you can."

Audu (*hurter still*): ??

K-G: "Isa, give Audu everything he wants from the store and we'll see what he can produce by the time I get back from the office. Meanwhile, make sure you lock him in the kitchen so that he gets no outside help on this."

On my return from the office for luncheon I personally unlocked the kitchen. Audu was sitting serenely at the kitchen table, reading a vernacular translation (I had sent him to the adult education classes when he was my small boy) of *A Thousand and One Nights*. Beside him on the table stood an Escoffier-worthy *bombe glacée*.

Another incident in Audu's "sweet" life, as it were, was when we agreed to take on an apprentice cook for a District Officer friend of mine. Just before the apprentice went back to his master in Kano, I came across Audu's handing over notes. He had listed twelve puddings and graded each as Class I, Class II or Class III. This grading he had apparently done on his estimate of the social importance of my guests—this in turn based on the number of times I, wifeless, fussed into the kitchen just before the guests arrived. If I were to quote any items from Audu's list, friends who remembered which pudding they had last had at my house might be shocked at his interpretation of the official Staff List.

Audu's newly-acquired literacy is sometimes as challenging to the brain as *The Times* crossword. Apparently last week, according to his shopping list, I ate the following: bekin, anyanz, tsikon, kopiploa, karim, kabeji, bota, kipa, ti. In addition, there generally features the West African egg triumvirate of saus-egg, cut-legg and om-leg.

But it is on tour, in the midst of nowhere with nothing to hand, that our cooks rise to unprecedented heights and deserve every word of the following praise sung by a *pukka sahib* a century ago: —

"Look into that kitchen. If your eyes are not instantly blinded with smoke, and if your sight can penetrate into the darkness, enter that hovel, and witness the preparation of your dinner. The table and the dresser,

you observe, are Mother Earth   . . .   Observe the kitchen-range, I
beseech you: a mud construction, with apertures for reception of charcoal, upon which repose pans of native mould, in which all the delicacies
are cooked   . . .   A spit, two native saucepans, a ladle and a knife
comprise all the requirements of the cook . . . with an aptitude and a skill
that gladdens the heart of the epicure on the march and affords to the
traveller, when far removed from the busy haunts of men, the certainty
of as excellent a dinner as ever graced his table in the land of the West."
G. F. Atkinson, who wrote this in *Curry and Rice*, with India in mind, would
have been interested to know that 100 years later African cooks were performing miracles with even less equipment, over a strip of corrugated iron and a
couple of stones.

The rest of the household are less colourful personalities, not inherently so
but because they have not, like Isa and Audu, been virtually an integral part
of my whole life in Northern Nigeria. Ephemeral, junior, reticent in The
Presence, they lack the bond the rest of us have—the bond of shared experiences, of tough treks in the bush now remembered with affection from the
relative ease of our P.W.D. 'cushion' chairs, safe in a Secretariat job; of fire
and storm and runaway horses; of midnight alarums and cornered cobras by
the thunder-box; of, in short, all the trials and thrills of life as a young
Administrative Cadet.

On the Coast we know the second steward as the 'small' boy. Actually, by
the rules of the game he doesn't have to be 'small,' though he generally is
since he is a learner, an embryo steward. But my first District Officer's small
boy was 6' 6" tall, a hilltop pagan with masses of muscle, and little else. He
didn't need anything else, for his sole job was to wield the starting-handle of
the Old Man's car. His name soon became Windie-Windie and he left when he
was strongly suspected of eating the Old Man's cat. Nor does another colleague
of mine quite abide by the rules. Admittedly, his small boy is only 4' 10", but
since he has been with John for ten years and has been married for seven, he's
not really a 'boy.' The third example illustrating the elasticity of interpretation in the term 'small boy' comes from an Old Coaster who, in the mid-30's,
was somewhat ruffled by the arrival on tour in his very up-country Division
of a new kind of Government official called a Woman Education Officer. She
turned out to be as prim, prudish and pussyfoot as he had feared, and barely
concealed her puritanical disapproval of the Old Coaster's ritual sundowner.
By dinner the chips were down.   At table, the vegetables were served by a

young Fulani of striking beauty, with eye-lashes long enough to sweep the cob-webs off any bachelor's heart, a pair of sparkling eyes enhanced by artfully applied antimony, and a rather suspicious fullness round the bosom.   Miss Prissymouth peered at the servant, then turned to her host: —

"Mr. X," she pursed her lips, "does the District Officer then keep a small girl in his house?"

Replied the Old Coaster: "Miss Y, I notice that your own staff consists of a cook and a small boy."

My own small boys have little to distinguish them in my memory. I have always allowed Isa to shortlist the applicants, my only demand being that he should select a local boy from the new Division that we have been taking over so that I could pick up something of the vernacular. But with the Government building flats and putting on the screws with its austerity budgets, the need for a small boy is gradually diminishing. We could really do without one in my bachelor household. But apart from the fact that the extra pair of hands is useful in coping with the current spate of transatlantic house-guests, Isa would think the world had come to an end if I dared to suggest that I, a *soi-disant* senior Administrative Officer, should dispense with a small boy. The status-symbol is too important for Isa. So we continue, the current small boy, Audi by name, doing, it always seems to me, 99 per cent. of the work, though admittedly under Isa's close supervision, and Isa undertaking the personal and therefore prestigeful tasks that involve access to The Presence. Thus Audi may run the bath but only Isa may communicate to me the news that it is ready; Audi may remove the early morning tea but it is Isa who brings it; Audi may wash and iron my clothes but it is Isa who puts them away in the chest of drawers; Audi may hand round the potatoes but Isa the meat; Isa alone may serve drinks.   These are all divisions of labour abrogated to themselves by themselves, and I would not dare, even if I wished to, to suggest a revision of rules that appear inviolate. Only in the informality and intimacy of bush tour-ing does such a strict domestic protocol stand a chance of being breached.

Of gardeners and horse-boys the less said the better.   I do not know whether I have less time for a horse or a garden, so my appalling indifference naturally colours my attitude towards the practitioners of such skills. My first Resident used to say, icily, but, alas, quite accurately, that it was perfectly easy to see which house his new Assistant District Officer had occupied: all you had to do was not to look *at* the garden but *for* it. The best gardener I ever had was Bagobiri. He was a long-term prisoner, inside for homicide, who because of his seniority among the convicts earned the 'cushy' job of working in the D.O.'s garden. Bagobiri and I understand each other perfectly.   We never interfered at all, either he by asking me for gardening tools or I by disturbing his long hours of sleep under the frangipani. The only time I did force myself into suburban zeal, lovingly inspecting my seed-bed every morning and murmuring words of encouragement above it, ended, I am happy to report, in utter disaster. Returning from a month's tour, I found an angry Agricultural Superintendent glowering over the seed-bed. "This," he growled, "is what I am paid to eradicate—one of the most deadly weeds in Africa! Yet you culti-vate it."

I kept—or, if the truth must out, I had to keep—a horse for four years. Now and again, I will admit, I got a lot of pleasure out of hacking. Muhammadu was a wonderful doki-boy on tour and he never let on that he how they really saw us. "Few men," Montaigne reminds us, "are admired by their servants." Meanwhile, many an Overseas Service officer will, particularly if he has now retired to Great Britain, join with me in paying this small tribute to those who, for all their vexing habits matched only by our own quirks of temperament, were yet part of us; and who, when the story comes to be told, played no small part in our success, or otherwise, in the work we went out to do.

Map Reading

by BUNDI

Smoothe out the creases; in these names are found
The touch of sun warm day and star cool night,
The laughter on long marches and the sound
Of sleepy voices in the camp firelight.
Here still these contour lines recall the slow
Climb to the thunderous mountain where we came
To stand in breathless gratitude and see below
The sunrise strike the mist-grey lake with flame.
Here rivers ran together in the plain
Flashing their silver to our tented hill,
And all creation in the scent of rain
Rose from the dark, replenished earth. Here still
When day is new
Do crested cranes dance in the dew ?
Still does the lonely eagle's cry
Ring down the dawn-emblazoned sky ?

Here, where no forests were, trees grew at our command.
Our medicine here dealt witchcraft's first defeat
And here we built a school and from the land
Fear and corruption turned into retreat.
Here in the court, disputing cow or wife,
The elders taught us patience and bestowed
On us the timeless verities of life.
Here was the rich green valley where our road
Evoked new commerce from the unspent earth,
And here the market where we took our fill
Of gossip, when a minute's chat was worth
An hour among the office files. Here still
When evening cools
Do wildfowl talk in reedy pools ?
Still does the ibis slowly fly
Across the dusk-enchanted sky ?

(d) Colonial Service Life Between the Wars

Although *Corona* was in existence up to 1962, and was committed to discussion of the work and problems of the contemporary Colonial Service, many of its readers had been in the Service since before World War II. In a number of cases, their service – and their recollections – went back to the very different context of the Colonial Service of the 1930s and even the 1920s. The editor, deriving his inspiration from his experience of his own senior officers in pre-war Tanganyika, made a point of encouraging the occasional contribution of the 'In Those Days' genre, where necessary guiding the writer away from any 'gone to the dogs' tendency or indulging in too much nostalgia for the perceived simplicity of colonial government 'in the good old days'. The historian as well as the comparative Colonial Service reader regularly found both profit and pleasure from this kind of article.

Forty Years Back

by SIR PHILIP MITCHELL, G.C.M.G., M.C.

THERE was, of course, no 'Colonial Service' to join in 1912. Each country had its own, recruited in various ways. First there were the 'failed I.C.S.' countries. You entered for the Indian Civil Service examination, as it was called. If you passed in the first ten or twelve you normally went to the Home Service, wore a black felt hat and worked from 11 a.m. to 6 p.m. daily with a generous gap in the middle for lunch at your club. The next forty or so were appointed to the Indian Civil Service. Then came what were called Eastern Cadetships, that is administrative appointments to Hong Kong, the Federated Malay States and Ceylon, under the Colonial Office; so incredibly idle had I been at Oxford that I failed even to find a place among the Eastern Cadets.

The second way into the Colonial Service then was to have a relative who was a Governor and took you out as private secretary, as often as not unpaid; once in his satrapy, there was no serious difficulty in obtaining a permanent appointment.

Finally, there was a simple process of applying for a post in some Colony. There was a Patronage Committee to select applicants and the Private Secretary to the Secretary of State ran the business; it seems hardly credible, but it is true, that in 1912 that post was occupied by Ralph Furse. A distinguished cousin of my father's, who had begun his career in the Indian Civil Service and ended it as Ambassador in Washington, peculiar as that may sound to-day, was chairman of the admirably named Patronage Committee. This seemed to me, rightly as the event proved, to be likely to result in the committee feeling a robust confidence in my suitability for colonial administration. A cynical uncle told me about this time that I could not hope for a post in a habitable country, because these all went to the Little Brothers of the Rich, and I certainly was not that. But, he added cheerfully, there was always the White Man's grave for which the Little Brothers were not applicants and Cousin Mortimer would no doubt see that I got a post there—that is to say in West Africa or the unhealthy parts of East.

So it proved; if memory is not playing tricks I had the choice of the Sudan at £400 a year, or Nyasaland at £250. Probably the Sudan post was for the contract districts in the south, for the central and northern Sudan was jealously guarded Little Brother country. It is in any case incredible that I should have refused £400 a year in a country of unlimited £10 ponies in favour of £250 in Nyasaland, even though I did not know until I got there that there were no ponies at all.

The next thing after being appointed was to attend a course at the Imperial Institute, which lasted ten weeks and in which lectures were given on criminal law by an agreeably convivial Irish barrister; on accounts by the then Director of Colonial Audit—who told us that the Colonial system of accounting was the most beautiful thing he had encountered in his life (what a life!); on tropical hygiene and on surveying. The surveying consisted of walking about Banstead Downs humping strange instruments and calling frequently at the local pubs for beer. We liked our instructor greatly, I remember, and viewed the mysteries in which he tried to instruct us without alarm, because we soon came to learn that, when the time came for the examination, his clerk was in the habit of supplying the 'students' with all the material necessary to answer the paper correctly for a modest fee.

The tropical hygiene lecturer was a gloomy leech who had been for a short time in Nyasaland, had contracted blackwater fever and returned to England. He took each tropical disease in turn, described its symptoms and so on and ended "And the result is death." One day, I suppose meaning to cheer us up, he varied this formula by saying: "But I do not want you to suppose that the result is in every case immediately fatal; sometimes the patient lingers on for a few days," then, after a pause for reflection, "in frightful agony." It seemed that Nyasaland was the White Man's grave all right!

On some days there would be three lectures, on others two, occasionally only one; so I went round to the Colonial Office and asked if there was any other form of instruction with which I might usefully fill in the ample spare time. A bright young man told me that if I was going to Nyasaland he advised me to learn to shoe a horse, "for," he said, "there is not a farrier in the Protectorate." So I arranged to learn, for a modest fee and certainly with toil, sweat and some blood, if not tears, on the vast feet of dray and 'bus horses at the forge which then existed near the Common end of Wimbledon High Street. I was brought up on horseback, but one of the things I had not learned was shoeing. It was then that I acquired that awe-struck respect for the vast knowledge of the Colonial Office that I have retained ever since. For that young man was perfectly right; there was not a farrier in Nyasaland. True, there was not a horse either, but that was no doubt the business of another department.

Well, at last all the preliminaries were over, even including the purchase of an incredible amount of quite useless junk. Every young man going out to Africa bought, for instance, a portable Berkefeld filter, an object called a Lord's lamp, another kind of lamp with no chimney and a clockwork-driven fan in the base, a fitted cook's box with a vast assortment of pots and pans, each neatly in its own compartment of Venesta wood—a challenge which no African cook could resist, of course. The partitions were soon broken or discarded and the gear reduced to frying pan, kettle and saucepan, and perhaps a knife, but that was more often worn at the cook's belt, like a dagger. We bought, too, vast pith helmets, spine pads, cholera belts and the Lord alone knows how much other junk. You could buy it all, new and unused, with the names of your predecessors stencilled on it, especially filters and lamps, for a few shillings at any of the junk sales that were such a feature of life in remote places in those days. But nobody told you that in London, and the admirable colonial outfitting firms who competed for our custom and cheerfully gave us long credit had a very persuasive way with them and sold these peculiarly useless and cumbersome things to us in great quantities. You could buy anything a man really needed, at half the prices paid in London, in the general stores of any African Colony—but, again, nobody told us that, in London; and if we had been told we should not have believed it. For the truth is, we all felt like a lot of young Stanleys and Spekes and the more exotic and peculiar the things we bought, the more we felt like intrepid explorers bound on some romantic 'Mission to the Interior.'

Junk and all I duly embarked on the German East Africa Line's *Feldmarschal*, and after a leisurely journey that included the Suez Canal, Aden, Mombasa, Tanga, Zanzibar and Dar-es-Salaam, arrived off the Chinde mouth of the Zambesi, and by stern wheel steamer and little wood-burning train at Limbe in the Shire Highlands.

Those were the great days of the big-game hunters. Wealthy men and even a few women—and there were many rich then—mostly from the United Kingdom, but a few Americans, Frenchmen and others, betook themselves via Mombasa and Nairobi to the vast game plains of Kenya, so that the Kedong Valley, the Lorian Swamp, Laikipia and other remote places were as full of Dukes, Marquesses and what have you as the Royal Enclosure at Ascot. And, if we impecunious cadets bought a lot of junk, these mighty hunters brought wagon loads of it, most of which they doubtless gave to their White Hunters unused—for even by then we could not be just hunters, we had to be white! The extraordinary obsession with 'Heads' and other trophies and records of big game was all the rage. Admirable men, the soul of honour in other things, would squeeze and twist their little steel tapes to try and make the horn of some unsightly mammal an eighth of an inch longer; would lie like lawyers to their cronies about the vast spread of buffalo horns or the weight of tusks, and would lie awake at night dreaming of the day when they might see in Rowland Ward's *Records of Big Game*, 'Hartebeeste, John Smith, Nyasaland, 12⅝ inches.'

I suppose there was some sense in it for the owners of ancestral halls, at any rate in the case of the more imposing and decorative heads, such as the kudus, the oryx or the buffalo; but what an impecunious Administrative Cadet supposed he was going to do with the smelly remains of heads that he so zealously collected, I cannot now imagine. And yet, when I first went on leave nine years later—seven years overdue because of the Kaiser's war—my baggage smelt to high heaven, for it consisted largely of skins and heads for the curing and mounting of which I paid large sums I could ill afford. Where they all went to in the end, I have long since forgotten.

Arrived in Zomba, I reported to the Secretariat, my first experience of that remarkable institution. I remember that I was told that I had been posted to Mzimba, some hundreds of miles away in the north. When I asked how I got there I got the, to me then, surprising answer, 'walk.' Being strongly of the same mind as Cobbett (of *Rural Rides*), who wrote 'Doubtless had God meant man to walk he would have given him four legs, like the beasts,' I took a poor view of this. But, as I have just said, it was my first experience of Secretariats; I need not have worried. In the next two or three weeks I was posted to Fort Johnston, to Liwonde, to Blantyre and to Zomba itself; in the end I found myself at Mlanje and was left there for fifteen whole months. I suppose the posting game was being played with someone else by then.

And when, being young, foolish and bursting with zeal to start this Saunders of the River business, I intruded upon my first boss as soon as he came to the office one morning and nervously asked if he could tell me what my duties were, he raised a pale, anæmic countenance, looked at me for a bit with pain and marked distaste and then replied: "Yes, I can; to keep out of my plurry sight."

Pacific Cadet

by SIR ARTHUR GRIMBLE, K.C.M.G.

I

I WAS nominated to a cadetship in the Gilbert and Ellice Islands at the end of 1913. The cult of the great god Jingo was as yet far from dead. Dominion over palm and pine (or whatever else happened to be far-flung) was still, for a vast number of Englishmen, the heaven-conferred privilege of the bulldog breed. Your uncles all said you'd never be a leader, my boy, if you weakened on that point. The Colonial Office said, more guardedly, that you could hardly pass your probation as a Cadet unless you showed qualities of leadership. Did Downing Street mean the same thing as your uncles? Well at least my Resident Commissioner on Ocean Island did not. Not for Cadets, anyhow. He told me at our first interview that he didn't want any of that heaven-born stuff from me, please. It would suit him best if I were to confine myself severely to learning just a few things not yet revealed to Cambridge or the Colonial Office. I was the first of the species Cadet to be injected into the Central Pacific, he continued: I should find a number of competent people more than eager to teach me what was truly what. By way of facilitating their business, he had decided to make me everybody's bottle-washer in turn. I was a mild young man, and it was a great relief to me.

" Everybody " meant, first, the Resident Commissioner, an expert on the Secretary of State's business; second, the Chief Clerk, an expert on the Resident Commissioner's; third, the Head Accountant and Customs Officer, an expert on the Chief Clerk's; and last, the Officer-in-Charge of Police and Prisons, who did practically everything for all of us but didn't talk about it. Between the four of them I was kept pretty busy at the various paper routines, but there were also outside jobs to learn. No Public Works Department existed in the Gilbert and Ellice Islands at that time. District Officers had to undertake quite a number of small building operations for themselves, and the idea was to get me a bit educated in such matters before I began to run away with Empire-building on a large scale. It was a very good idea indeed, and I liked it, but it occasionally cost the taxpayers a lot of money. Take, for example, the case of the Residency cistern.

Water was a problem on Ocean Island, and they were trying to meet it when I arrived. One of the first odd jobs I had to learn was how to blast twenty foot pits in the rocky earth for laying down concrete storage tanks. The actual work wasn't difficult. You got someone to drill holes in the rock; you pushed sticks of gelignite, with detonators and fuses attached, into the holes; then you tamped them in, lit the fuses, and ran for your life. I chose the Residency back-yard for my first independent blasting operation. A tank had been ordered for it. My only real mistakes were that I chose a Saturday afternoon, warned nobody, and used 300 per cent. too much gelignite. The immediate result was an explosion of volcanic force. The surface of the back-yard rose bodily into the air, and boulders of gigantic size fell crashing through the Residency roof into the dining room. The Resident Commissioner and his lady were taking their siesta at the time. They addressed me at once, and both at once, from the verandah, in their underclothes. I could not help feeling that the things they said of me were extraordinarily true. It was time I learned about the Customs.

The Customs work on that reef-bound island could be exciting, because it took in, as a side-line, the landing of mails and small cargo for the Government. Our boat's crews were made up of hand-picked Ellice Islanders. There are no better oarsmen in the world, and nothing less than all their skill was needed in rough weather. The ships lay out in an unsheltered bay; the entrance to the boat-harbour was a narrow passage blasted through the reef, wide open to the ocean swells. In the westerly gales that blew up between September and March, the passage became a hell's cauldron of raging surf and snarling back-suck.

Two days before Christmas, 1914, a trading steamer bound for the Gilbert Group came wallowing into the bay and signalled at about 4 p.m. that she had on board a new porcelain bath and three cases of whisky for the Residency. Would we take delivery at once, please, as a westerly blow was starting and the captain wanted to make for Tarawa that night.

The boat-passage looked awful to me. I certainly should not have tackled it ordinarily, but, as a matter of fact, the whisky wasn't only for the Resident Commissioner: it was for everyone on the Government Station. The cheeriness of our Christmas festivities was at stake. I had in mind what my four masters would say to me if the stuff wasn't landed. So out we went.

We found the porcelain bath already waiting for us in the ship's slings. Have you ever tried to catch a bath in a boat from a ship that's rolling twenty degrees? There it goes at one moment, hurtling up and away from you, as the vessel wallows to windward; and there it comes now, roaring down at you with the whole ship's side, as she takes her leeward lurch. There's just an occasional moment or two between rolls when you can snatch it on board without scuppering yourself. We waited half an hour for our chance in that brutal seaway; but we did get away with it when it came, thanks to the superb boat's crew. I was so braced with the thing that I actually enjoyed shooting the boat-passage on the way home. "This is the life", I thought, as I opened a note that was waiting for me on the boat-jetty. The Resident Commissioner had watched us through his telescope. He had written to congratulate and thank all of us. "And please", his letter ended, "have the whisky brought straight up to the Residency, and join us in a drink". It was the proudest moment of my life— except that the whisky wasn't there. In the excitement about the bath, I had left the ship without it.

There was only one thing to be done. Dusk was falling as we got out to the ship again. I was greeted by a torrent of abuse for holding her up, but we got the three cases aboard somehow. Then, off we started on the homeward pull . . . and we pulled, and we pulled, and we pulled, and we gained not a yard shorewards. No boat's crew in creation could have made it against that current. We were in the wrong end of a tide-rip that was scouring the bay. We found ourselves being swept round a point into the open Pacific. In the end, after dark, the ship had to take us all on board, and we slept the night there. It was only three o'clock the next afternoon that the weather abated, and the captain got rid of us. The ship was standing away round the point as we landed.

"Well", I thought, "we've done the trick anyhow. It's Christmas Eve, and here we are with the goods". Yes, that again could have proved one of my life's high moments—if the whisky had been there. But it wasn't. The boat captain and I scrabbled wildly through every nook of the boat, but it just wasn't there. And then the piteous truth came out. Two men of that devoted crew had risked a lot the night before to get the liquor safely back on the ship when I had left the boat. Only, they had forgotten to say so before our return to shore. Not a thing more could be done about it now. There was the whisky merrily steaming away to Tarawa.

When I got to the Residency, the whole Government staff, with wives attached, was waiting to greet me. They cheered me from the front steps as I approached. They clapped me on the back. They were waiting to divide the whisky. Was it following me up at once? My word, young Grimble, they said, we'll drink the first one for you when it arrives . . . but let the curtain fall.

Salad Days in Tanganyika

by SIR REX SURRIDGE, C.M.G.

AFTER A BRIEF, but at times not unexciting, period spent in the Army in France in 1918 and a very enjoyable holiday in the Army of the Rhine in Germany in 1919-20, I decided to take advantage of a Government grant to Oxford for two years. As my eldest brother had previously joined the Cyprus Administration, I thought that I would also try for the Administration, and after a year's delay, which was spent schoolmastering in Hampshire, I was offered appointment to Tanganyika in August, 1923.

The new cadets for the African Colonies foregathered in October for the Tropical African Services Course of four months at the Imperial Institute in London. There we were taught map reading, Mohamedan law, accounts, tropical hygiene, elements of agriculture, etc. It was not, however, a very serious business and we all thoroughly enjoyed ourselves, even though some of us did not do a great deal of work. For example, one of our number managed to get no marks in one of the papers, mainly because he found the atmosphere in the bar of a nearby hotel more congenial than the stuffy rooms of the Imperial Institute. This same cadet had an unfortunate *viva* in agricultural products which consisted in naming the various products on a large table. The candidates coming out of the *viva* told those waiting to go in where the products were placed, and by the time this particular cadet went in he had memorised the most important. Unfortunately, the examiners had moved the products round and he got none right. In the end he was allowed to proceed to Tanganyika but was warned that he would have to do better in future, particularly when he faced the Swahili and Law examinations in the Territory. The rest of us got through without much difficulty, due perhaps to the fact that the examiners were apt to set the same papers course after course and that the maps for the map reading examination were obtainable for five shillings each—not from the examiners, I should hasten to add.

At that time we were informed of our stations; the above-mentioned cadet to Lushoto and I to Moshi. But this was changed before we sailed as the Senior Commissioner, Moshi, had asked specially for the other cadet and I was sent to Lushoto. I well remember a visit I subsequently paid to Moshi when I was collecting taxes from the railway employees, for when I saw this cadet I mentioned to him the difficulties I had been having over Treasury queries on our accounts. He replied with a smile that he never had less than a hundred a month and that he already had six months' supply in his drawer which he had not attempted to answer. Perhaps it was just as well for him that he was transferred to Dar-es-Salaam to be aide-de-camp to the acting Governor.

On the journey out to East Africa we were a party of six, one ex-Royal West African Frontier Force subaltern for Uganda, two cadets for Zanzibar and three for Tanganyika, and we had a wonderful voyage. I arrived in due course at Tanga where I stayed with the Senior Commissioner and of this visit I still remember three things vividly. First my host's great kindness to me, secondly the intense heat which put me fast asleep every afternoon after lunch, and lastly my host's peculiar habit of returning to the offender, irrespective of rank or sex, any matches, cigarette ends, or ash deposited anywhere except in the ash trays provided for the purpose. Luckily, he had explained this little foible to me in forcible language so I managed to avoid that particular hazard.

After a few days in Tanga, I got on one of the twice weekly trains and arrived at Mombo (the station for Lushoto) at about 11 p.m. Here a very ancient Ford took me on to Lushoto and I arrived at the District Commissioner's house soon after midnight, having seen nothing of the scenery on the way. Imagine my feelings the next morning when walking round the Boma garden, prepared for something fairly tough, I found carnations, roses and violets in bloom, a lovely running stream and a glorious climate. So good, indeed, that many Europeans and Asians had settled in the area; there was a country club with golf course and tennis courts, and even a few horses—plus the odd lion. It was not long before I came into close contact with the latter by way of a Senior Forest Officer, a small but enthusiastic hunter who owned a double-barrelled six hundred rifle nearly as big as himself.

The first call came from a nearby headman who reported that a lion had been surrounded in thick bush and would the D.C. come and deal with it. The D.C. was away, so the Forest Officer and I set forth on his motor bicycle and sidecar, armed to the teeth, and in due course took up our positions on a small path about fifty yards away from one another in very thick bush where the only field of fire was down the path where the other stood. After much beating of tin cans and shouting, the lion eventually sauntered out in front of the Forest Officer who was so taken aback that he let off his rifle at point blank range and missed it altogether. I got a running shot at the lion which was by then over a hundred yards away, going fast, and, of course, missed.

A few days later this same headman reported about 5-30 p.m. that they had caught a lion in a trap and would we go and dispose of it—I suppose he thought we couldn't miss that target. The Forest Officer and I had not yet learned sense and agreed to go at once. After disposing of the lion by the aid of a Dietz lamp the Forest Officer said that he wanted to take the skin back that night. As the Africans with us were taking the lion out of the trap, I heard some very unpleasant grunts and groans from the bush nearby—oh, I was told, that's mother lion and her other cub. So the whole operation of moving the lion and skinning it had to be covered by me with my rifle, while one of the locals held a lamp. This lasted nearly an hour and that was the last time I went lion hunting in the dark, or indeed at any other time, with that particular Forest Officer.

As Lushoto was a two-man station and my D.C. was nearly always on safari, I had very little travelling but found plenty of time for studying law and Swahili. I also found time to persuade my future wife to marry me— she and her family lived conveniently close to the Boma, at least her father did when he was not on safari which was the breath of life to him. It was clear that I was almost a city dweller in his eyes but he tolerated me, I think because I had soldiered in France, albeit not very well and only for a short time.

It was not long before the acting Governor and his wife decided to visit Lushoto officially, and the fullest preparations were made, reminding me of earlier visitations by G.O.Cs. The paths and roads were cleaned, the station tidied up and the stones whitewashed. His Excellency and his wife stayed at the D.C's house and as was the custom ran it with their staff from Government House. About two hours after the gubernatorial party and the D.C. had left for Tanga, the latter's wife came down to me and said: "All my silver has gone—will you tell W... at once; the G.H. servants must have taken it." We went upstairs and she searched the whole place again without success. She again insisted on telephoning her husband, which very reluctantly I did, stopping the train at Korogwe for him. Some two hours later a very flustered wife came down and said she had found all the silver in a drawer. I suggested that she should telephone her husband to give him the glad tidings but she refused and I had to do it, to find that all the loads on the Governor's train had been put on the platform and searched but that, naturally enough, nothing had been found. I was not very popular with my D.C. for a bit nor, I fear, was his wife.

After I had been in Lushoto about a year "they"—possibly egged on by the D.C. still smarting from the silver incident—decided that I should change places with one of the Dar-es-Salaam district Assistant District Officers. I packed up and went down on my motor cycle *via* Mombo, Korogwe, Turiani and Kilosa. There were, of course, no proper roads from Korogwe to Turiani and although my future father-in-law said that I couldn't miss the way I did manage to do so more than once. But the biggest hazard was the tsetse flies which seemed to be in their millions and a more unpleasant ride I have never had. I just managed to get to Turiani by nightfall after a tremendous storm had almost washed the path away, and there I stayed with the Mission who were most kind to all travellers. The Turiani—Kilosa portion of the road was easier except that one of the main bridges was down and I had some difficulty in getting my bicycle across the river—luckily the Public Works Department were there to help.

At Dar-es-Salaam I was one of three or four A.D.Os. under the Senior Commissioner, Geoff Webster, and was at once sent on two long safaris up and down the coast, collecting taxes. Although the long rains were at their height and we were seldom dry for long, I found these safaris most enjoyable. I took my motor cycle with me on my first trip down the Utete road but soon had to abandon it as most of the road was hopelessly eroded, and I found on that safari that a push bicycle was the only possible means of conveyance and that only for short distances. It took some little time to get used to the inherent politeness of the coastal people after the shy Wasambaa of Lushoto, and also to their reckless promises to get things done at once, which later on I realised were mainly made to get rid of one. Tax collecting was an unpleasant task as all the money had to be collected personally by the Administrative Officer and the exemption certificates issued by him. The result was that a normal day's work consisted of rising at 3-30 a.m. and moving off at 4 a.m. Then followed a 16-25 mile walk depending on the distance of the next call, arriving there between 10 and 11 a.m. or possibly later and, after a breakfast/lunch, starting collecting tax about noon. That went on until about 4 p.m., followed by tax exemptions and *shauris* (discussion of general affairs). Supper at 6-30 p.m., or earlier if the mosquitoes were bad, and they often were, and bed at 8 p.m. Off again the next day at 4 a.m. The reason for the very early start was, of course, the humid heat on the coast at that time of the year. I usually managed to keep Sunday as a rest-cum-*shauri* day and stayed in one of the larger villages. The people were very hard up for the most part and many of them found difficulty in getting their tax, though the fishermen near Dar-es-Salaam had no such excuse and they were some of the worst offenders. In one village not far from the capital I found that nearly all the taxpayers, hearing of my arrival, had cleared off, leaving me with the women and children. But the outstanding memory I have of those safaris was the great kindness and courtesy of all those with whom I came into contact, and their sense of humour—no doubt my leg was pulled a lot but on the rare occasions when I discovered it, it was never treated as other than a joke which had failed to come off.

After these two months of safari I found myself back in Dar-es-Salaam Boma where I was responsible for the cash, the administration of small estates and the supervision of the Liwale's (African Magistrate) court among other matters. The Liwale was a fine old man who brooked no nonsense from anyone and when he received it he promptly ordered his court clerk to put the offender into the cupboard where he remained until he realised his error. On one occasion I nearly found myself there for I had been foolish enough to remonstrate with him over a case of adultery in which he had fined the man the large sum of five shillings but had despatched the erring woman to goal for fourteen days. He was most upset over my interference and it was only after a great deal of discussion that he accepted my suggestion that we should seek the advice of the Kathi of Zanzibar, the only person in East Africa whom he admitted to be (just slightly) his superior. I am thankful to say that the Kathi agreed with me and even more that the Liwale bore me no grudge.

In the Season

by W. B. COLLINS

The leaves spin lifeless from the cotton trees
And noiseless kiss the ground that gave them birth;
Hot from the desert the Harmattan flees
In hurried gusts to desiccate the earth.
A red cloak masks the green as lorries tear
Southwards, groaning beneath a weight of beans
From golden pods soon to make sumptuous fare
For those who live far from these sun-drenched scenes
Set in a tangled leafy living coil.
How few do know that this is the true gold?
Not dug from vaults but budded from the soil
Of a country shaded by monarchs bold
Which, stripped of mantle green by fiery wind,
Yet keep this living gold for all mankind.

Along the Road

by SIR REX NIVEN, C.M.G., M.C.

A LONG valley winds gently upwards between rounded hills in the heart of Nigeria. A stream runs down its length. Tall trees stand beside it. On the foothills there are more, but lower, trees; between them is old farm land. Up the valley can be seen a broad cleared track, not particularly straight, but persevering in its direction towards a large village on the higher ground. The huts are close together: their roofs are the uniform grey of good thatch; their walls are old brown. By the track is a wide open space with rows of smooth stones—obviously a market: on the village side of the road is a huge fig tree; its bare grey roots form not only a wide network on the ground but also the seats of the village council.

People can be seen coming and going round the village and in its tilled fields nearby; a string of women comes up from the stream with heavy pots on their heads; behind them totters a very small girl child, in her first apprenticeship, with her minute pot slopping water over her face. Just outside the village stands a large round rest house, conspicuous with its lofty thatched roof: its arc of small staff houses stands respectfully behind it and fine trees are about it.

Coming into the picture now is a small column in single file. A policeman in navy blue, his rifle slung and glinting in the sunshine, leads the way. Thirty or more carriers follow him spread out along the road. The metal fastenings on the chop-boxes catch the light: the flat top of the bath, polished by years of wear, gleams suddenly; the dull awkward shape of the bedding catches the eye: a pile of chairs and tables contrasts with the prim lines of a black steel trunk and the smug office box. The light flickers on the buttons and arms of a couple more policemen. The Office Messengers look startlingly clean in their white *rigas*, the black and gold crown badges show boldly. The carriers are a shabby lot in rags and tatters, but you should see them when they want to impress the village girls in the evening.

At the end of all this, the prime mover, and of course the paymaster of this tired column is a solitary white man. He is, at the moment, not a terribly good advertisement of the breed, for he is very weary: the sun is scorching; his helmet is heavy; his khaki bush clothes are black with sweat; his feet are sore and hot; there is a slight sway in his walk; he has come a long way but the rest house is in sight at last. Let us rise in our places and remove our headgear, for here is a member of an extinct race: the old style District Officer on tour.

We need not follow him to his deck chair where he collapses and waits for a tepid drink, or into his bath and clean clothes. Soon he will sit on the verandah and talk to the Village Head and his elders on their affairs; he will listen to the complainants who spring out of the ground (and tenfold, if they think he is a new man); and in the cool of the evening he will walk and talk with all, the men and women and the children, the old men and the shy young people, and they will be happy, for they will have held converse with the Government.

The years pass and a great war is waged far away, but not too far to affect even this remote valley. When we see it again the winding track has disappeared; a fine new road has been cut and with it have gone the shady trees of the old path. The village has opened out and the houses are bigger, some with shiny tin roofs. Many of the trees on the hillsides have gone and there is little of the fine timber that stood by the stream. A rough heap of red earth marks the site of the rest house and only one tree stands there. Just outside the village is a long building in a fenced compound, it is a school; and not far off is the dispensary, its square verandah shading the usual crowd come up for medicine and a gossip. But the people in the farms are using the tools they used since time began: a man is cutting a fallen tree with an axe no bigger than a large chisel, as his fathers did before him: the women come up from the stream with their water-pots on their graceful heads and behind them comes the toddler, a daughter of the child we saw before.

Now comes the sound of an approaching vehicle, and down the valley an ugly smudge of dust rises above the trees. The people in the farms turn away from it, but the Village Head recognises the car and starts to rise from his seat under the great fig tree. It goes too fast for him and he sinks back again.

And that, too, is the District Officer on tour, working in an era separated from that of his predecessor by a deep gulf, not only of time but of outlook and conditions.

In our primeval days, or so they seem now, if you were in a one-man station you were in fact alone—in our first tour my wife saw ten white faces in the year: everyone had to walk to get to us, five days' trek from Provincial headquarters. The distance to a doctor was probably the most serious worry and didn't do anyone's health any good. Now motor transport and the light aeroplane have changed all that: people can still be lonely but they are not cut off. There is the radio to keep them in touch and they no longer have to rely on the Reuters' telegram, not only hopelessly abbreviated but also mutilated—and it seldom got beyond Provincial headquarters. Now, too, if you are near an air route the London papers arrive at most three days old and not three weeks at the best and six at the worst. Even in the far bush they come reasonably quickly.

Then, there are other things. The decision of the Nigerian Government to give every officer a refrigerator, free of charge and maintenance, has made the greatest difference to personal comfort and well-being. Again, gratitude should go to those few brave men who first went in the midday sun not only without a sun-helmet but also without that curious haddock-shaped object, the now forgotten spine-pad. Mad we thought they were as we made ready for the funeral, but how right they have been proved. And white children, so long prohibited, are all over the place now, with a profound effect on the general tenor of the country—whether for better or worse, who can say?

Nevertheless the electric lights fail and the water supply is cut off and telephones drive to frenzy and the old hands say it never used to happen. Even in these days people do suffer some hardship who go out to the Coast. There are still no theatres, and though most of the large towns have cinemas, the films are often very old. There are still in general no hotels which would come up to even the three star class; and outside Lagos and Ibadan, and possibly Kano, there is nowhere one can get a good meal. There are no concerts, and public libraries, though they are coming on, are rare. Churches are rare, too, and services in African churches are often conducted in a vernacular, which does not take the European very far.

The failures of modern services in the larger places are a nuisance but the shortages of this and that in the smaller stations are even now more than a nuisance. The insect life of the country has in no wise diminished with the years. The mosquito and the tsetse fly are very much with us: the cantharis raises its ghastly blister as it did in the old days.

But let us look back beyond the last war, with its privations and difficulties, its uncertainty and lack of news, long tours and separations from families, to the years of the Great Depression, the greatest shock that any young Government could suffer; and back to the beginning of what many foolishly thought was the peace they had fought for and others had died for. Then was the time of the deficiencies in obvious public necessities. Hardly any of the desiderata existed—indeed most of them had not been thought of—and lack of money, staff and equipment prevented action.

Most serious was the absence of roads. In 1922 in Kabba Province we had four miles of motorable road (admittedly there was only one car—the Resident's) and I took it upon myself to build a motor road from my headquarters to Lokoja, the Provincial headquarters. No one asked me to do so: no one gave me any money (fortunately there was £500 in the Native Administration Estimates and that paid for 45 miles of road, including quite a number of bridges); no one gave me any advice and certainly no one gave me any encouragement, though the Marine were kind enough to forge me some steel plates for a patricularly difficult bridge. In less than a year the road was through and five days' trek was reduced to two hours in a Ford kit car which mysteriously made its short appearance, before it fell over a precipice (on, I might say, another road for which I was not responsible). I might also add that no one ever officially said 'thank you' for that road, though the local people were deeply appreciative.

Again, there was no map beyond a distorted sheet of tracing linen with a few vague names. There were some fine traverses by a predecessor but there was no key to put them together. Once more I had to start from scratch, as many others did at the same time, and after months of exhausting work a section of 2,500 square miles of country was added to the map of Nigeria where it still appears—and so do the efforts of my friends. This time there was a single line of thanks from the Governor.

Perhaps the best of the appreciations was the result of a long and, I thought, comprehensive report on the life and activities and economics of a section of the Province, running into a gross or so of pages. The Resident took an interest in it and asked a number of quite unanswerable questions. Months afterwards I received, very formally, the comments of the Lieutenant-Governor: they read: "Surely 112 lbs. of guinea corn per acre is low?" Perhaps it was an off-day in Kaduna.

These extra activities were interesting and instructive and I am sorry for the modern official whose lot cannot include them. The jack-of-all-trades has gone and a great deal of fun has gone with him: Governments will never realise how much they saved financially when any job could be thrown to the District Officer.

But there were so many things that *we* could not put right of our own initiative. There were no schools in the Province: there was no agricultural guidance or research: there were no police beyond the pitiful Native Administration *dogarai* in faded scarlet rags, untrained, uncared for, and miserably paid: there was no works organisation beyond a few picks and shovels and headpans, no trained men, though fortunately we did not lack for sensible leaders and some good masons, trained on the Railway. It is funny to think of all this nowadays when it seems to be quite impossible to carry out any major work without the most complicated of modern equipment, regardless of its original cost and the difficulties of maintaining it.

But the gravest of all the deficiencies was in health. There was simply no one, black or white, to take any interest in the health of the people outside the rare Provincial Headquarters. In Kabba Province we did not have a singe dispensary, or indeed any trained man, outside Lokoja. Even the Missions were unable at that time to fill the gap as they have done so well in places since. It was an unconscious lack for the African population who had never enjoyed any medical help but for the Europeans it was a serious worry indeed. The Medical Department's duties were officially confined in the first instance to the health of the Government staff: but even this they were not able to ensure.

The Government stations were small. There were less than a thousand Europeans in Lagos and about two hundred in Kaduna. It was quite normal to know most of the people in the station: now it is difficult to know many as they are so numerous. Then the danger was the boredom of seeing the same people all the time, now the danger is loneliness from knowing hardly anyone. High costs now reduce the amount of entertainment—in any case, I think many people nowadays are not normally given to entertainment (though they expect to be entertained by the Resident and senior people, who are wrongly supposed to be well off!).

In official work people now tend more to deal with the immediate problem as presented to them in a file as an unrelated matter. There seems to be less care or interest as to past action on the same thing or to its consequences, whether direct and immediate or in distant ramifications. The body of historic and almost instinctive knowledge is fast disappearing.

The Ministers and the new senior African staff started by knowing little outside their own boundaries and lacked the great knowledge of the senior British staff. But they have made up for this very quickly and are helped greatly by their phenomenal memories. The development of the Ministers has been one of the remarkable features of these times. I remember the first time one of them spoke in the Assembly. He was sitting next to me and showed me the few lines of his speech scribbled in pencil on a scrap of paper. When he rose slowly to his feet I thought that he would collapse with nervousness and fright. By the time he had finished I was nearly as terrified as he was. Now he can talk for twenty minutes without a note and without a qualm, with conviction and impressiveness.

It has been said that the British bored their subject people to tears, but our last gesture has removed this slur. When we gave them elected Assemblies we brought in the finest, the most exciting, the most highly rewarded game there is—party politics; and the Assemblies are impressive and well-conducted and as noisy as Westminster—and as surprising. Yet in spite of all this, the Village Head, under his tree, is still responsible for the most precious thing that we brought here. For the Peace is in his hands and he and his friends must preserve it.

Times change and new faces come and go. The peasant remains the same, but he doesn't get much of a look in now. No one wanders through his village and passes the time of day with him. If he wants to complain he must take the 'proper channel'. There is little oppression: he gets good prices for his produce: there is a dispensary not too far away: there are roads: there is a reasonable degree of security and peace: he can listen to far off news and stories and music on the radio and of course he can own and ride a bicycle and carry his lady friend on the upper frame—"He's no good," say the girls, "he's got no bike".

Travelling Hopefully

by SIR ROBERT ALFORD, K.B.E., C M.G.

"SIT DOWN and I will tell you the story of my life" is not a conversational opening that I often employ; but *Corona*, having come to the end of its run, is fading out at the moment when I have come to the end of mine and have faded from the Colonial scene myself, and so *Corona* will perhaps let me take a short retrospect, a very selective one, of the thirty-four years which I have spent in Colonies and Protectorates.

Soon after I went to the Northern Provinces of Nigeria in 1928, somebody said to me quite seriously: "The African will never be able to govern himself." (I did not contradict him because I was an Administrative Cadet on probation and he was the Resident of a Province—and a good and very experienced Resident at that). The remark, by an intelligent senior administrator, gives as good a measure as any of the road that Africa has travelled since I first went there.

The kind of travelling I noticed then, however, was what I did myself, since I did little else. Having ridden a pony all over Kano Province for a year or two I was sent with many others to the Benue to fight a locust invasion. There I found that since there were tsetse flies instead of horses I was allowed to travel from point to point on a motor-bicycle (when there was a road joining the two points, which was not often). Indeed I was encouraged to do so, because if I used my feet or a push-bike I tended to pay insufficient attention to mending holes in the bridges, which were contraptions of logs, earth and white ants, and that meant that my District Officer, who liked to drive his car rather fast, had to drive it rather slowly — thereby giving me more warning of his approach when he dashed out into the bush from Divisional Headquarters (three houses and a dispensary) to see what I was up to.

I stayed in Benue Province after that particular plague of locusts, and though it was not the last one I never found an effective means of combating the principal gambits of the adult locust against the motor-cyclist, which are shorting the ignition by getting electrocuted across the sparking plug, and tickling the rider into hysterics by getting scooped up in his shorts.

Marriage put an end to solo motor-cycling, to my relief, and thereafter for the most part my wife and I travelled by push-bike, usually on paths a foot wide and up to a foot above or below the level of the ground on each side. At first my wife used to get very annoyed when she fell off, her annoyance being proportioned to the distance the rest of the procession had travelled before her absence was noticed; but she passed her test before long, on a night when she successfully negotiated a particularly violent thunderstorm on a German bicycle with low-pressure tyres and a back-pedalling brake borrowed from an Alsatian missionary. The remoter parts of the Benue Province were fairly testing for delicately nurtured females in those days, especially as the tropical outfitters sent them out with a fearsome kind of hat called a double terai, which looked as if it had been made for two Boy Scouts going to the North Pole. But my wife's biggest shock was probably on her first arrival, when she saw our cook. When the day came on which we had to abandon our car (those bridges—it was bound to happen sooner or later) and do the last few miles of our day's journey on foot wearing pyjamas and sun helmets (through no fault of our own), I doubt if she minded. She did mind being woken one night by a tremendous sigh from a cow which had come into the hut and lain down against her camp bed.

Much as I loved the cheerful Tiv, among whom most of my time in Benue Province had been spent, I was glad to go back to Kano and horses and cheap and inexpert polo. Plenty more travelling, but an interlude in idyllic surroundings just outside the Dan Agundi Gate of Kano City while I was in charge of the Printing Press and Survey Department of the Kano Native Administration. What good I was expected to do to a professional printer and a professional surveyor is no longer clear to me but I learnt a certain amount about printing, which plays a large part in the life of a Secretariat officer such as I became later, and a certain amount about surveying which came in useful long afterwards when an optimistic prospector applied for a licence for the extraction of some improbable mineral from St. Helena, where there are no surveyors.

In the nine years I spent in the Northern Provinces I got to know the Kano and Benue Provinces pretty well, but not much of the rest of the country except Kaduna (where I had a short time in the Northern Provinces Secretariat) and the places I saw briefly when accompanying the Lieutenant- Governor as his Private Secretary on his far-ranging visitations.

Eventually, after some mild horse-trading with my Resident (he wanted me to postpone my leave, and I wanted to be posted to the Nigerian Secretariat after it), my wife and I found ourselves in Lagos. I was put in the Establishment Branch of the Secretariat, where I learnt that the proper study of mankind is personnel, and that when my immediate superior, who was an African, corrected my English, he was usually right. There was a phenomenal amount of work, but time nevertheless for the consolations of life in Lagos—sailing in the harbour, on the lagoon and up the creeks, and swimming and surf-boarding on the magnificent beaches.

We were back in Lagos again after the war, where I was obliged to occupy myself with finance. I was also Custodian of Enemy Property. Both these occupations had consequences for my wife and me. The latter, by obliging us to go to the Cameroons to hand over the ex-German banana plantations to the Cameroons Development Corporation, reminded us that after eighteen years it was time to take some local leave. The former presumably was why I was offered the post of Financial Secretary in Zanzibar. Why I accepted it is another matter; when the Financial Secretary of Nigeria came to press me for a decision I was in bed with a fairly severe fever and wished to be left alone, and certainly that had something to do with it..

Zanzibar was a big contrast to Lagos. Coming in over a sea of coconut palms in a biplane with pointed wings, and being received in airport buildings consisting of a small shed with a thatched roof, were things that might happen as well in West Africa as in East. But having arrived I found myself living in an eastern city under the rule of an Arab sultan, surrounded by Arabs and Indians as well as Africans, and attending an office that closed for the day at one o'clock in the afternoon; none of these interesting circumstances had obtained in Lagos. It was a pleasant change to have something to think about besides oilseeds. In Nigeria I had been concerned with encouraging people to produce groundnuts, benniseed, palm nuts, palm kernels and to a lesser extent coconuts, and dealing with the consequences of their producing too little, or too much or the wrong kind. In Zanzibar the principal crop, the principal topic of conversation, the principal prop of the Government revenue and the principal smell in the town, was cloves (and to a lesser extent coconuts). A row of warehouses stacked to the roof with cloves is an impressive sight to those whose consumption of cloves runs at an approximate rate of one per apple pie, and when such people were told that the demand was largely due to the Indonesians' habit of mixing chopped-up cloves with their cigarette tobacco they were often incredulous. (When I actually smoked the cigarettes I found the story even harder to believe).

Working for His Highness's Government called for some adjustment of a Colonial Civil Servant's previous ideas, especially as the British Resident was at the same time both the Queen's adviser to the Sultan and the head of the Sultan's Government; but nobody could have made it easier than that very charming and kindly old gentleman, Seyyid Khalifa bin Harub, on whom be peace.

Zanzibar Island is pretty, though rather too flat; it has splendid beaches of white coral sand and a properly heated sea; and the sea is ideal for sailing small boats. So these were occupations that we left with regret when after five years as Financial Secretary and another five as Chief Secretary I left Zanzibar to govern St. Helena, which is mountainous, is surrounded by a chilly ocean and offers to small sailing boats a good chance of being blown to leeward and seeing no land again for four thousand miles.   There were plenty of other things to do, however. At frequent intervals I had to stop being the Governor in order to be the Chief and only Justice. This admirably economical arrangement (there is no provision in the Estimates for paying the Chief Justice) had its inconveniences; some versatility is expected of the Governor of a remote island, but when a certain involuntary resident applied to the Supreme Court for a writ of *habeas corpus* directed to the Governor it was decided that however deftly the wearer might change his cocked hat for a wig and *vice versa* it was too much to ask the Governor to try himself.   Other arrangements were therefore made.   That, however, though it happened twice, did not happen every day.   For most of the time St. Helena kept out of the news and was a pleasant place to live in. Our four years there went all to quickly, and my wife and I were very sorry to leave the island and its friendly people.

So that is that. Looking back on thirty-four years as a Colonial administrator there is one thing I can be sure of: from start to finish I never wished to be doing anything else. As the whaling captain said on getting home after a three-year voyage, "We didn't catch anything, but we had a grand sail."

Those were the Days

by A. H. M. KIRK-GREENE

JUST fifty years ago, in 1905, there appeared a remarkable book called *Verb. Sap. on Going to West Africa*. The author was a Mr. Alan Field, F.R.G.S., who had seen service in the Royal Scots, the Bombay Famine Relief Department, the Indian Staff Corps and the Colonial Political Service. It was written to help travellers about to make their first acquaintance with what was then widely acknowledged as the White Man's Grave (and who would be so bold as to dismiss the story as apocryphal that shipping companies to the Coast refused to sanction the printing of such a *non sequitur* as a return ticket?), "primarily for the Protectorate of Northern Nigeria, the latest and the least civilised of our West African possessions. It must be remembered that what would often be appropriately termed as 'molly-coddling' in a good climate is ordinary 'horse-sense' in a bad. The happy mean between hypochondria and folly is not hard to attain."

That this volume was of considerable value is self-evident: the *African World* declared it to be "a boon to the man going out . . . it brims with precisely the information for which the average man diligently searches in vain a few weeks before sailing from Liverpool," while the *West African Mail* acclaimed it as "a little book which no one going to the Coast can afford to miss reading . . . good enough to save time, money, temper, health and life, and it only costs half a crown." Its wisdom has never been in doubt; indeed, much of its advice is pertinent to the present-day Coast-bound tiro. Yet such an immense advance has there been over the past half-century that much of what was written only a generation or so ago now appears humorous, perhaps dated. This jubilee review of "*Verb. Sap.*" is made in honest admiration of the original; and if we can bear in mind that there is no denigratory intention in these excerpts, then we can enjoy—and probably, even to-day, profit from—a glance at its contents.

As a background to the outfitter's scene we must recall the 1905 historical setting of West Africa. Northern Nigeria was the latest acquisition in the Empire. Only in 1900 had the Government taken over those territories formerly administered by the Royal Niger Company, and not till March, 1903, had Kano and Sokoto been finally occupied. The telegraph had just been established at Bauchi and Yola, and its extension was planned to Sokoto and Lake Chad so that the country would soon boast of two thousand miles of line. "The native up-country may occasionally be reckoned as a factor in the death rate. Out of fifteen fellow-travellers with the present historian, two were killed within four months of arrival . . . truly the alligator and the poisoned arrow are ever ready."

"No one really goes out for the fun of it, but either for pay or glory. If the reader goes out for the pay, he is probably not rich and will want to cut down his expenses. He must not cut down anything in the least essential, or he will not live long to draw his pay. If he goes out for the glory, he must pursue fame with a complete trousseau, or all the public notice he will attract will be a short obituary." With these words of advice ringing in our ears we turn to the chapter on Outfit, suitably followed by its next of kin, Estimate of Expenses.

Uniform for the Civil side was based on the Dress Regulations issued for the Colony by the Colonial Office, and at the then stage of Northern Nigeria's development the complete outfit was not considered necessary. A khaki-drill Norfolk jacket and trousers, with three pairs of riding-breeches, were the mainstay, together with two sets (31s. complete) of white-drill mess jacket and trousers and a silk mess cummerbund—"not a made-up, so-called 'shyster,' but a correct length of silk to wind four times round the waist." Mess kit was necessary only for Lokoja, the gateway to Northern Nigeria, and Zungeru, the Protectorate Headquarters, but an adjacent asterisk warns the reader that "it is good to wear it at Bush stations—refer to Chapter IV on Slackness" . . . a caution that we shall examine later. Headgear consisted of a sun-topi, a grey double-terai hat, a panama and a cap: "It is *very important* to ascertain that the brim of the sun hat is not touched by the arm when a gun is raised to shoot. If the arm touches the sun hat, the hat is no good to a sportsman." These, of course, were the days of the spine-pad, a *sine qua non* to ward off "fever, sunstroke and retching." Perhaps old sweats will forgive a brief description of this museum-piece, which has ever aroused the curiosity of my greenhorn generation. "A spine-pad may be of any material, padded with cotton wool and quilted. Easily home-made with a sewing-machine. Worn outside or inside. Fixed on by buttons or safety pins. Two to be taken, for wearing down the spine."

The ubiquitous rubber knee-boots, invaluable for swamp work in the South, were *not* recommended, and we read that Lokoja was full of discarded boots. Under Linen (Body), appears the formidable item of "eight celluloid stand-up double collars"—what price aertex open-necks!—followed by the warning that "wool vests MUST be worn underneath, or fever fit to catch master!" Six all-wool vests and short drawers, four flannel cummerbunds to be buttoned *over* the all-wool pyjama coat, and two thick, long, wool drawers for voyage and fever are the highlights of the underclothes department: "one of the worst features of prickly heat is that there is a temptation not to wear wool next the skin." We are reminded to choose white or coloured socks, as mosquitoes show a preference for black ones.

The camp furniture lists differ little from present day ones (except in the vital matter of prices: one Lord's lamp at 30s. 6d., bedstead and rods at 35s., two mosquito nets at 18s. 6d., a tin bath in a wicker case at £1 14s. 6d., and so on until tears well up in our bankrupt 1955 eyes), and for crockery we are assured that the best glass for Bush work is aluminium and the best crockery is enamelled tin. Fittings for the tiffin basket loom large, tacked on to an important note:—"When travelling in Bush, always see that the most reliable man carries the tiffin basket. A mosquito net should be with this, and if both the tiffin basket and net are with you, it does not matter so much if the rest of the baggage is late or astray." Saddlery is remarkable for its modest cost of £10 9s. 2d. for a very generous equipment, after which we come to the powerful battery of rifles, guns, revolvers and 1200 cartridges including 200 man-stopping revolver rounds . . . all for £36 3s. Books recommended include "Malaria," "Family Medicine in India," language and professional books, one copy Shakespeare and two copies "*Verb. Sap.*" so that one may be permanently on loan to the incautious novice on your station.

The contents of the medicine chest included one pint of best Cognac at 7s. 6d. and twelve pints of dry Champagne at 6s. 6d., the latter strictly for that tired feeling. Under miscellaneous articles that we might so easily have overlooked we find a water-bottle ("aluminium are lightest, but whisky affects the metal"), two balls of string, two tape measures "if for nothing else but to measure sporting trophies," pipe clay for blancoing, gramophone records—"band pieces are specially cheerful"—and a regretful veto that the damp heat precludes either a banjo or a guitar. Detailed information on prices and purchases is given, with the final *nota bene* of 1955: "it is better to anticipate one's salary by an arrangement with an agent or banker or make an agreement to pay by instalments rather than to go out to a bad climate incompletely fitted out."

Thus superbly equipped we can progress from Liverpool to Lokoja-along-the-Coasts. "It always comes as rather a shock to a man to learn that his interests and career lie in a land of which many of his contemporaries have never even heard." Indeed, the "man in the street" told a certain lady that his brother, "the man in the sun hat," was in Northern Nigeria; to which the good lady replied, having caught the sound but not the context, that she always thought it was such a pretty creeper!

"If you are black, speak Hausa, and conceal your valuables with your fear of death together, you may, with luck, get through Tripoli. But as you are assumedly not the first, cannot speak the second, and have no desire to perform the third requisite, to ship from Liverpool were best." The first landfall is at Sierra Leone (greenhorns to note that it is pronounced Salleone), the Port Said to the Coast "in the sense of being the demarcation which ends Europe for us now, as does that hybrid sink of the sins of three continents for the Eastern Voyager." Here you post your first letters, have a cocktail at the Club, and learn that "the washed-out, limp, dead-white European" who passes in a hammock is not on the way to die in hospital but is merely representative of the Salleone complexion. From Salleone to Calabar—on which stretch of the voyage "there is a washer-man on board for his own exceeding profit and the cleaning of passengers' underwear"—the Old Coasters, once they have sniffed the subtle airs of the coast, are in their element. "They hold a ghoulish terrorism, a tyranny of corpse yarns and prophecy over all new voyagers to these seas. Certes, the climate is deadly bad, treacherously, murderously bad, but 'poor Jones' never could have died in such contortions of such pain in so short a time under such depressing circumstances as they will tell to a shuddering circle."

Twenty-five pounds was recommended as being more than enough for the voyage from Liverpool to Lokoja. Large items might be cards and the bar on board—"Treating is customary. The wine bills are settled weekly. 30s. a week is an ordinary bill"—and there was the "conscience salve" at the Forcados customs to offset the official's self-persuasive casuistry that all the property he had with him was necessary to preserve his life and enable him to carry out his duty efficiently: "many estimable persons, it is feared, have been smugglers with less reason."

Thus the voyage approaches its end: in Lagos Roads, over Forcados Bar, and finally to Burutu, where transhipment takes place from the liner to the Niger stern-wheeler which has just brought down the red-sealed mail bags from Lokoja. But the oily, mangrove-swamps of Burutu do not "engender other than sad brooding. Perhaps there are letters in those bags whose writers are already for ever beyond sending any more messages to their homes, their loves, and their duns—that is the thought bred in the new arrival's brain by the atmosphere of Burutu, by the sight of the little, overfull cemetery in the water-logged soil. This is the last resting-place of many who have thought that they have got away in time, but it has been just in time to see the home-bound steamer at her moorings, and then the tired, fever-wasted and so lonely exile has gone 'on leave' for good."

On the up-river journey to Lokoja, the port of Northern Nigeria as it then was, it used to be the practice for travellers to form a mess. There was on board the stern-wheeler a cook, who received 2s. 6d. a head, and one of the travellers acted as Mess President: "Vote one of the congenial spirits to be caterer, but do not get voted to it yourself, as it means all work and little thanks." Each member of the party contributed a share from his fortnight's box of provisions that he had brought out from England specially for this part of the journey. This list makes interesting reading, from both a menu and a monetary point of view:—

For a fortnight's stores purchase:				*s.*	*d.*
7 lb. ship's biscuits at 5d.	..	..	..	2	11
6 lb. flour	..	..	..	1	0
3 tins roast beef at 1s. 11d.	..	..	..	5	9
1 tin spiced beef (2 lb.) ..	..	..	..	1	7½
1 tin lamb and peas (2 lb.)	..	..	..	2	3
2 tins tongue at 1s. 2d.	..	..	..	2	4
1 tin turkey (2 lb.) ..	..	..	..	3	2
6 tins vegetables at 2½d.	..	..	..	1	3

Carried forward £1   0   3½

				Brought forward £1		0	3½
4 tins sausages at 7½d.	..	..	..	..		2	6
6 tins sardines at 5¼d.	..	..	..	..		2	9
3 tins bacon	..	..	..	..		3	0
2 lb. sago at 2¼d.	..	..	..	..			4½
2 lb. rice at 2¼d.	..	..	..	..			4½
12 small Bovrils at 11½d.	..	..	..		11	6
6 squares dessicated soup at 4½d.	..	..		2	3
1 lb. tea	..	..	..	..		2	0
12 tins unsweetened milk	..	..	..		5	6
1 tin figs (3 lb.)	..	..	..	..		1	10
4 tins Plasmon cocoa at 9d.	..	..	..		3	0
1 tin cheese at 10d. lb. (3 lb.)	..	..		2	6
2 tins jam at 7½d.	..	..	..		1	3
			Total	£2	19	1½

For the remaining months of the tour officers could either take out supplies, specially packed at home in suitably-sized boxes for head-loading (the original "chop-box") or trust to the canteens, which at Lokoja had a considerable range of tinned provisions.

The following quotation from F. P. Crozier's *Five Years Hard* reveals what the Lokoja canteen recommended at the beginning of the century:—

"Six months' chop," says a thin, cheery looking clerk from Liverpool; "well, the usual, I suppose. A case of flour, a case of meat, four dozen soup, four dozen veg., a gross of sardines, three dozen bloaters in tomatoes, two dozen whitebait, two dozen salmon, a dozen lard—them's the essentials."

"You said 'essentials,' " says B., "you never mentioned drink!"

"Ah," replies the clerk, "tastes vary."

"Let me see," says B., "six months, roughly a hundred and eighty days, a hundred and eighty bottles of whisky—fifteen dozen—that sounds awful—half that amount of gin—a bottle of Angostura, a case of beer—four dozen—a case of champagne—that should do. What do you think?"

"Rather a lot," says the clerk, "why not make it half: you might be dead in three months. I should be if I drank half as much in double the time!"

AS we are creeping upstream, we have time to assimilate the author's advice on other subjects; and the first of them is, not surprisingly in the White Man's Grave, a homily on health. "Now the West Coast is a notoriously bad climate, but it is not so black as it is painted. It must be acknowledged that until recent years the best class of man has not been attracted to the country, and the Coast was to a very large extent a dumping ground for undesirables . . . men, often the black sheep of good families, who by dissipation and by those very courses which were the cause of their exile, arrived with nervous tissues worn and stamina undermined, in a physical condition least qualified to ward off the results of fever and hardships. Neither were they in a mood to be prudent, and malaria loves the reckless. Furthermore, they understood the mixing of cocktails too well and the might of the sun too little."

But now that England had started to send out her best picked men to the Coast to replace those of unhallowed memory—apart, it appears, from the gold-mining companies, who dealt in "some very queer fish, who like to journey with a cigarette stuck behind each ear and eccentric red-hued language on their lips"— the thermometer of the death-rate was dropping from "deadly" and "dangerous" to a less ominous "unhealthy," below which mark the latitude would never permit it to fall. Admittedly, the Coast Colonies were falsifying their vital statistics by refusing to count those who "die at sea or almost immediately on landing at the Canaries or Plymouth," but the pestilential climate was now claiming less victims each year. Quinine, to be taken daily in a small dose or twice a week in a 15-grain dose, with an extra 5–10-grain dose when tired, damp or much mosquito-bitten, was the first precaution against malaria; a Coaster who ignores this protection "is a fool, and the sooner he dies, the better for the work he is sent out to do: let him make way for a man better suited for the country." Everyone, of course, gets fever sometime, but let him remember; "Keep smiling, the fever will soon be gone."

The correct tucking-in of the mosquito-net, the wearing of mosquito boots, aperients, prickly heat ("the rubbing of the skin with lemons relieves"), stagnant water, ventilation and sanitation are all dealt with, but above all "cocktails and their relations are much preached against. There are old stagers who certainly do not stint themselves, after sunset. But note that these old stagers are the survival of the fittest: they do not forget quinine even when d——k!" Nevertheless, the final pages of this *vade mecum* contain a number of "Recipes for a Thirsty Land," culminating in the warning that a single one of these Curses of the Coast is ample and that the "one-finger whisky-soda or a small bottle of good claret is the best drink with the evening meal."

This leads us on to *verb. sap.* on food. "The ubiquitous bird called chicken is a mainstay of the table. By the aid of sound teeth, a sausage machine and much cooking, it can be assimilated. A mincing machine is a *sine qua non*. There are some Coast joints which are only suited for inclusion in geological museums. These will be recognised when met. They are hopeless . . . Eggs may be quickly tested. Put the lot into a calabash, those which do not sink and lie still may at once be discarded. They are fit for election purposes only." Two principal meals are recommended, at 10 or 11 a.m. and at 7 p.m., with a light meal between times. "Do not have many curries or palm-oil chop, they are heating."

So, too, are "boys," classified (a little unkindly, perhaps) under the heading of Servants and Other Pests. "It remains for a Neuropath to gauge how many degrees of rise of temperature in a fever-patient are owing to his boys." A steward and a cook should be engaged at Forcados at 20s. to 30s. a month. The best cooks came from Accra, but the Roman Catholic Fathers at Onitsha ran a very fine cookery school, whose products were worth seeking. "Remember that you want a man who can cook bread. Do not flog your boys if you can possibly avoid it, and preferably not the cook. He *might* poison you." Other pests in the chapter range from "obnoxious insects to the-man-above-you-in-the-scale-of-seniority-who-will-live-on."

There is much rich reading in the chapter on Life and Social Amenities, at the head of which we find the Ladies. "The Lord of Creation when travelling in the tropics somewhat resents the keeping up of appearances which the presence of ladies demands of him, but he will nevertheless acknowledge, when he reaches home again, that the little effort against slackness did him good . . . Ladies come on board at the Canaries on the voyage home: two dinner shirts are suggested to be taken."

The West Coast was not impossible for ladies, and there were some along the wide littoral, but apart from the very few nurses at Zungeru and Lokoja hospitals, there were in 1905 only three ladies in Northern Nigeria. "On arrival in a place it is well to preserve the decencies of social amenity and call at once on each of the government officials, on the doctors, on the regimental mess, and, of course, on any ladies there may be." Here follows the promised severe lecture on Slackness: an officer of the West African Frontier Force is held up to us who was awarded a D.S.O. for shaving under adverse circumstances when other officers were not so keen about their personal appearance, and the not-so-mythical gentleman who invariably changed for dinner, however tired or feverish, makes his appearance. "If you are in the Bush and run into a white man's camp, and the European is unshaven, with pyjamas or dirty flannels tucked into mosquito boots, you can confidently look for a dirtily kept outfit, dirty servants, and slack police. The shaven boss in comfortable old but clean kit, on the contrary will welcome you to a camp like himself, old and worn in outfit perhaps, but all smart and workmanlike. You will get a cooler drink quicker at the latter camp than in the former, and without your host having to shout and rave for it." "No apology is offered for this preachment," concludes the author; none is needed, the modern reader echoes, for everybody in the tropics recognises that happy medium between slackness and stuffiness that is such an important factor in maintaining self-respect and in promoting good tone in an outstation.

Other items of the social side include the weekly mail. "Oh, reader! arrange that you get a good, fat budget! Write to aunts, old loves, anyone and everyone, to get answers. The mail means more to exiles than the exiles themselves remember, when at home." Games, photography, taxidermy, curio collecting and pets all get a paragraph each, and the cool comfort of a mud-hut with its "couple of home rugs and a dozen Christmas number chromos to give a quite Belgravian air to the exile's home" is contrasted with the death-trap Europe-made houses imported to Lokoja and Zungeru, consisting of a central chop-room flanked by a sleeping-room on either side for two or more occupants.

A special chapter was contributed, On Sport—Shot and Saddle, whose description of the local shikari is worth quoting in full. "He cannot understand the idea of your shooting an animal yourself if you can pay a man to do it for you. When your interpreter first explains that you want such and such a beast, the locality accepts the fact and sits still. Then the interpreter announces that money, much money, may be obtained by gratifying you. Thereupon, perhaps two or three villagers may arouse themselves by the prospect of cash and they leave the village. The chief tells the interpreter, who tells you, that everything is being done, that, yes, there are herds of elephant, hartebeest, panther, everything close by, and that all the neighbourhood is locating them. After two or three days' wait you are wakened at 4 a.m. by a tremendous row in your camp, and, on emerging from your mosquito net, find that a slim cow hartebeest or a doe waterbuck lies on the ground near you, with the proud two or three villagers demanding immediate recompense: they have slain the beast you said you wanted!" A further note on elephant-hunting: "you must be on the ground in order to get full value for your elephant licence, *and* for your life insurance premium."

Merchants and missionaries, so often the forerunners of the flag in our history, have their niche in this booklet. "Salary varies for a clerk, but the average is about £80 to £120 for the first and second years respectively. In addition to the pay, all board, lodging and laundry are provided free—in fact, everything is provided but clothing and outfit." Prospects were good, and if a man survived his first tour in "an up-river trading station of a little tin-roofed house in the middle of wild nothingness," he would become a proud *second-term* man, whence promotion might be expected to sub-agent or even agent on £500 to £1500. "It may be said that a clerk can save all his salary, for there is nothing on which he *must* spend money except. clothing and luxuries, and for these an allowance of £25 for the two years should suffice." The pioneer educational and medical work of Missions is noted.

So there is our starry-eyed Empire Builder of fifty years ago, safely arrived at Lokoja and ready to trek forth to his first station in the Northern Nigeria hinterland. "It is very hard to realise, accustomed as we all are to roads and to wheeled vehicles, what a land is like where there are no roads and no wheels of any kind. The coast towns, and in Northern Nigeria, Lokoja and Zungeru, have roads in the station itself only, but outside is bush. The villages and towns are connected by bush paths, only one man wide, and these wind about to make a crow-fly march other miles into fifteen. All transport is by head porterage, the load of each carrier being from 56 to 60 lb. The wages of carriers are 6d. a day. An ordinary march would be 12–15 miles, while 25 can be done. The number of carriers when you are in a tranquil region is not, except from the point of view of expense, a matter of importance but it becomes somewhat difficult when in a troublous zone the length of your line of carriers has to be cut down to such dimensions as the escort can safely convoy. The sort of jumble that can develop, when going through a jungly bit of hostile country and a shot is fired in front or rear, has to be seen to be believed. Off the narrow path is impenetrable bush. Front, middle and rear are escort, with the unarmed and alarmed carriers in the middle spaces. Through the middle of deposited loads towards the source of alarm *he* comes, followed by police or soldiery, pushing through the squatted carriers. Thumbs are stuffing home cartridges in case things are serious, and most of the fighting men's faces wear a grin, a reflection of the smile on *his*: *he* knows that every soul is taking his cue from *him*, and that *his* smile is worth, to the morale of his little ' push,' another Maxim." A whistle blows; excited chatter as the loads are hoisted aloft again; a wave of the hand; and the party moves on . . .

From the bowler-hatted suburbanity of the daily 8.18 to Waterloo or from behind a formidable barricade of Secretariat files, our aching hearts bid *him bon voyage*. 1955 may safely echo 1905: "West Africa has a great future speedily unrolling, a future for the country and for all those willing to identify themselves and their careers with it. To each of these I would say with all my heart:—Go—and prosper."

Index of Authors